FAIRY TAIL

フェアリーテイル

25

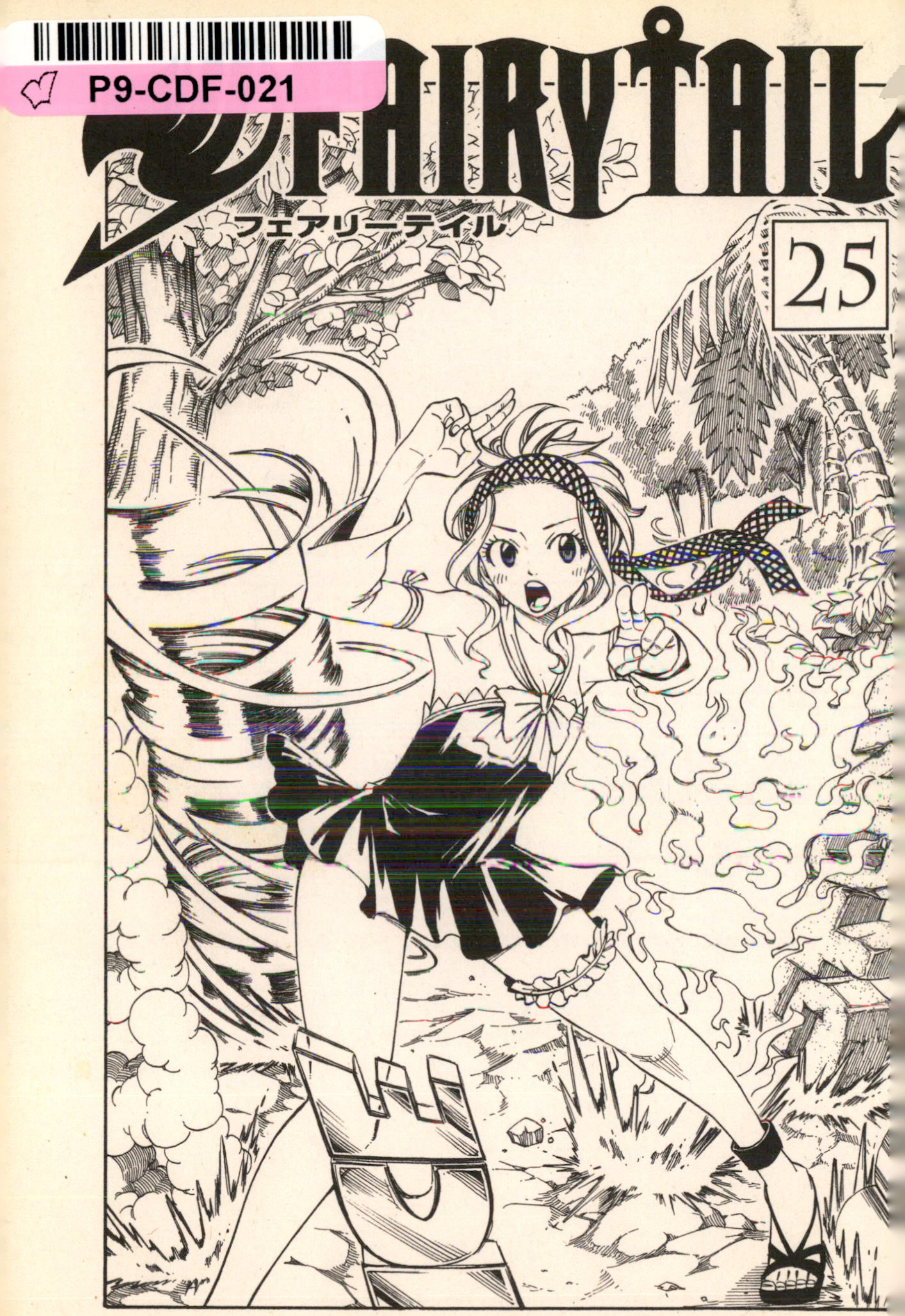

HIRO MASHIMA

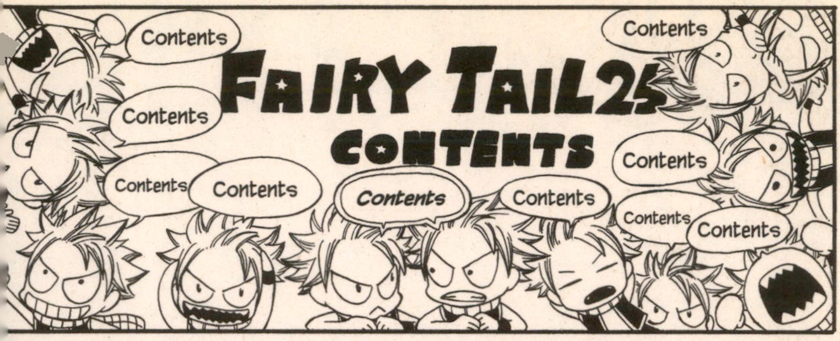
Contents
Contents
FAIRY TAIL 25
CONTENTS
Contents
Contents
Contents
Contents
Contents
Contents
Contents
Contents
Contents

Published in serial form by Weekly Shônen Magazine 2010-2011 Volumes 47-55

FAIRY TAIL

フェアリーテイル

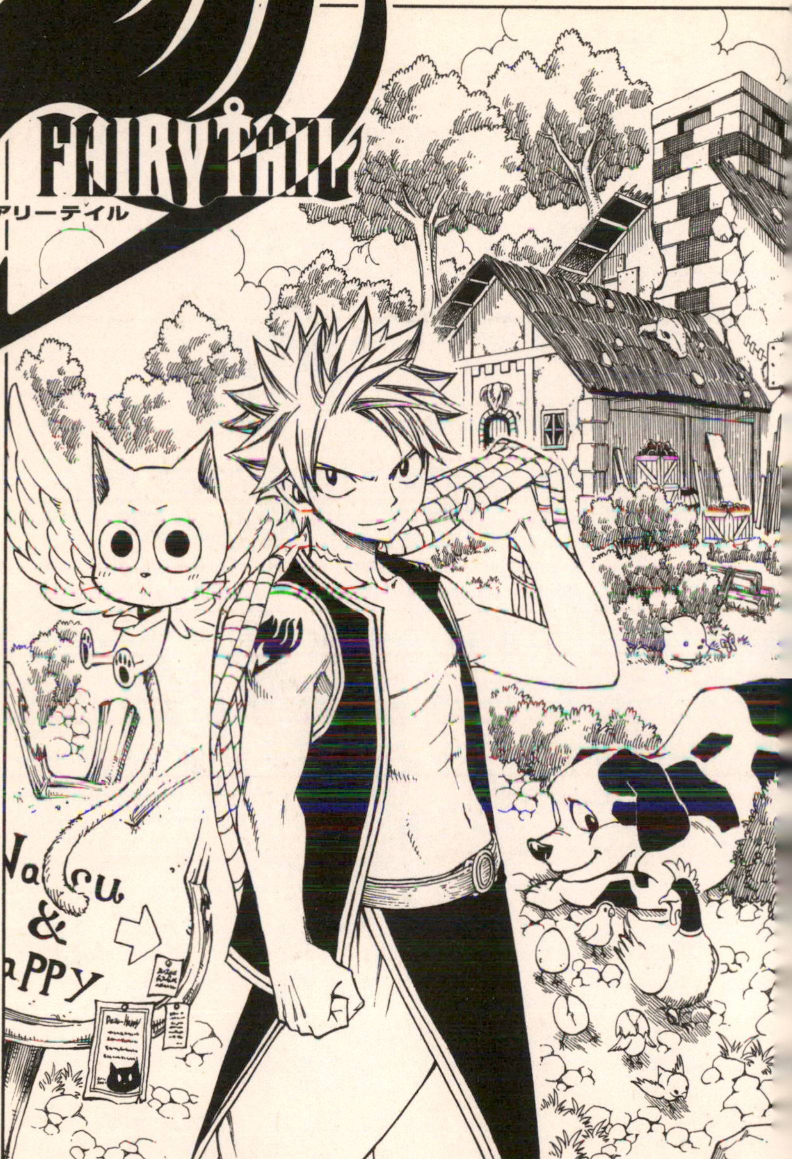

Chapter 205: Natsu vs. Gildarts

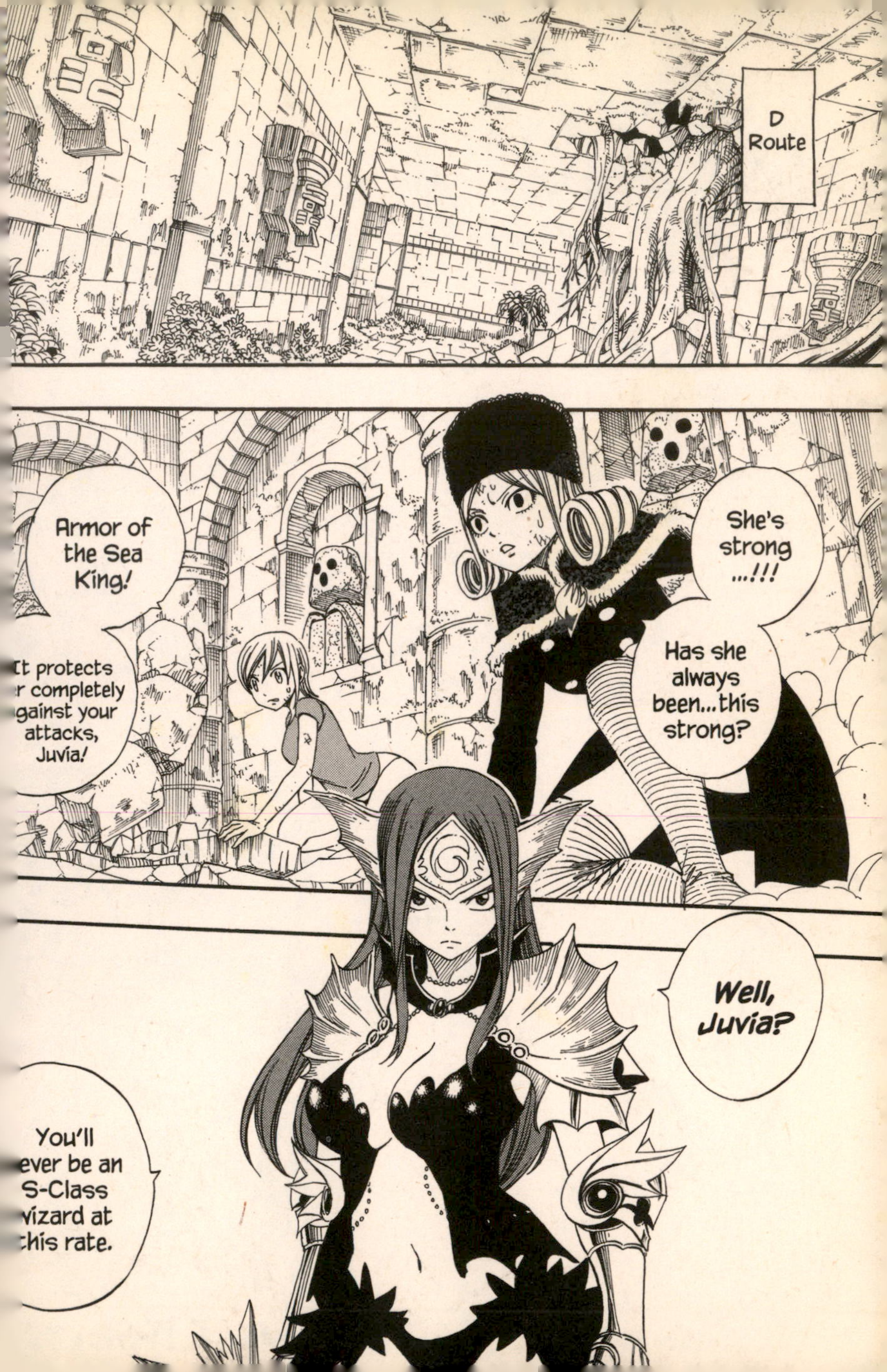
D Route
She's strong ...!!!
Has she always been...this strong?
Armor of the Sea King!
It protects r completely gainst your attacks, Juvia!
Well, Juvia?
You'll ever be an S-Class vizard at his rate.

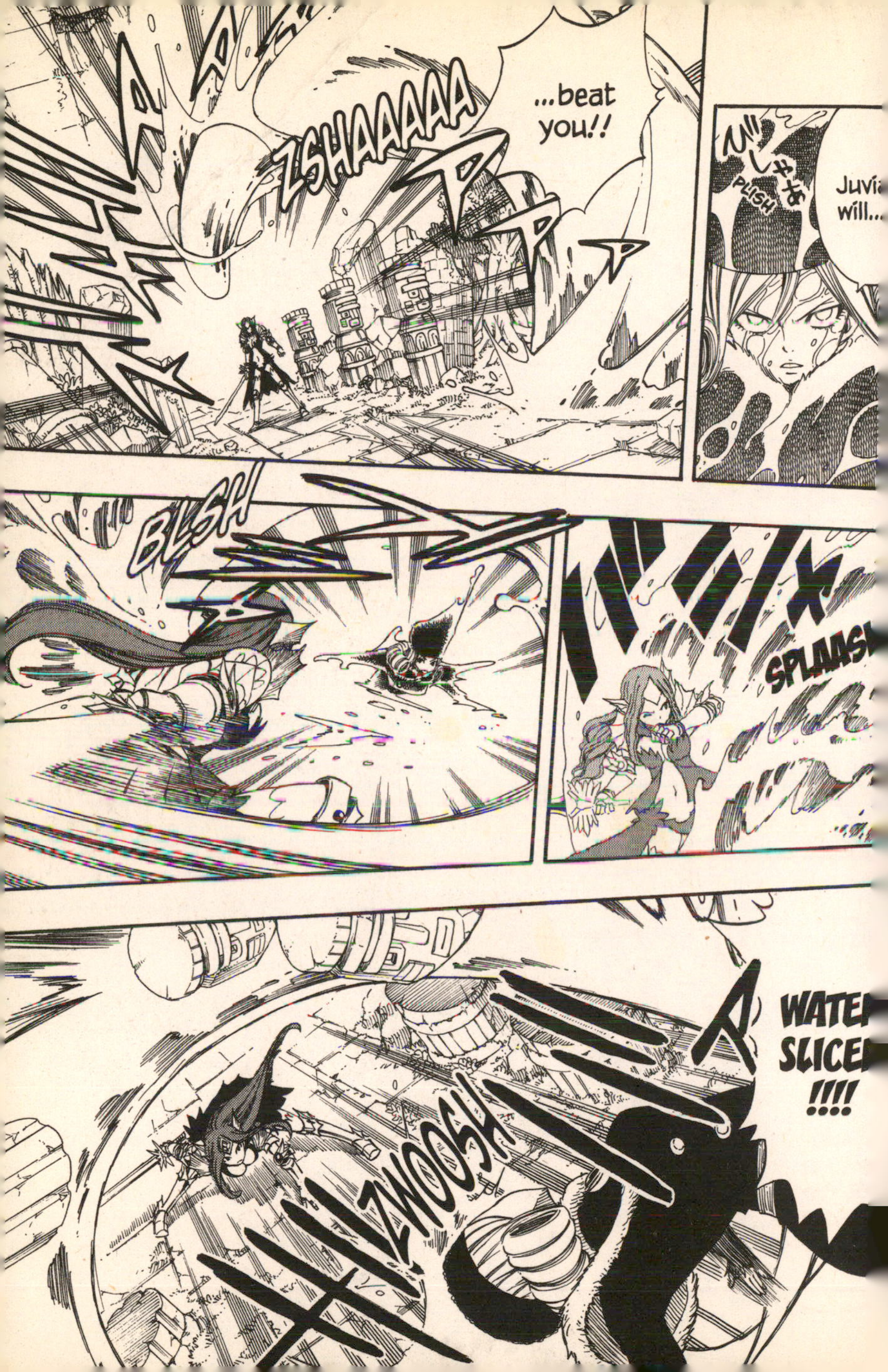
びしゃあ
PLISH
Juvia will...
...beat you!!
ZSHAAAAA
SPLAASH
BLSH
WATER SLICER!!!!
ZWOOSH

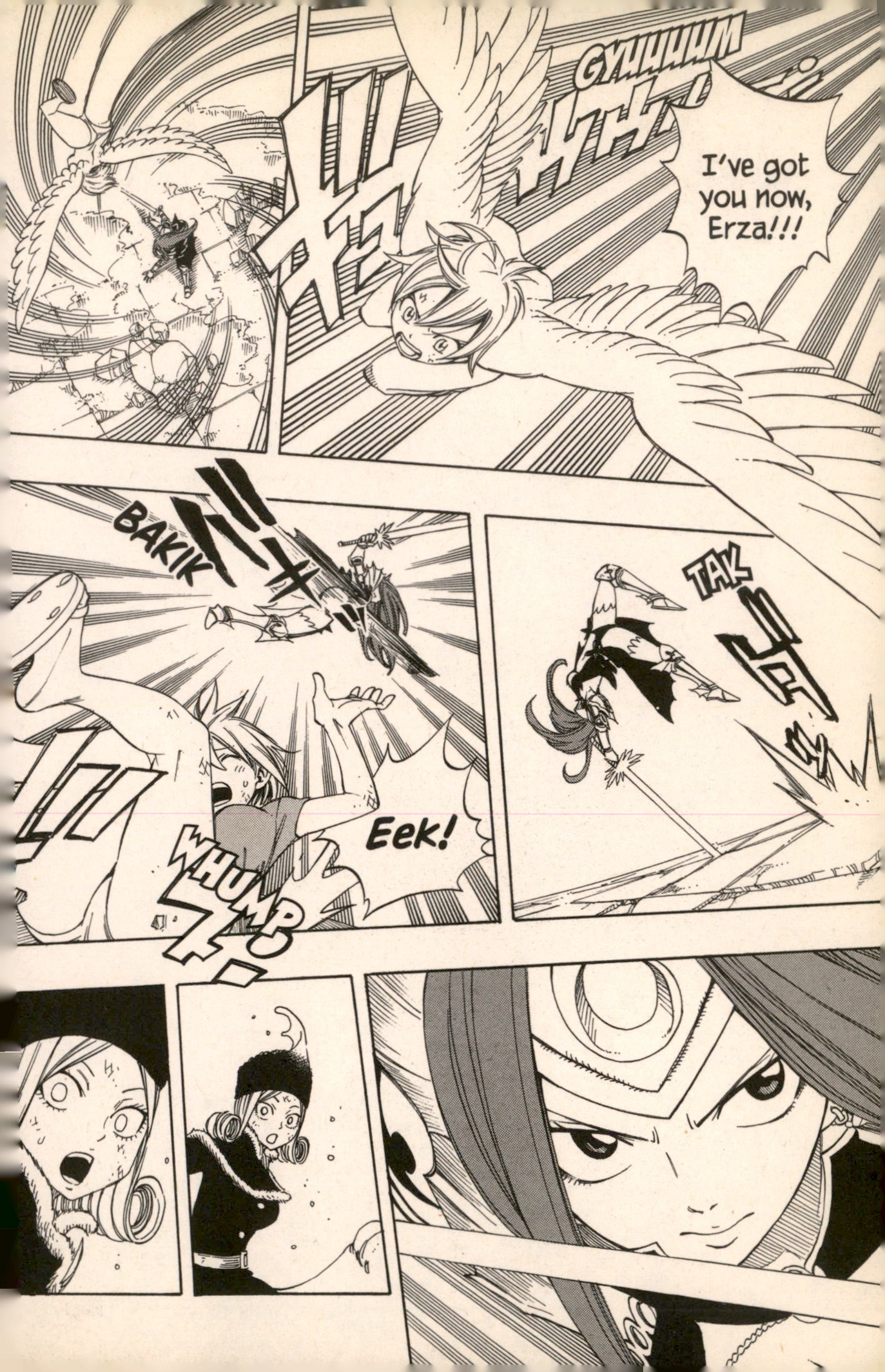
GYUUUUM
I've got you now, Erza!!!
TAK
BAKIK
Eek!
WHUMP

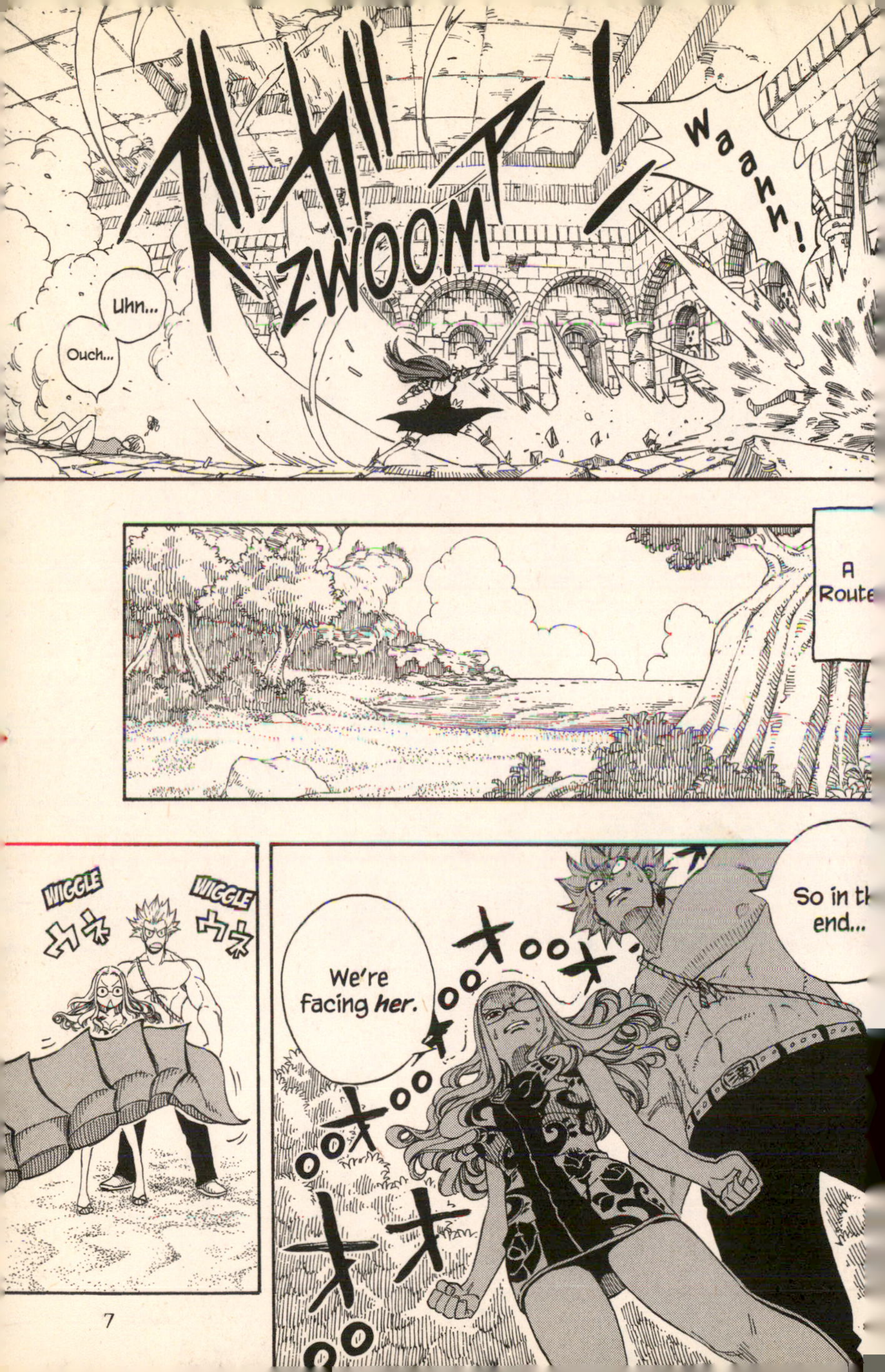
Waann!
ZWOOM
Uhn...
Ouch...
A Route
So in th
end...
We're facing *her*.
WIGGLE
ウネ
WIGGLE
ウネ

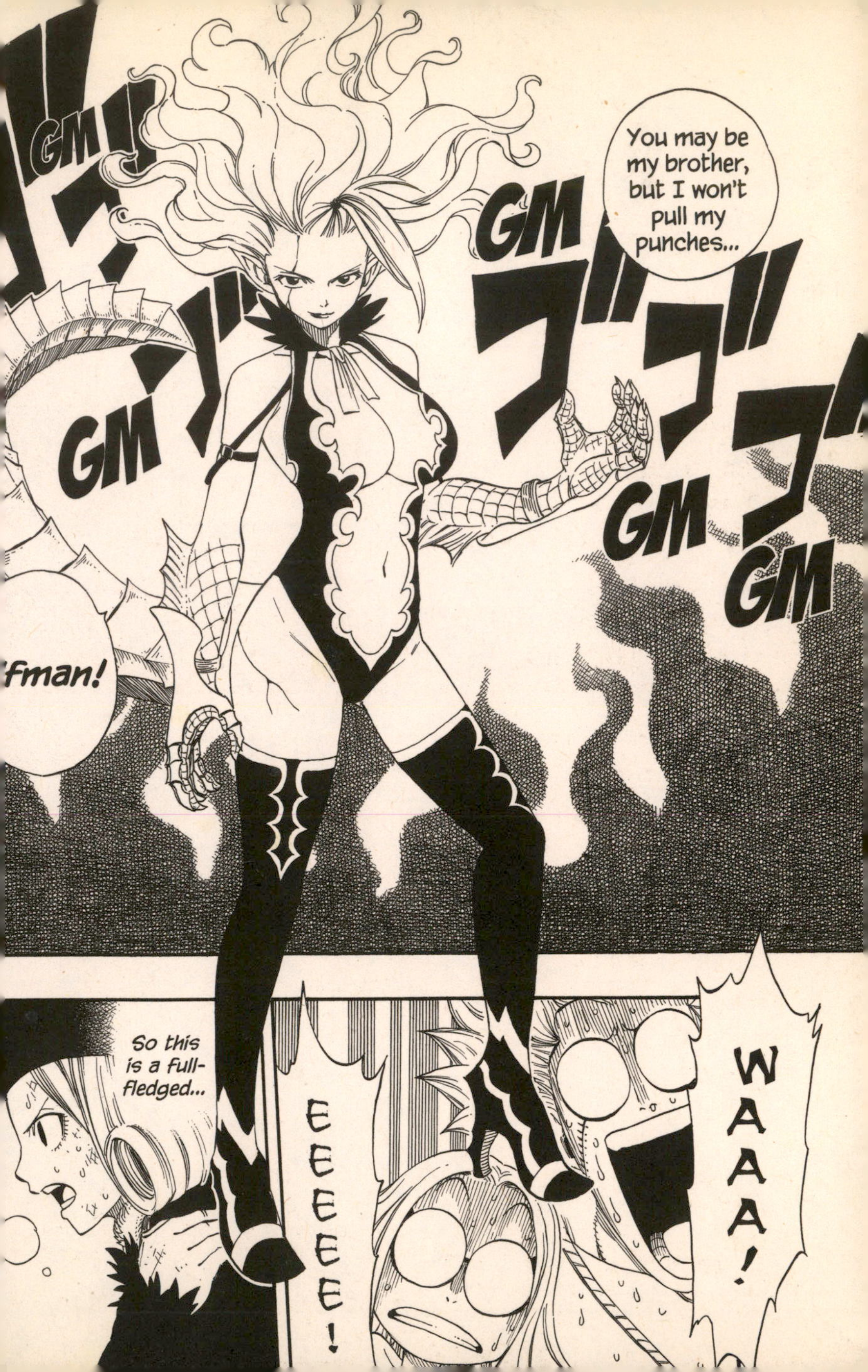
You may be my brother, but I won't pull my punches...
GM
GM
GM
GM
GM
GM
fman!
WAAA!
EEEEEE!
So this is a full-fledged...

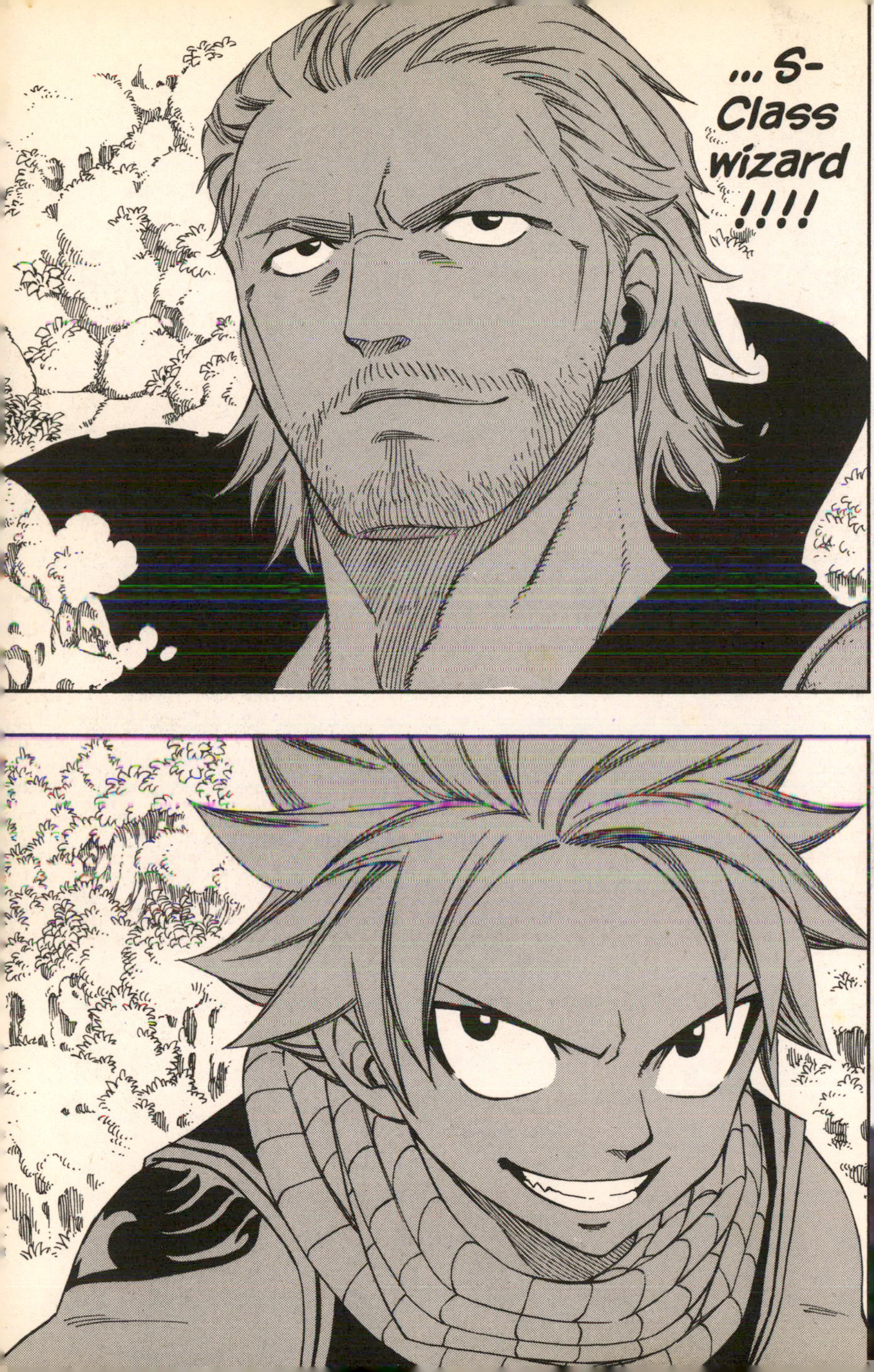
... S-Class wizard !!!!

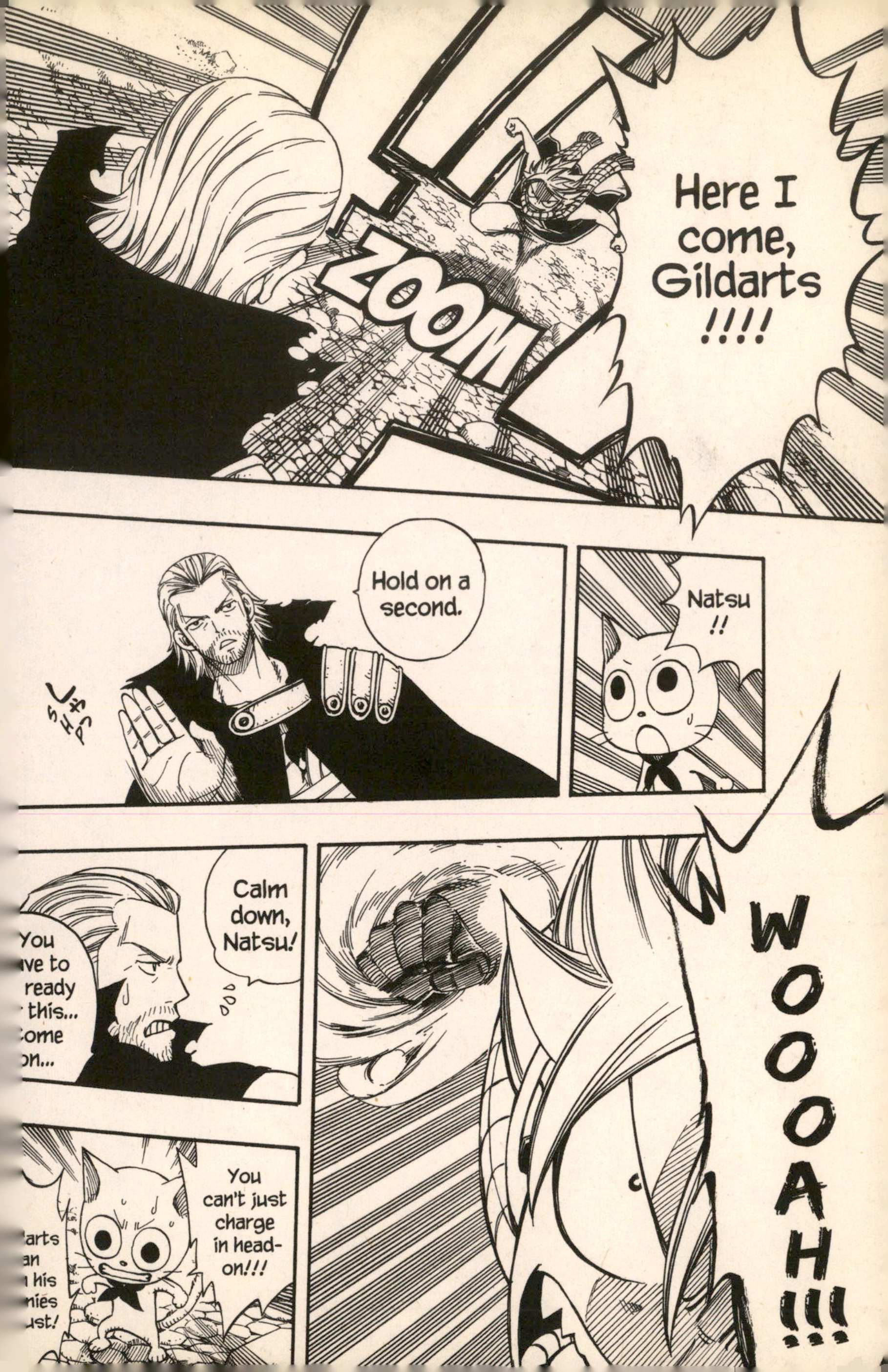
ZOOM
Here I come, Gildarts!!!!
Natsu!!
Hold on a second.
WOOOAH!!!
Calm down, Natsu!
You ave to ready this... ome on...
You can't just charge in head-on!!!
arts an his mies ust!

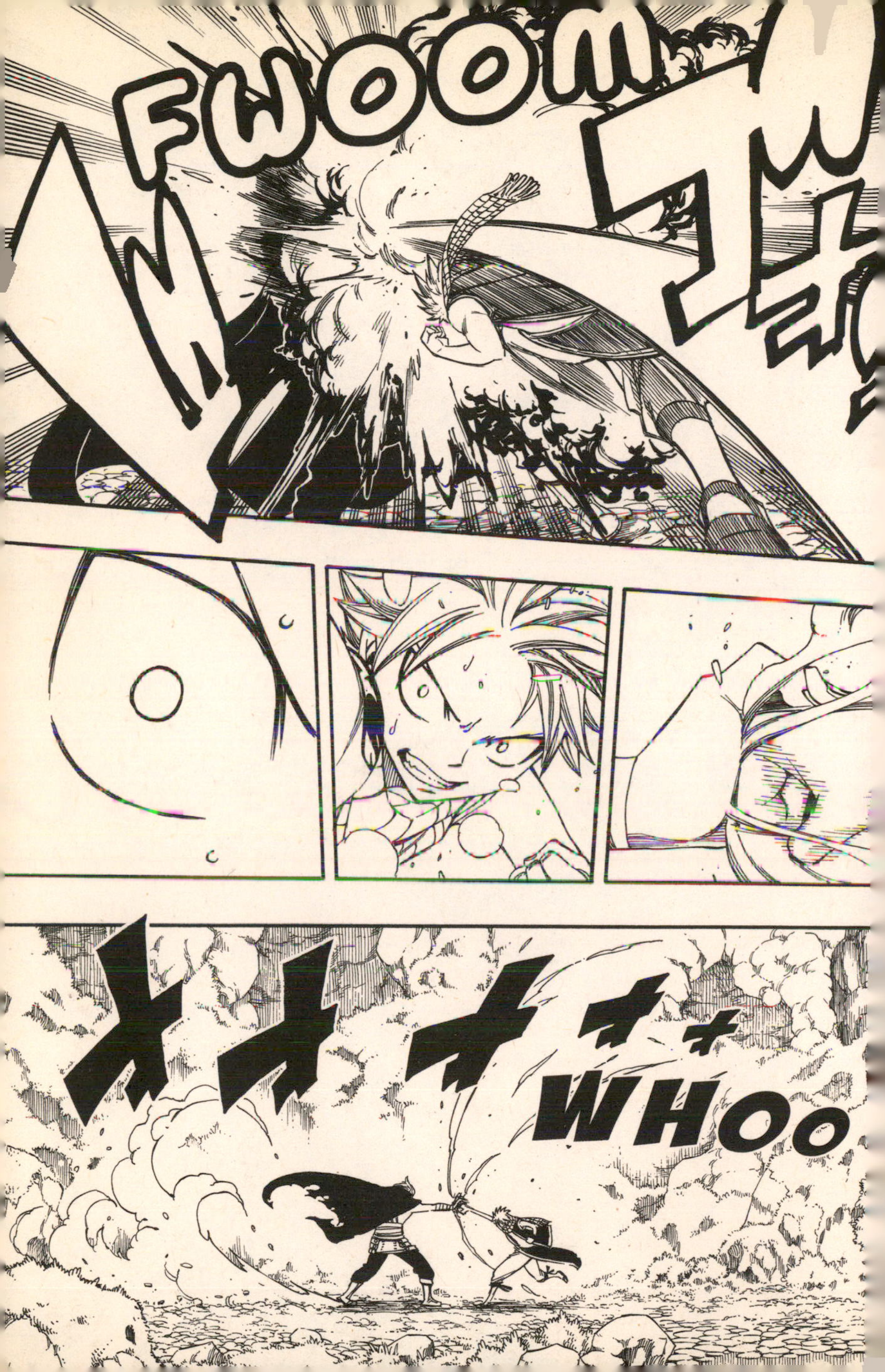
FWOOM
WHOO

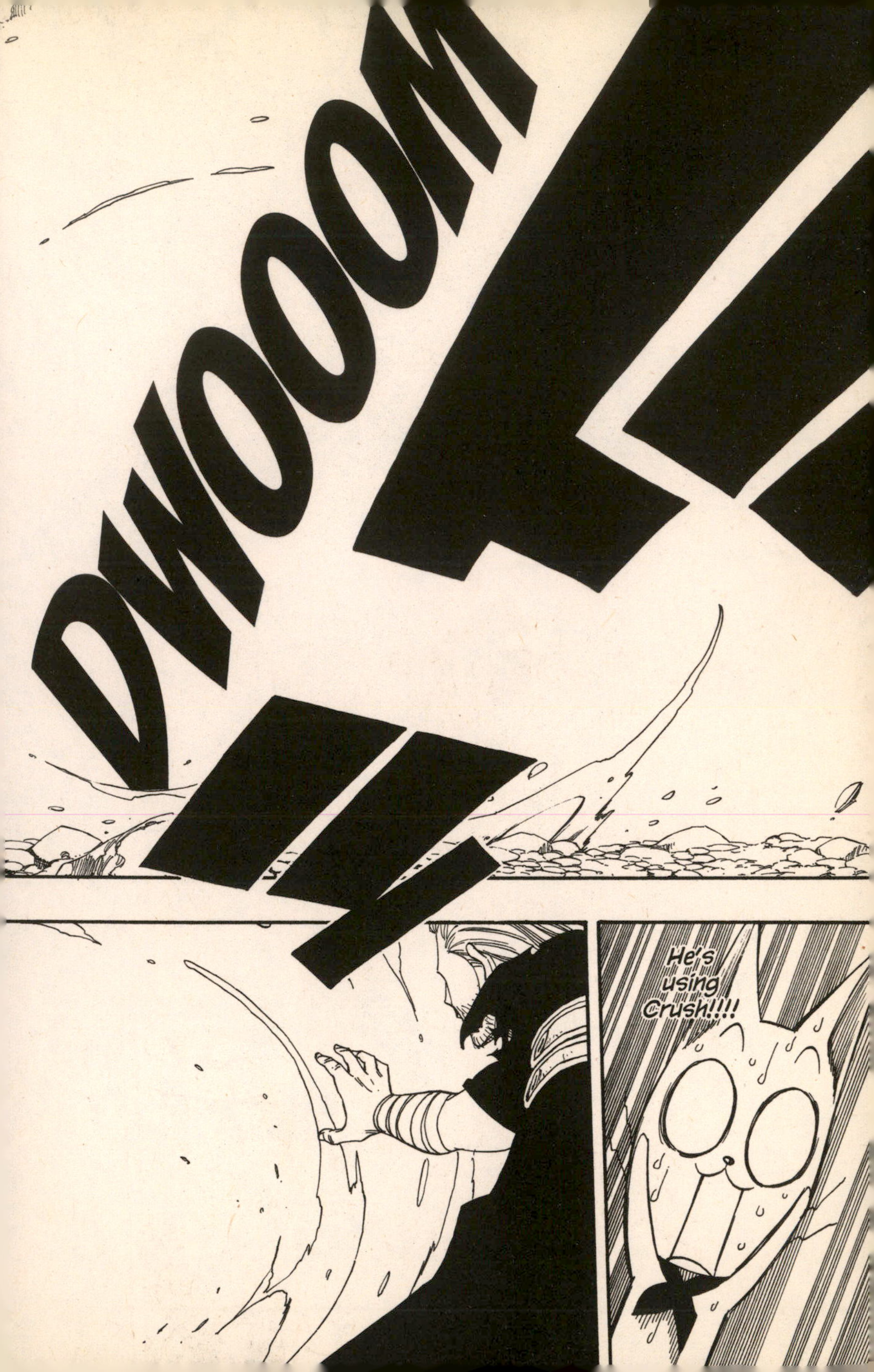
DWOOOM
He's using Crush!!!!

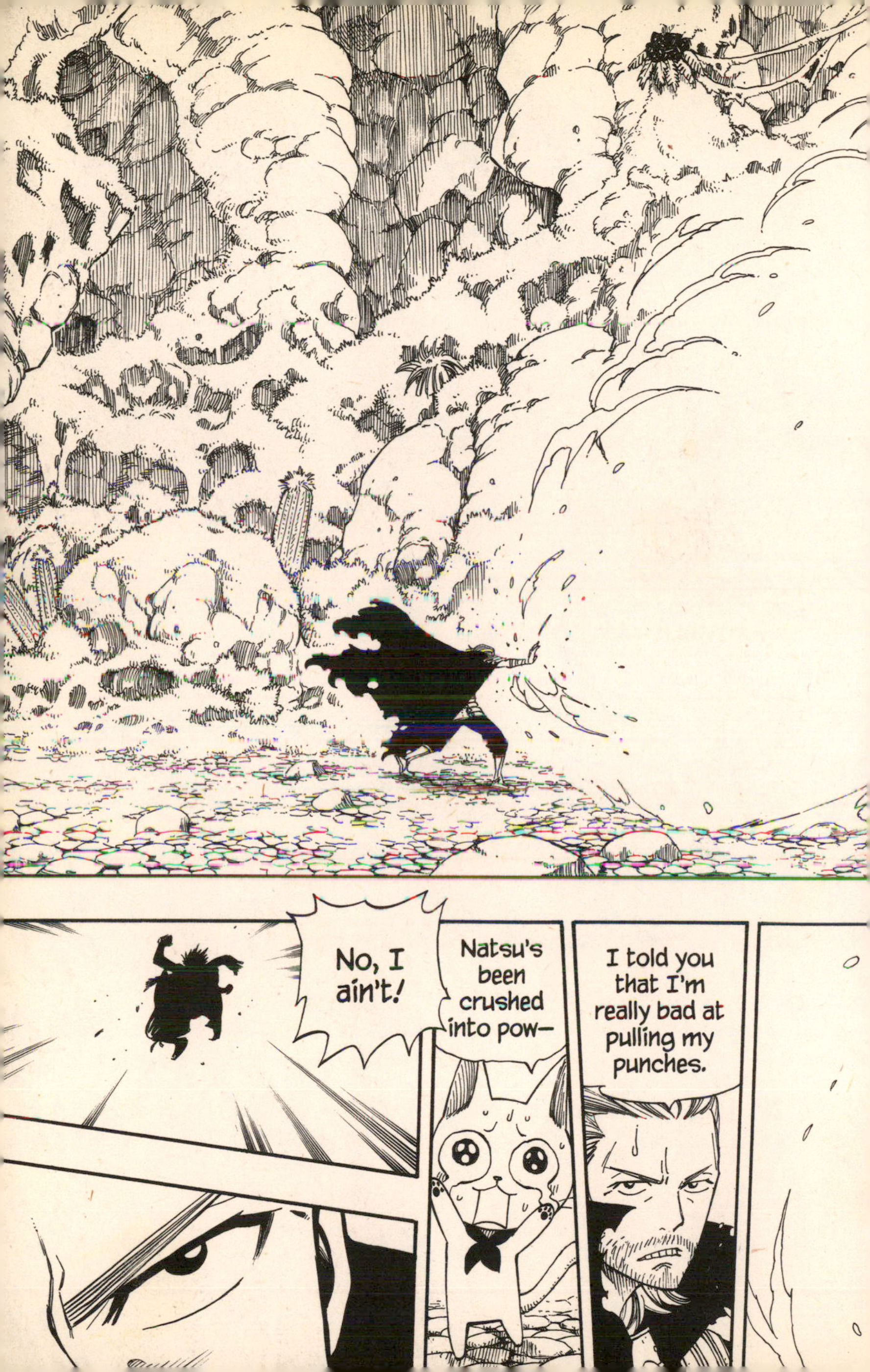
I told you that I'm really bad at pulling my punches.
Natsu's been crushed into pow—
No, I ain't!

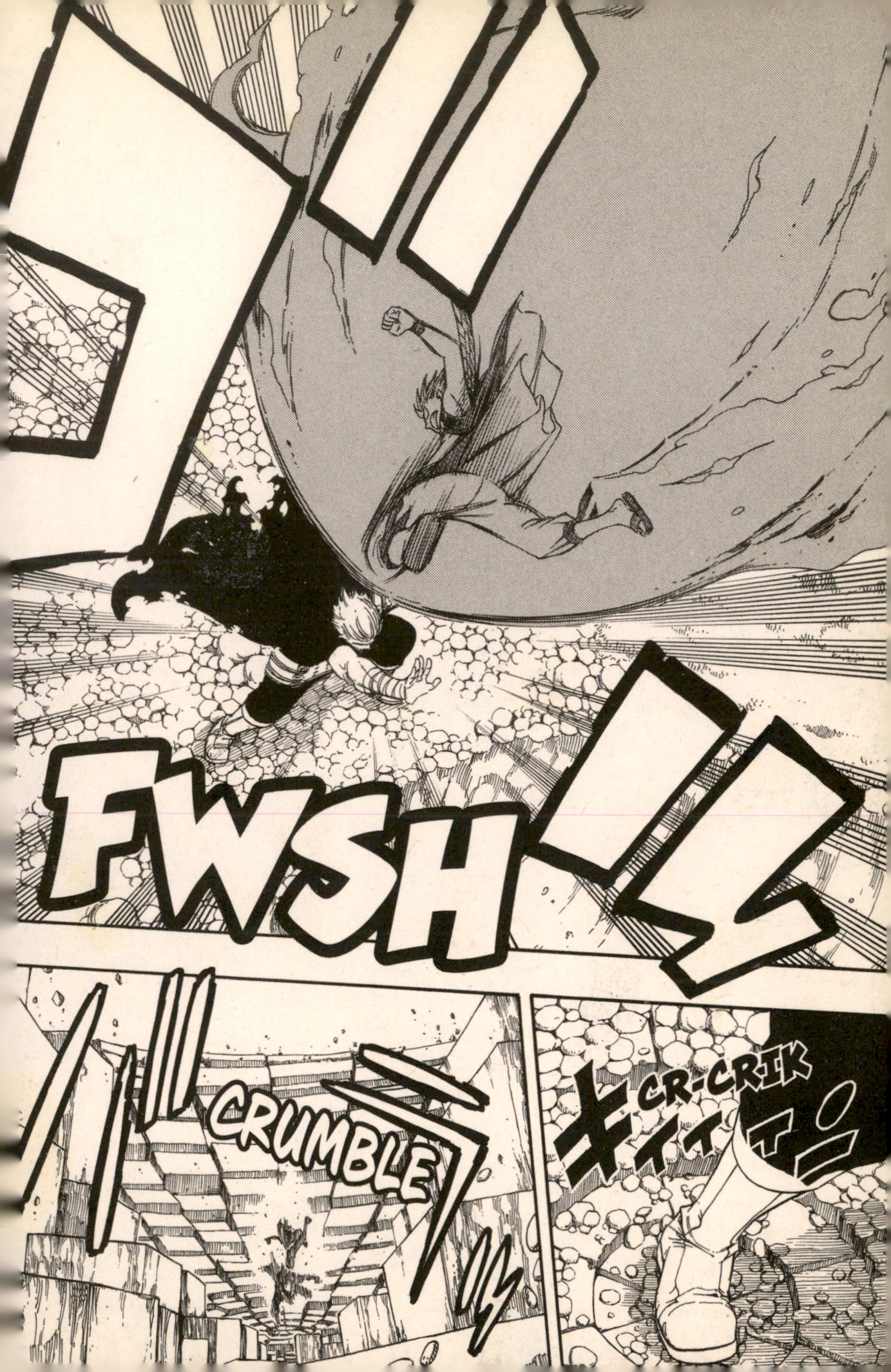
FWSH
CR-CRIK
CRUMBLE

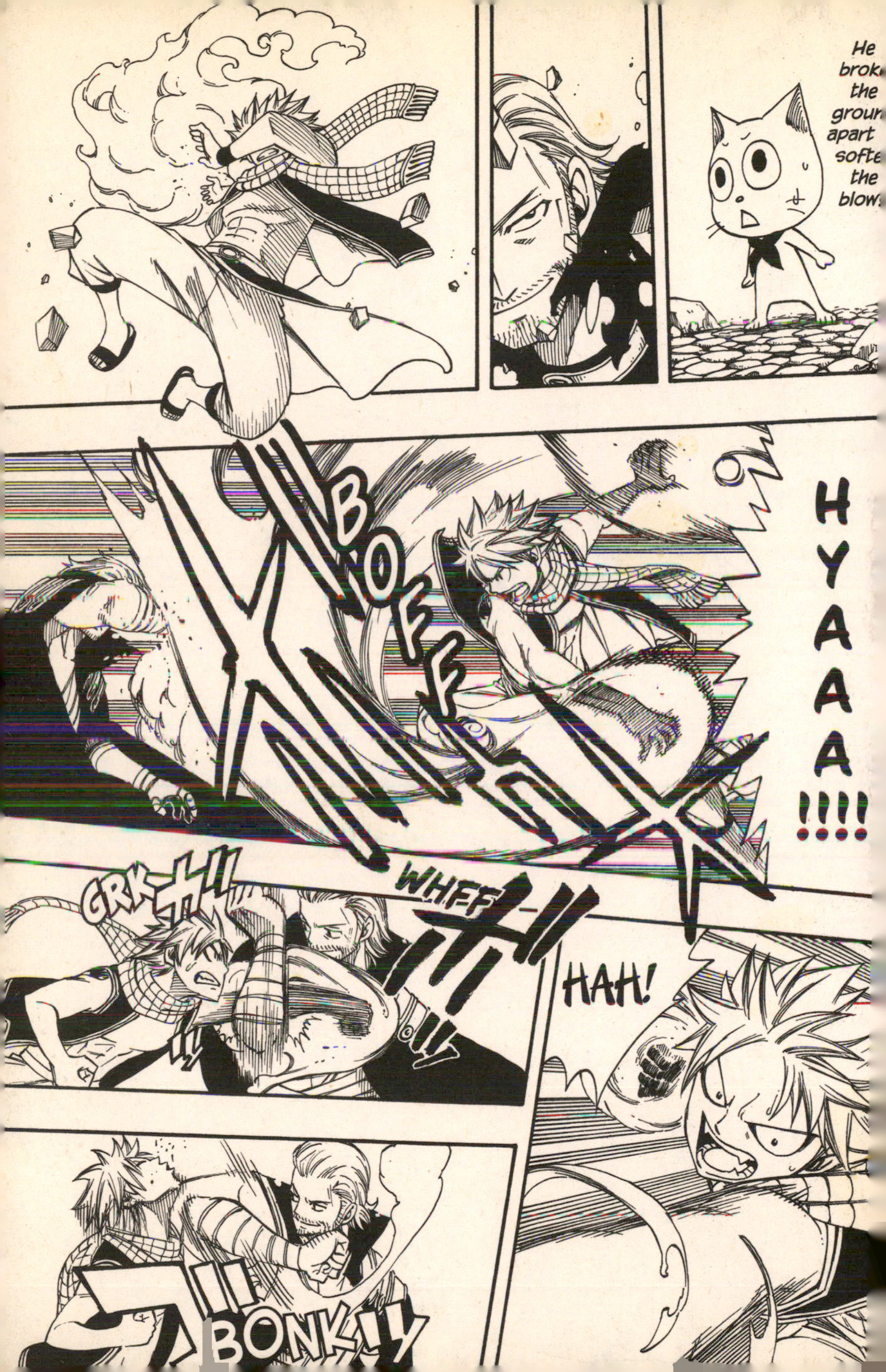
He brok the groun apart softe the blow
HYAAA!!!!
BOFF
HAH!
WHFF
GRK
BONK!!

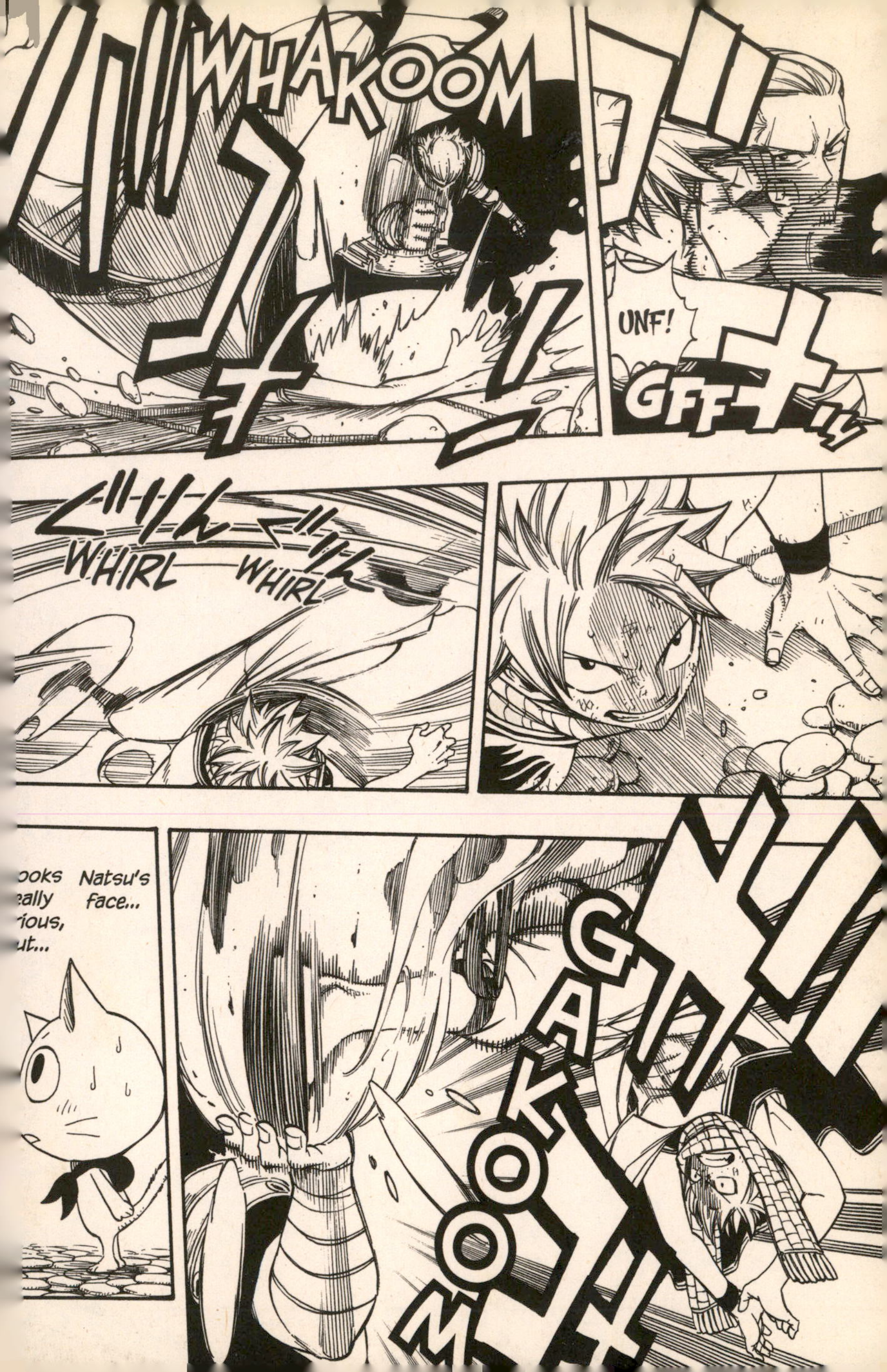
UNF!
GFF
WHAKOOM
WHIRL
WHIRL
GAKOOM
Natsu's face...
ooks eally rious, ut...

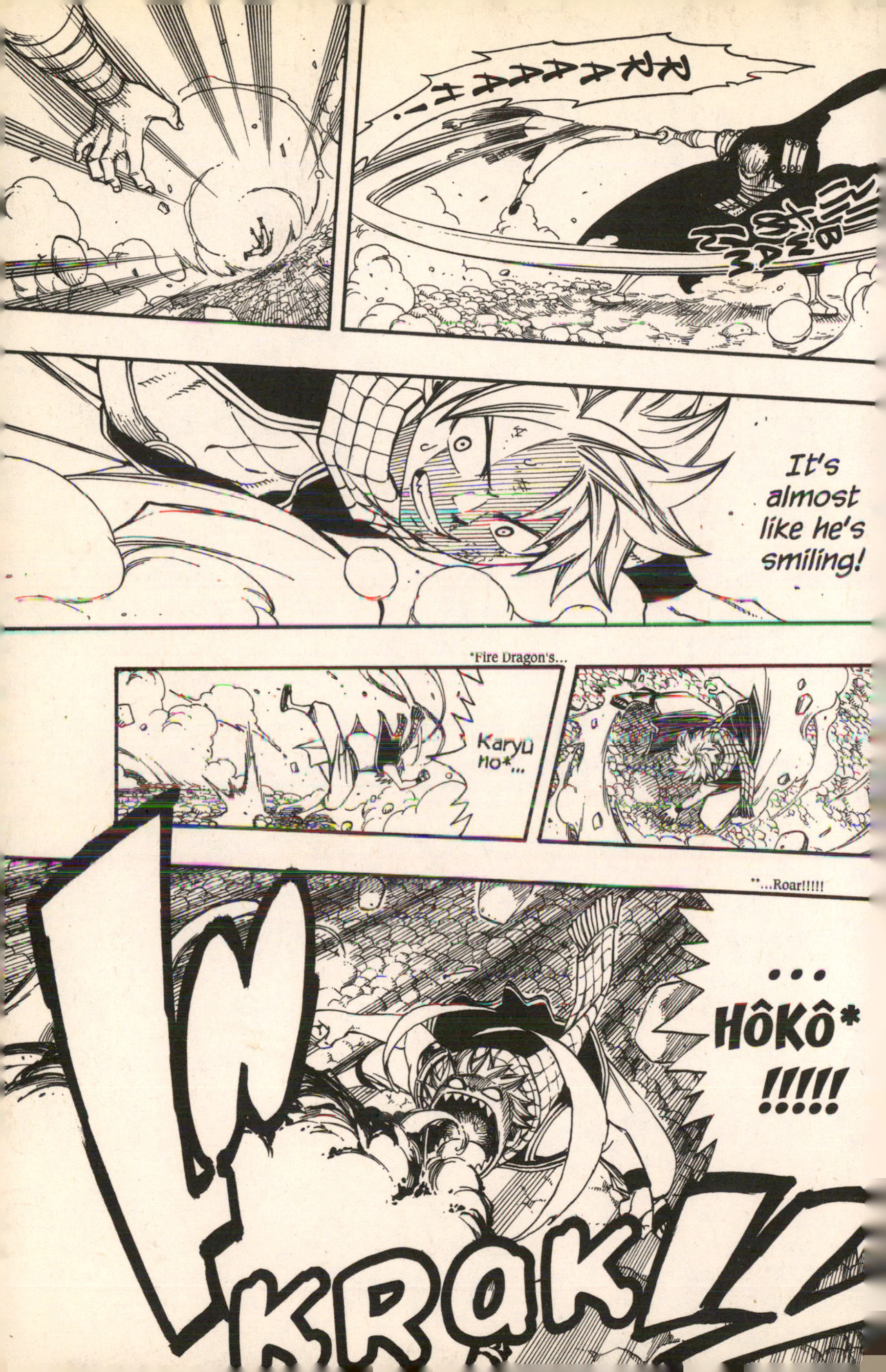
RRAAAAH!
It's almost like he's smiling!
Karyû no*...
...Hôkô**!!!!!
KRAK
*Fire Dragon's...
**...Roar!!!!!

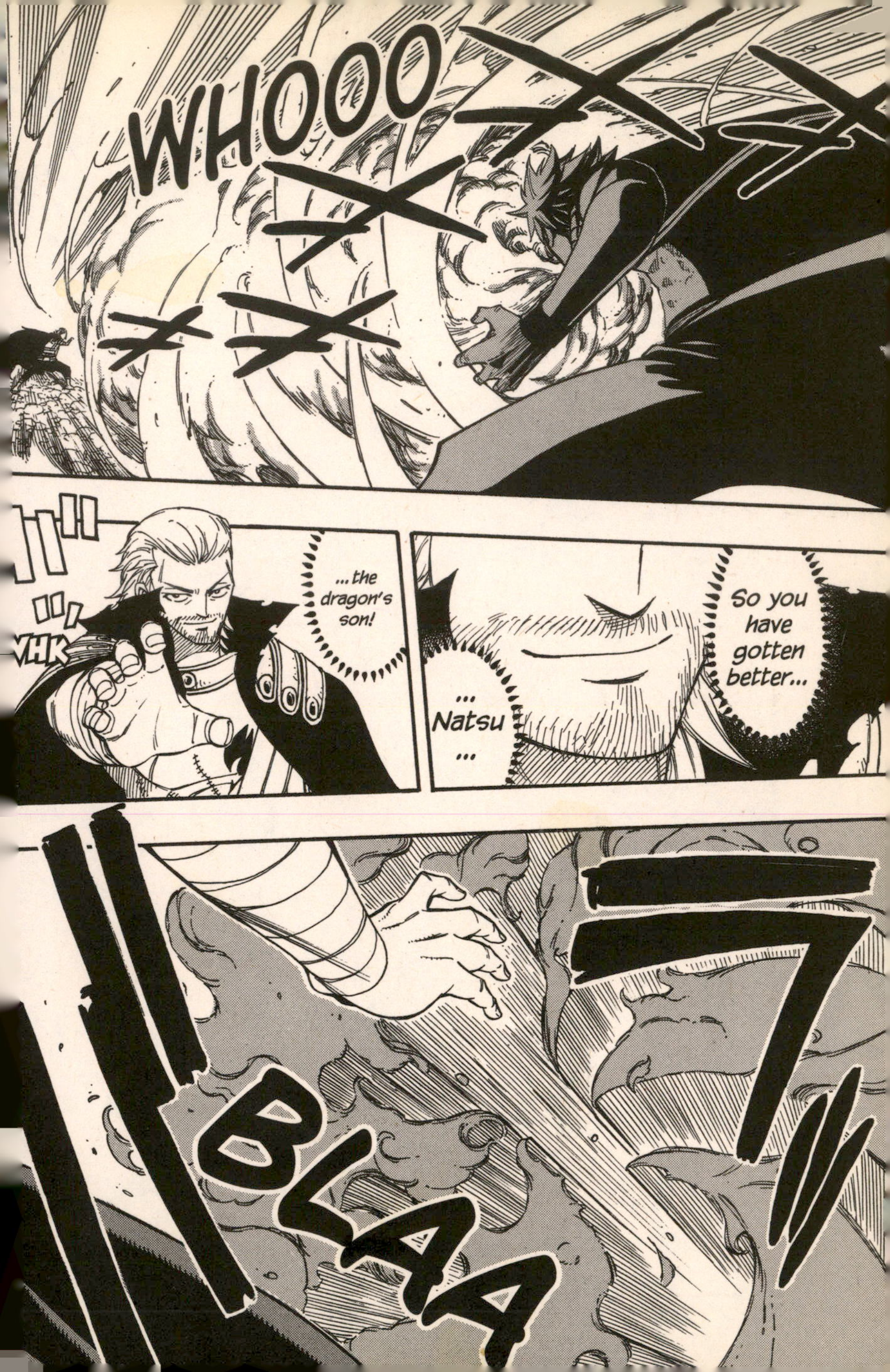
WHOOO
So you have gotten better...
... Natsu ...
...the dragon's son!
VHK
BLAA

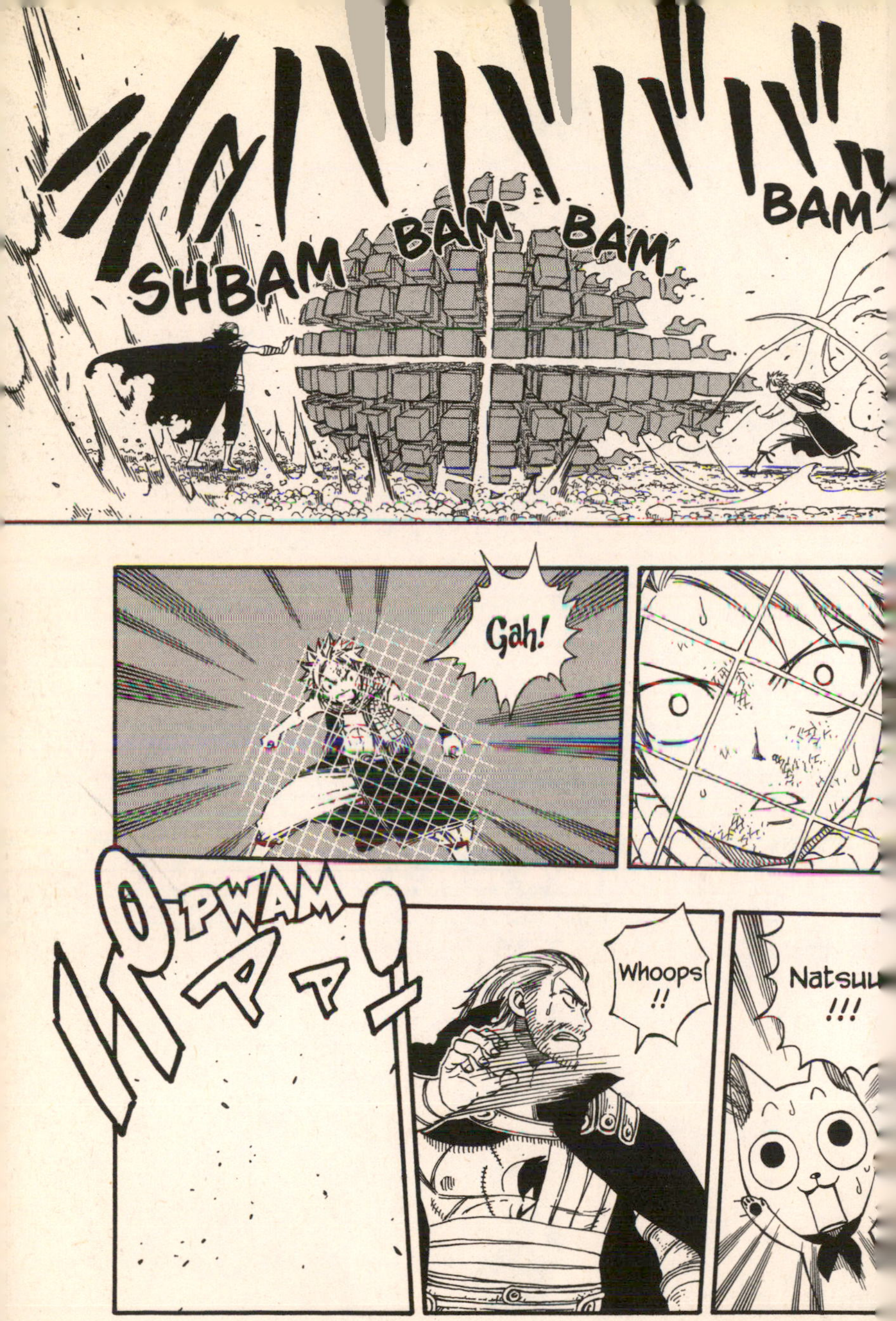
BAM!!
BAM
BAM
SHBAM
Gah!
Natsuu!!!
Whoops!!
PWAM

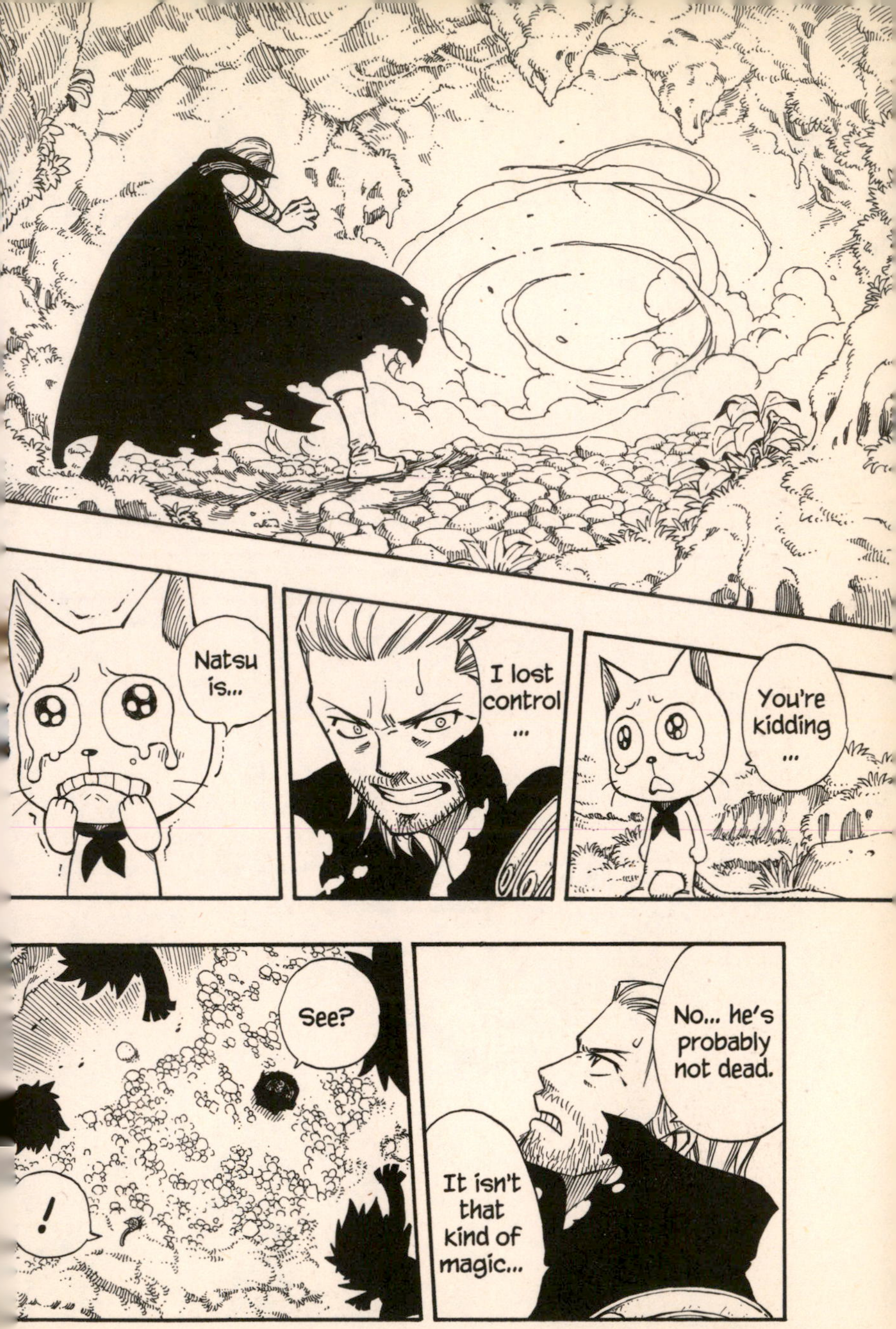
You're kidding ...
I lost control ...
Natsu is...
No... he's probably not dead.
It isn't that kind of magic...
See?
!

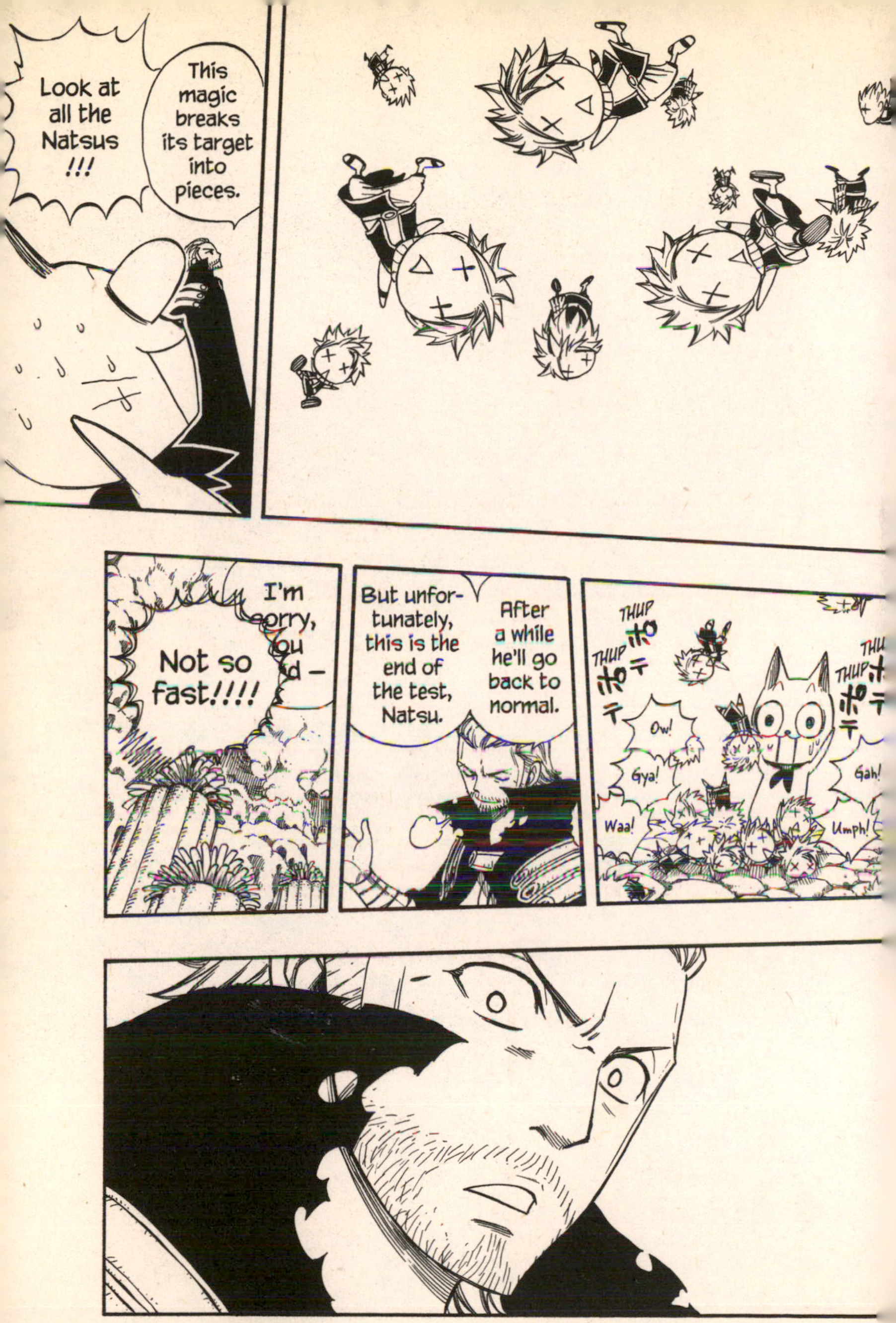
This magic breaks its target into pieces.
Look at all the Natsus!!!
THUP THUP
THUP THUP
Gah!
Umph!
Ow!
Gya!
Waa!
After a while he'll go back to normal.
But unfortunately, this is the end of the test, Natsu.
I'm orry, ou d –
Not so fast!!!!

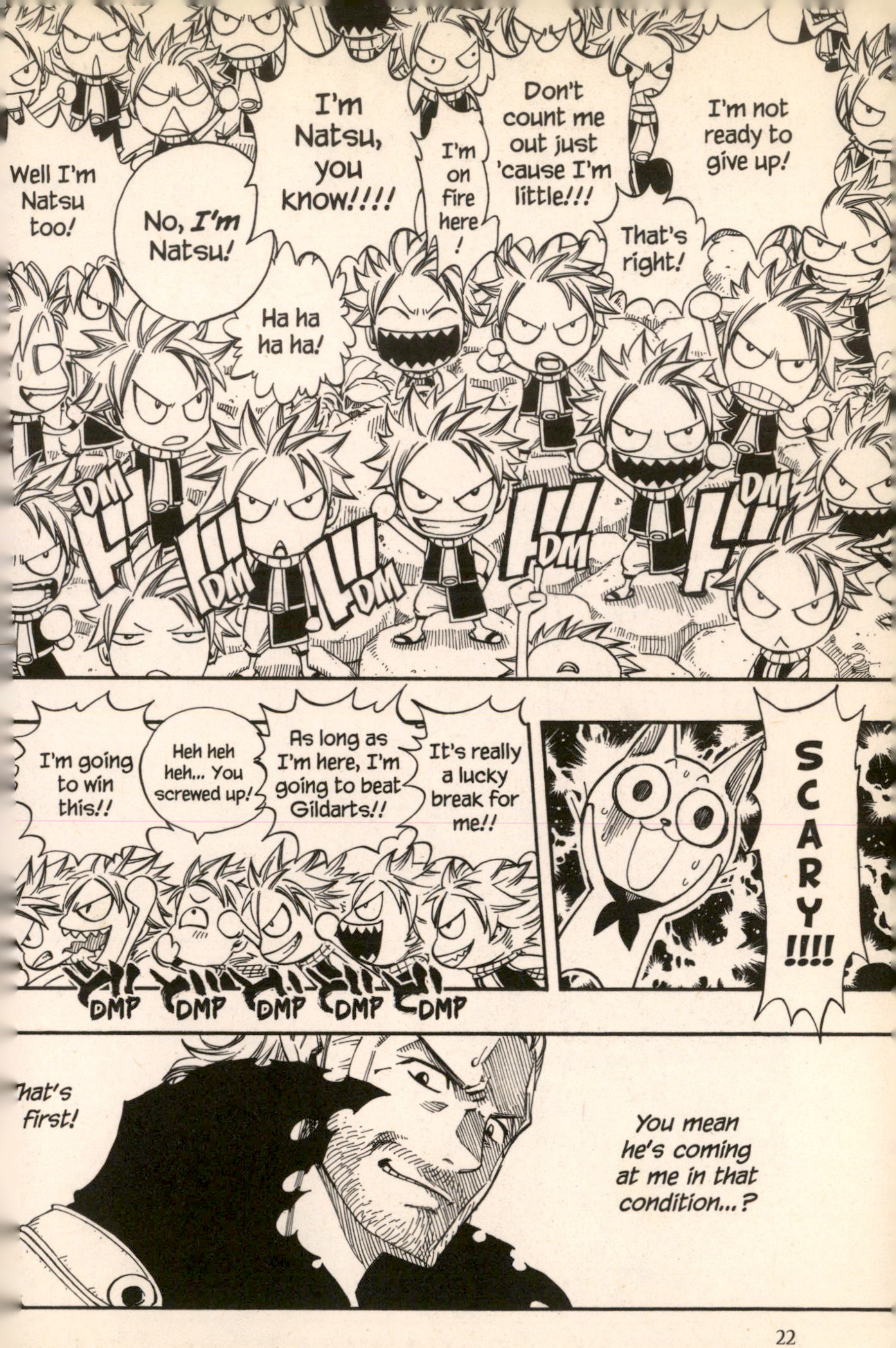

I'm not ready to give up!
Don't count me out just 'cause I'm little!!!
That's right!
I'm on fire here!
I'm Natsu, you know!!!!
No, *I'm* Natsu!
Well I'm Natsu too!
Ha ha ha ha!
DM DM DM DM DM DM
SCARY!!!!
It's really a lucky break for me!!
As long as I'm here, I'm going to beat Gildarts!!
Heh heh heh... You screwed up!
I'm going to win this!!
DMP DMP DMP DMP DMP
You mean he's coming at me in that condition...?
hat's first!

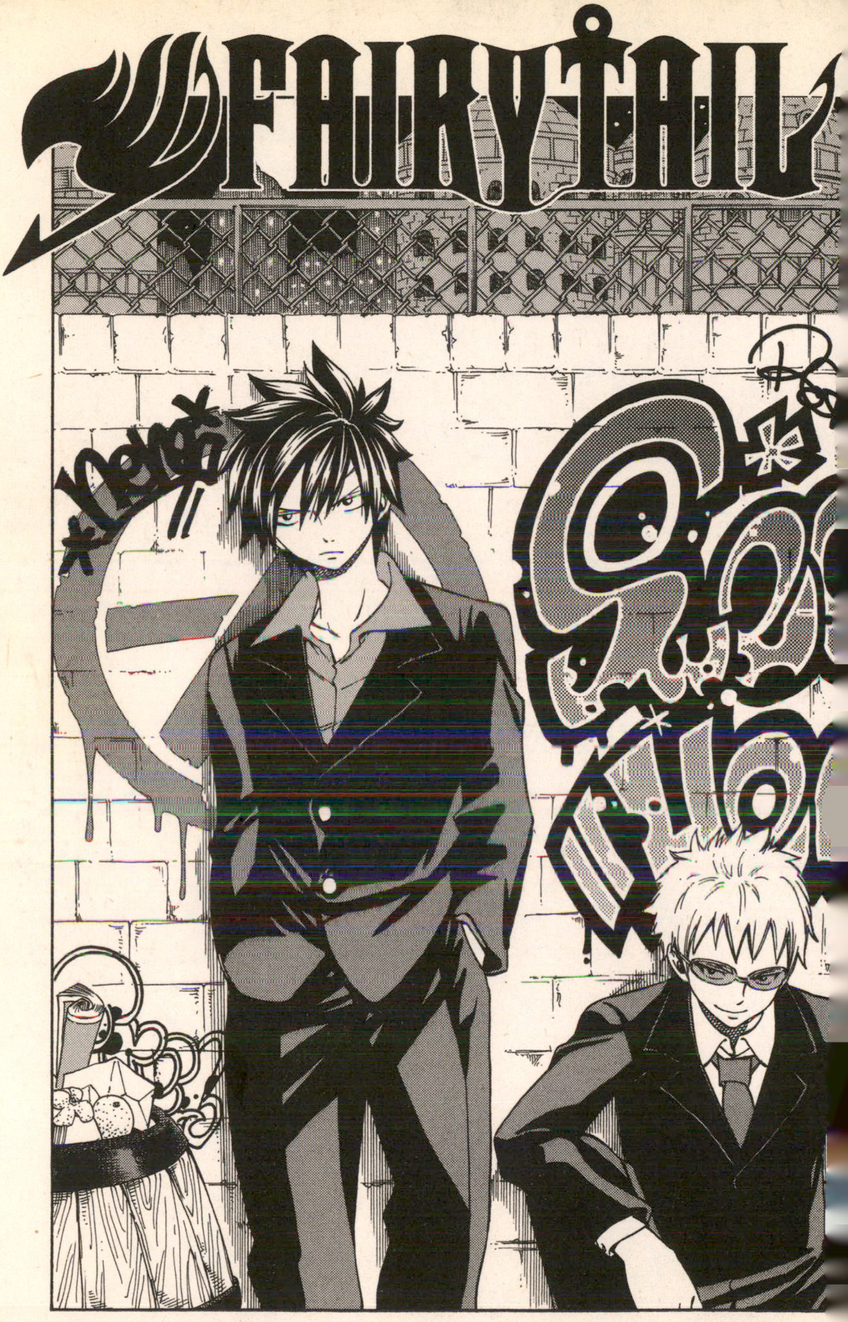
FAIRY TAIL

Chapter 206: To Continue Down This Pa

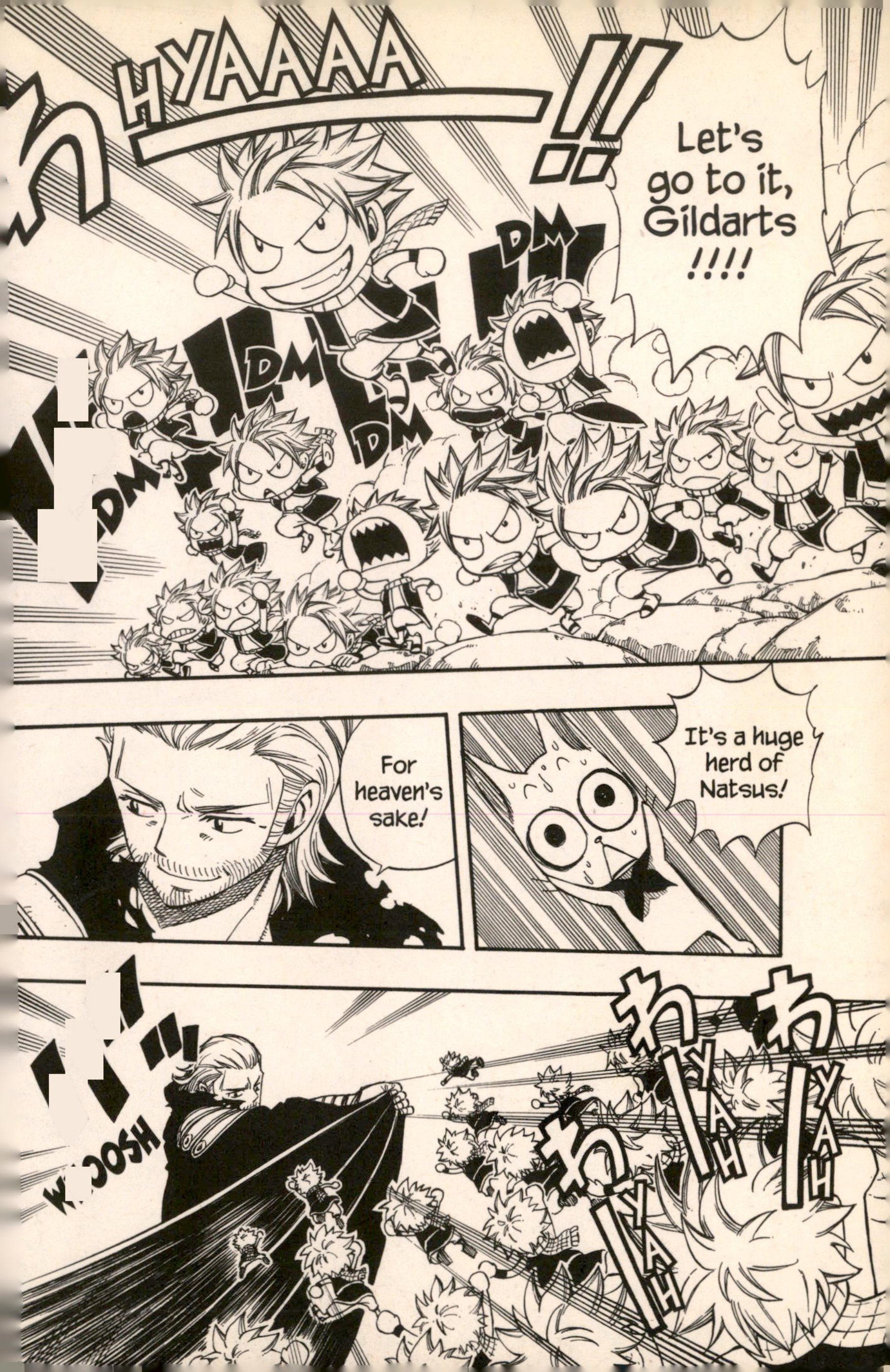

HYAAAA!!
Let's go to it, Gildarts !!!!
DM
DM
DM
DM
DM
It's a huge herd of Natsus!
For heaven's sake!
YAH
YAH
YAH

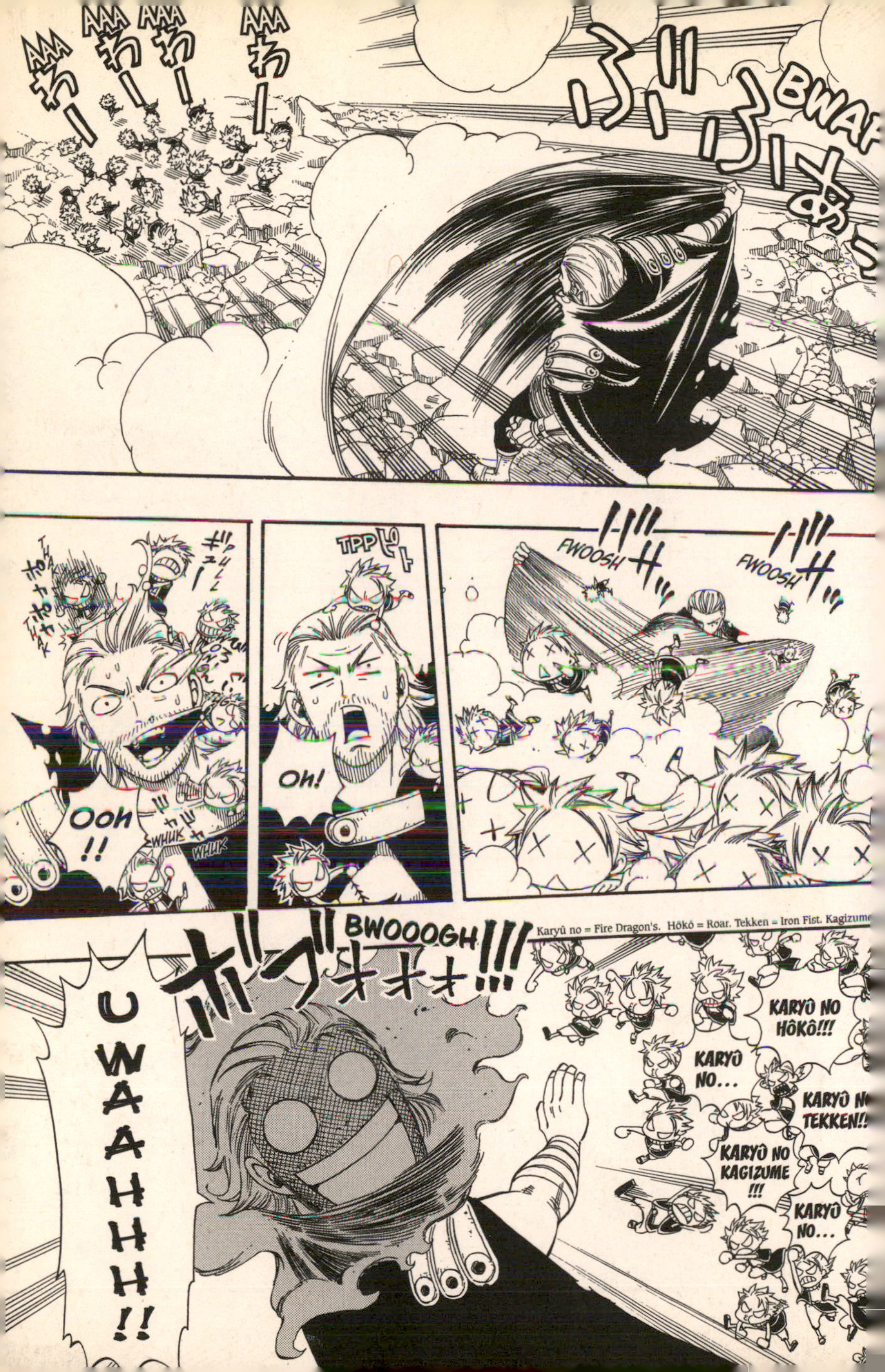
BWAH
AAA
わー
AAA
わー
AAA
わー
AAA
わー
FWOOSH
FWOOSH
TPP
Oh!
THWACK
WHUK
WHUK
Ooh!!
Karyû no = Fire Dragon's. Hôkô = Roar. Tekken = Iron Fist. Kagizume
KARYÛ NO HÔKÔ!!!
KARYÛ NO...
KARYÛ NO TEKKEN!!
KARYÛ NO KAGIZUME!!!
KARYÛ NO...
BWOOOGH!!!
UWAAHHH!!

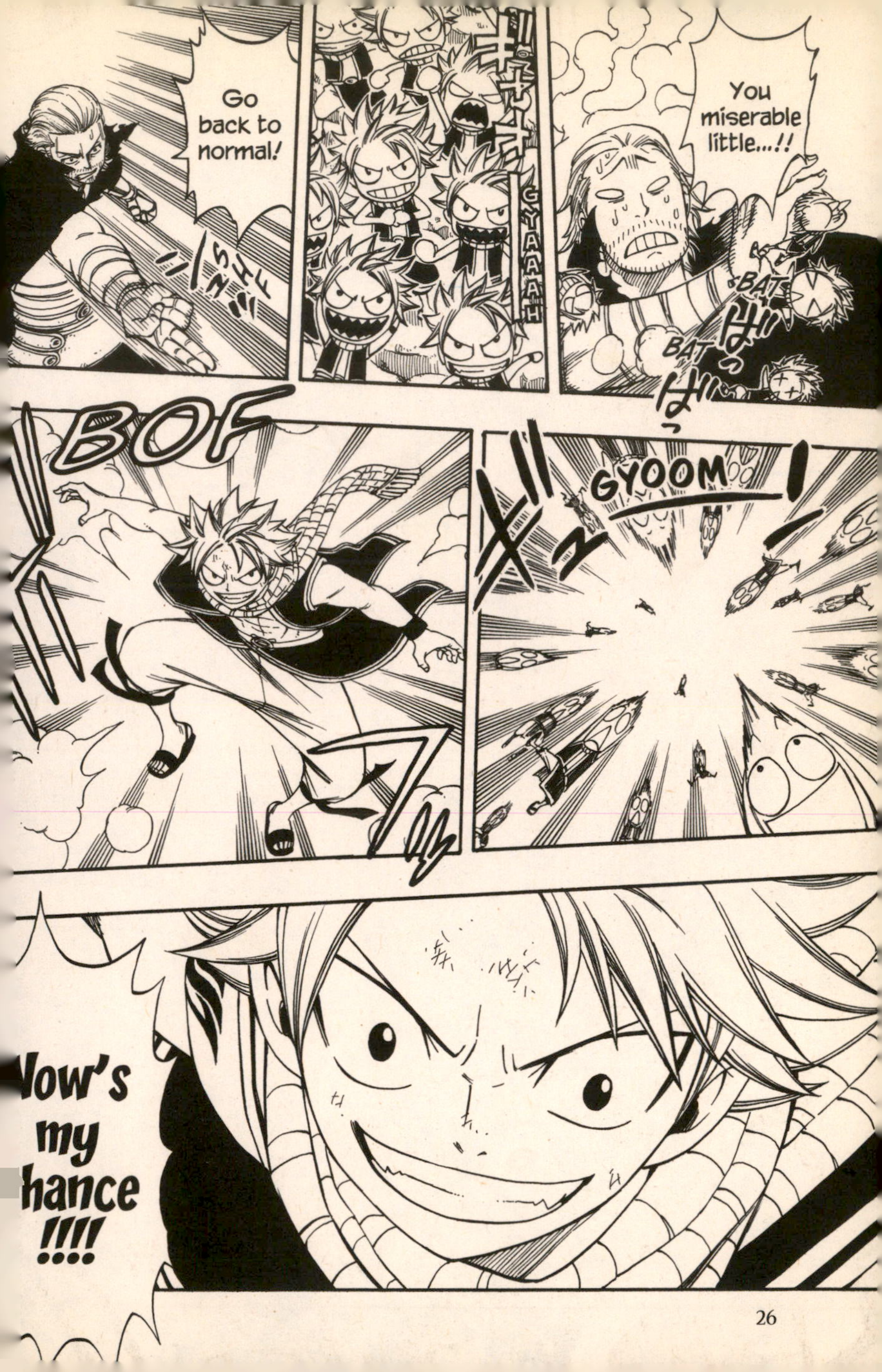
You miserable little...!!
BAT
BAT
GYAAAAH
Go back to normal!
GYOOM
BOF
low's my hance !!!!

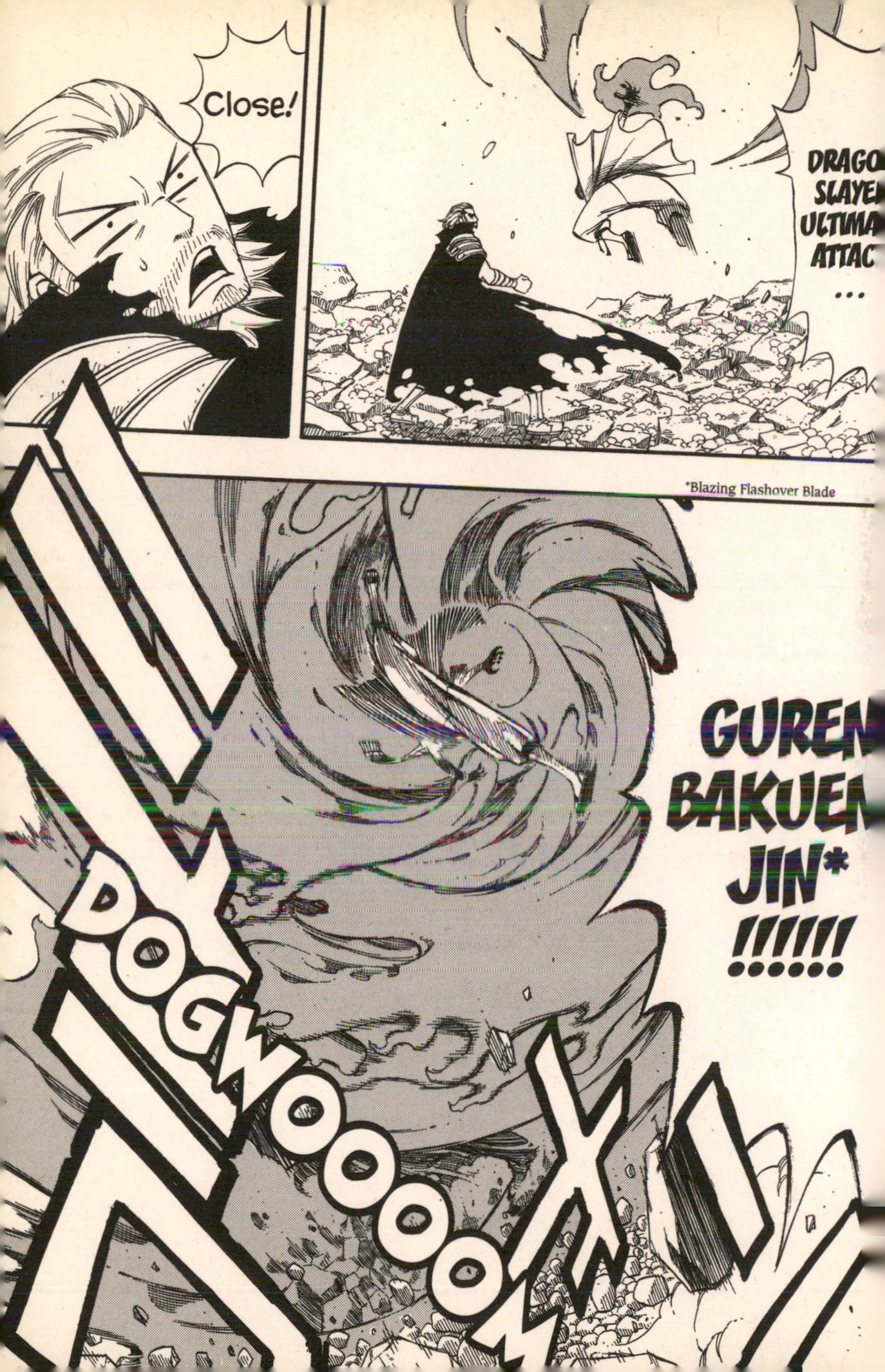
DRAGO
SLAYE
ULTIMA
ATTAC
...
Close!
GUREN
BAKUEN
JIN*
!!!!!!
DOGWOOOOOM

*Blazing Flashover Blade

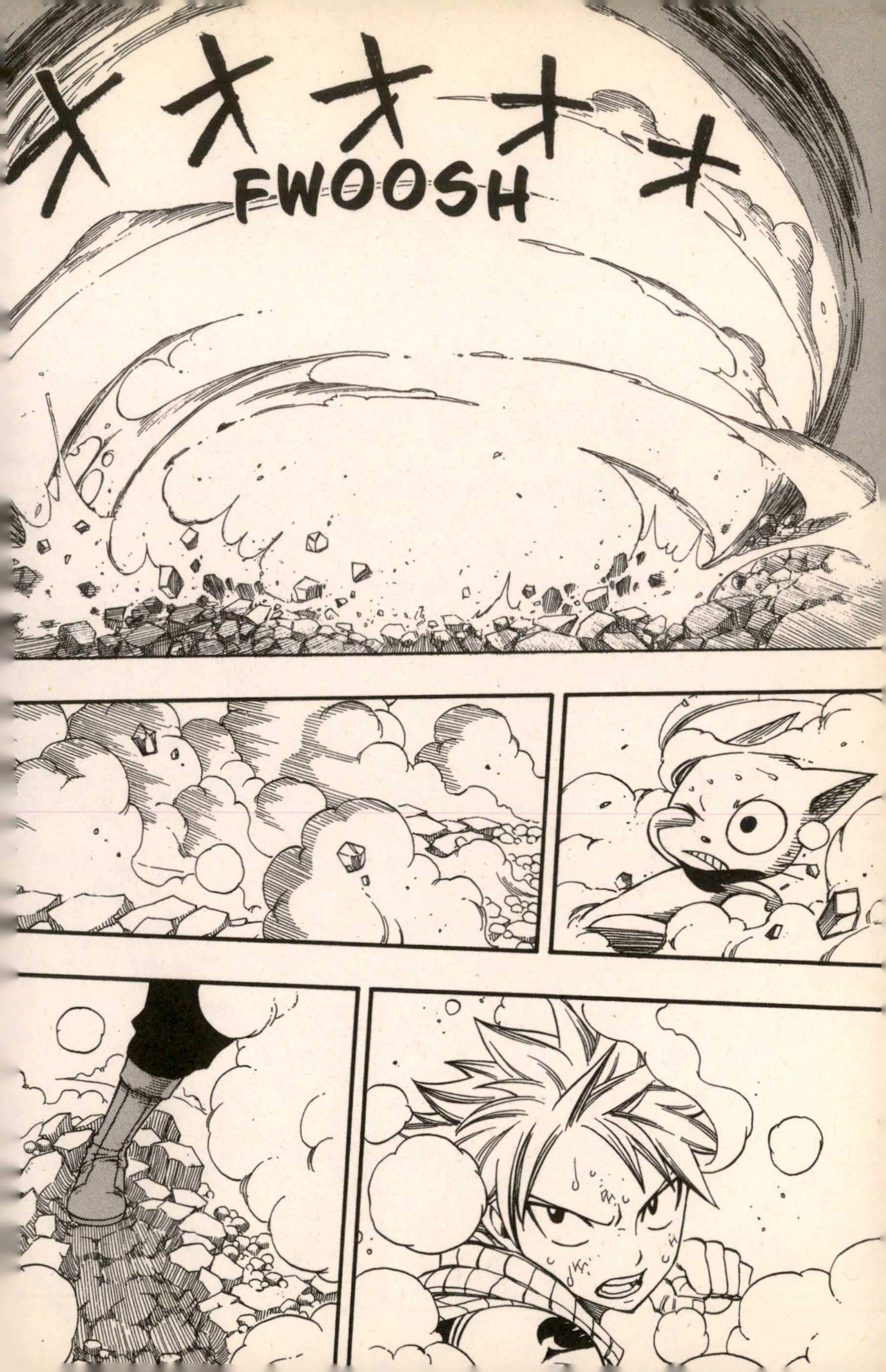
オオオオオ
FWOOSH

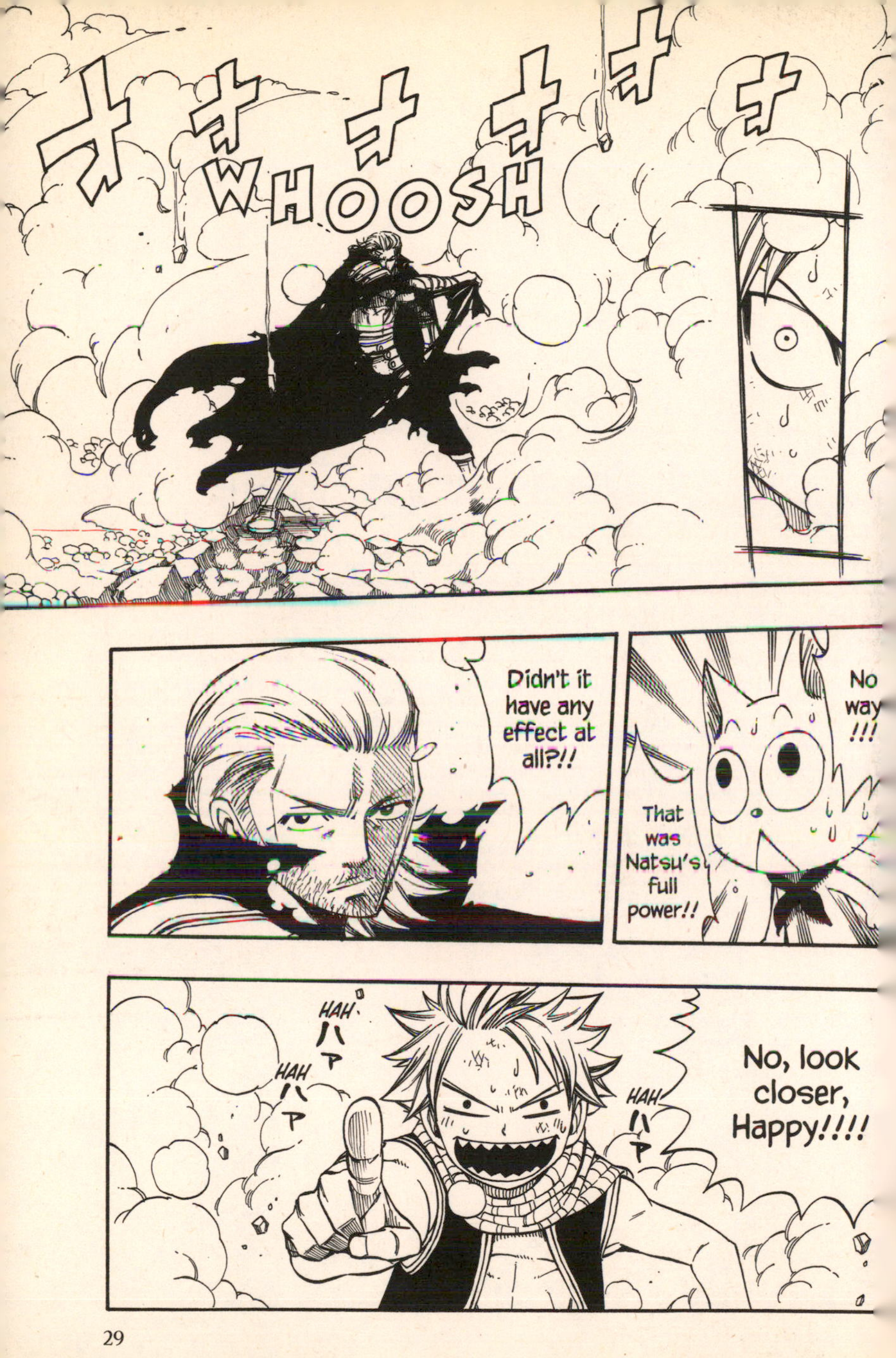
オオオオオオ
WHOOSH
No way!!!
That was Natsu's full power!!
Didn't it have any effect at all?!!
HAH ハア
HAH ハア
HAH ハア
No, look closer, Happy!!!!

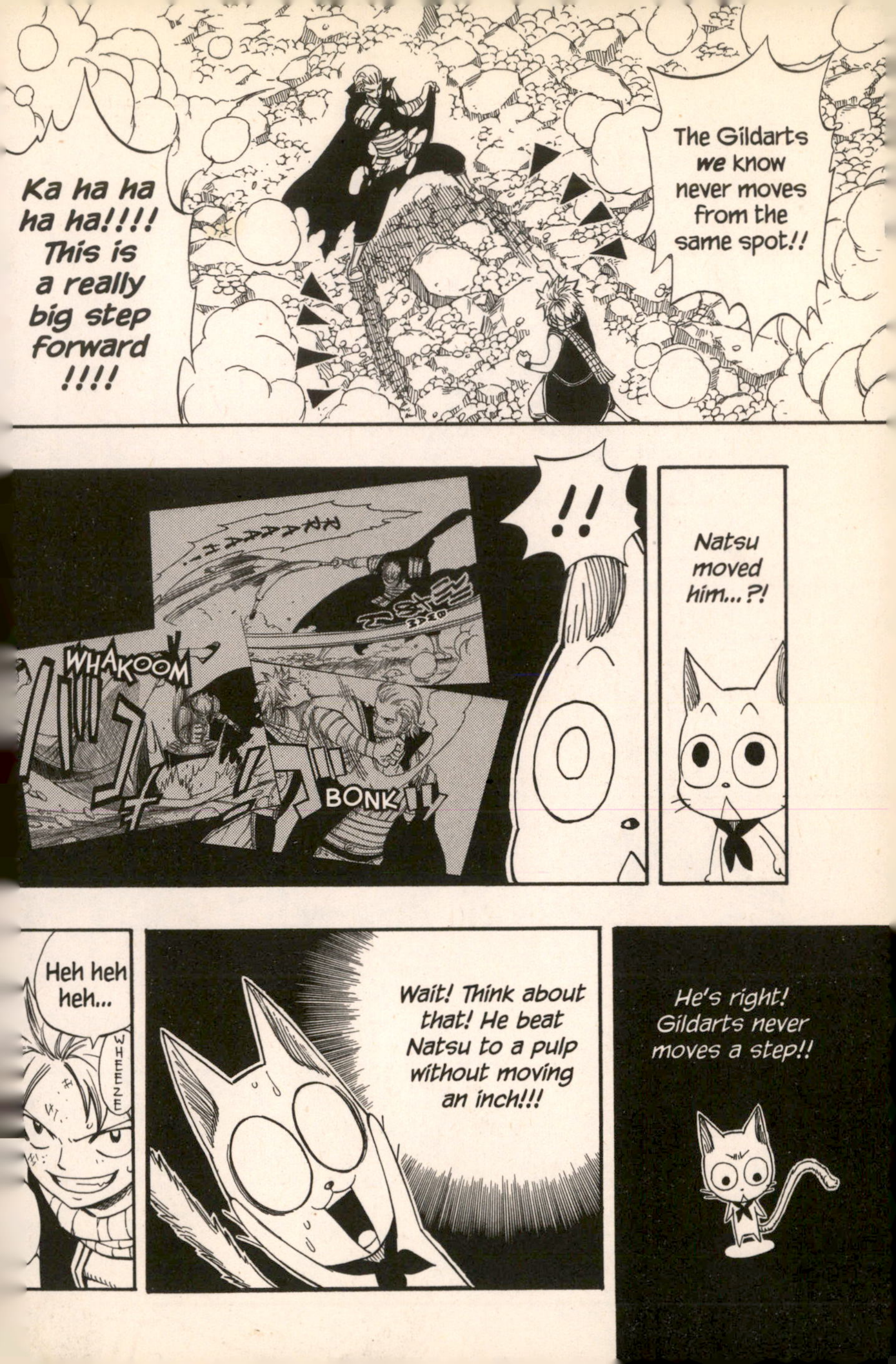
The Gildarts *we* know never moves from the same spot!!
Ka ha ha ha ha!!!! This is a really big step forward !!!!
Natsu moved him...?!
!!
WHAKOOM
BONK!!
He's right! Gildarts never moves a step!!
Wait! Think about that! He beat Natsu to a pulp without moving an inch!!!
Heh heh heh...
WHEEZE

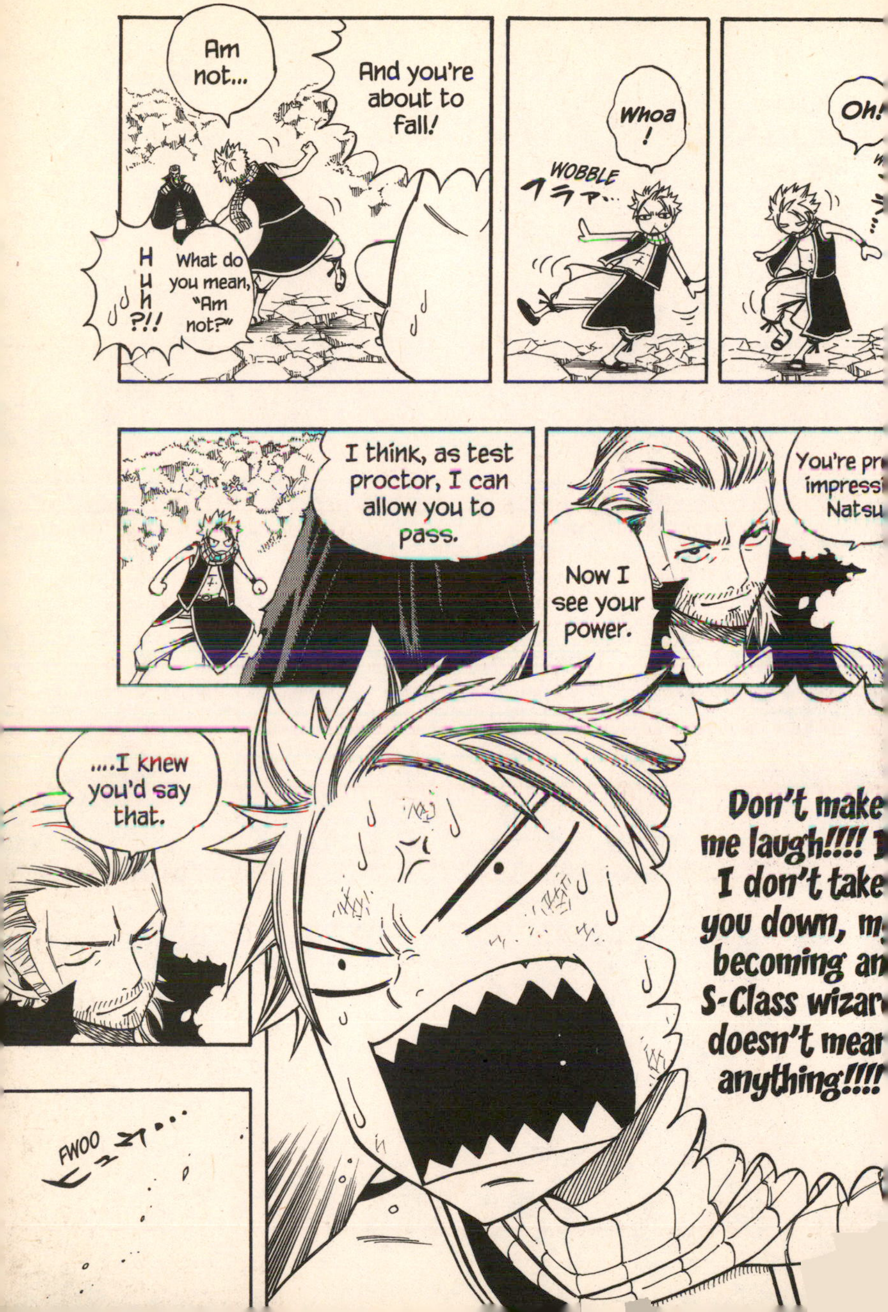
Oh!
WOBBLE
Whoa!
And you're about to fall!
Am not...
What do you mean, "Am not?"
Huh?!!
You're pr impressi Natsu
Now I see your power.
I think, as test proctor, I can allow you to pass.
Don't make me laugh!!!! I don't take you down, m becoming an S-Class wizar doesn't mean anything!!!!
....I knew you'd say that.
FWOO

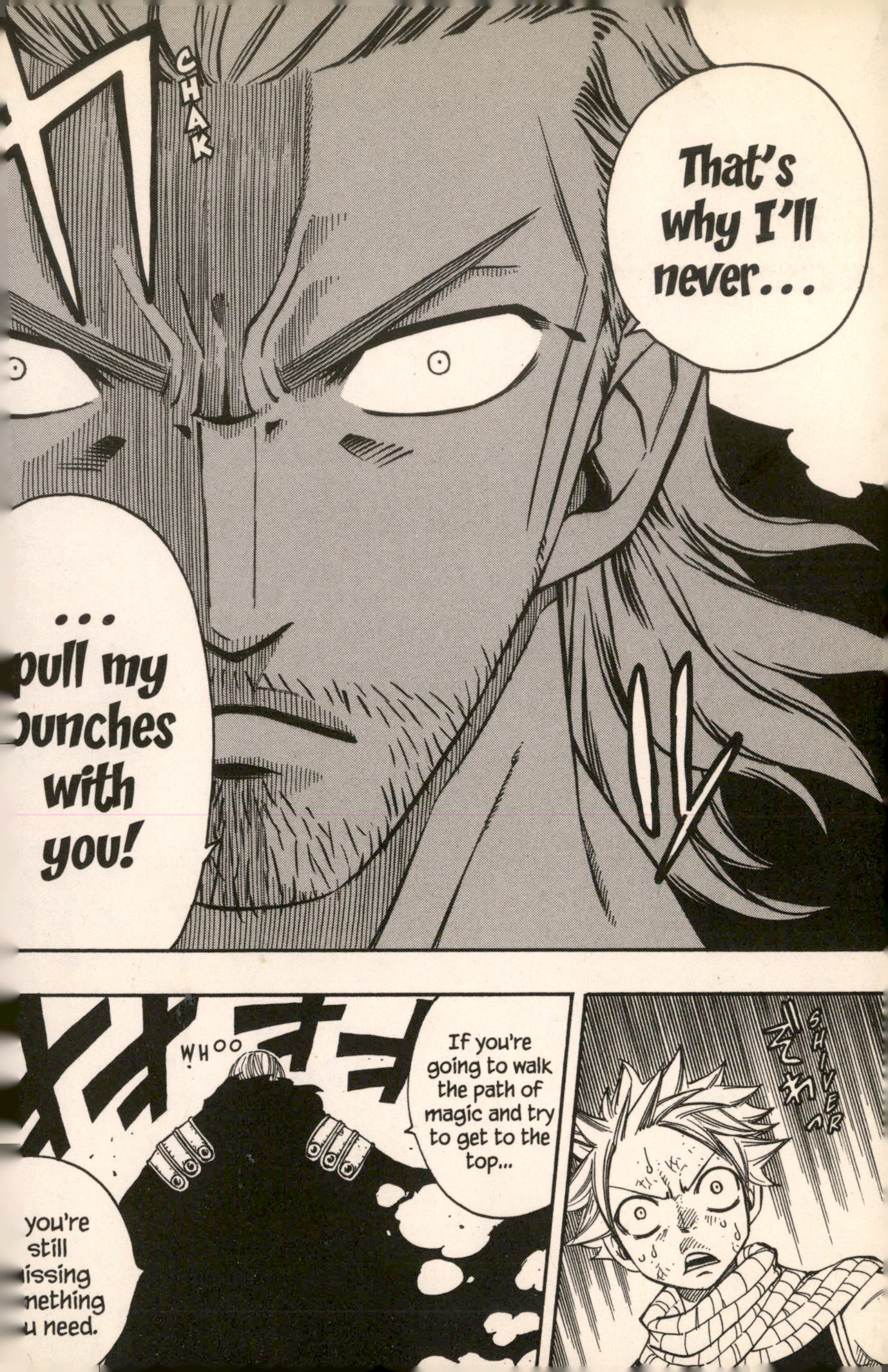
CHAK
That's why I'll never...
...pull my unches with you!
SHIVER
If you're going to walk the path of magic and try to get to the top...
WHOO
you're still issing nething u need.

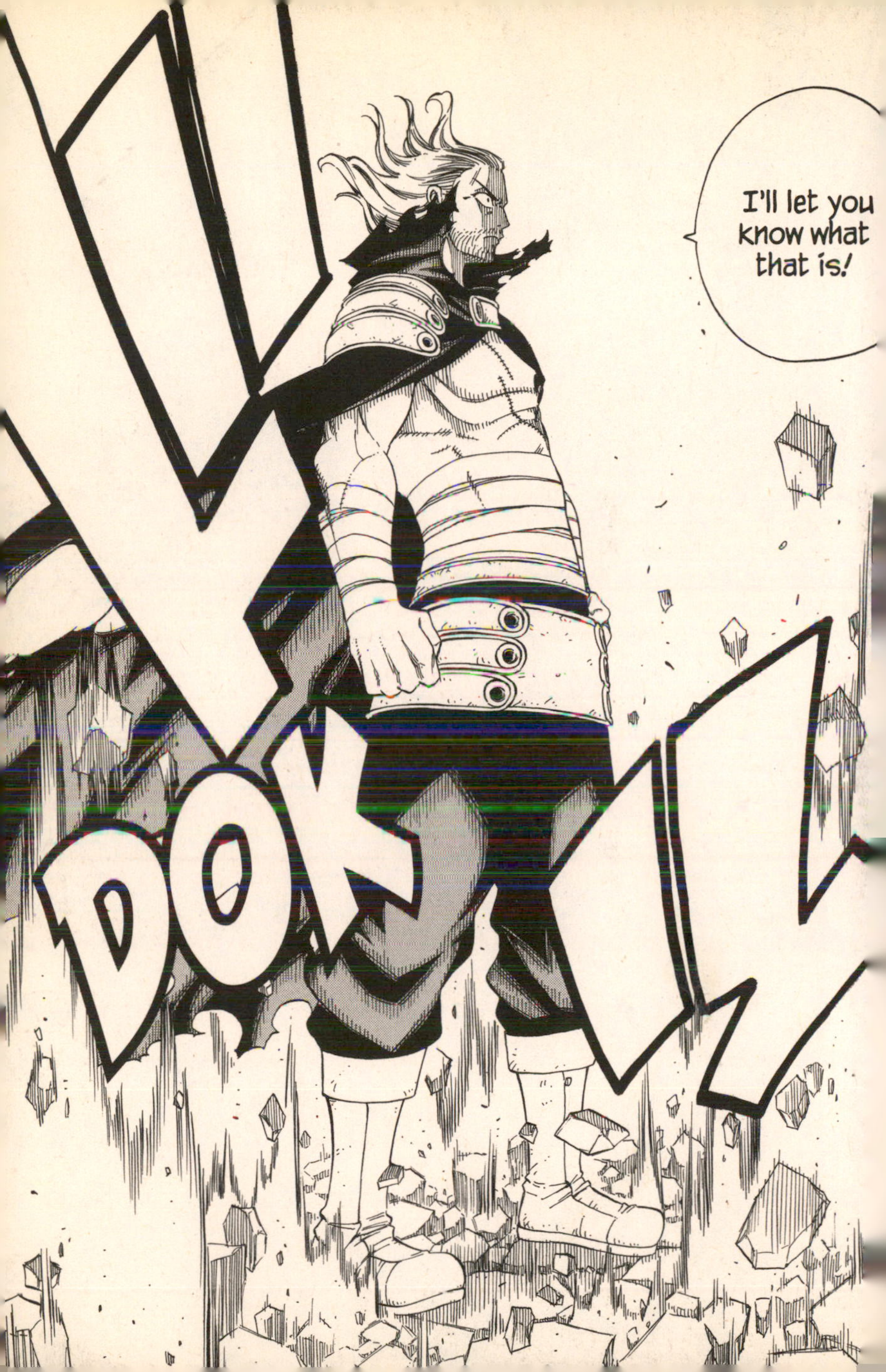
I'll let you know what that is!

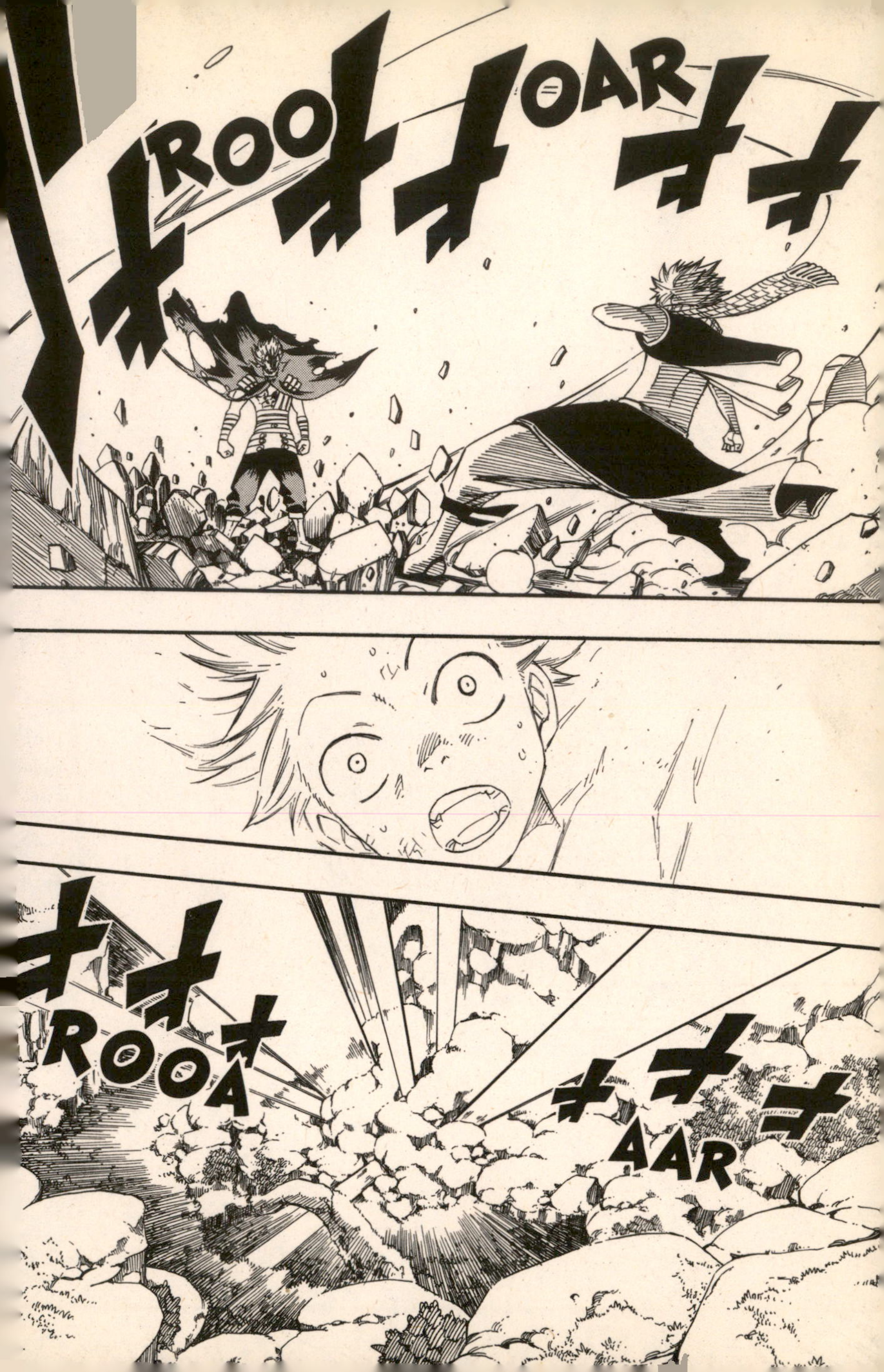
ROOOAR
ROOA
AAR

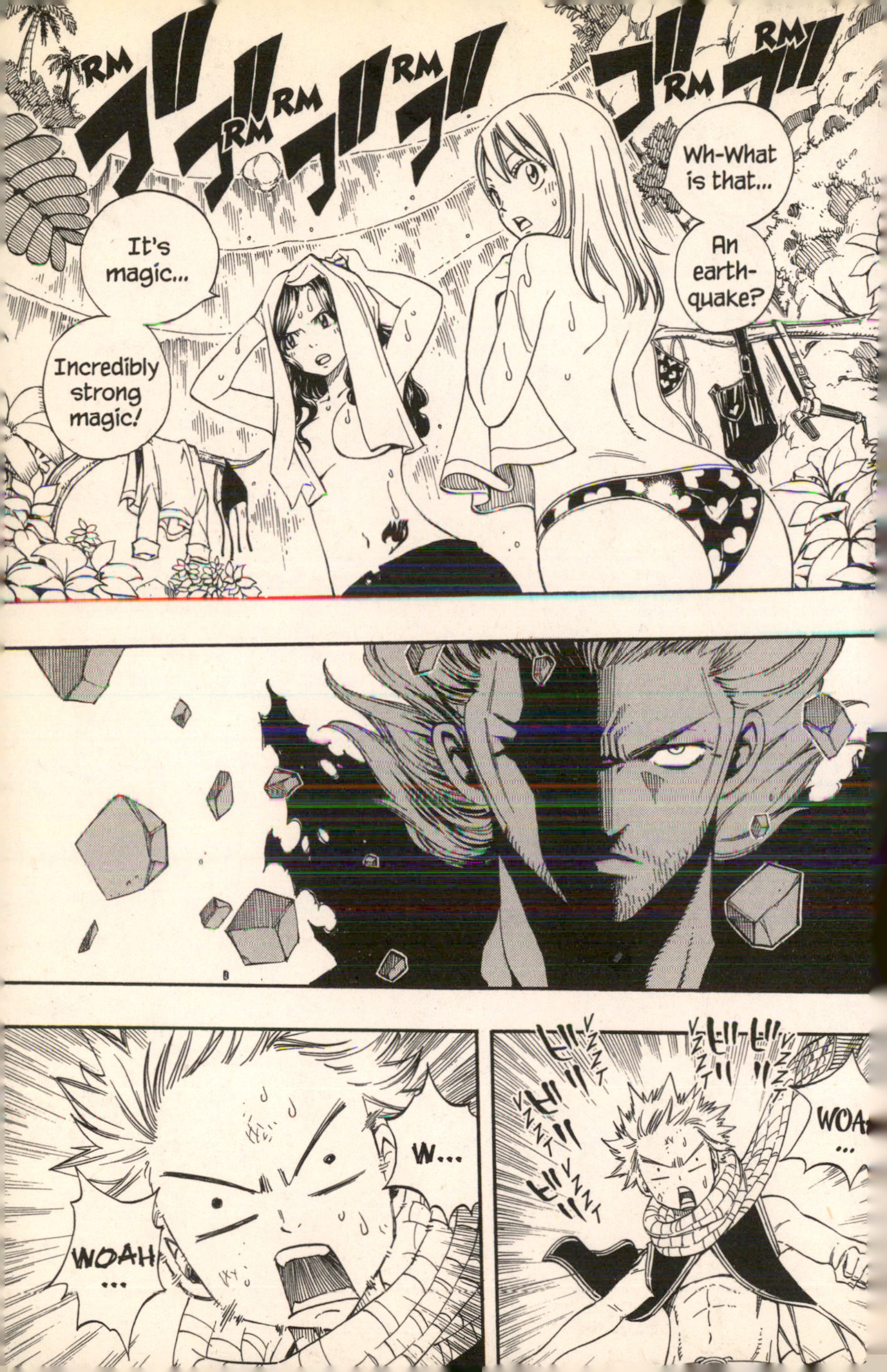

RM
RM
RM
Wh-What is that...
An earthquake?
RM
RM
RM
It's magic...
Incredibly strong magic!
VZZZT
VZZZT
VZZZT
VZZZT
VZZZT
WOA ...
W...
WOAH ...

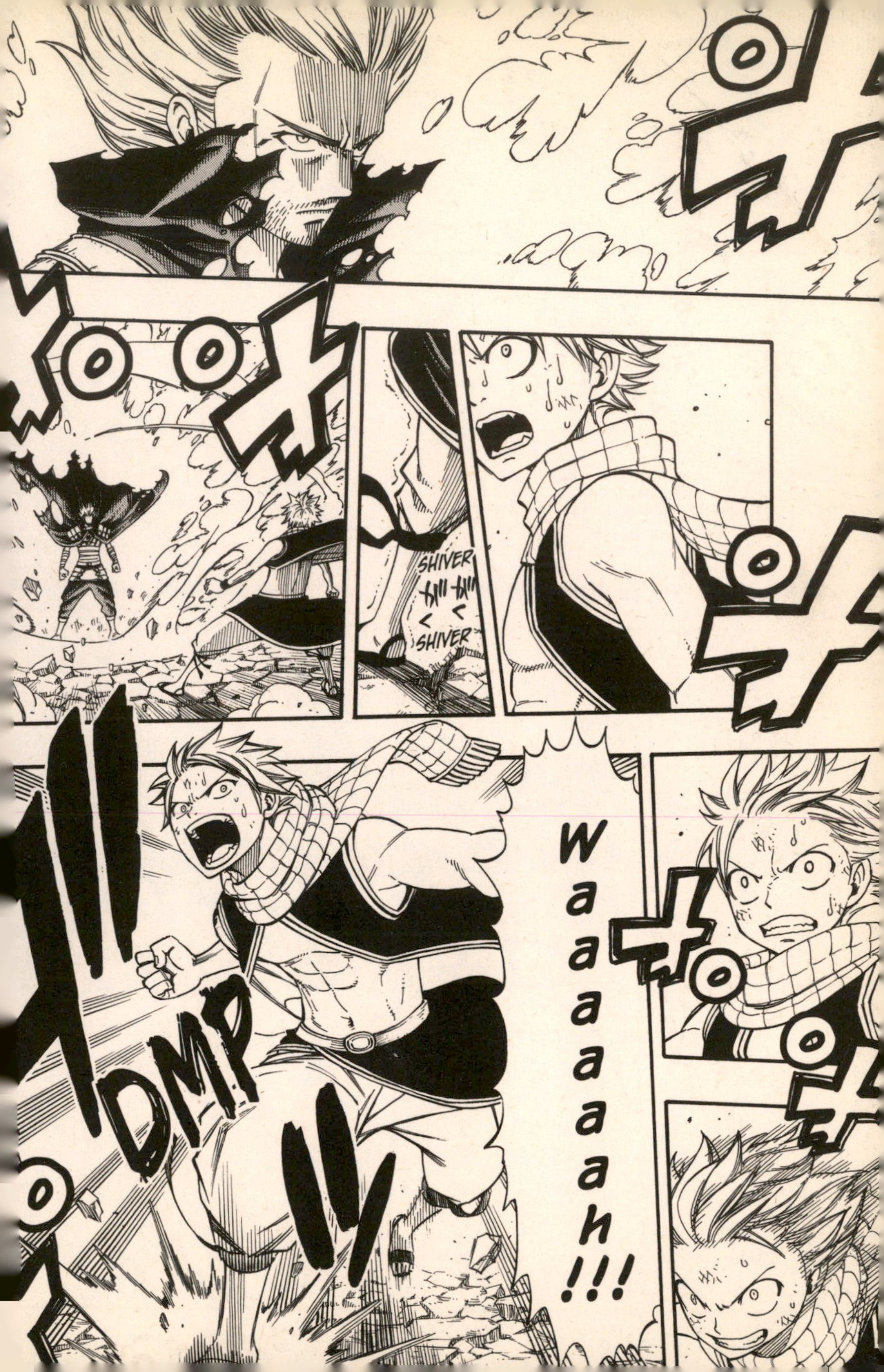
SHIVER
SHIVER
Waaaaaaah!!!
DMP

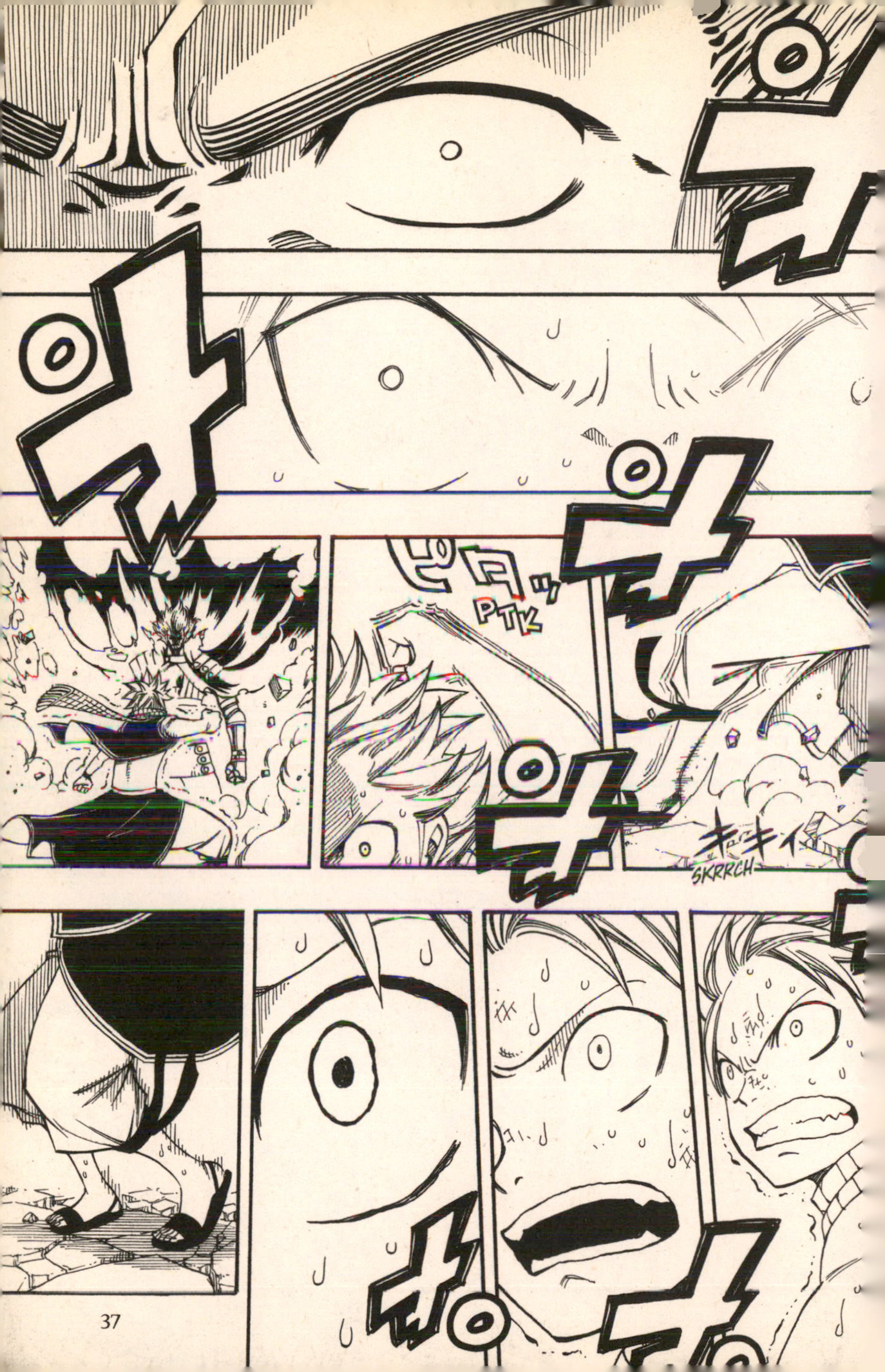
SKRRCH
PTK

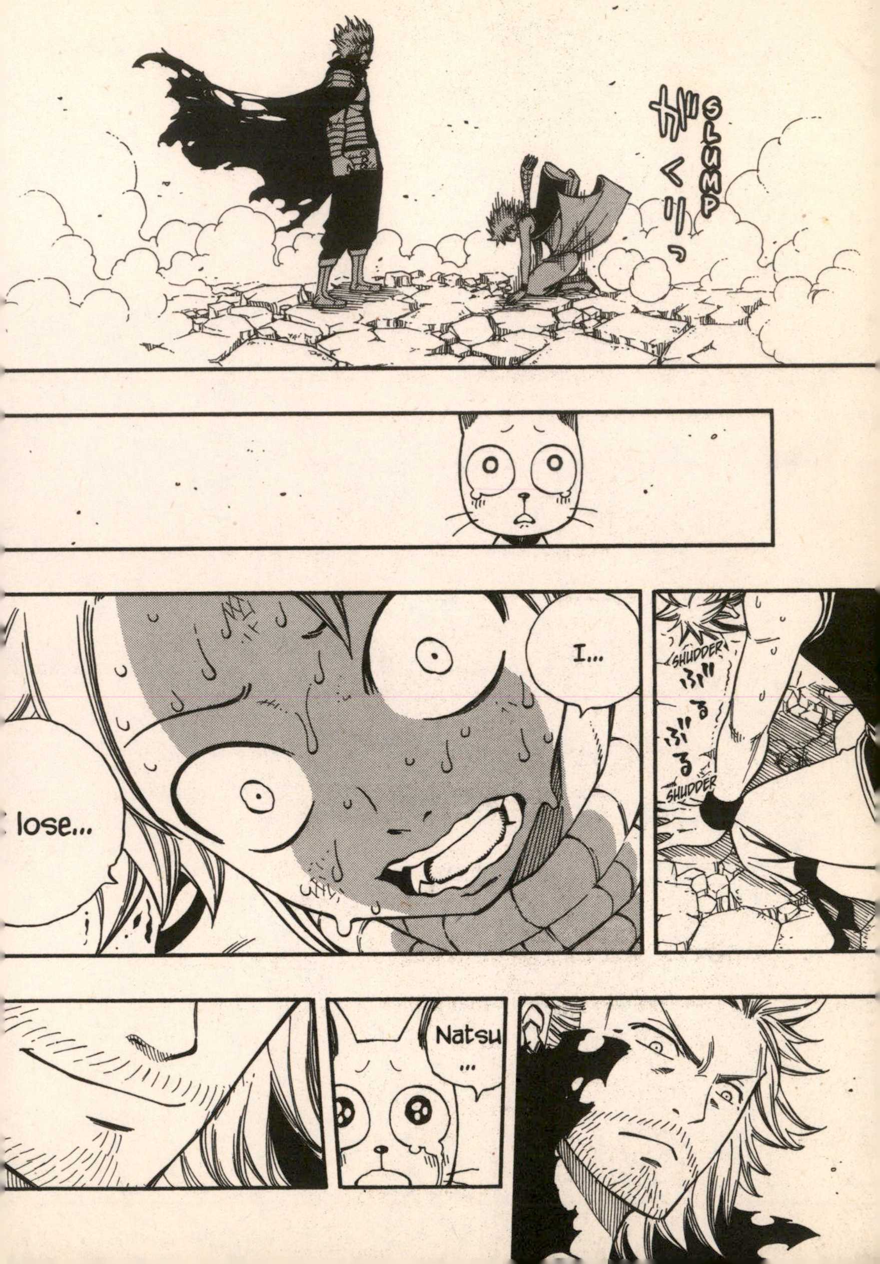
SLUMP
SHUDDER
ぶるぶる
SHUDDER
I...
lose...
Natsu
...

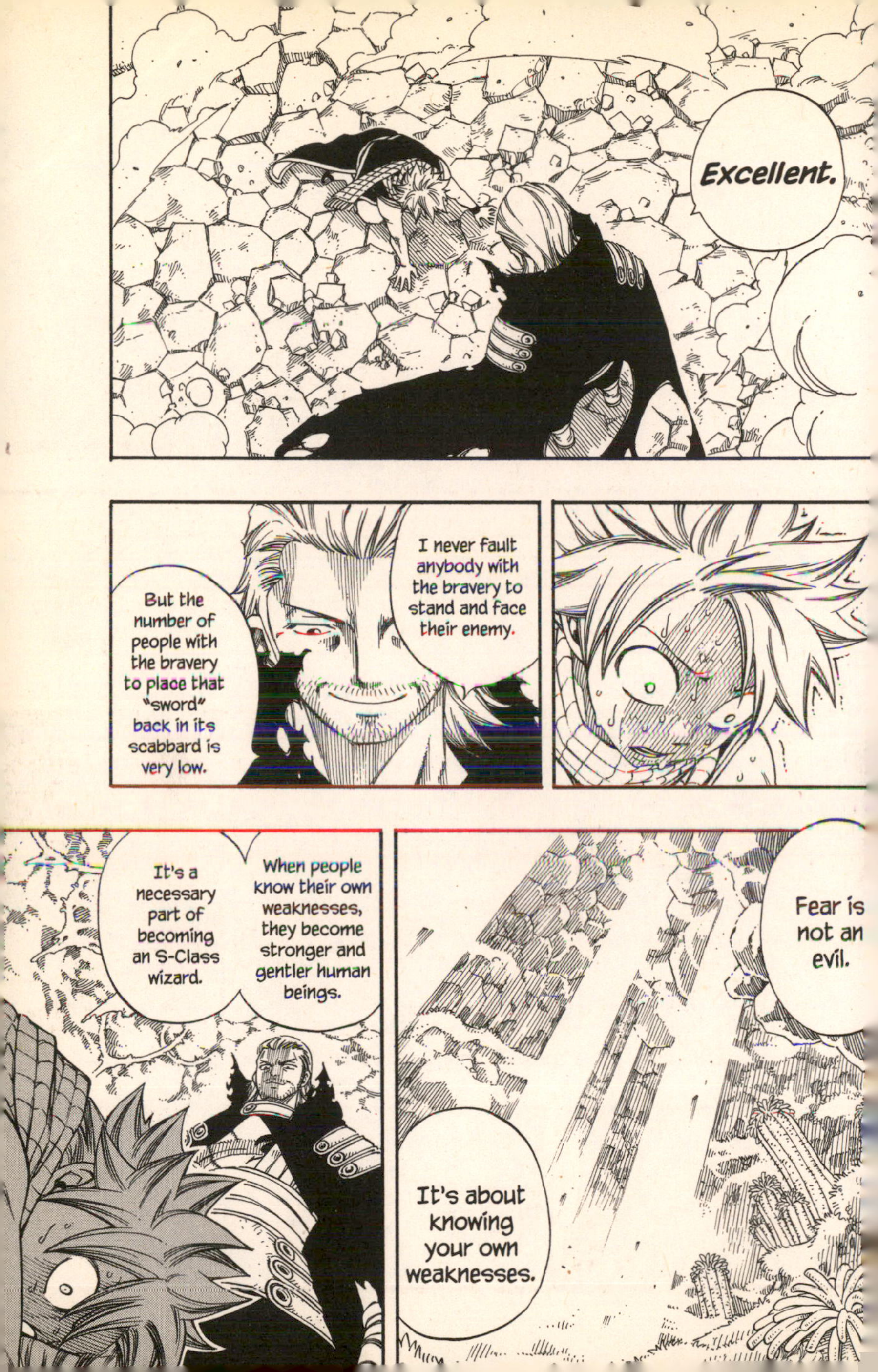
Excellent.
I never fault anybody with the bravery to stand and face their enemy.
But the number of people with the bravery to place that "sword" back in its scabbard is very low.
Fear is not an evil.
It's about knowing your own weaknesses.
When people know their own weaknesses, they become stronger and gentler human beings.
It's a necessary part of becoming an S-Class wizard.

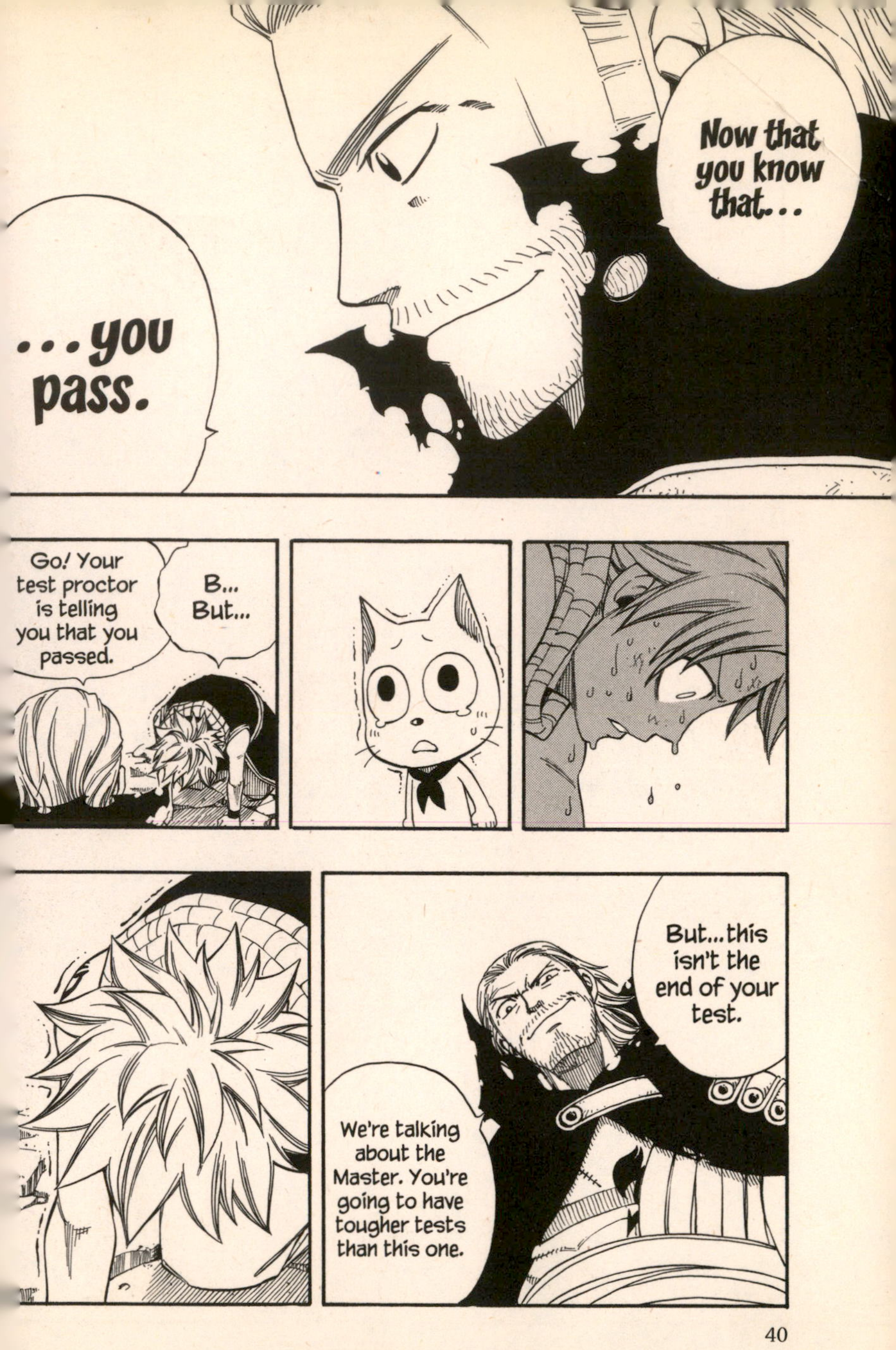
Now that you know that...
...you pass.
B... But...
Go! Your test proctor is telling you that you passed.
But...this isn't the end of your test.
We're talking about the Master. You're going to have tougher tests than this one.

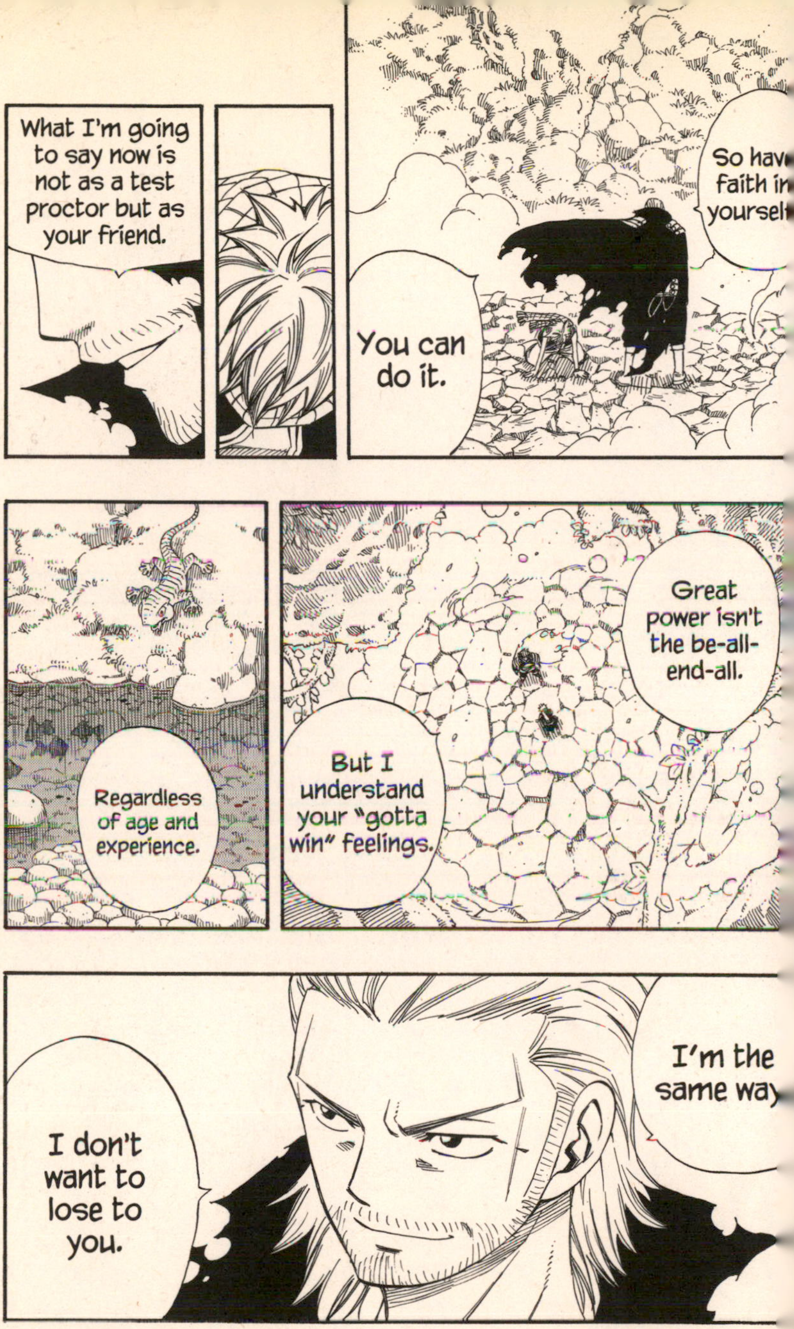
So hav faith in yoursel
You can do it.
What I'm going to say now is not as a test proctor but as your friend.
Great power isn't the be-all-end-all.
But I understand your "gotta win" feelings.
Regardless of age and experience.
I'm the same way
I don't want to lose to you.

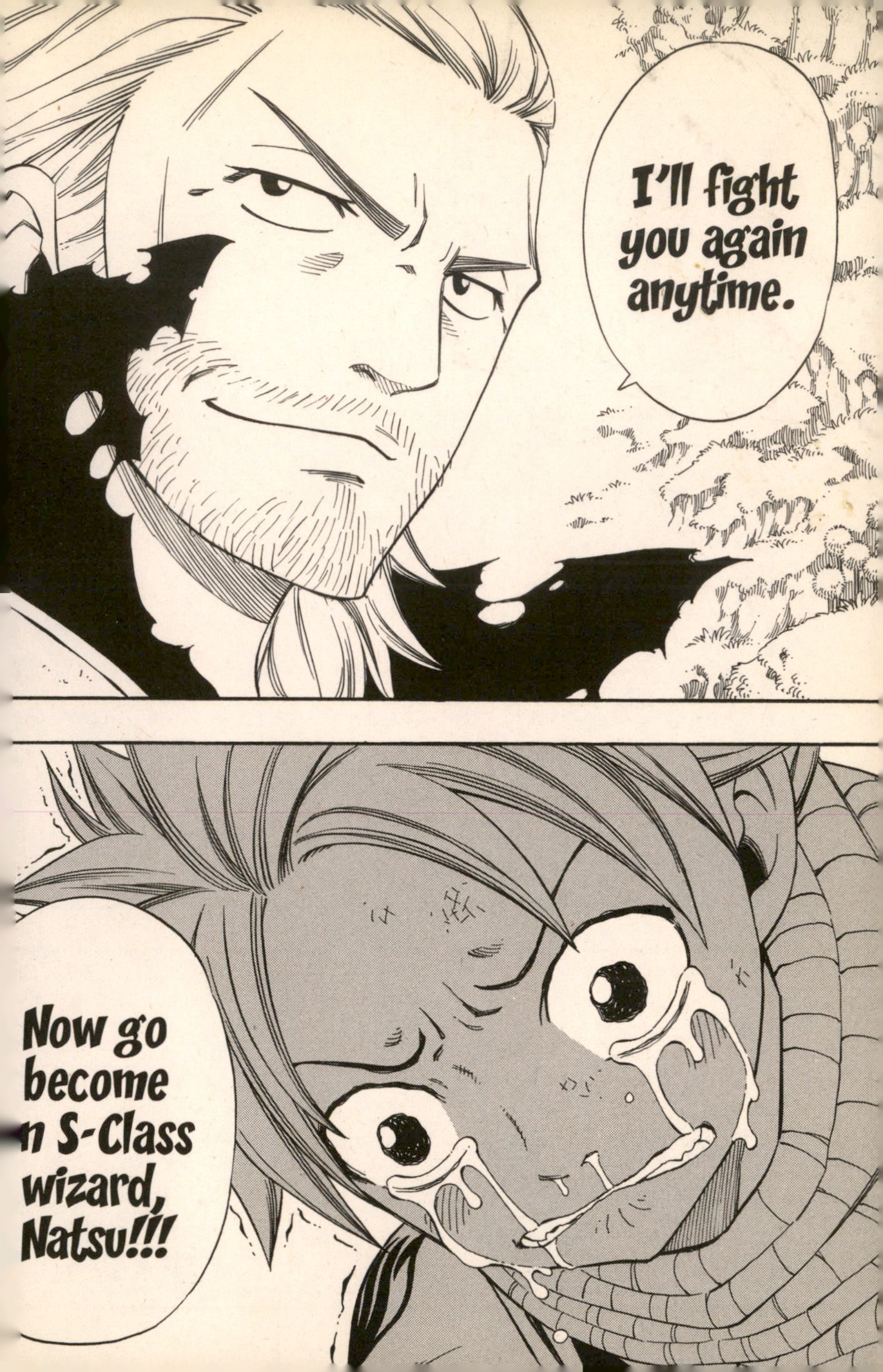
I'll fight you again anytime.
Now go become n S-Class wizard, Natsu!!!

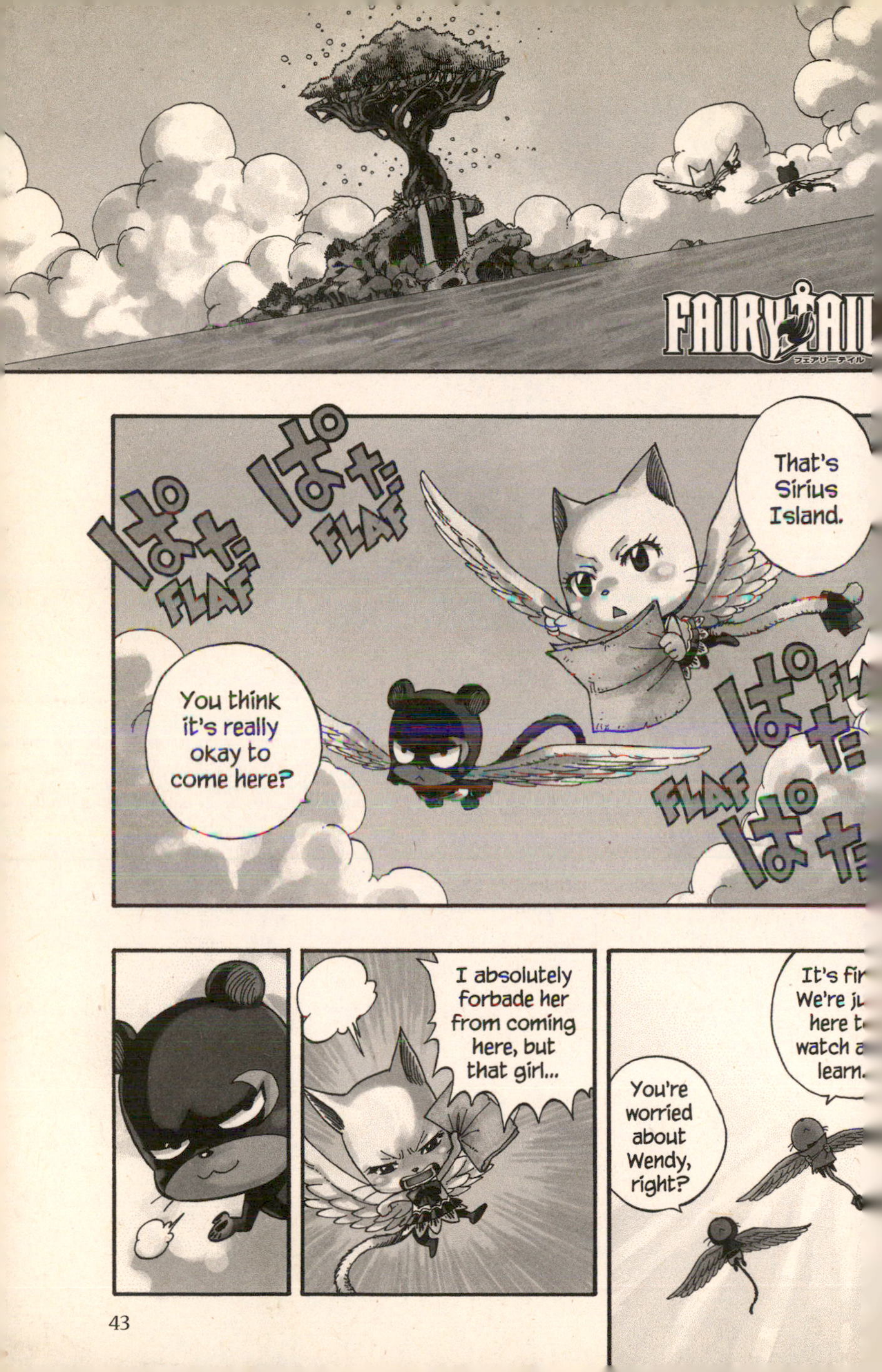
FAIRY TAIL
フェアリーテイル
That's Sirius Island.
ぱた FLAF
ぱた FLAF
ぱた FLAF
ぱた FLAF
You think it's really okay to come here?
It's fir We're ju here t watch a learn.
You're worried about Wendy, right?
I absolutely forbade her from coming here, but that girl...

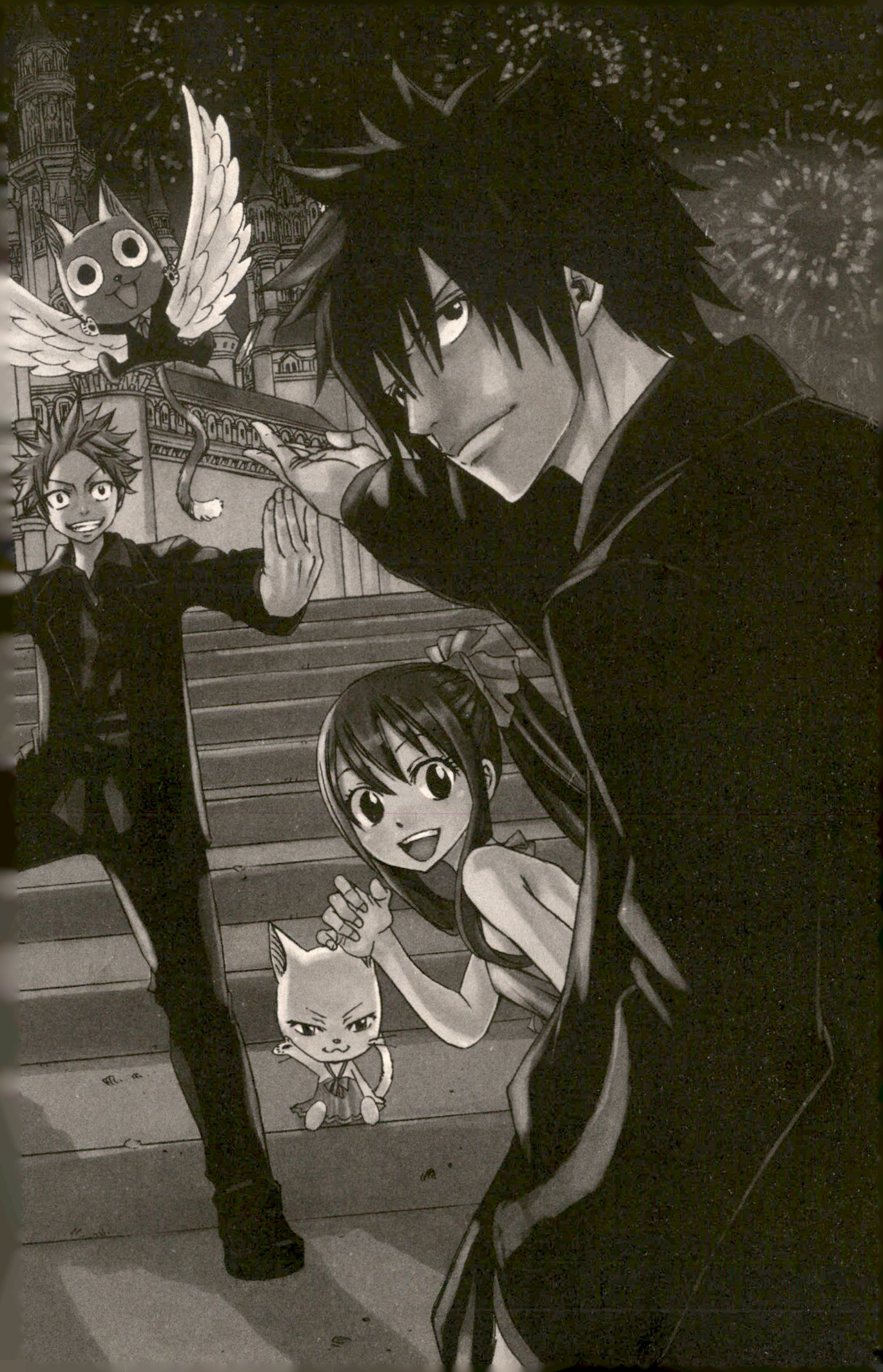

Chapter 207: Mest

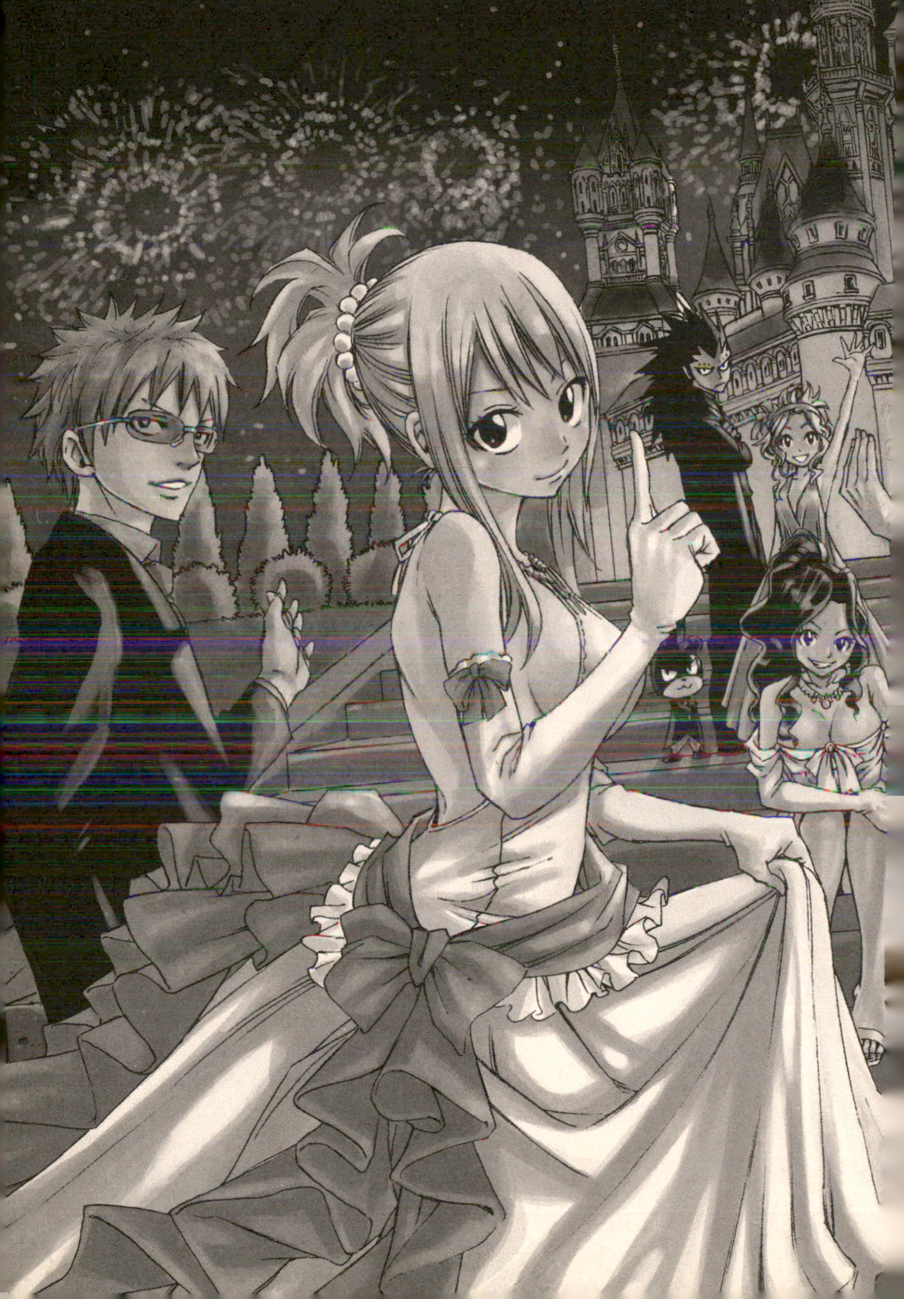

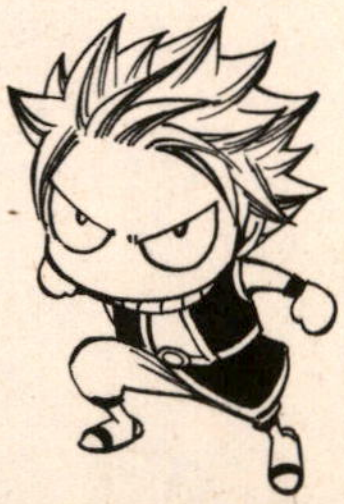

FAIRY TAIL

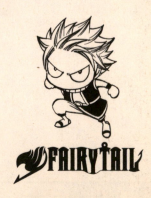

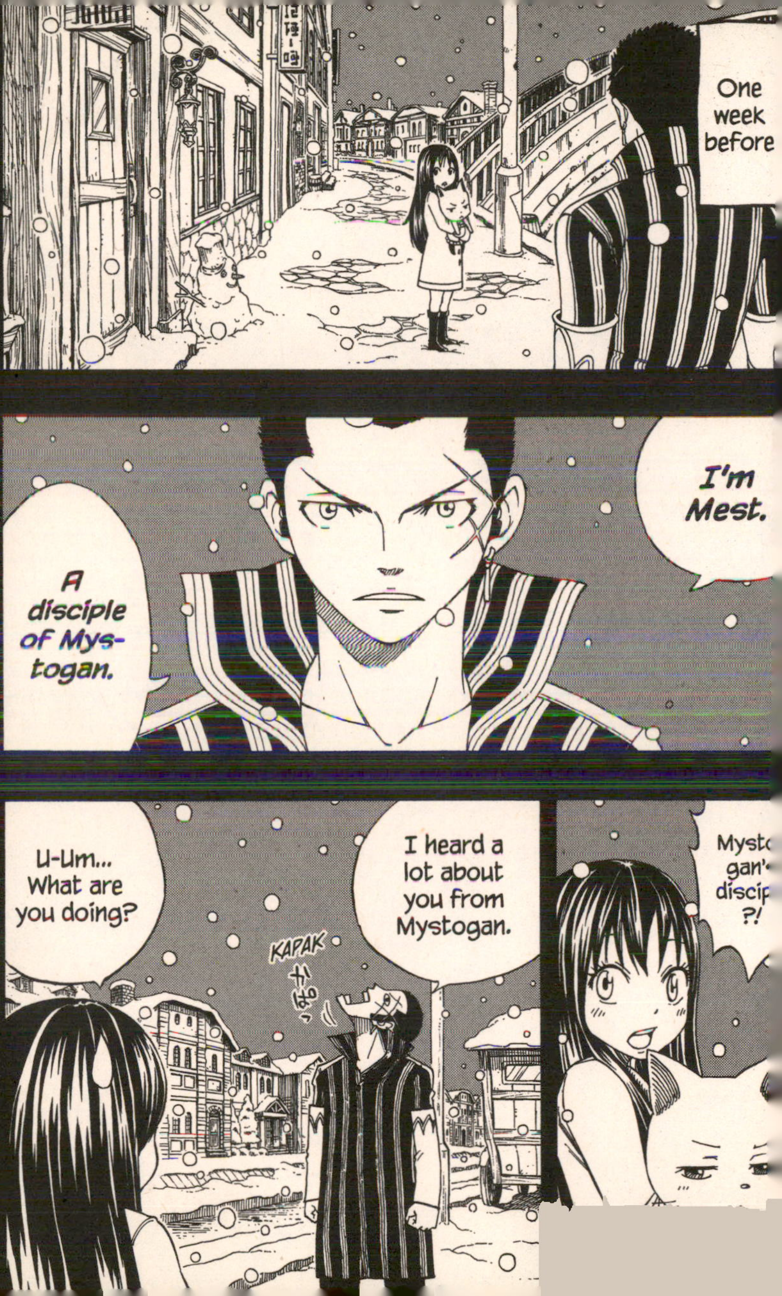
One week before
I'm Mest.
A disciple of Mystogan.
Mysto gan's discip ?!
I heard a lot about you from Mystogan.
KAPAK
かぱっ
U-Um... What are you doing?

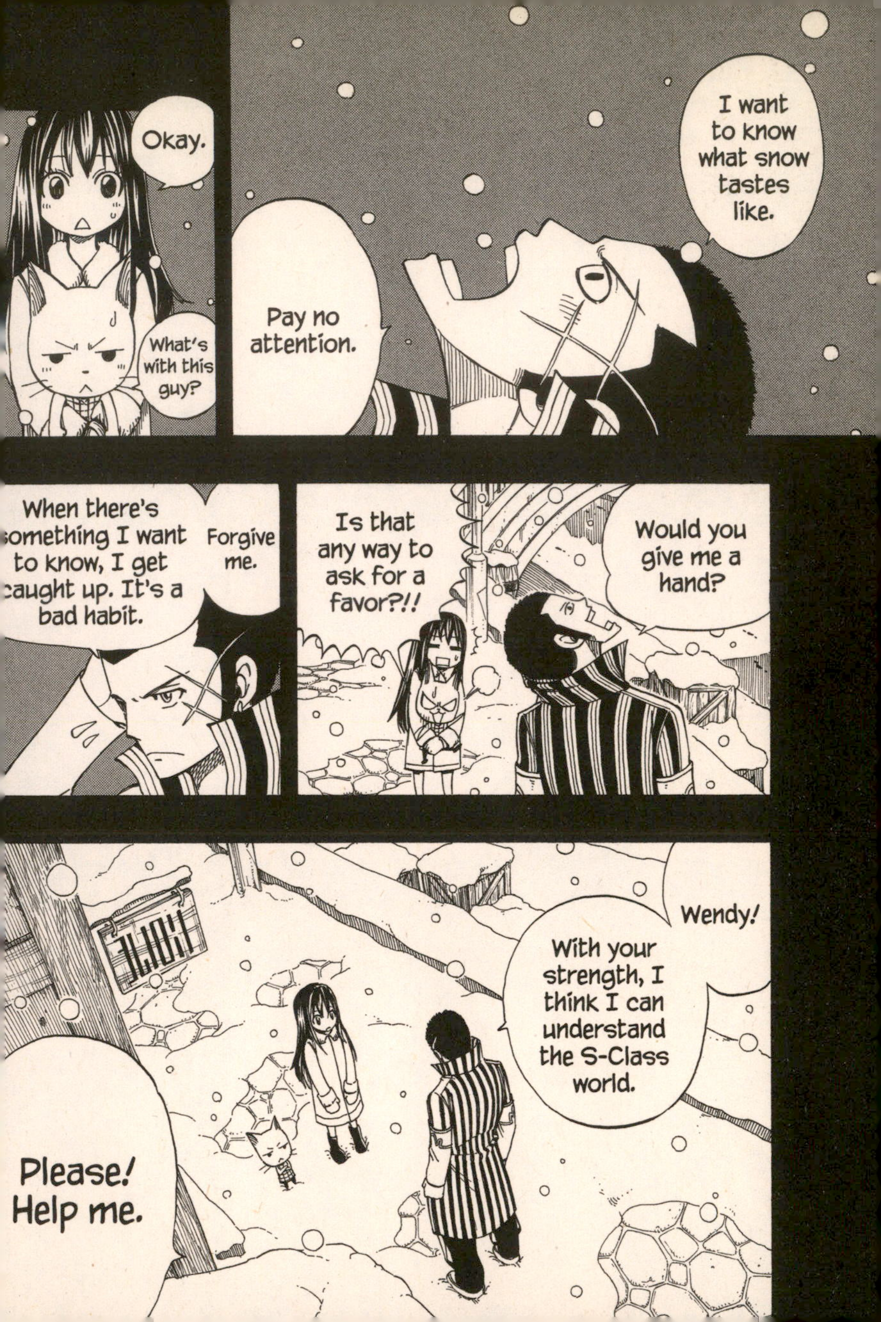
I want to know what snow tastes like.
Pay no attention.
Okay.
What's with this guy?
Would you give me a hand?
Is that any way to ask for a favor?!!
Forgive me.
When there's something I want to know, I get caught up. It's a bad habit.
Wendy!
With your strength, I think I can understand the S-Class world.
Please! Help me.

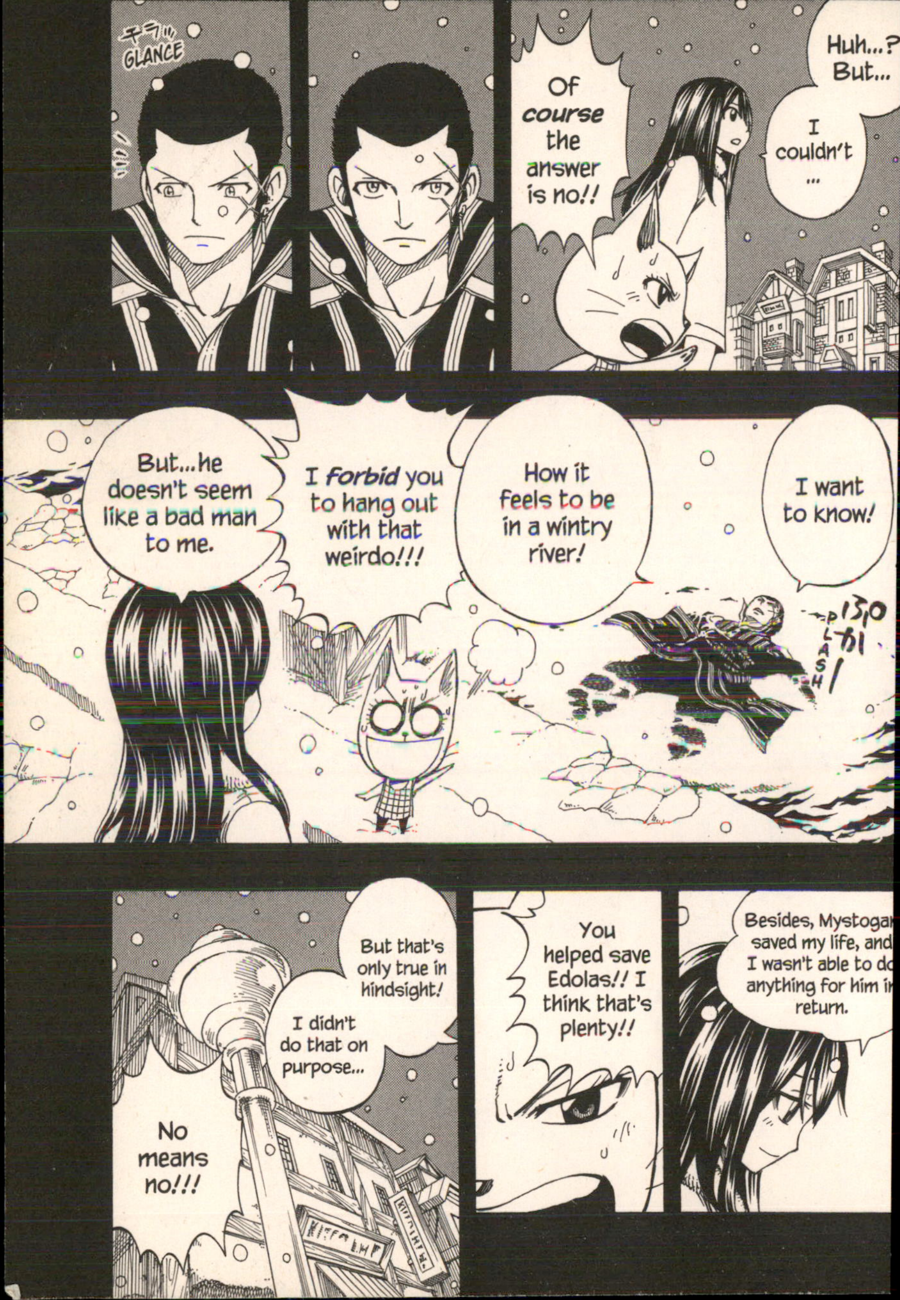
Huh...? But...
I couldn't ...
Of course the answer is no!!
チラ GLANCE
I want to know!
How it feels to be in a wintry river!
SPLASH
I forbid you to hang out with that weirdo!!!
But...he doesn't seem like a bad man to me.
Besides, Mystoga saved my life, and I wasn't able to do anything for him i return.
You helped save Edolas!! I think that's plenty!!
But that's only true in hindsight!
I didn't do that on purpose...
No means no!!!

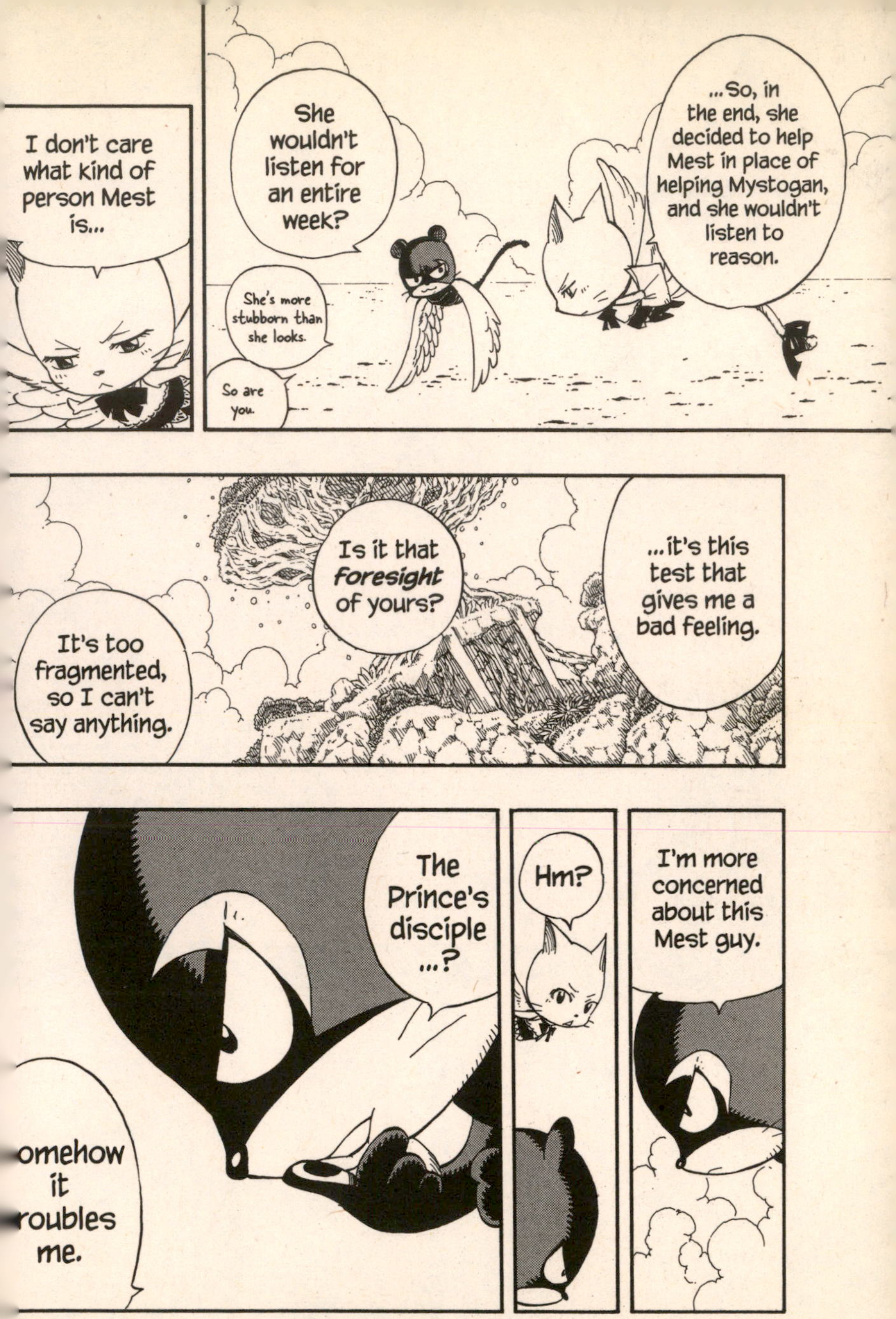
...So, in the end, she decided to help Mest in place of helping Mystogan, and she wouldn't listen to reason.
She wouldn't listen for an entire week?
She's more stubborn than she looks.
So are you.
I don't care what kind of person Mest is...
...it's this test that gives me a bad feeling.
Is it that *foresight* of yours?
It's too fragmented, so I can't say anything.
I'm more concerned about this Mest guy.
Hm?
The Prince's disciple ...?
omehow it roubles me.

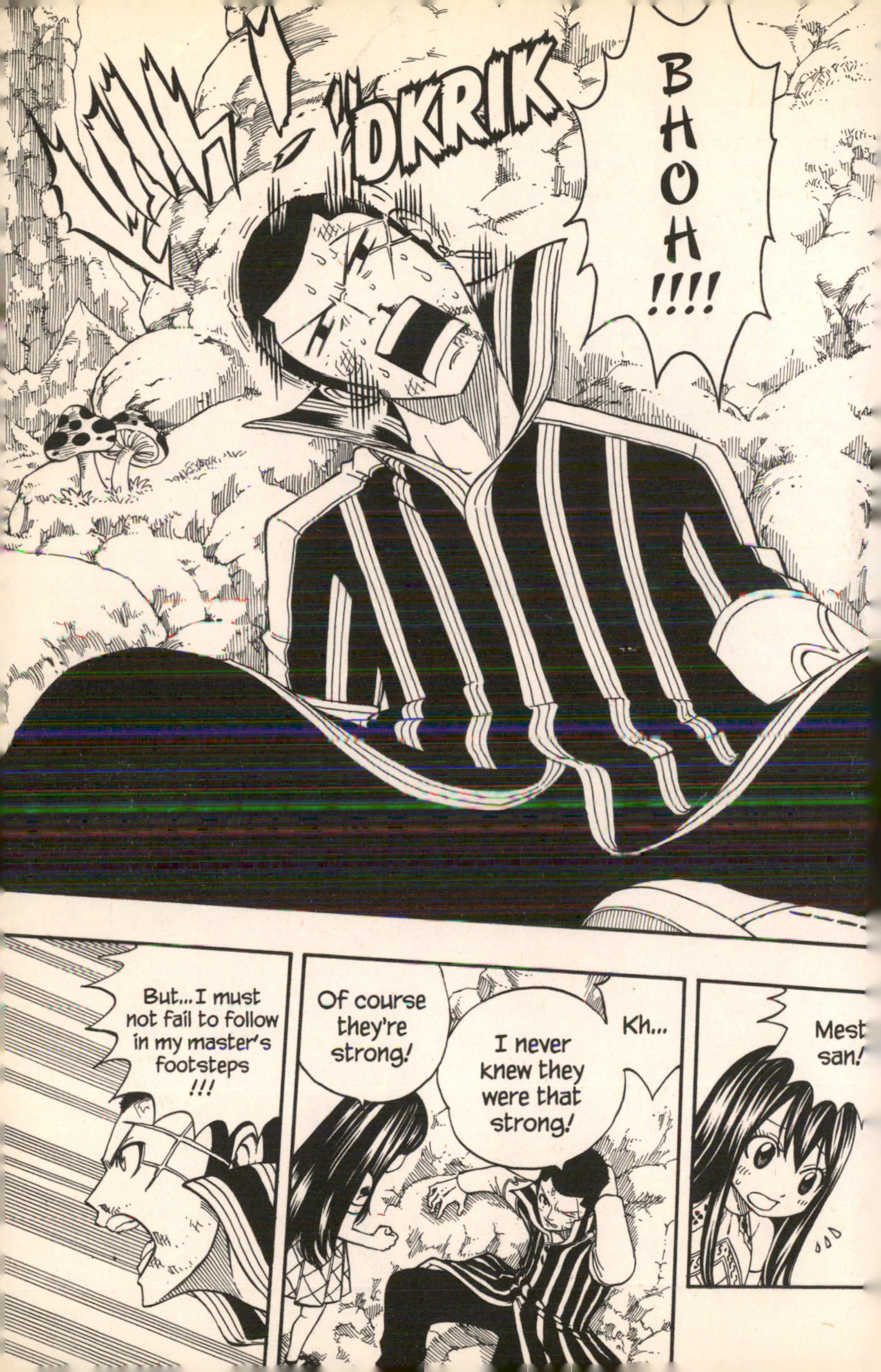
BHOH!!!!
DKRIK
Mest san!
Kh...
I never knew they were that strong!
Of course they're strong!
But...I must not fail to follow in my master's footsteps!!!

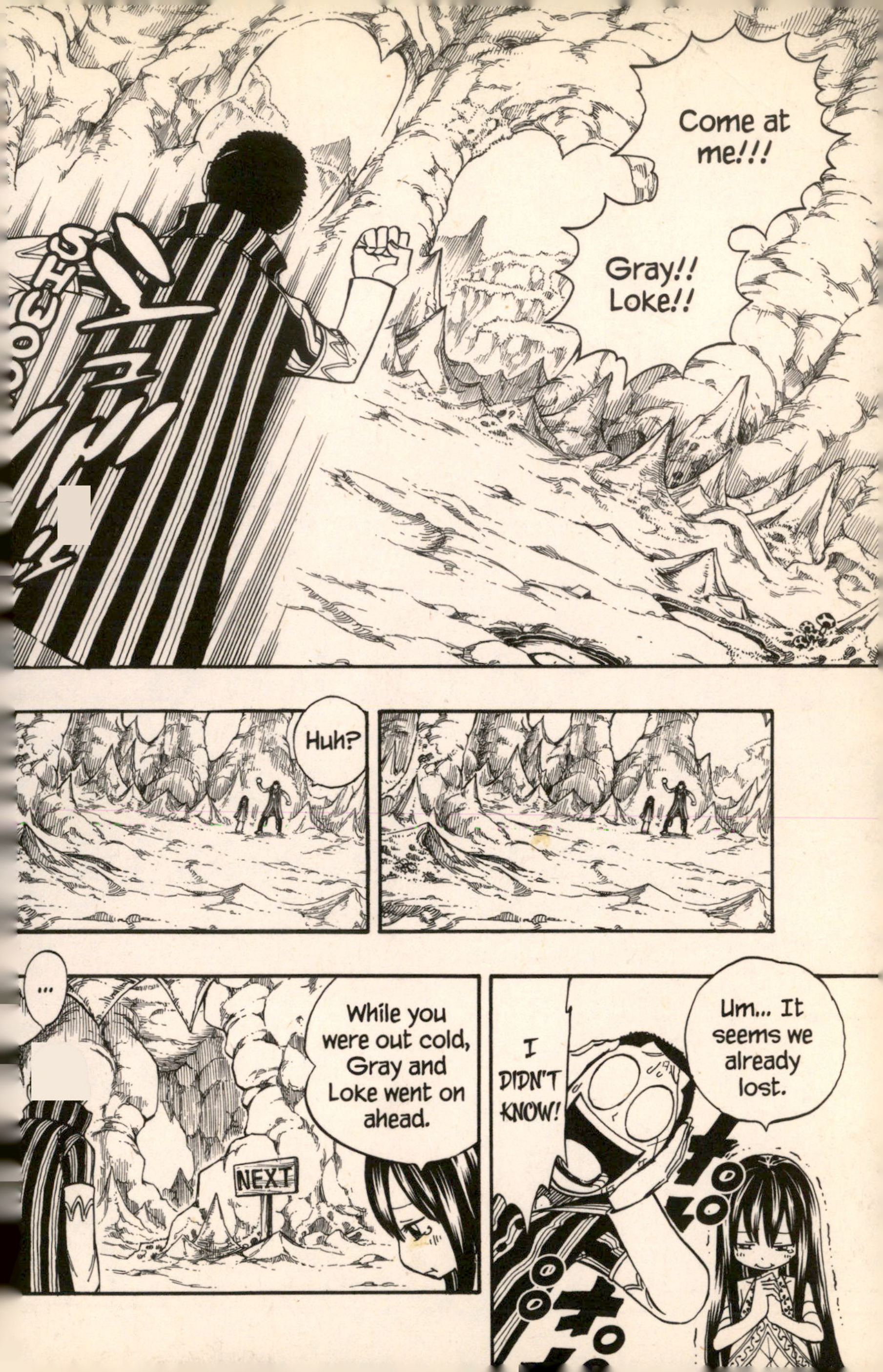
Come at me!!!
Gray!! Loke!!
Huh?
Um... It seems we already lost.
I DIDN'T KNOW!
While you were out cold, Gray and Loke went on ahead.
...
NEXT

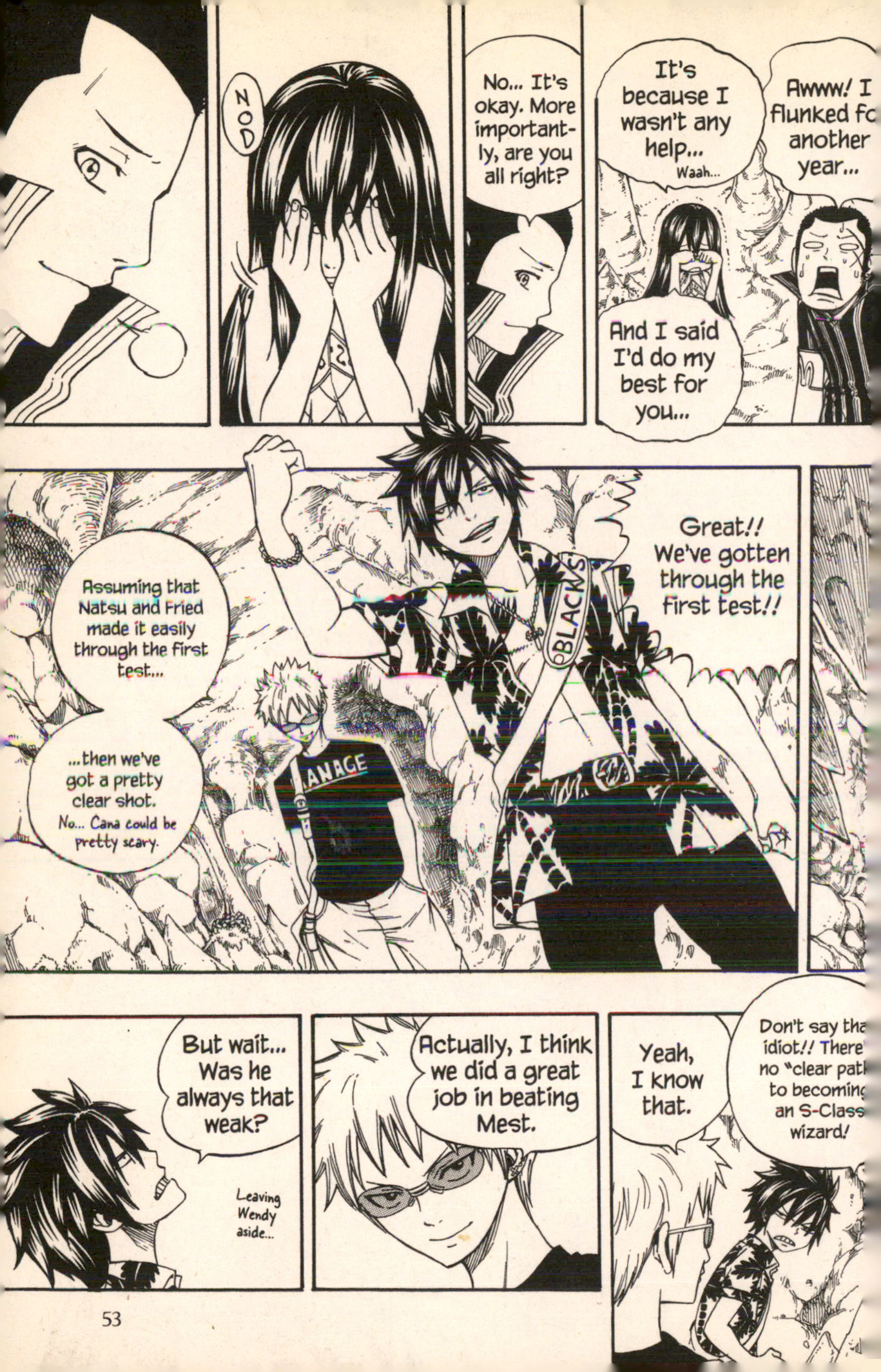
Awww! I flunked fo another year...
It's because I wasn't any help...
Waah...
And I said I'd do my best for you...
No... It's okay. More important-ly, are you all right?
NOD
Great!! We've gotten through the first test!!
Assuming that Natsu and Fried made it easily through the first test...
...then we've got a pretty clear shot.
No... Cana could be pretty scary.
Don't say tha idiot!! There' no "clear pat to becomin an S-Class wizard!
Yeah, I know that.
Actually, I think we did a great job in beating Mest.
But wait... Was he always that weak?
Leaving Wendy aside...

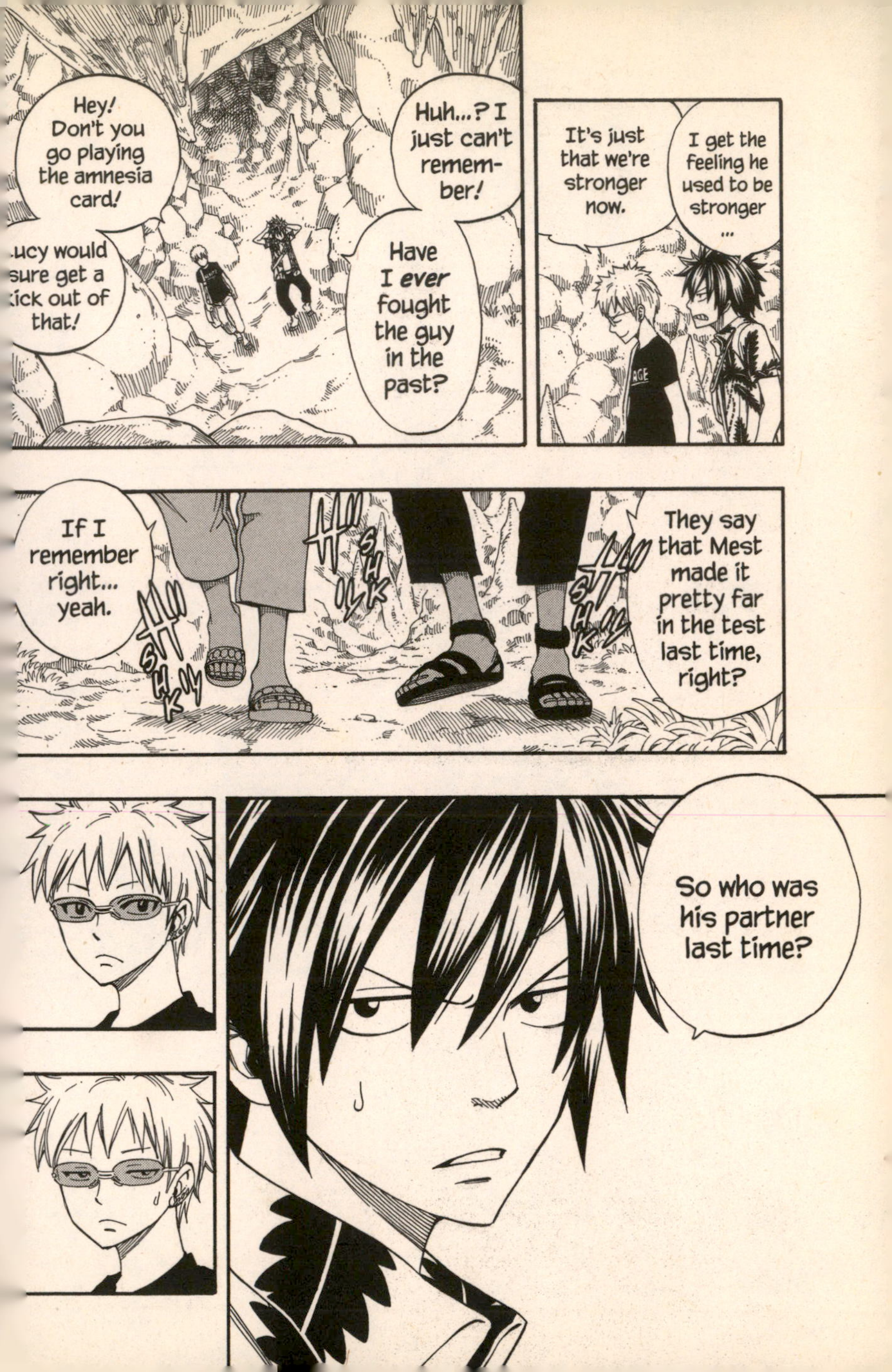
I get the feeling he used to be stronger ...
It's just that we're stronger now.
Huh...? I just can't remember!
Have I *ever* fought the guy in the past?
Hey! Don't you go playing the amnesia card!
ucy would sure get a ick out of that!
They say that Mest made it pretty far in the test last time, right?
SHK
SHK
If I remember right... yeah.
So who was his partner last time?

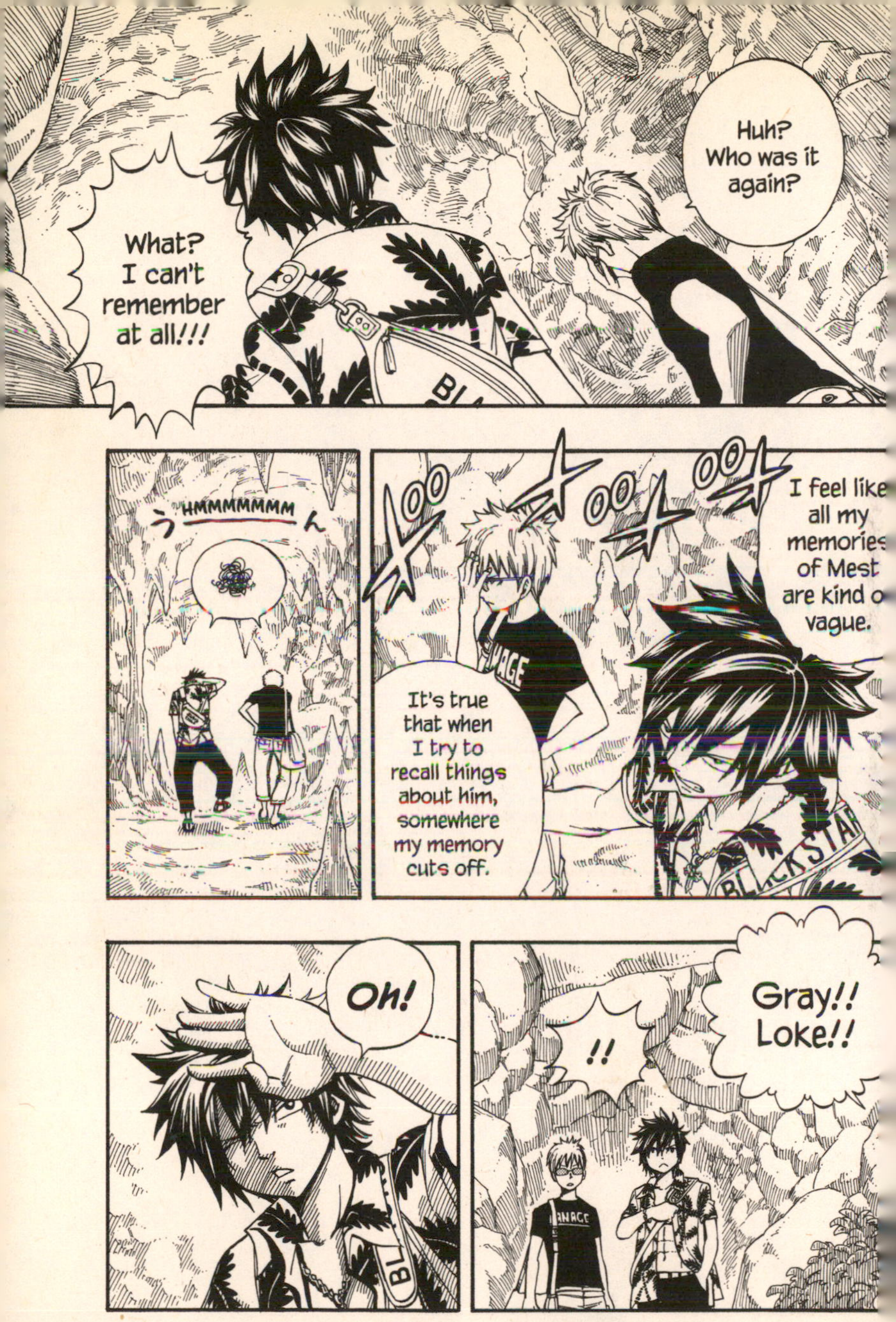
Huh? Who was it again?
What? I can't remember at all!!!
I feel like all my memories of Mest are kind o vague.
It's true that when I try to recall things about him, somewhere my memory cuts off.
う HMMMMMMM ん
Gray!! Loke!!
!!
Oh!

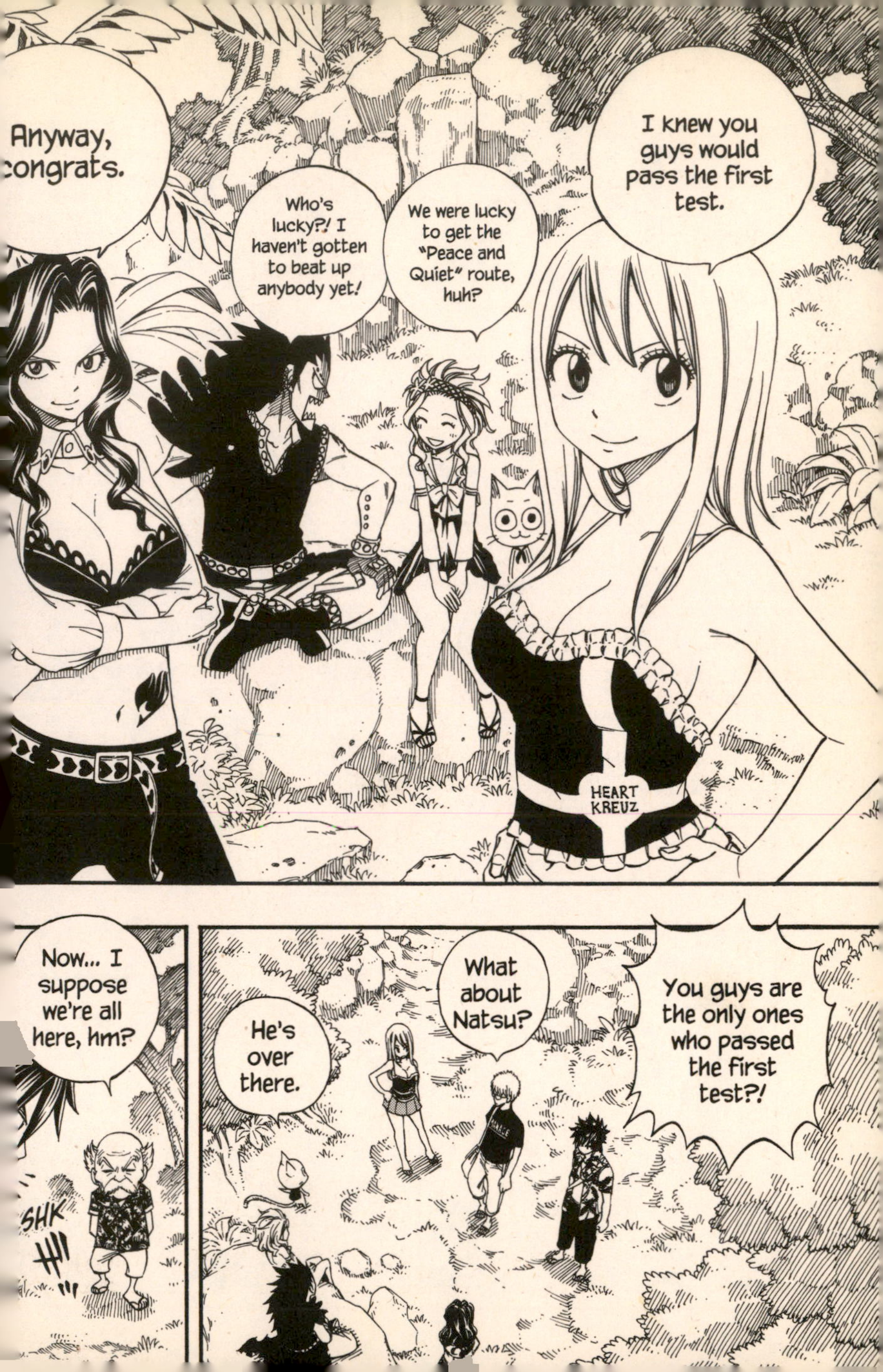
I knew you guys would pass the first test.
We were lucky to get the "Peace and Quiet" route, huh?
Who's lucky?! I haven't gotten to beat up anybody yet!
Anyway, congrats.
HEART KREUZ
You guys are the only ones who passed the first test?!
What about Natsu?
He's over there.
Now... I suppose we're all here, hm?
SHK

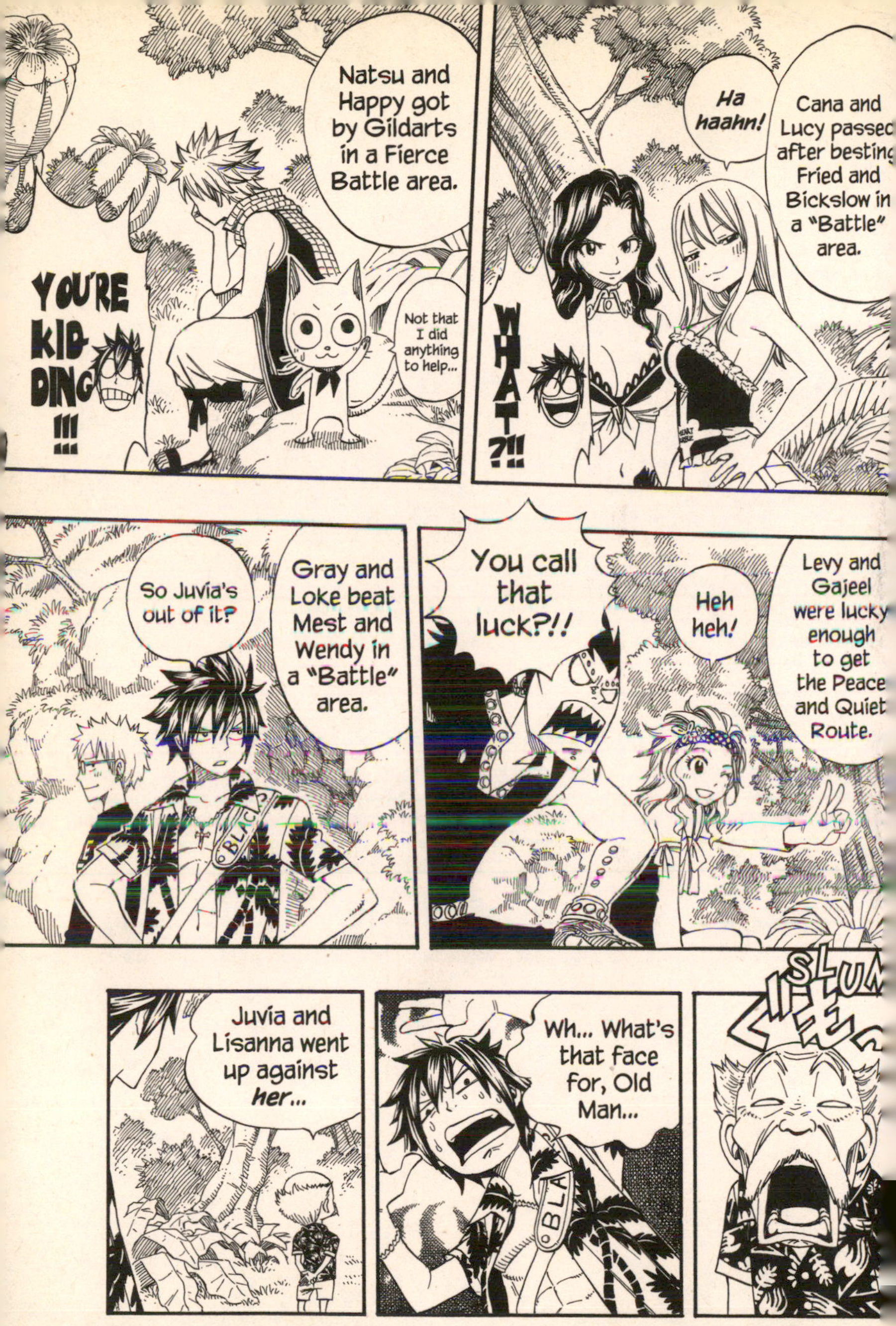
Cana and Lucy passed after besting Fried and Bickslow in a "Battle" area.
Ha haahn!
WHAT?!!
Natsu and Happy got by Gildarts in a Fierce Battle area.
Not that I did anything to help...
YOU'RE KIDDING!!!
Levy and Gajeel were lucky enough to get the Peace and Quiet Route.
Heh heh!
You call that luck?!!
Gray and Loke beat Mest and Wendy in a "Battle" area.
So Juvia's out of it?
SLUM
Wh... What's that face for, Old Man...
Juvia and Lisanna went up against *her*...

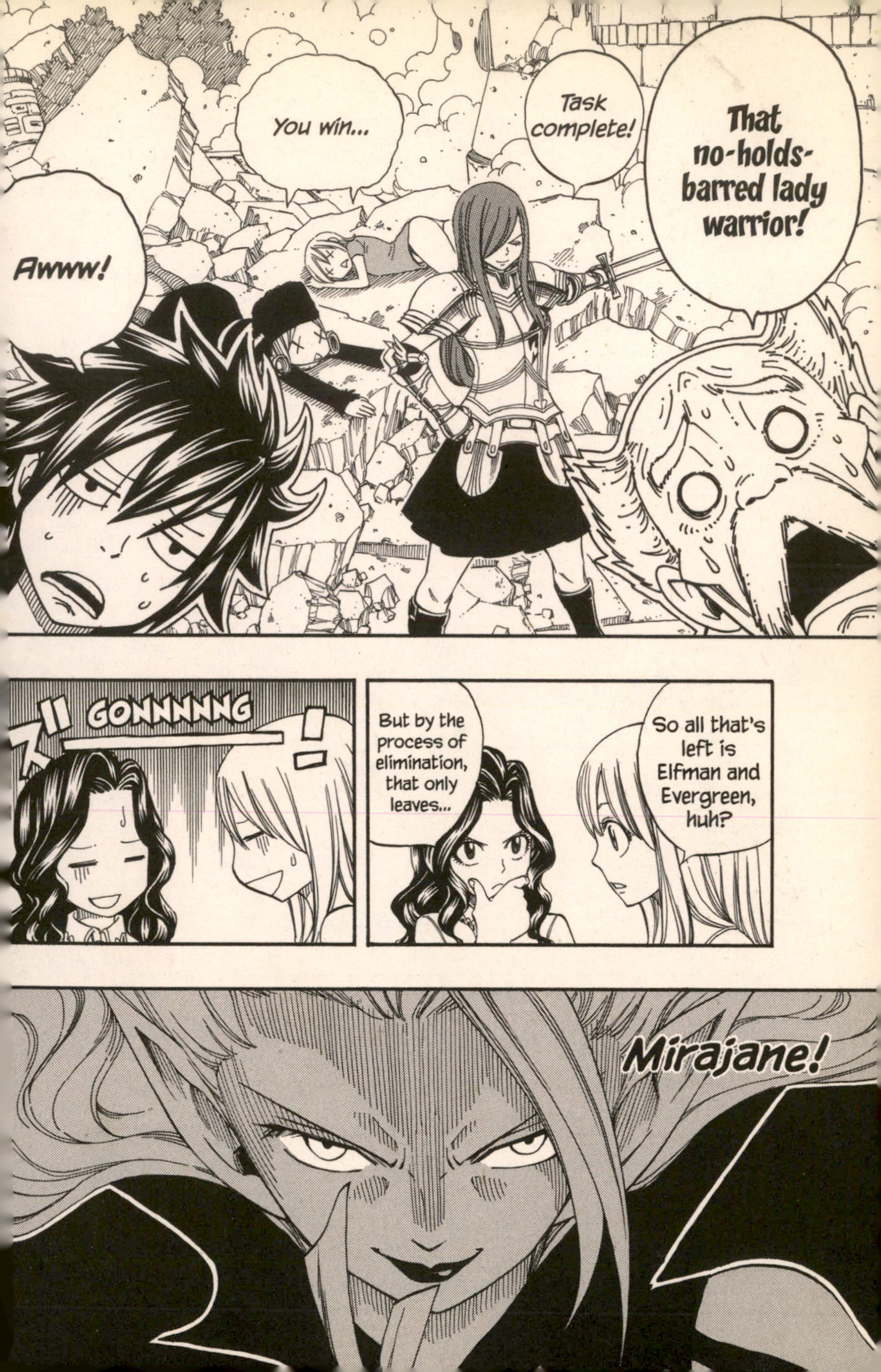
That no-holds-barred lady warrior!
Task complete!
You win...
Awww!
So all that's left is Elfman and Evergreen, huh?
But by the process of elimination, that only leaves...
GONNNNG
Mirajane!

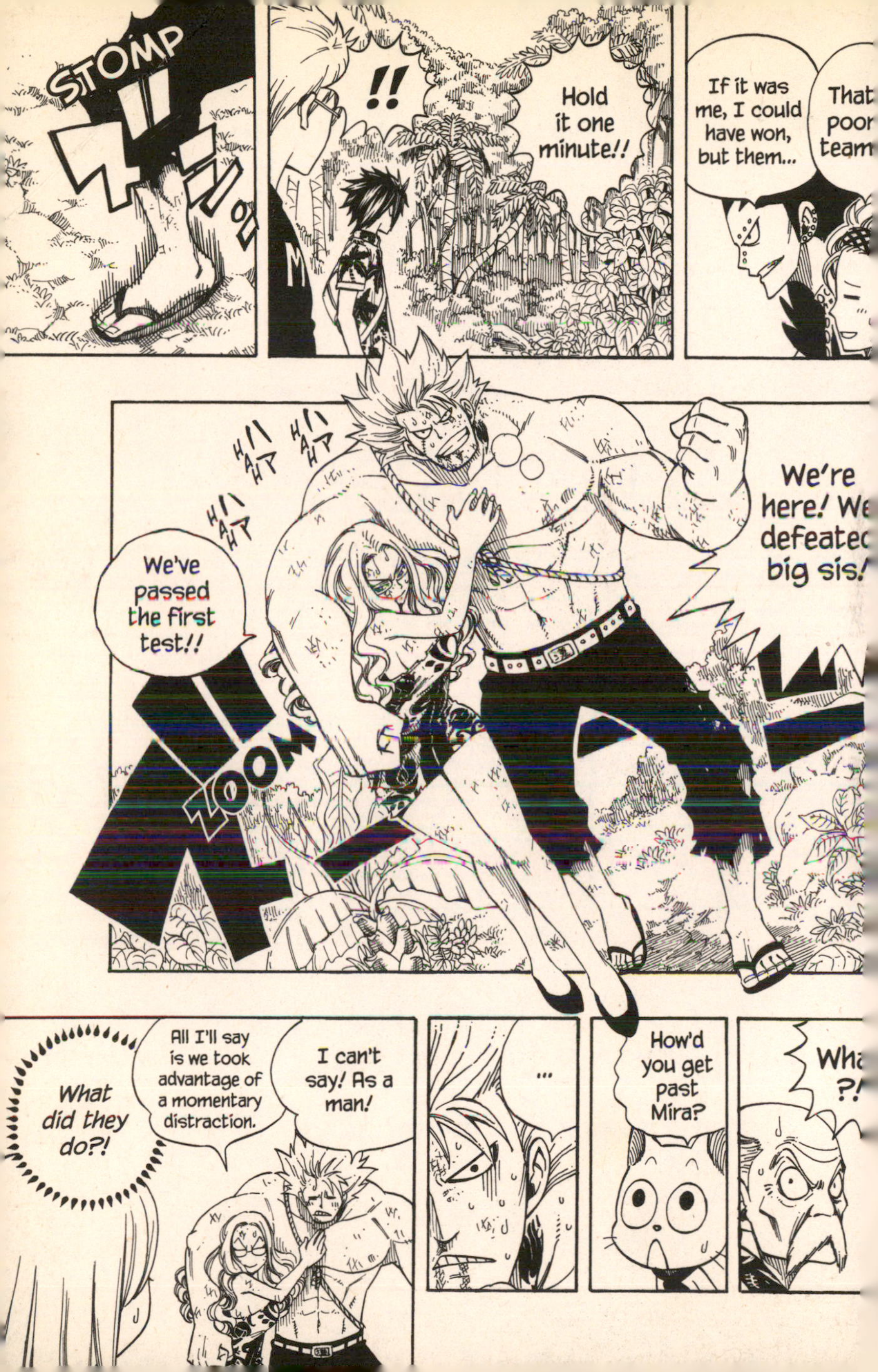

That poor team
If it was me, I could have won, but them...
!!
Hold it one minute!!
STOMP
We're here! We defeate big sis!
HAH HAH
HAH
We've passed the first test!!
ZOOM
Wha ?!
How'd you get past Mira?
...
I can't say! As a man!
All I'll say is we took advantage of a momentary distraction.
What did they do?!

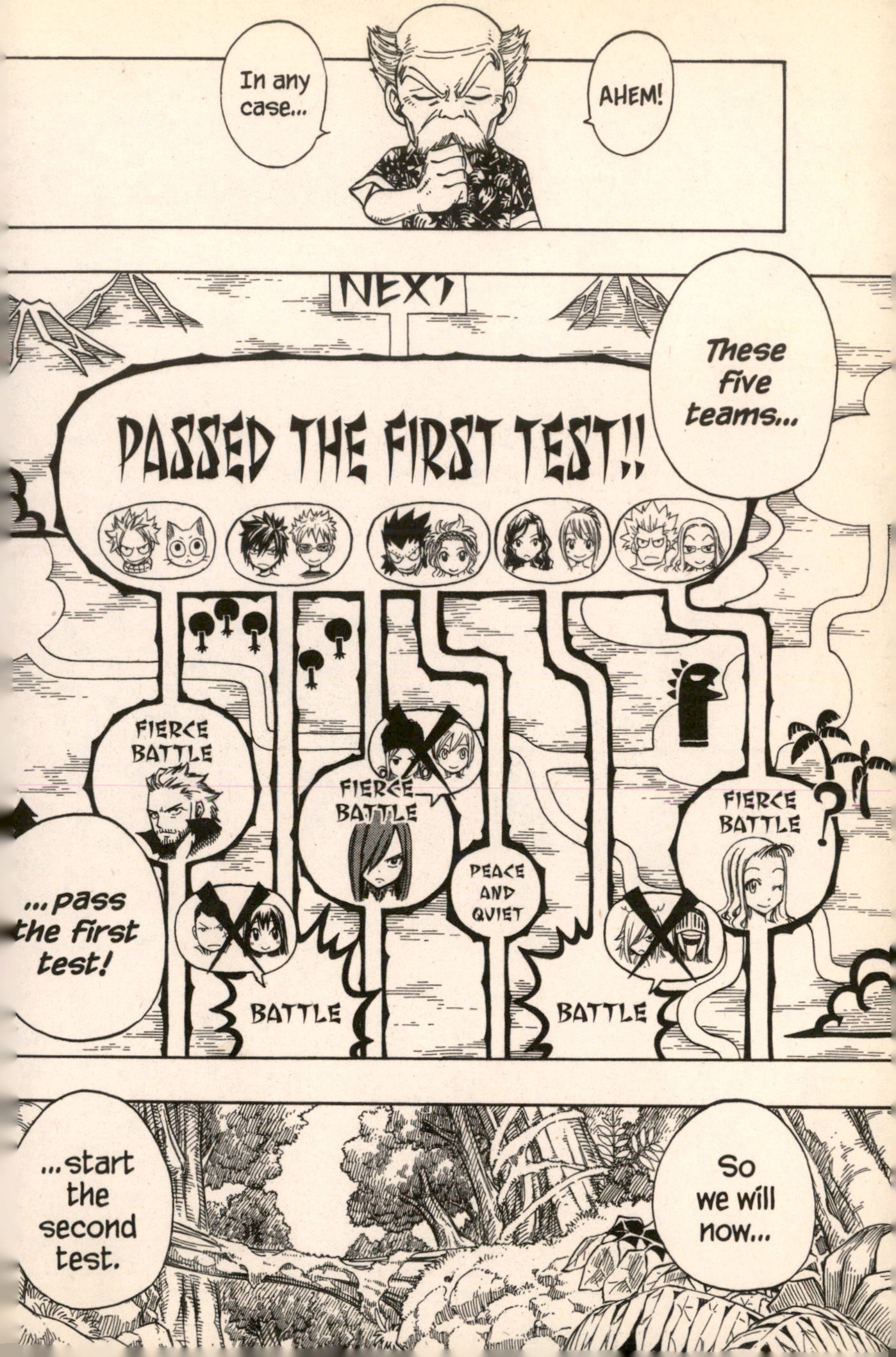
AHEM!
In any case...
These five teams...
NEXT
PASSED THE FIRST TEST!!
FIERCE BATTLE
FIERCE BATTLE
FIERCE BATTLE
PEACE AND QUIET
BATTLE
BATTLE
...pass the first test!
So we will now...
...start the second test.

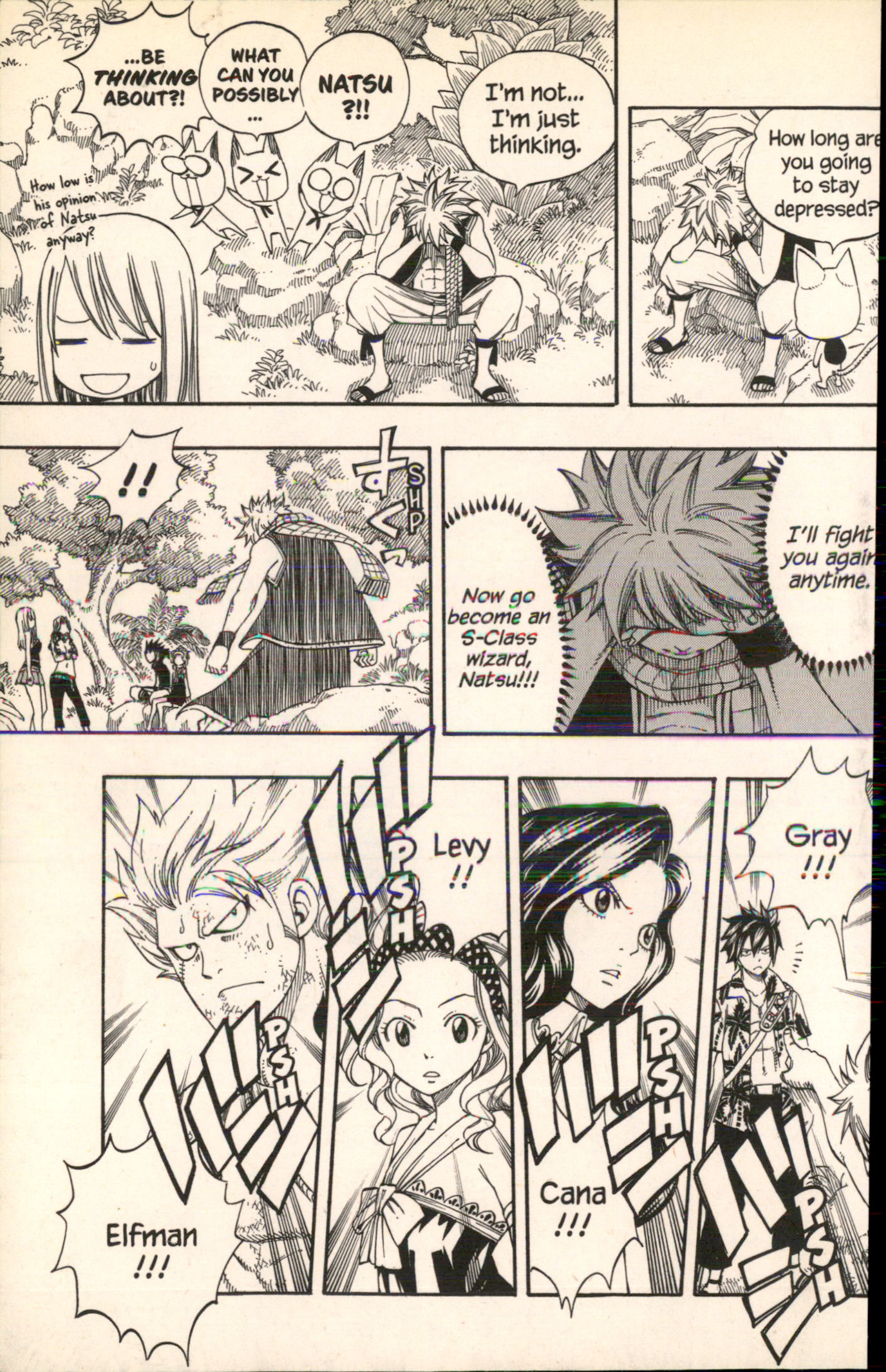

How long are you going to stay depressed?
I'm not... I'm just thinking.
NATSU ?!!
WHAT CAN YOU POSSIBLY ...
...BE THINKING ABOUT?!
How low is his opinion of Natsu anyway?
I'll fight you again anytime.
Now go become an S-Class wizard, Natsu!!!
SHP
!!
Gray !!!
PSH
Cana !!!
PSH
Levy !!
PSH
Elfman !!!
PSH

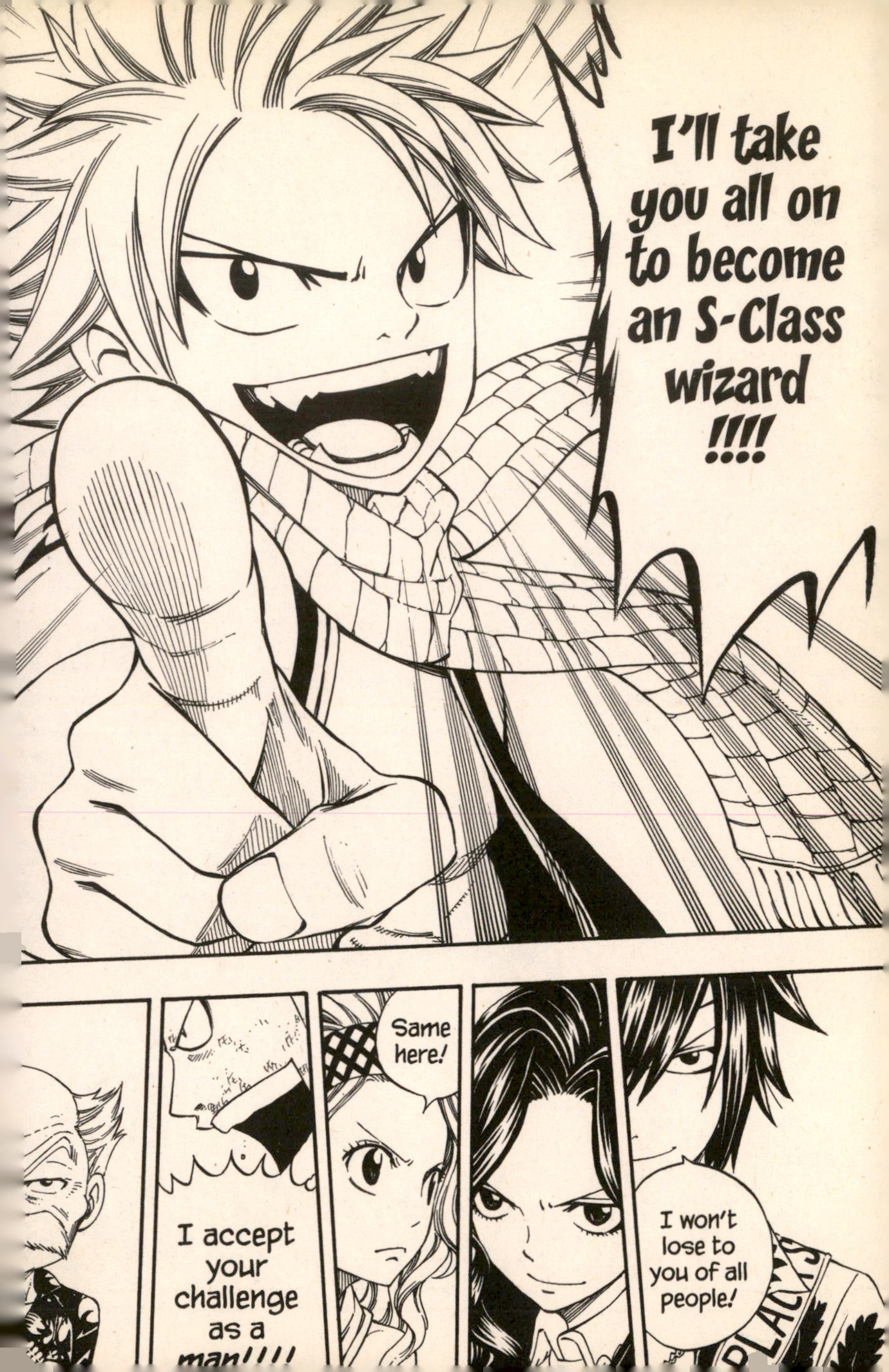
I'll take you all on to become an S-Class wizard !!!!
I won't lose to you of all people!
Same here!
I accept your challenge as a man!!!!

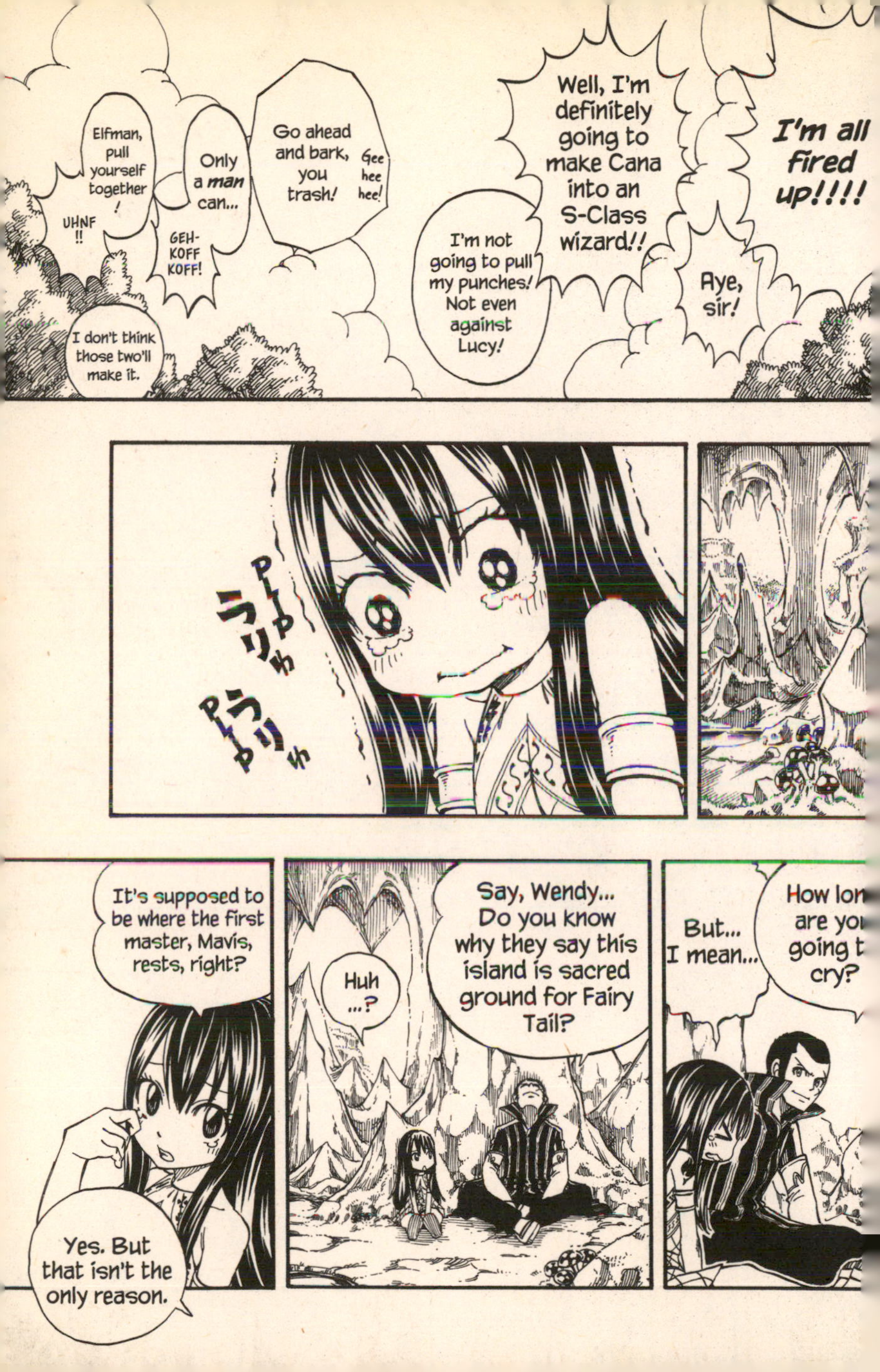
I'm all fired up!!!!
Aye, sir!
Well, I'm definitely going to make Cana into an S-Class wizard!!
I'm not going to pull my punches! Not even against Lucy!
Go ahead and bark, you trash!
Gee hee hee!
Only a *man* can...
GEH-KOFF KOFF!
Elfman, pull yourself together!
UHNF!!
I don't think those two'll make it.
PLIP
PLIP
How lon are yo going t cry?
But... I mean...
Say, Wendy... Do you know why they say this island is sacred ground for Fairy Tail?
Huh ...?
It's supposed to be where the first master, Mavis, rests, right?
Yes. But that isn't the only reason.

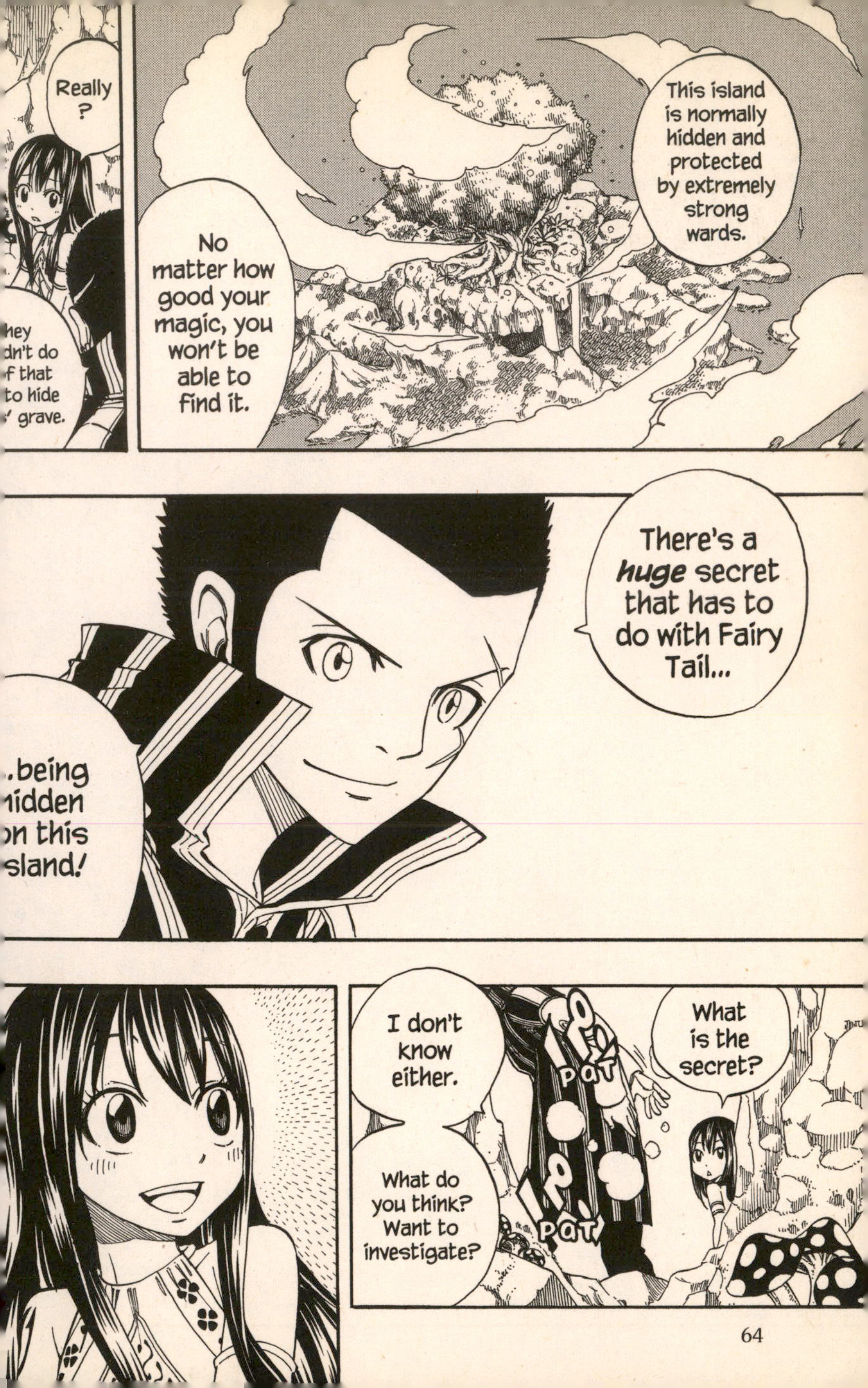
This island is normally hidden and protected by extremely strong wards.
No matter how good your magic, you won't be able to find it.
Really?
hey dn't do f that to hide ' grave.
There's a ***huge*** secret that has to do with Fairy Tail...
.being hidden on this island!
What is the secret?
PAT
PAT
I don't know either.
What do you think? Want to investigate?

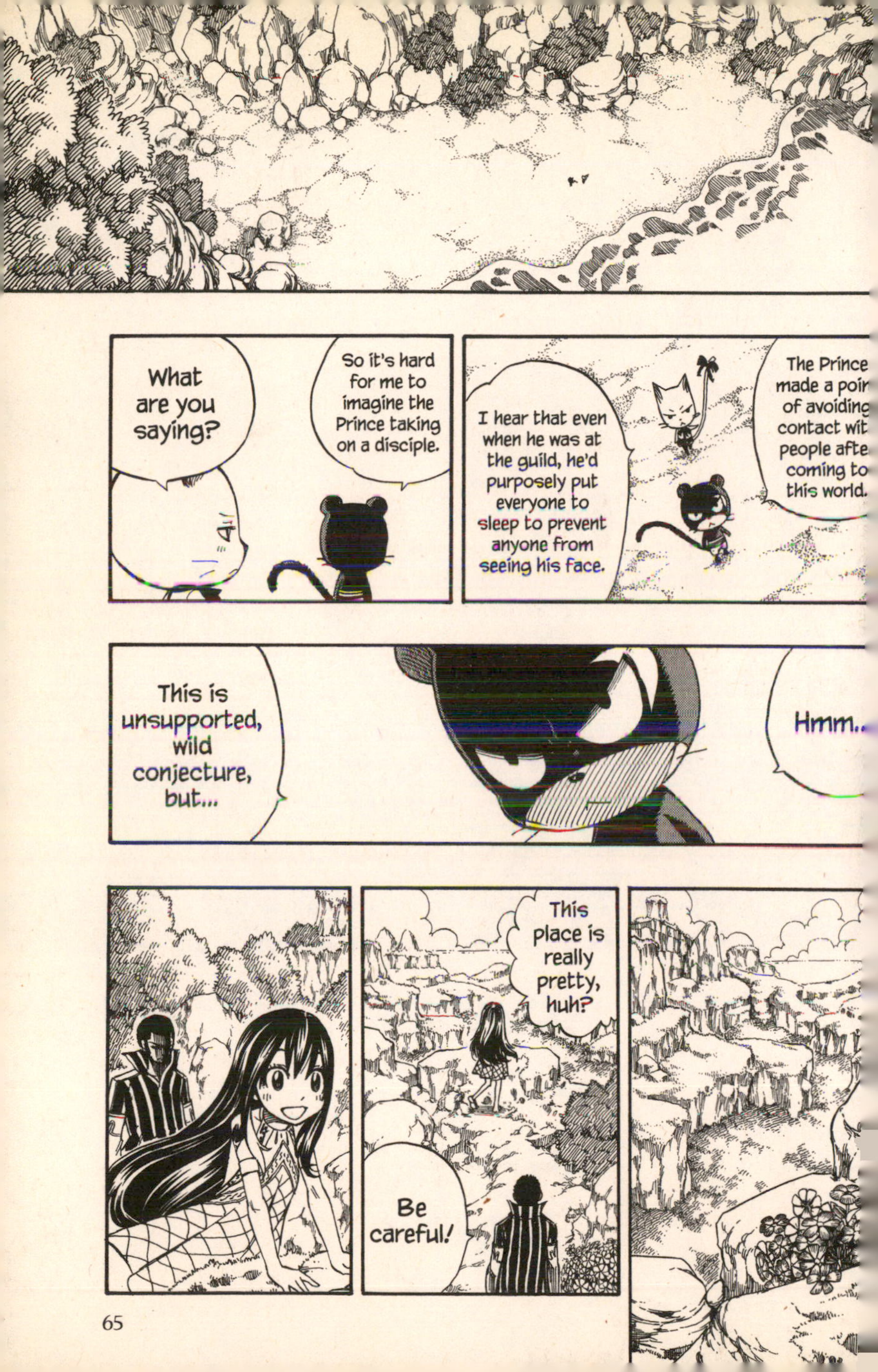
The Prince made a poir of avoiding contact wit people afte coming to this world.
I hear that even when he was at the guild, he'd purposely put everyone to sleep to prevent anyone from seeing his face.
So it's hard for me to imagine the Prince taking on a disciple.
What are you saying?
Hmm..
This is unsupported, wild conjecture, but...
This place is really pretty, huh?
Be careful!

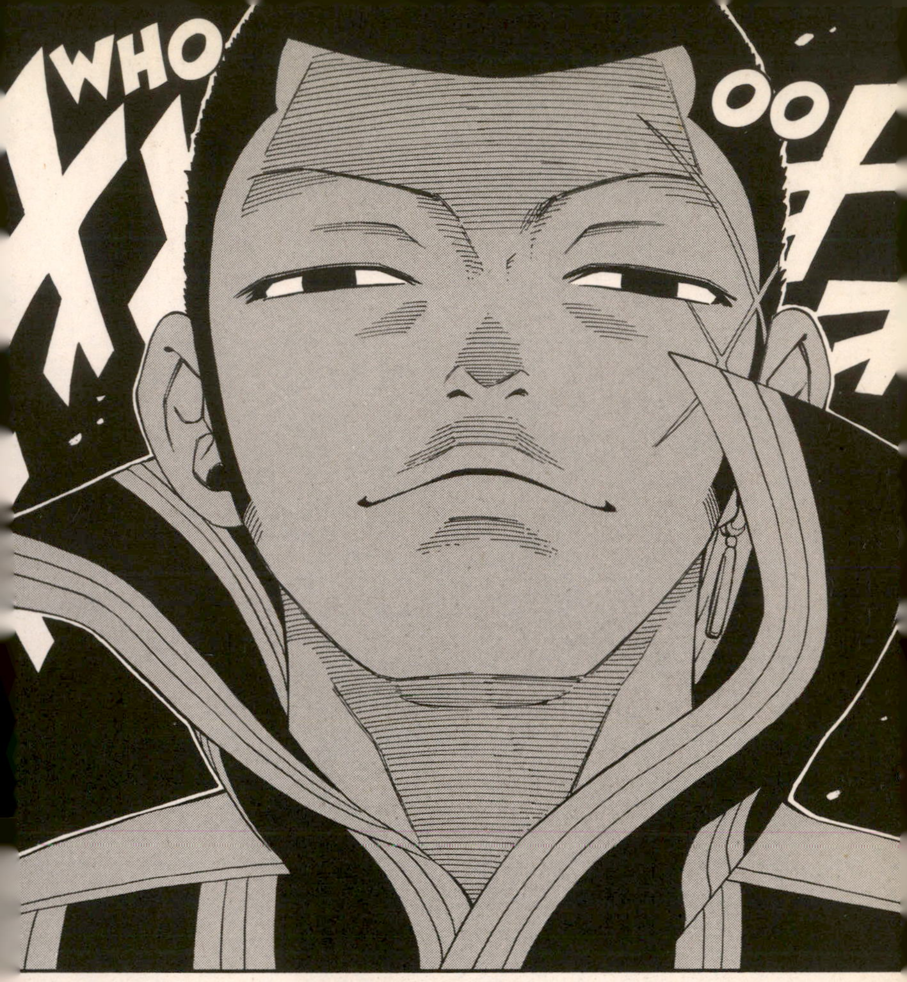
WHO
OO

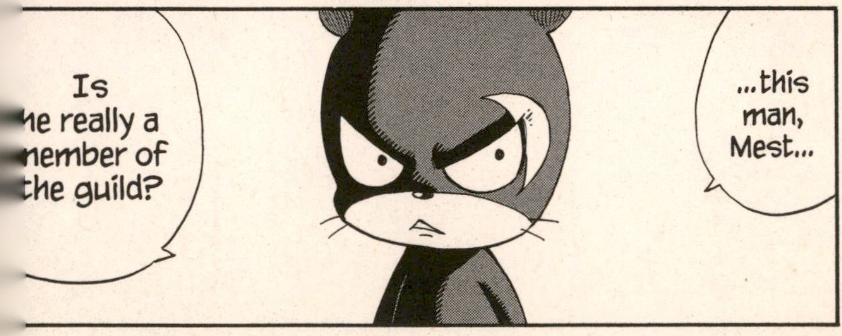
...this man, Mest...
Is he really a member of the guild?

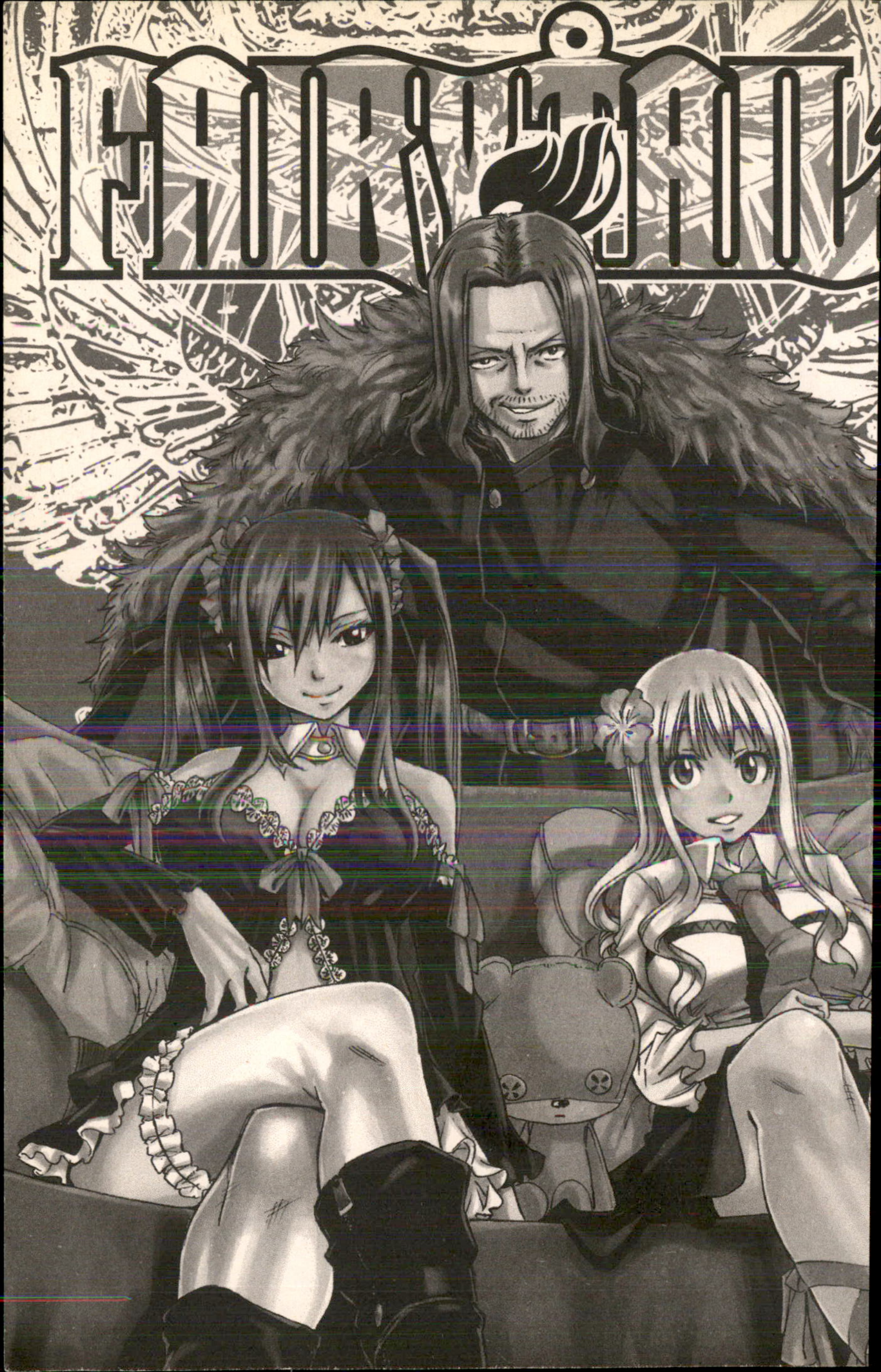
FAIRY TAIL

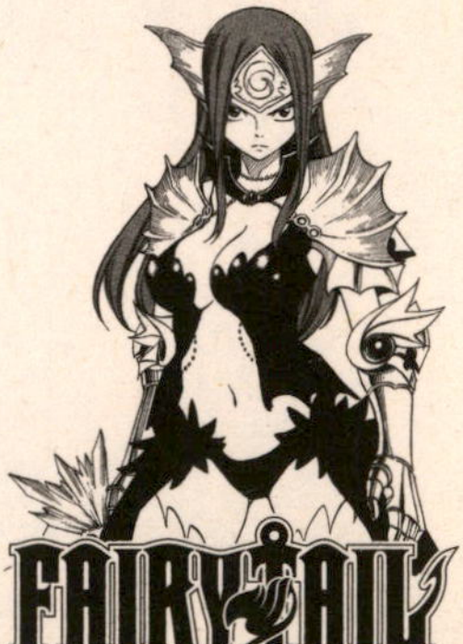
FAIRY TAIL
フェアリーテイル

Chapter 208: Predator of Death

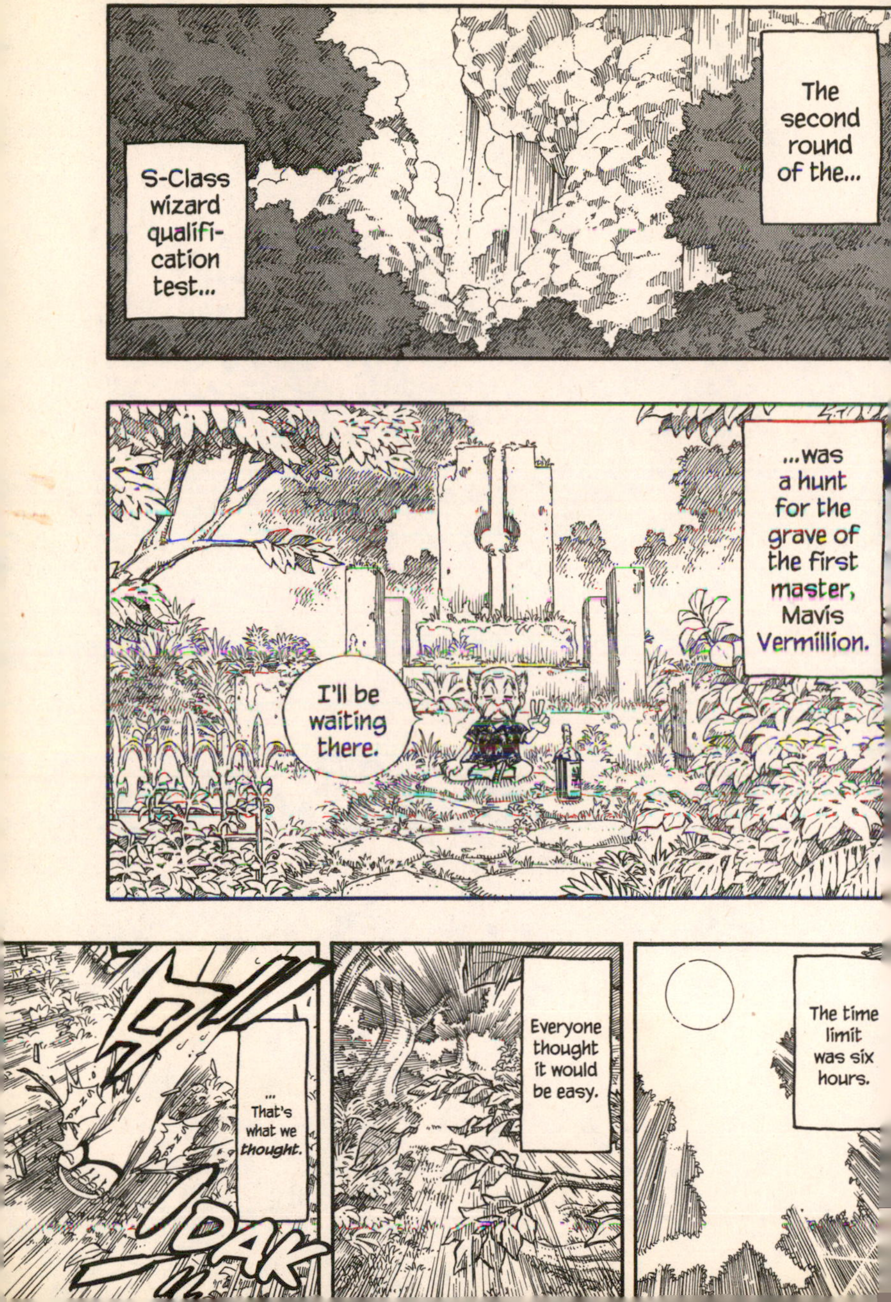
The second round of the...
S-Class wizard qualifi-cation test...
...was a hunt for the grave of the first master, Mavis Vermillion.
I'll be waiting there.
The time limit was six hours.
Everyone thought it would be easy.
...That's what we *thought*.
DAK

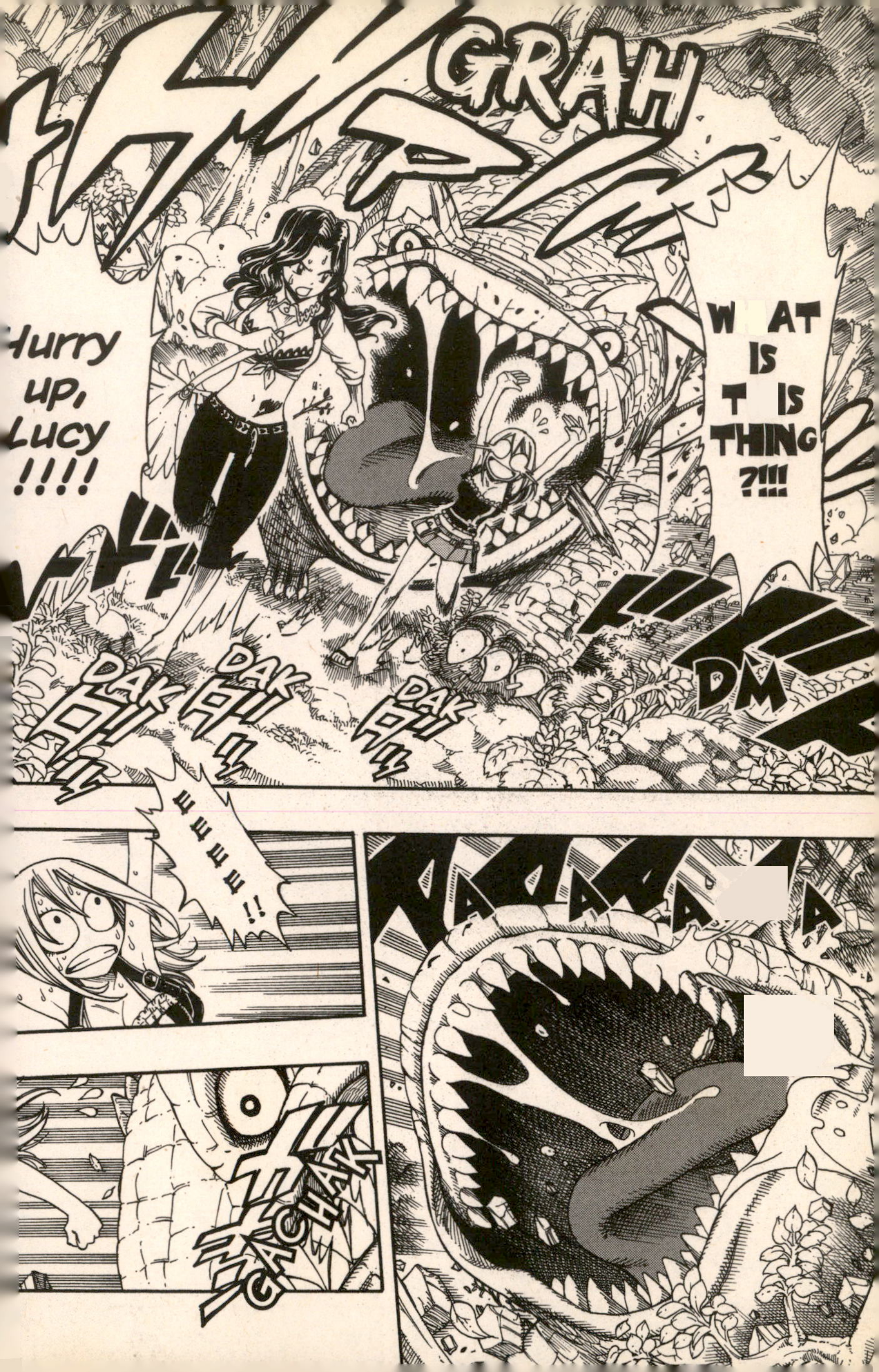
GRAH
WHAT IS THIS THING?!!!
Hurry up, Lucy!!!!
DM
DAK
DAK
DAK
EEEEE!!
GACHAK

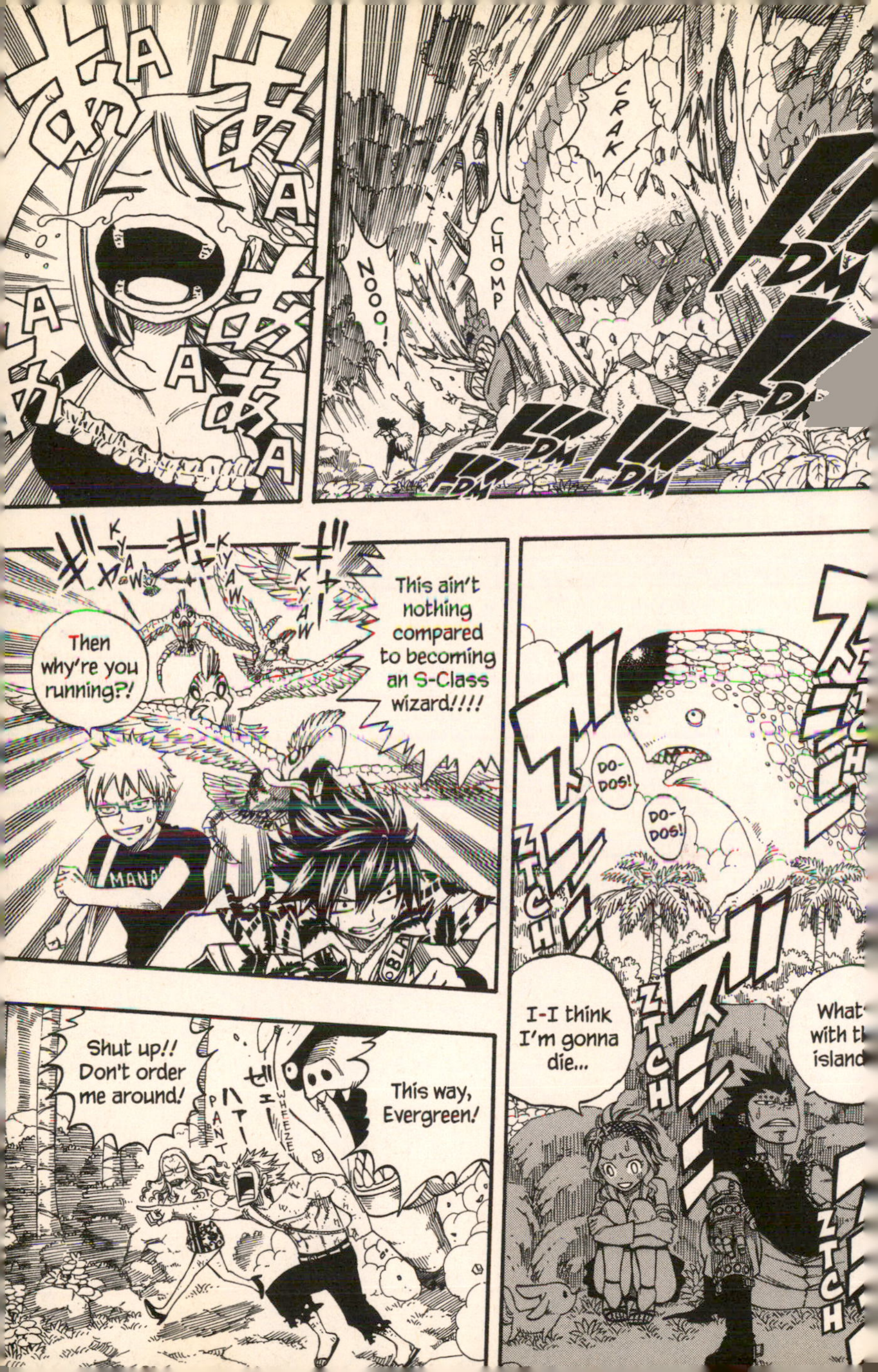
CRAK
CHOMP
NOOO!
DM DM DM DM DM
A A A A A A
DO-DOS!
DO-DOS!
ZTCH ZTCH ZTCH
This ain't nothing compared to becoming an S-Class wizard!!!!
Then why're you running?!
KYAW KYAW KYAW
What
with th
island
I-I think I'm gonna die...
This way, Evergreen!
Shut up!! Don't order me around!
PANT
WHEEZE

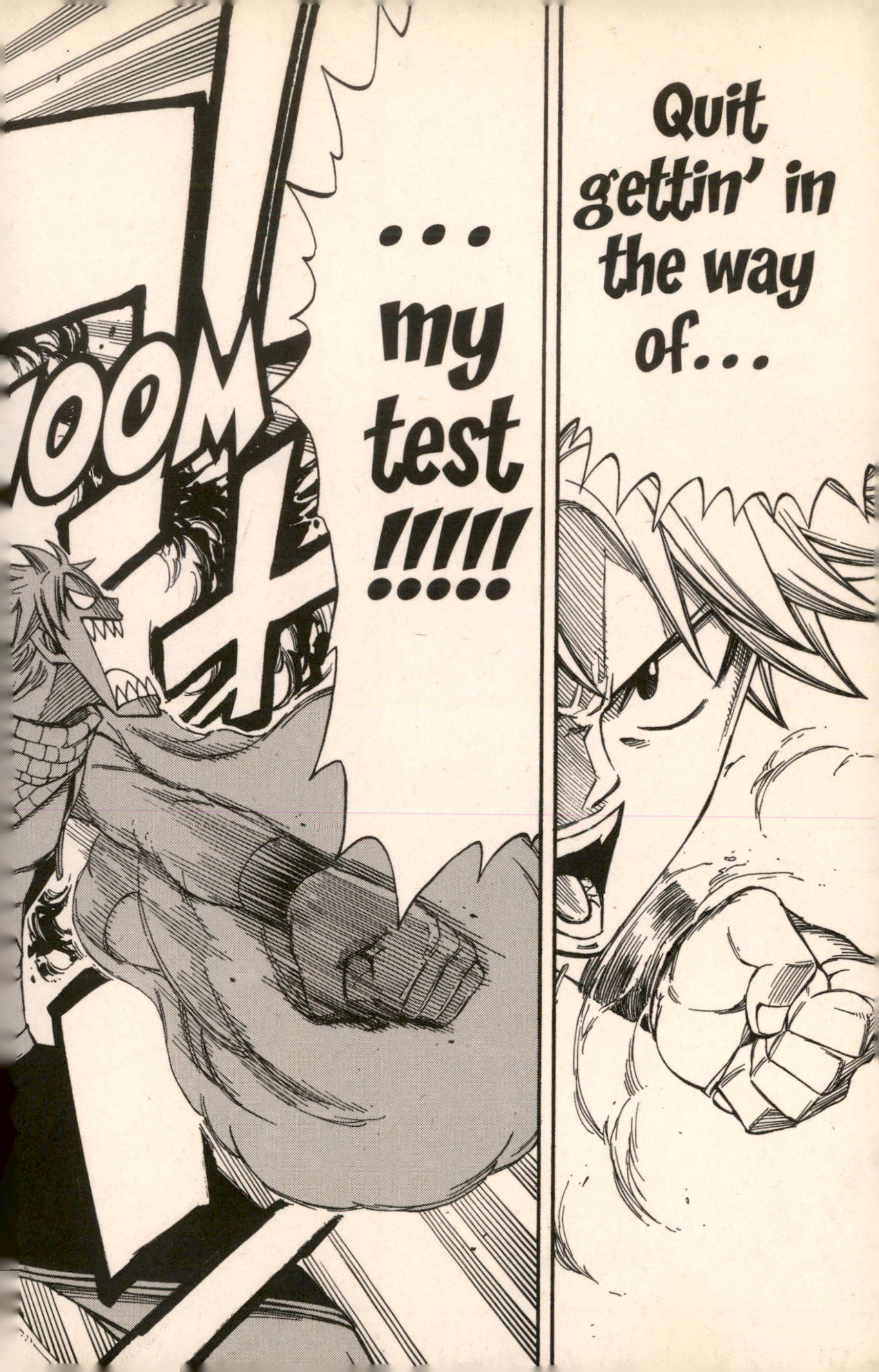
Quit gettin' in the way of...
...my test!!!!!
OOM

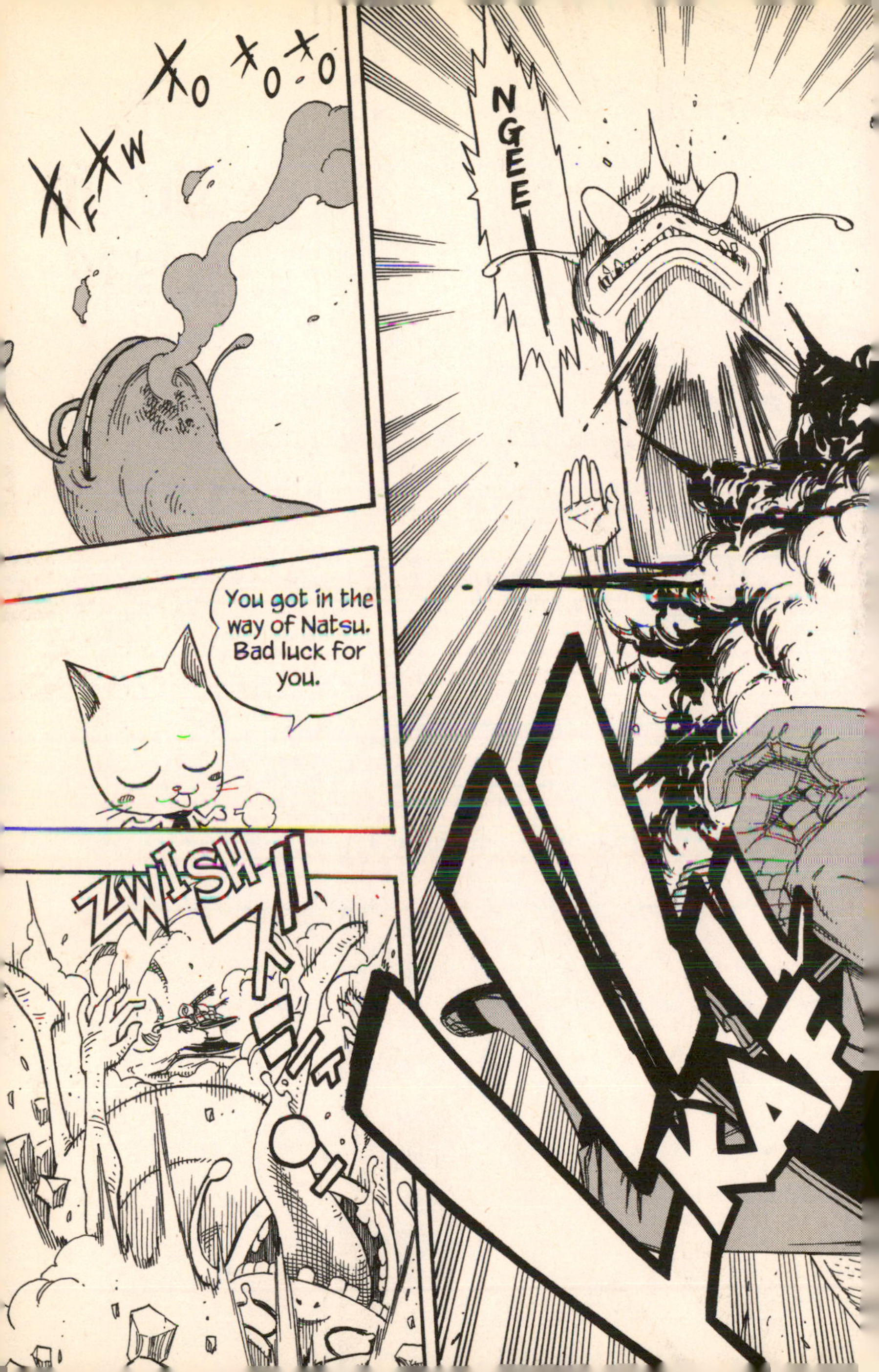
NGEE
You got in the way of Natsu. Bad luck for you.
ZWISH

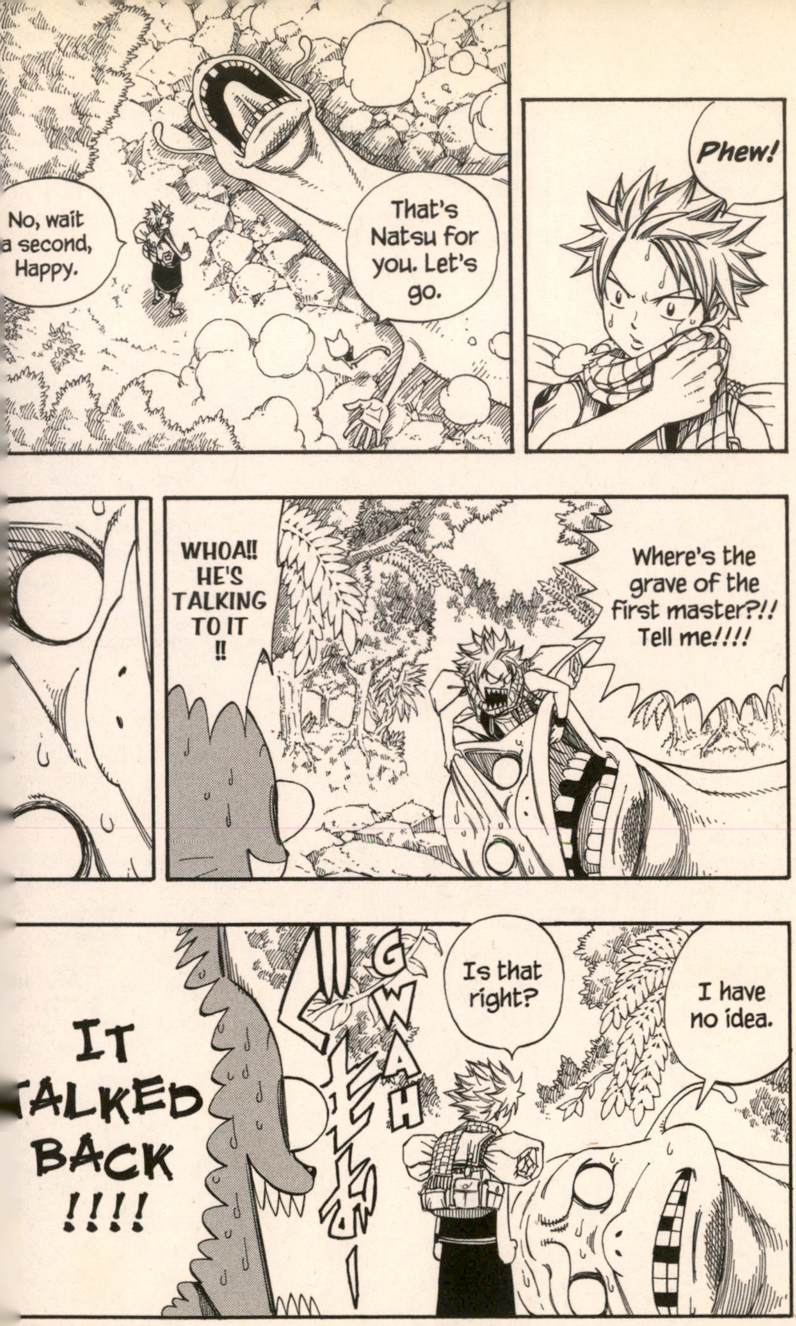
Phew!
That's Natsu for you. Let's go.
No, wait a second, Happy.
Where's the grave of the first master?!! Tell me!!!!
WHOA!! HE'S TALKING TO IT !!
I have no idea.
Is that right?
GWAH
IT TALKED BACK !!!!

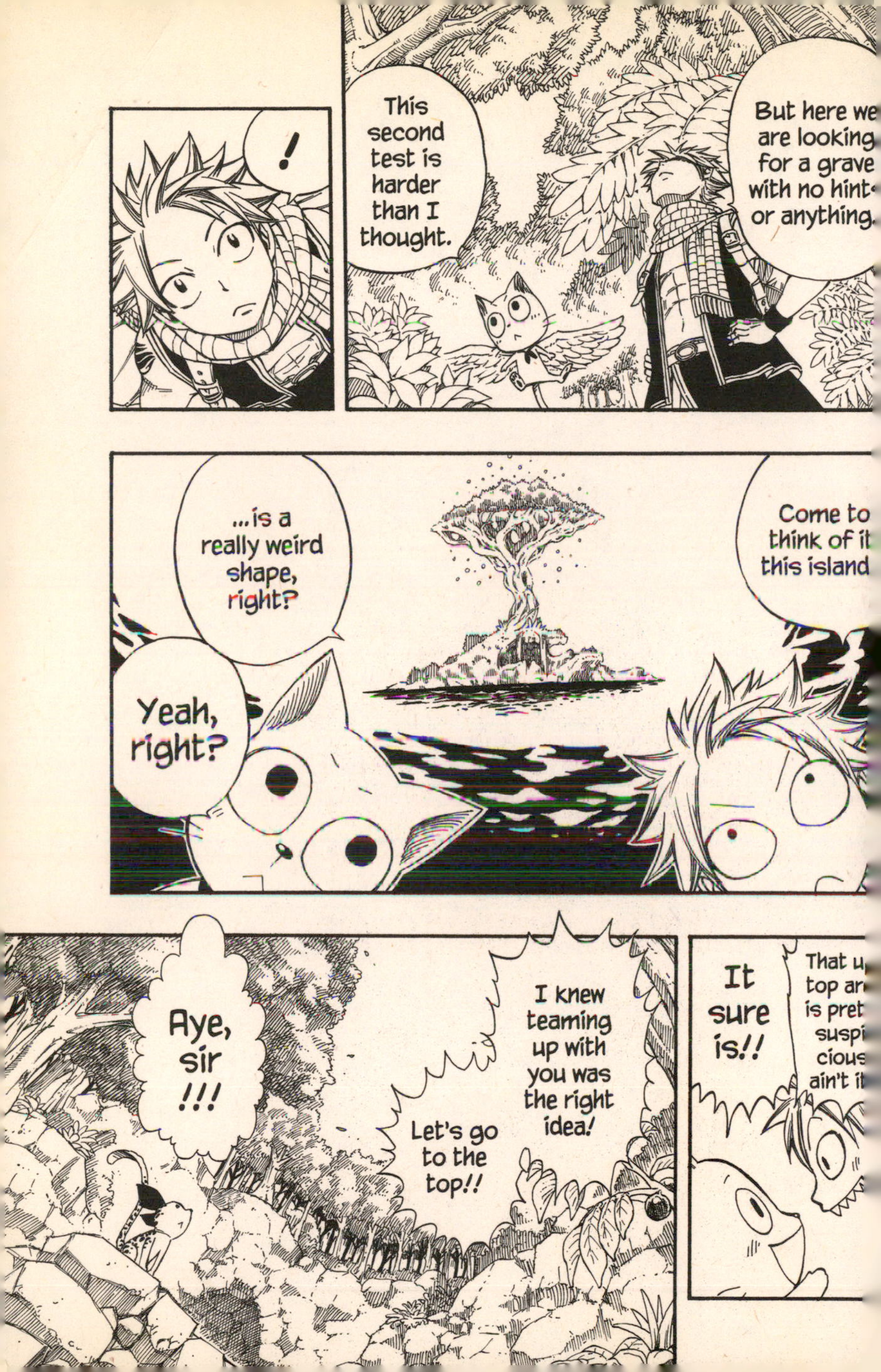
But here we are looking for a grave with no hint or anything.
This second test is harder than I thought.
!
Come to think of it this island
...is a really weird shape, right?
Yeah, right?
That u top ar is pret suspi cious ain't it
It sure is!!
I knew teaming up with you was the right idea!
Let's go to the top!!
Aye, sir!!!

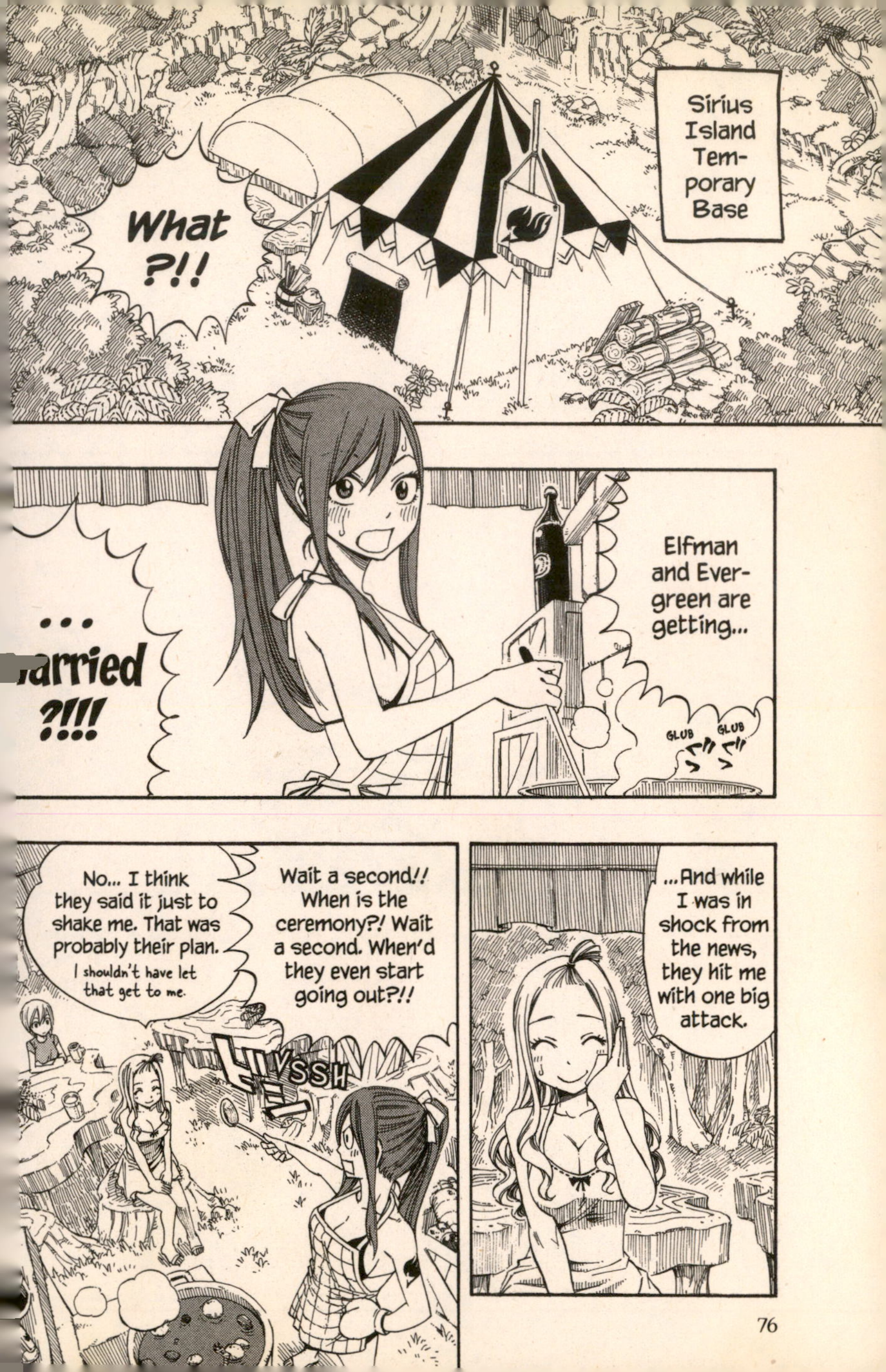
Sirius Island Temporary Base
What ?!!
Elfman and Evergreen are getting...
... arried ?!!!
GLUB GLUB
...And while I was in shock from the news, they hit me with one big attack.
Wait a second!! When is the ceremony?! Wait a second. When'd they even start going out?!!
No... I think they said it just to shake me. That was probably their plan.
I shouldn't have let that get to me.
VSSH

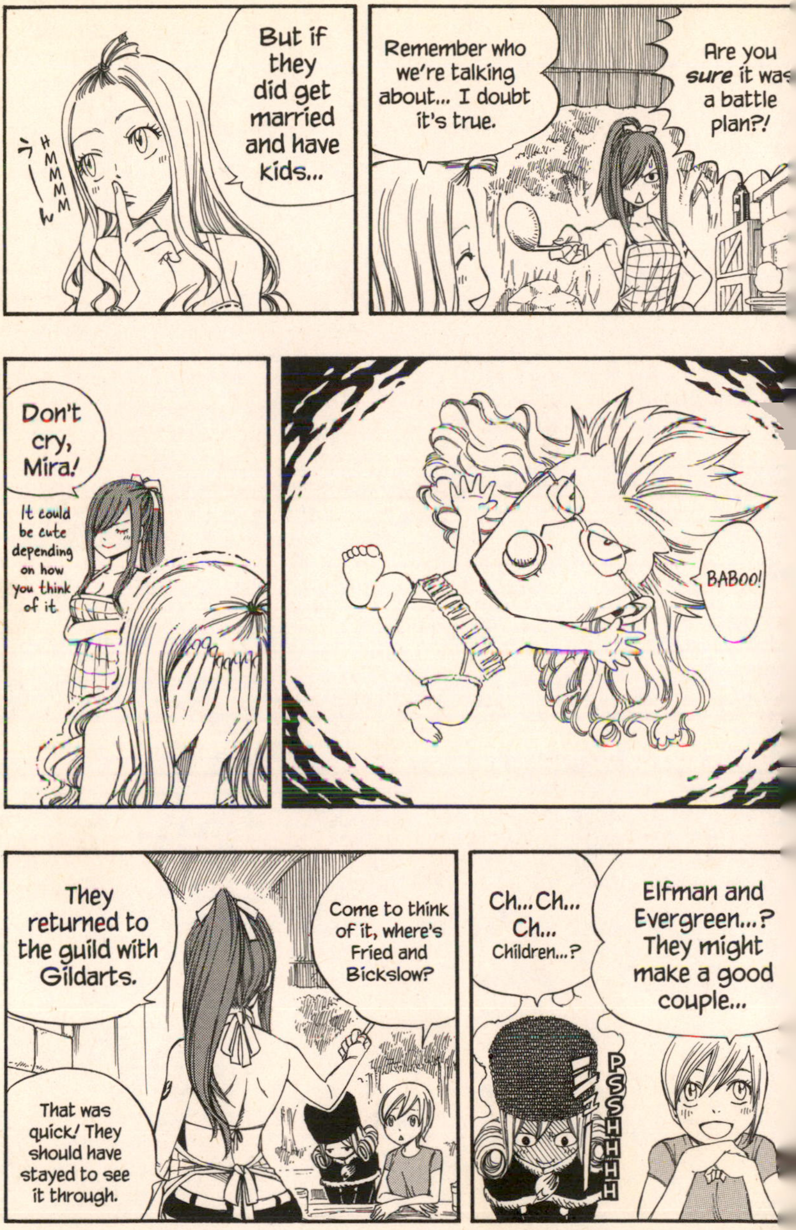
Are you sure it was a battle plan?!
Remember who we're talking about... I doubt it's true.
But if they did get married and have kids...
HMMMM
BABOO!
Don't cry, Mira!
It could be cute depending on how you think of it.
Elfman and Evergreen...? They might make a good couple...
Ch...Ch... Ch... Children...?
PSSHHHH
Come to think of it, where's Fried and Bickslow?
They returned to the guild with Gildarts.
That was quick! They should have stayed to see it through.

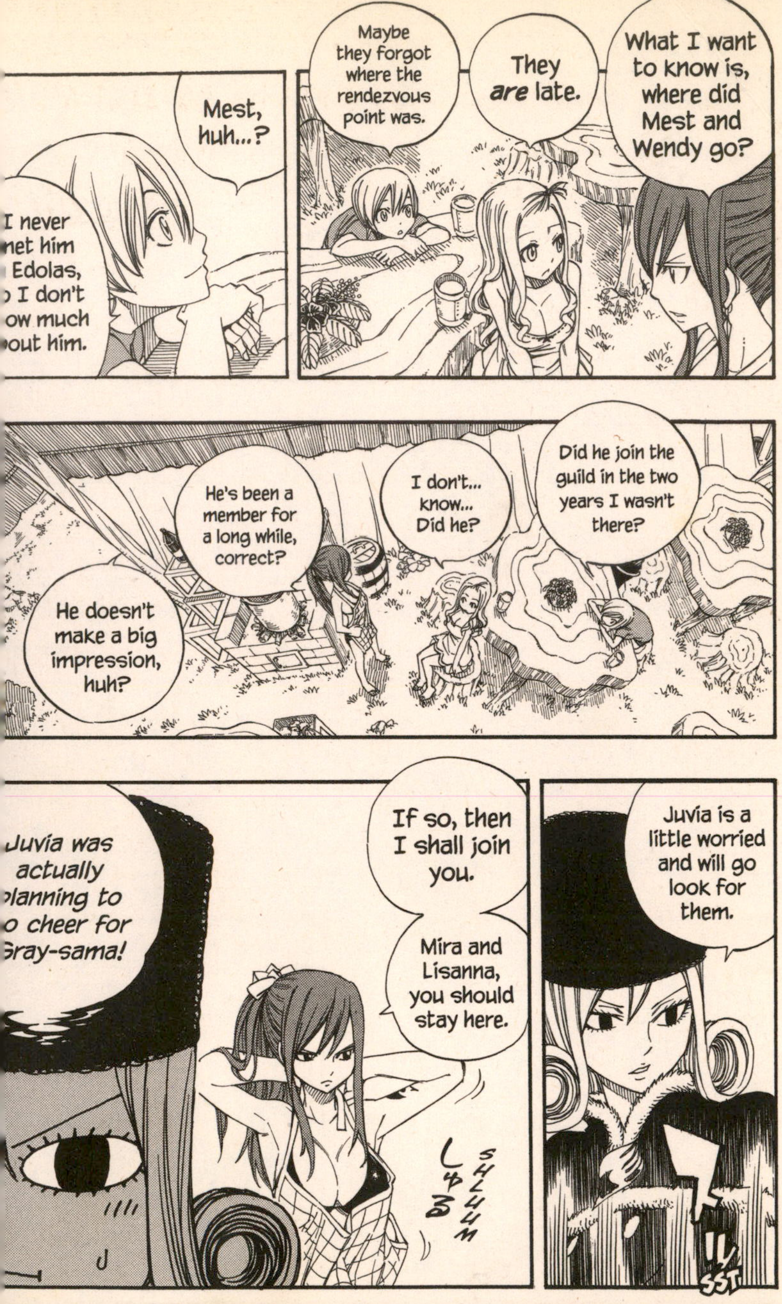
What I want to know is, where did Mest and Wendy go?
They *are* late.
Maybe they forgot where the rendezvous point was.
Mest, huh...?
I never net him Edolas, I don't ow much out him.
Did he join the guild in the two years I wasn't there?
I don't... know... Did he?
He's been a member for a long while, correct?
He doesn't make a big impression, huh?
Juvia is a little worried and will go look for them.
SST
If so, then I shall join you.
Mira and Lisanna, you should stay here.
SHLUUM
Juvia was actually lanning to o cheer for Gray-sama!

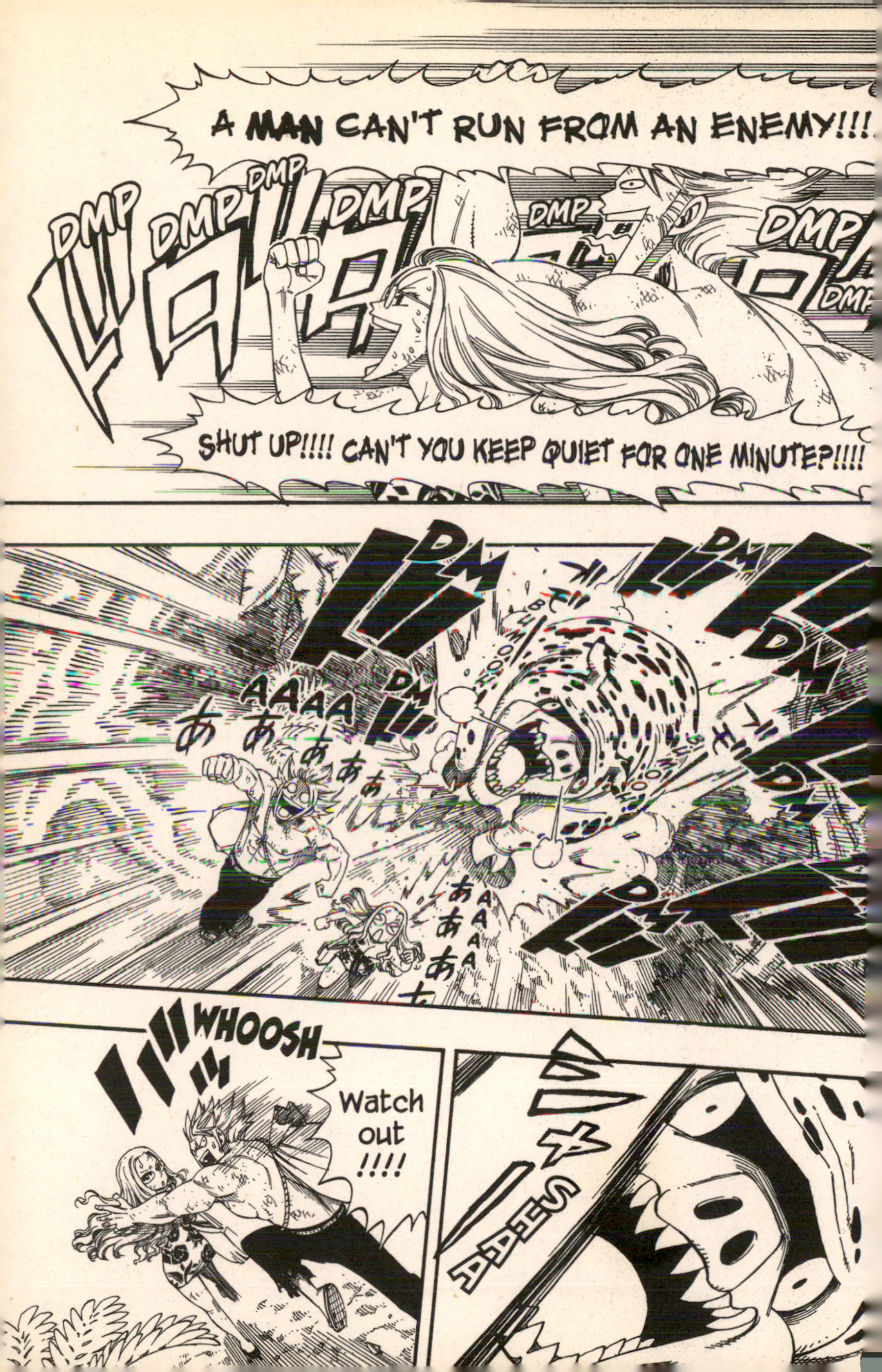
A MAN CAN'T RUN FROM AN ENEMY!!!!
DMP DMP DMP DMP DMP DMP DMP
SHUT UP!!!! CAN'T YOU KEEP QUIET FOR ONE MINUTE?!!!!
DM DM DM DM DM
AAAAA
ああああああ
AAAA
あああ
WHOOSH
Watch out !!!!

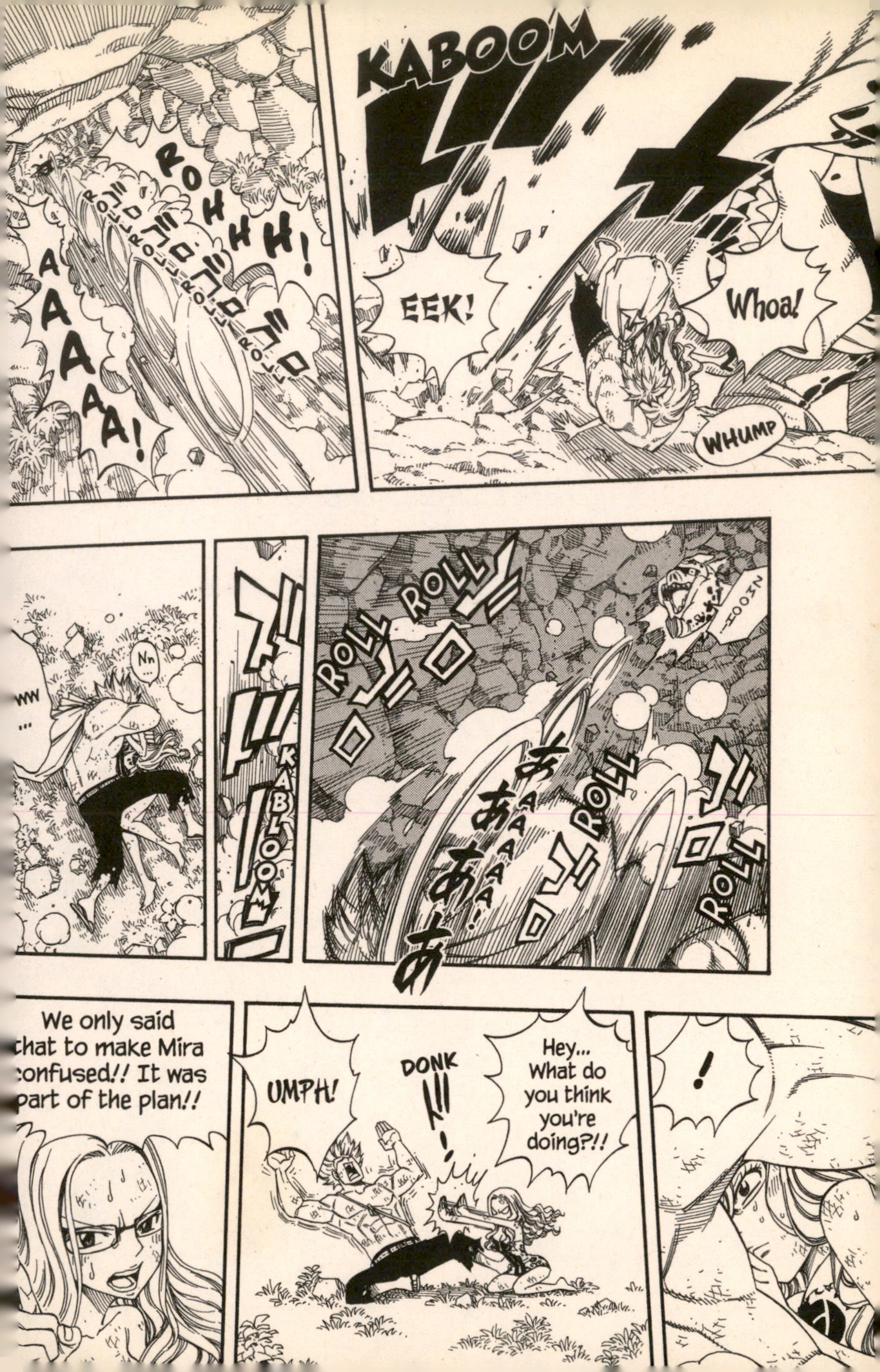
KABOOM
EEK!
Whoa!
WHUMP
ROHHHH!
AAAAAA!
ROLL ROLL ROLL ROLL
ROLL ROLL
ROLL ROLL
AAAAAA!
ROLL
ROLL
KABLOOM
Nn ...
!
Hey... What do you think you're doing?!!
DONK
UMPH!
We only said that to make Mira confused!! It was part of the plan!!

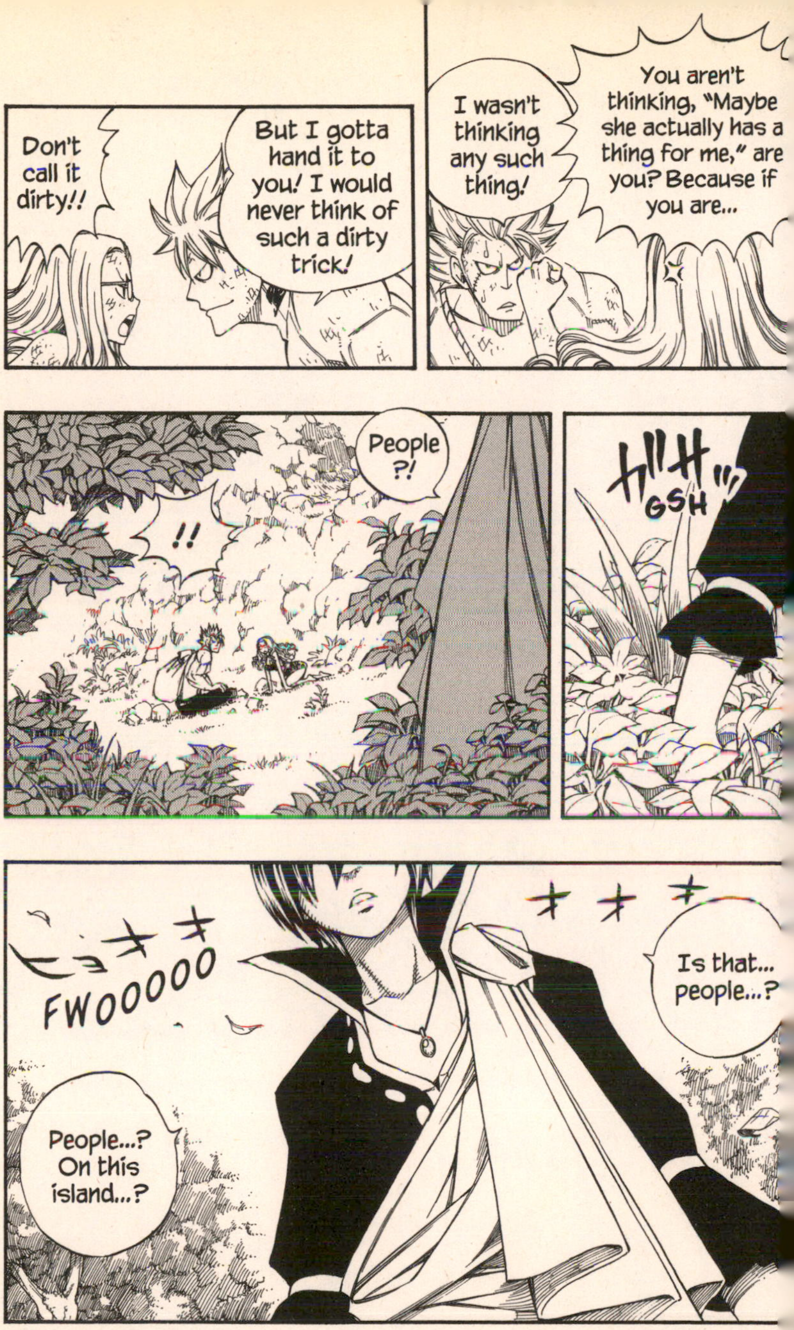
You aren't thinking, "Maybe she actually has a thing for me," are you? Because if you are...
I wasn't thinking any such thing!
But I gotta hand it to you! I would never think of such a dirty trick!
Don't call it dirty!!
GSH
People?!
!!
Is that... people...?
FWOOOOO
People...? On this island...?

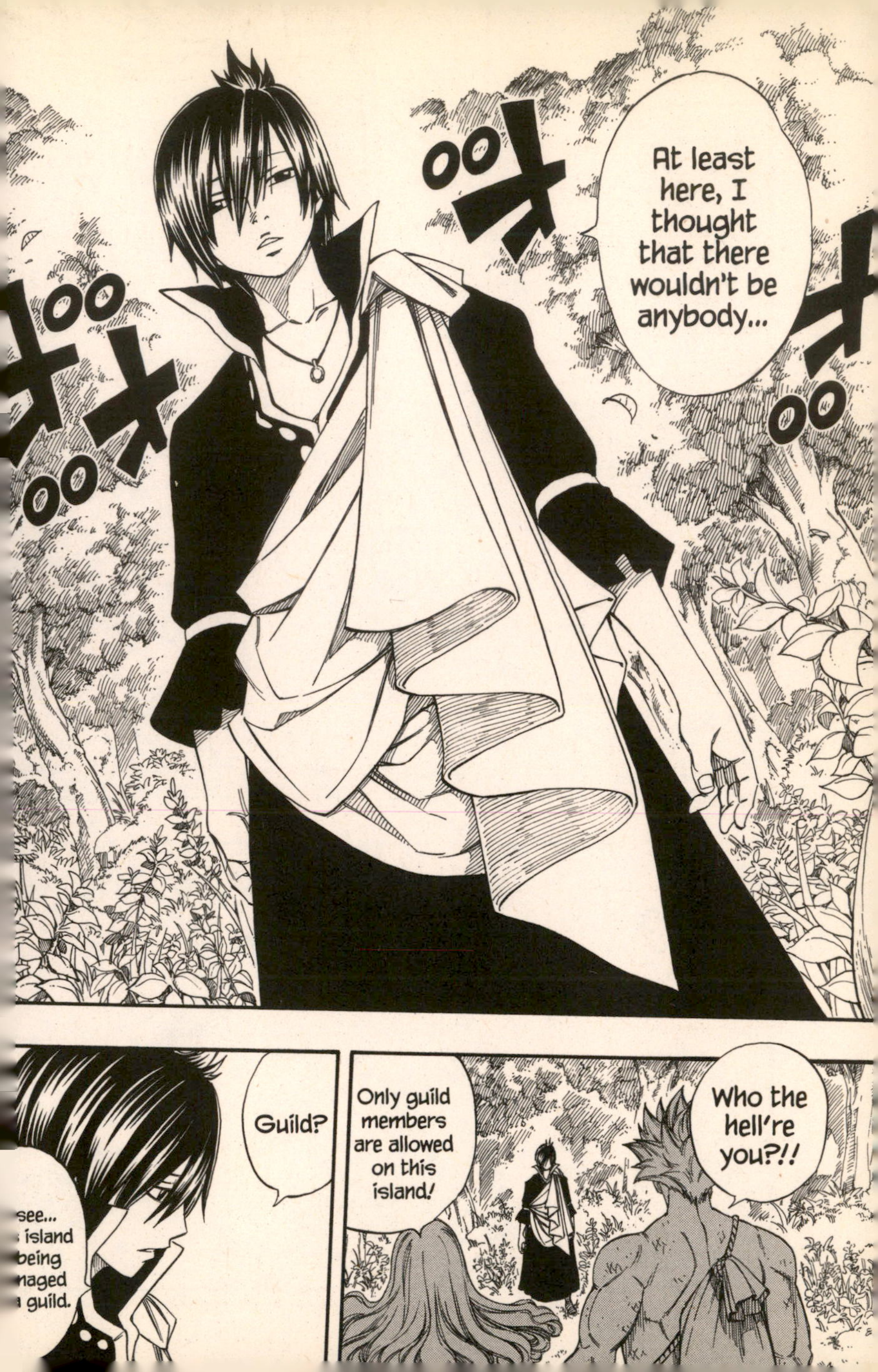
At least here, I thought that there wouldn't be anybody...
Who the hell're you?!!
Only guild members are allowed on this island!
Guild?
see... island being naged guild.

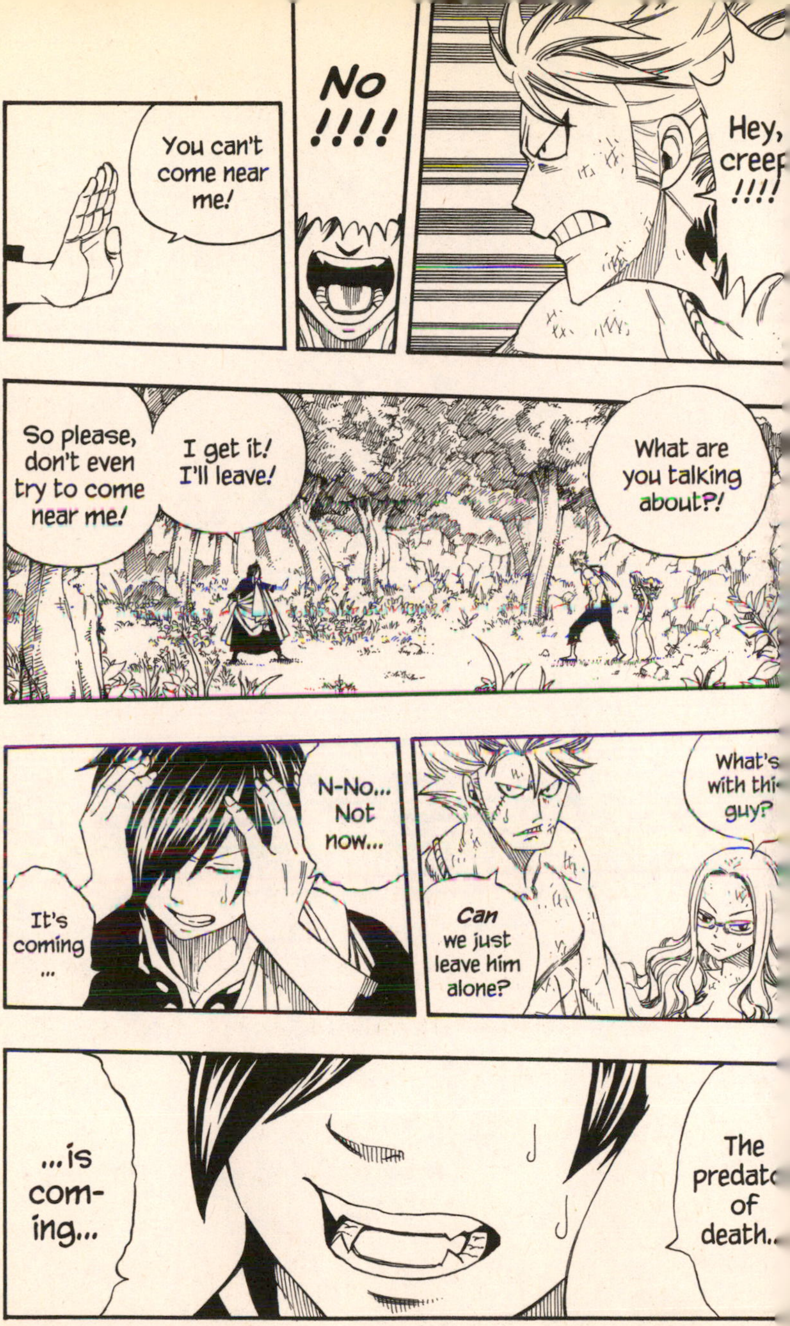
Hey, creep !!!!
No !!!!
You can't come near me!
What are you talking about?!
I get it! I'll leave!
So please, don't even try to come near me!
What's with this guy?
Can we just leave him alone?
N-No... Not now...
It's coming ...
The predator of death...
...is com-ing...

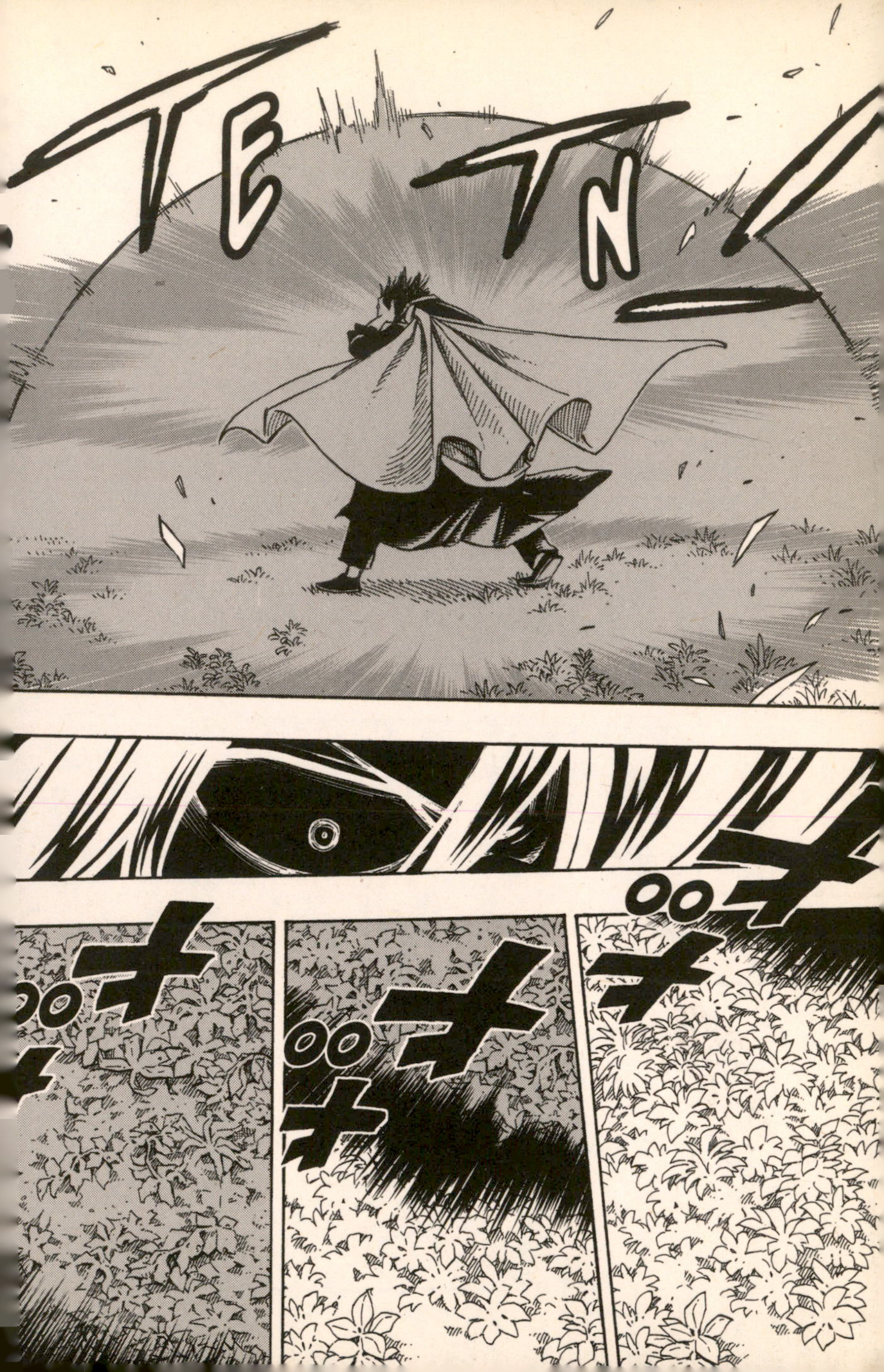

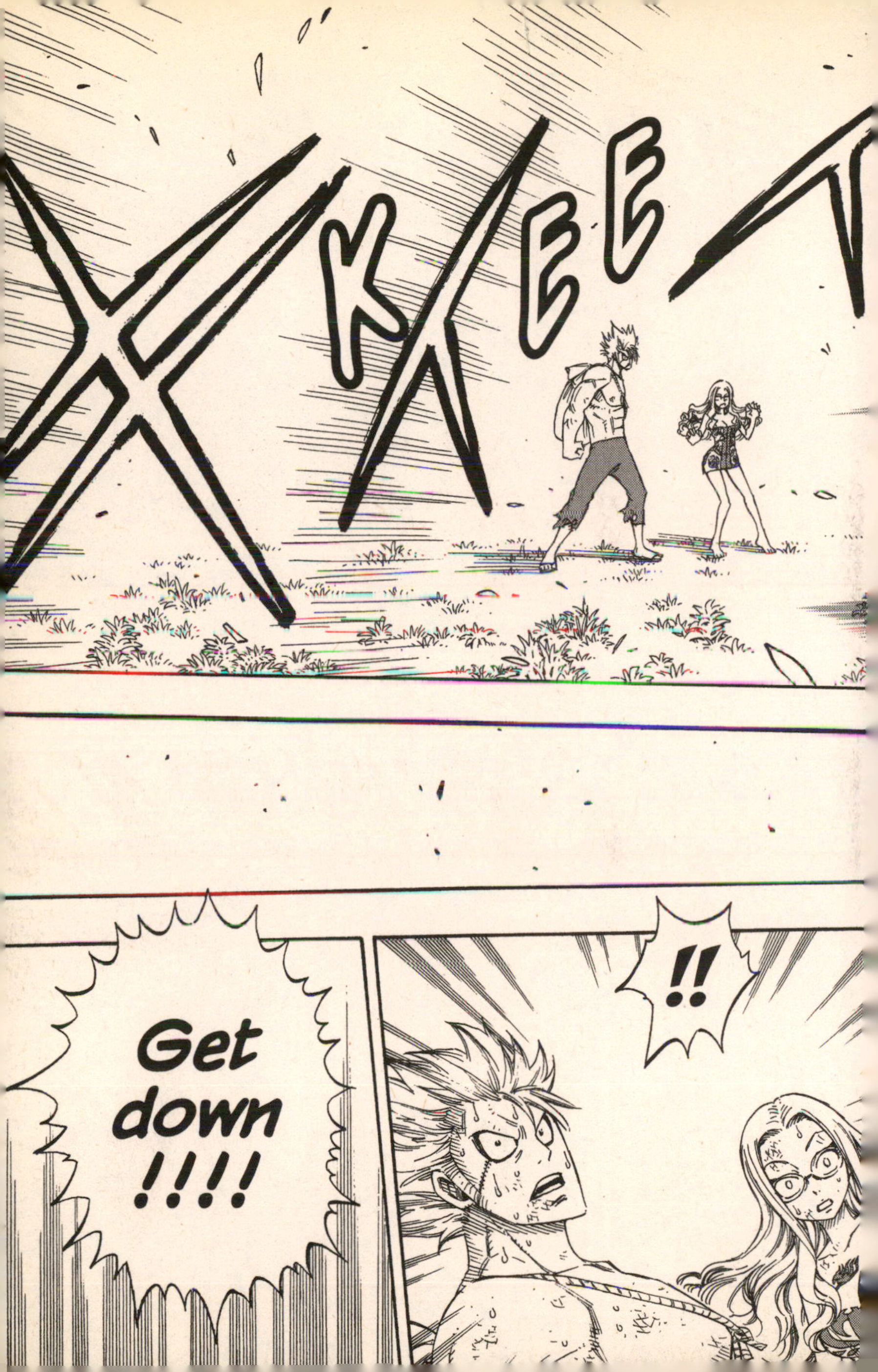
!!
Get down !!!!

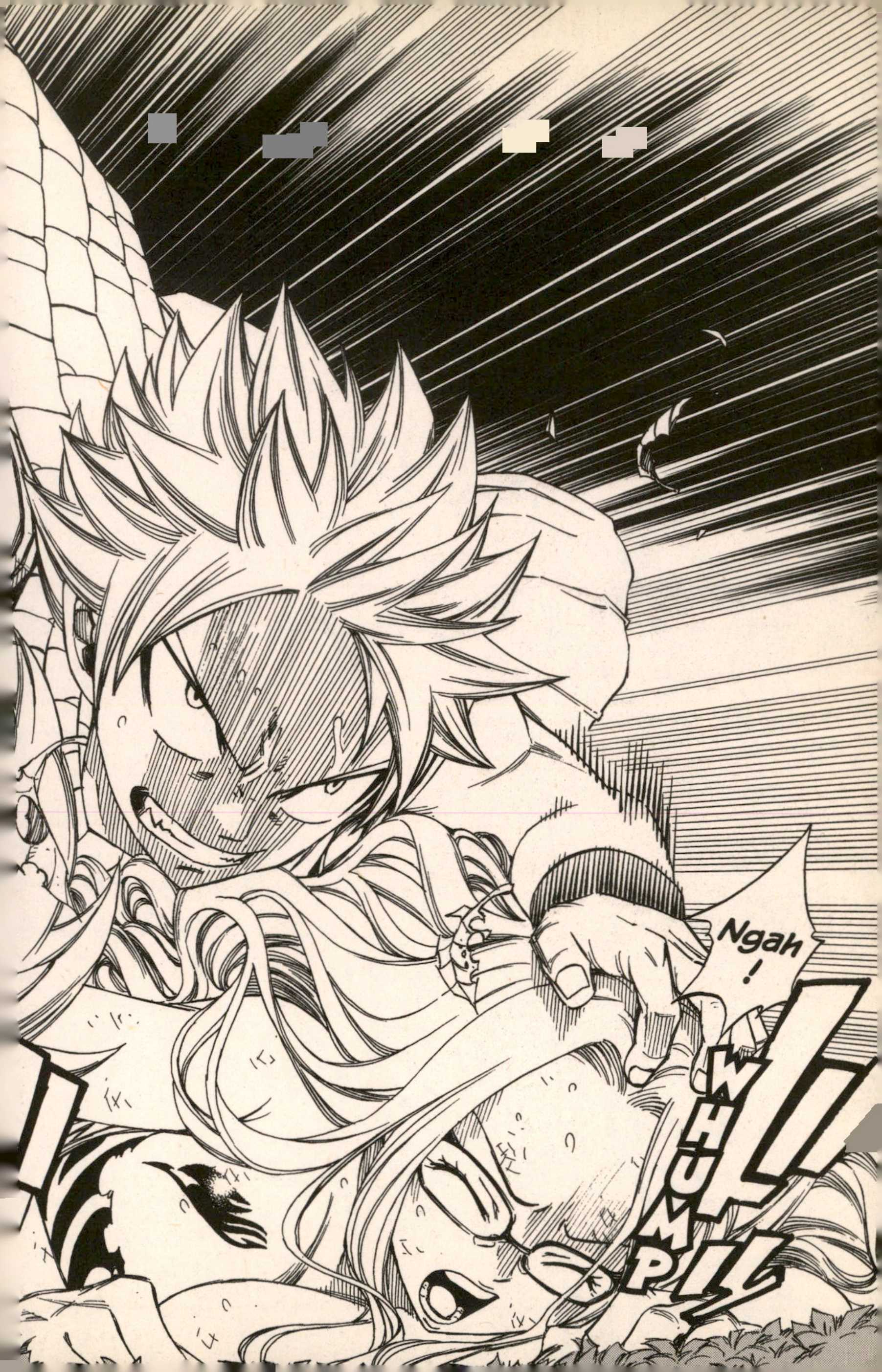
Ngah!
WHUMP!!

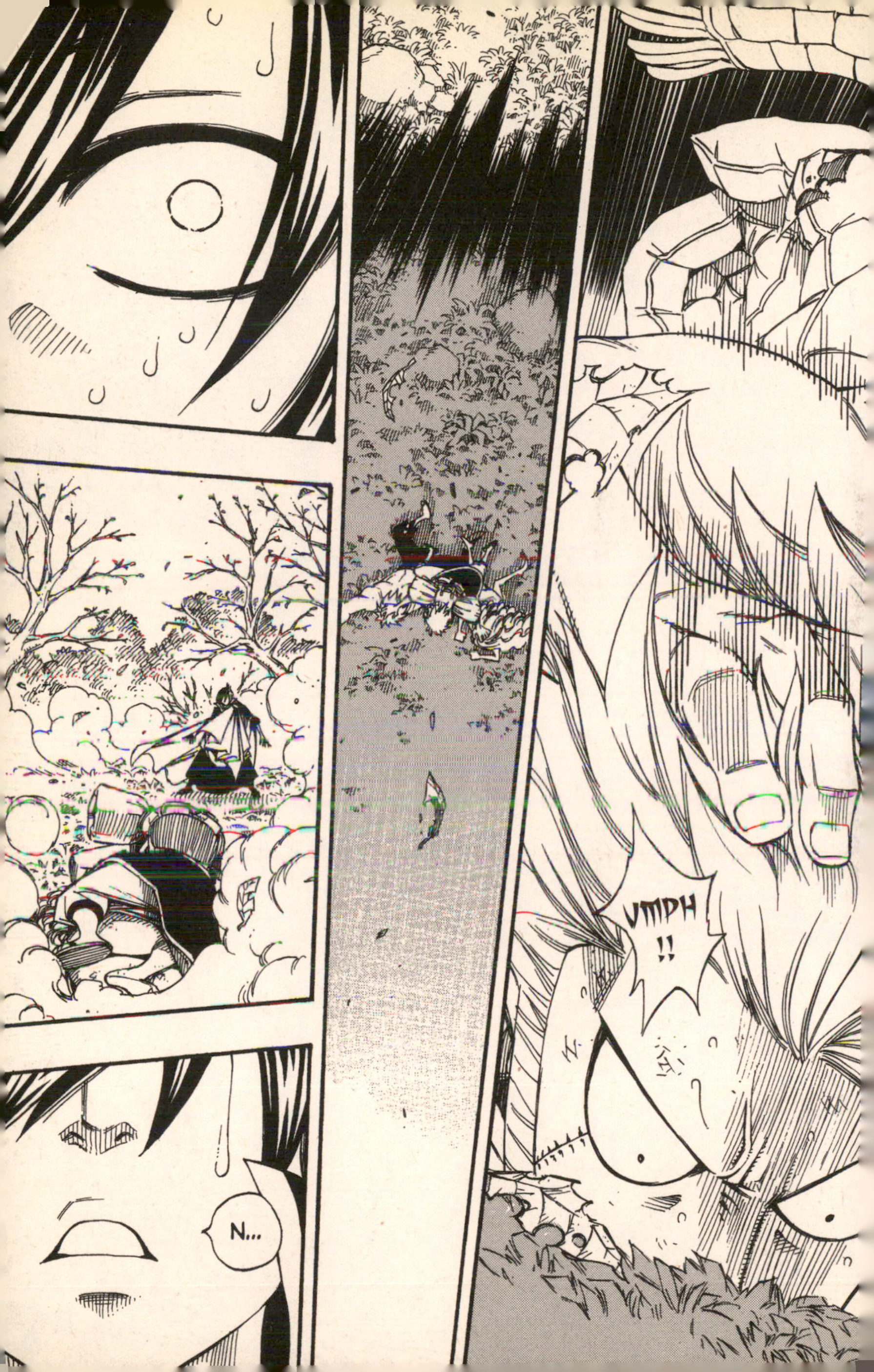
UMPH !!
N...

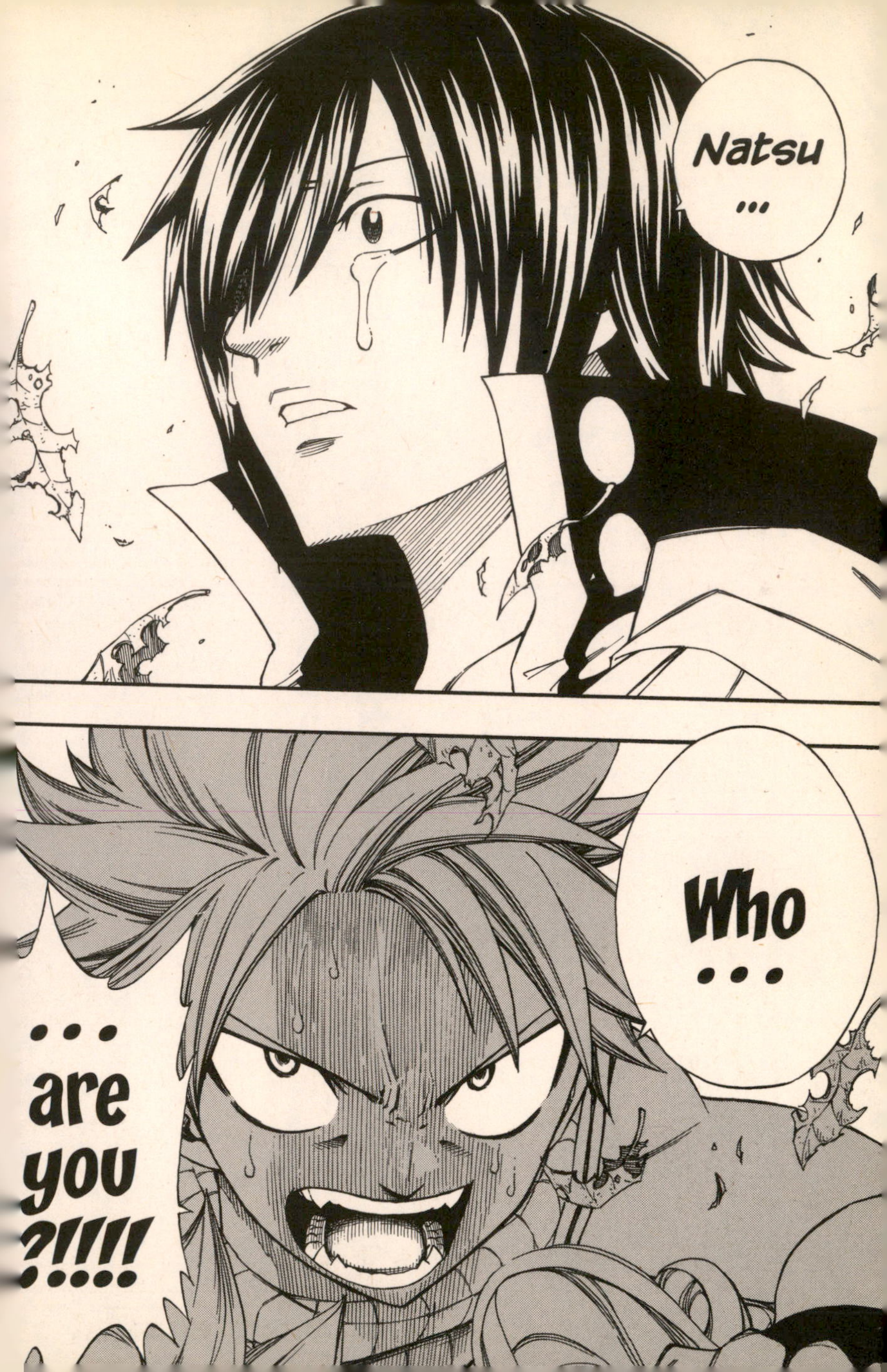
Natsu ...
Who ...
... are you ?!!!!

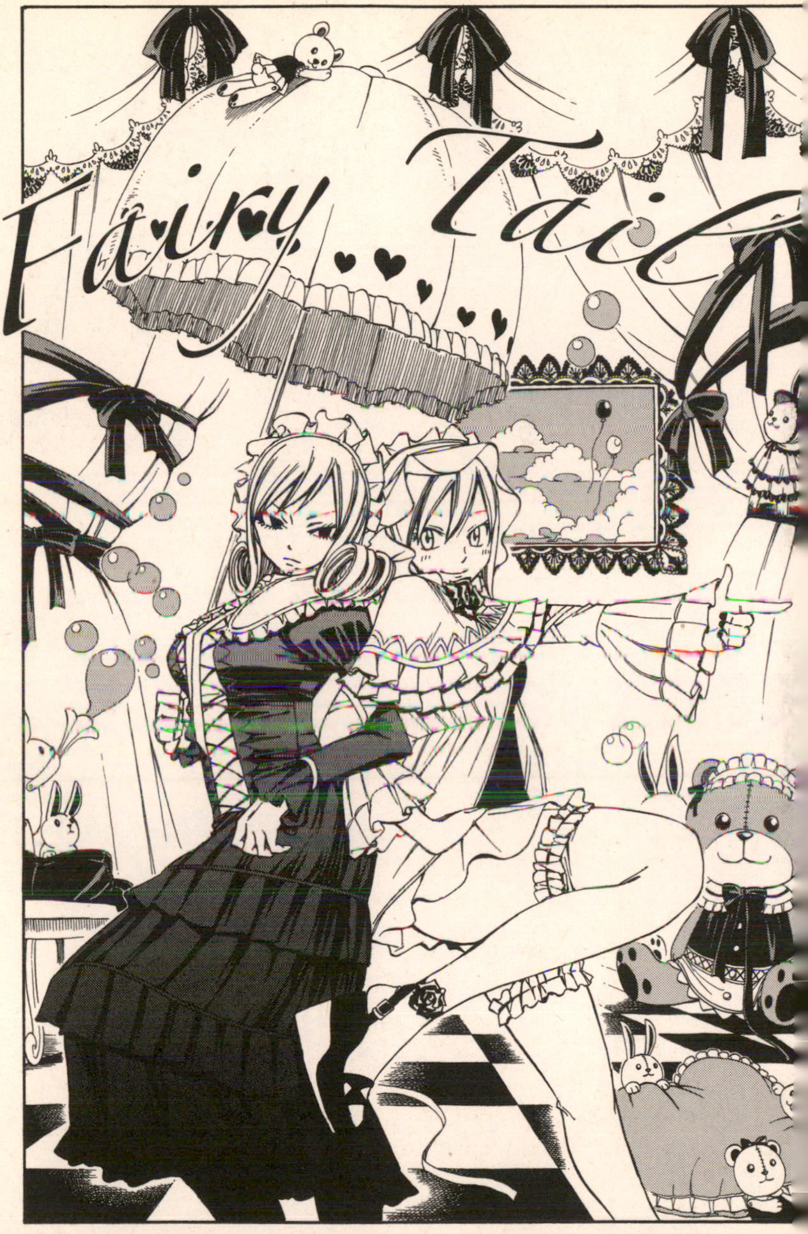
Fairy Tail

Chapter 209: The Black Wizard

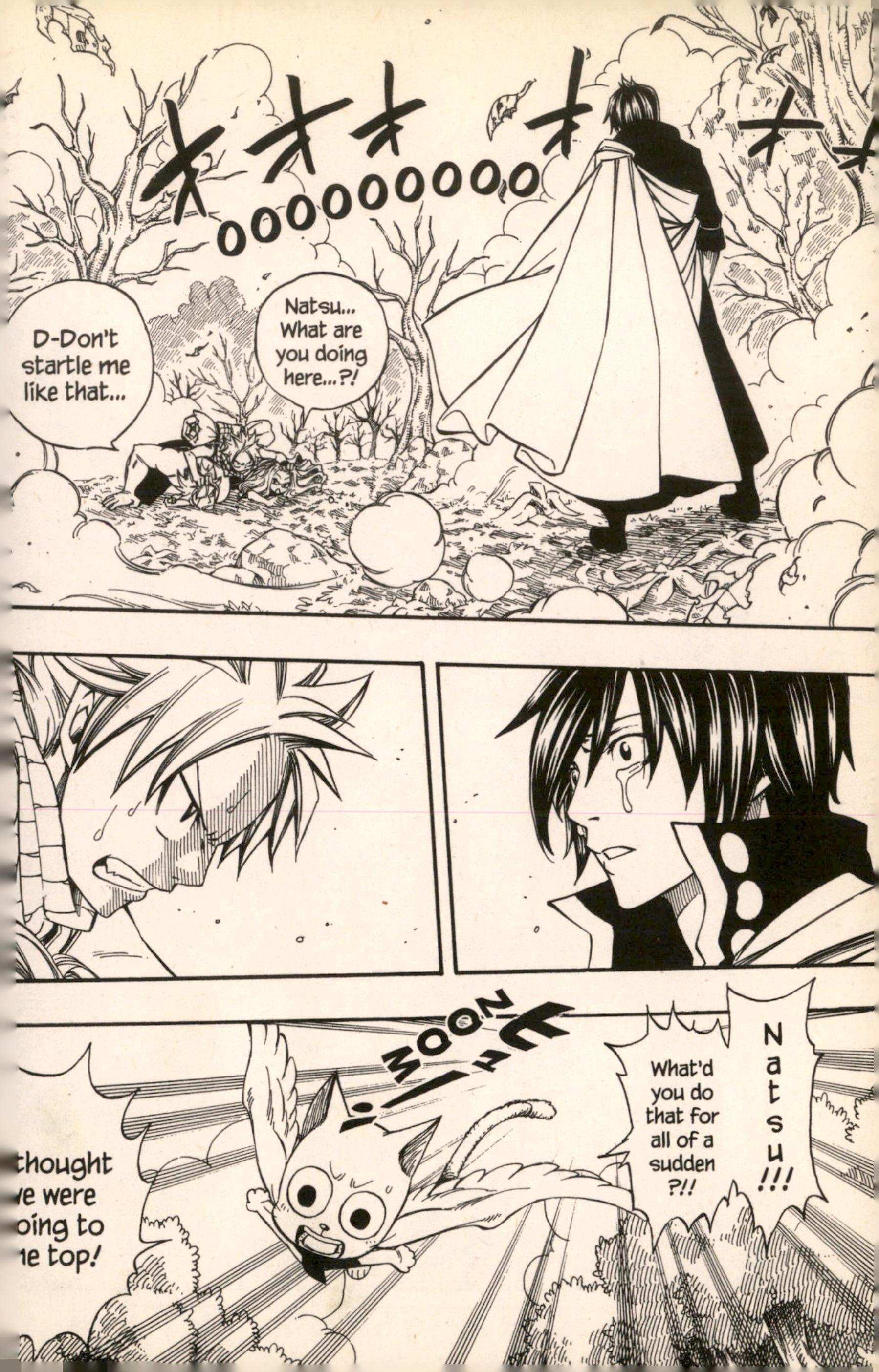

オオオオ オ オオ
OOOOOOOOOO
Natsu... What are you doing here...?!
D-Don't startle me like that...
Natsu!!!
What'd you do that for all of a sudden?!!
ZOOM!!
thought
e were
oing to
e top!

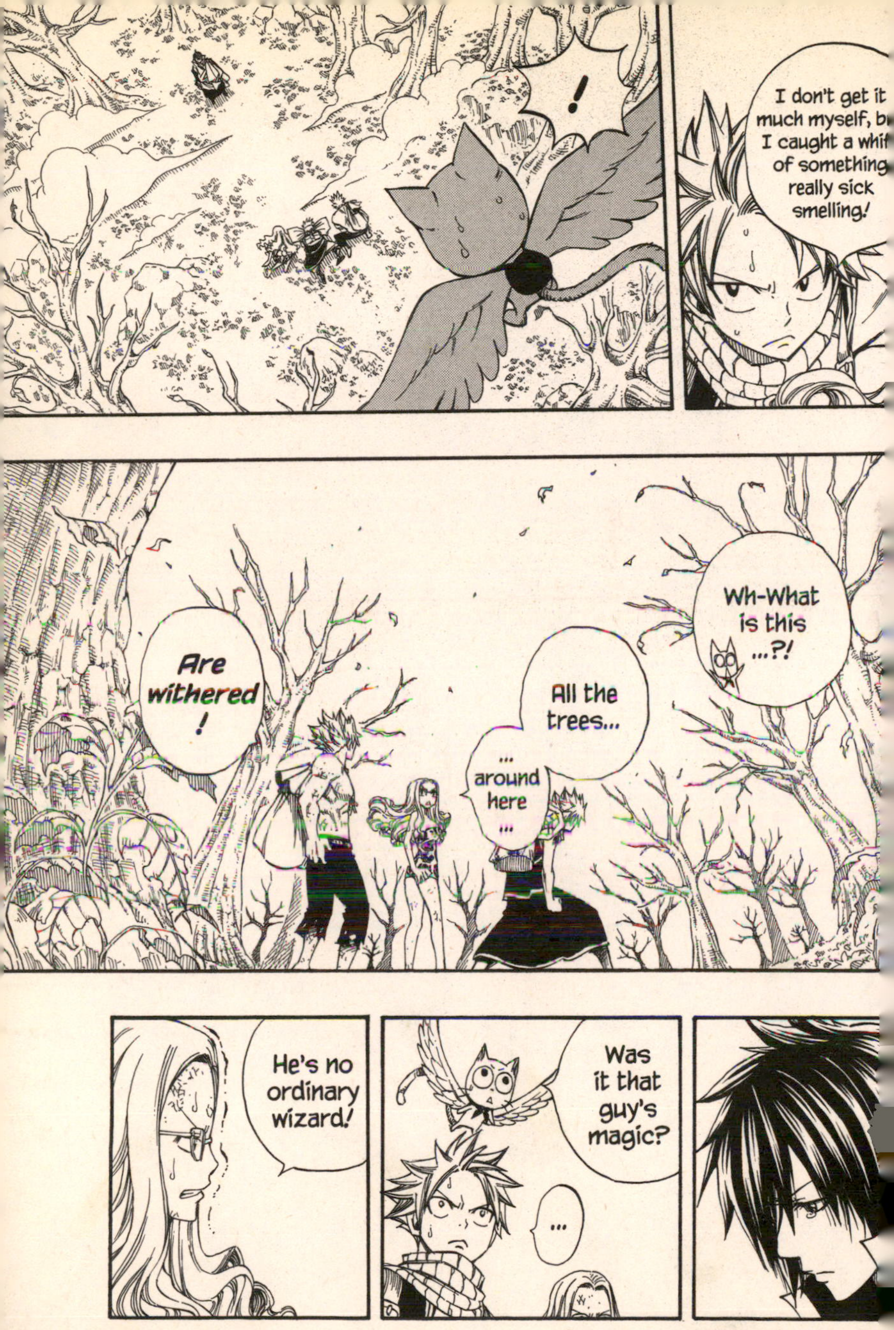
I don't get it much myself, b
I caught a whif of something really sick smelling!
!
Wh-What is this ...?!
All the trees...
... around here ...
Are withered !
Was it that guy's magic?
...
He's no ordinary wizard!

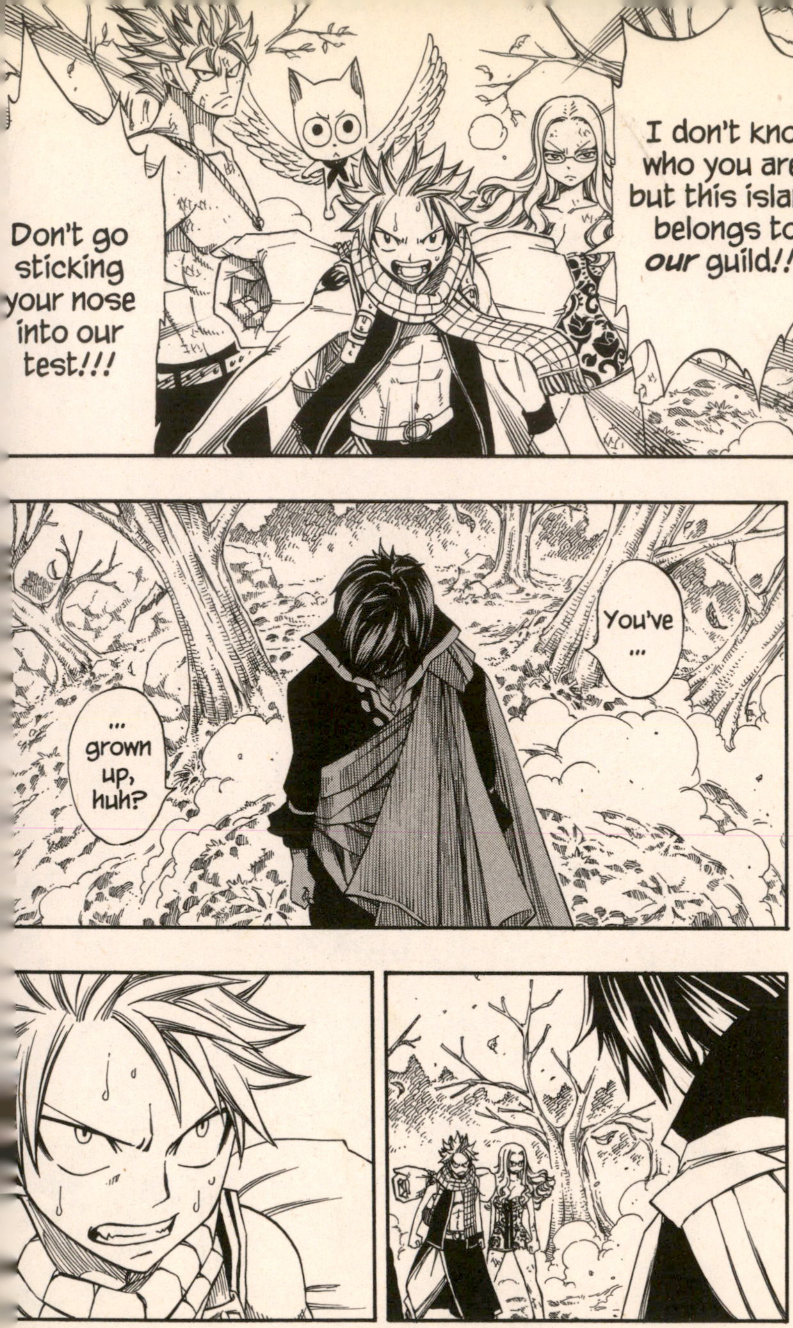
I don't know who you are, but this island belongs to *our* guild!!!
Don't go sticking your nose into our test!!!
You've ...
... grown up, huh?

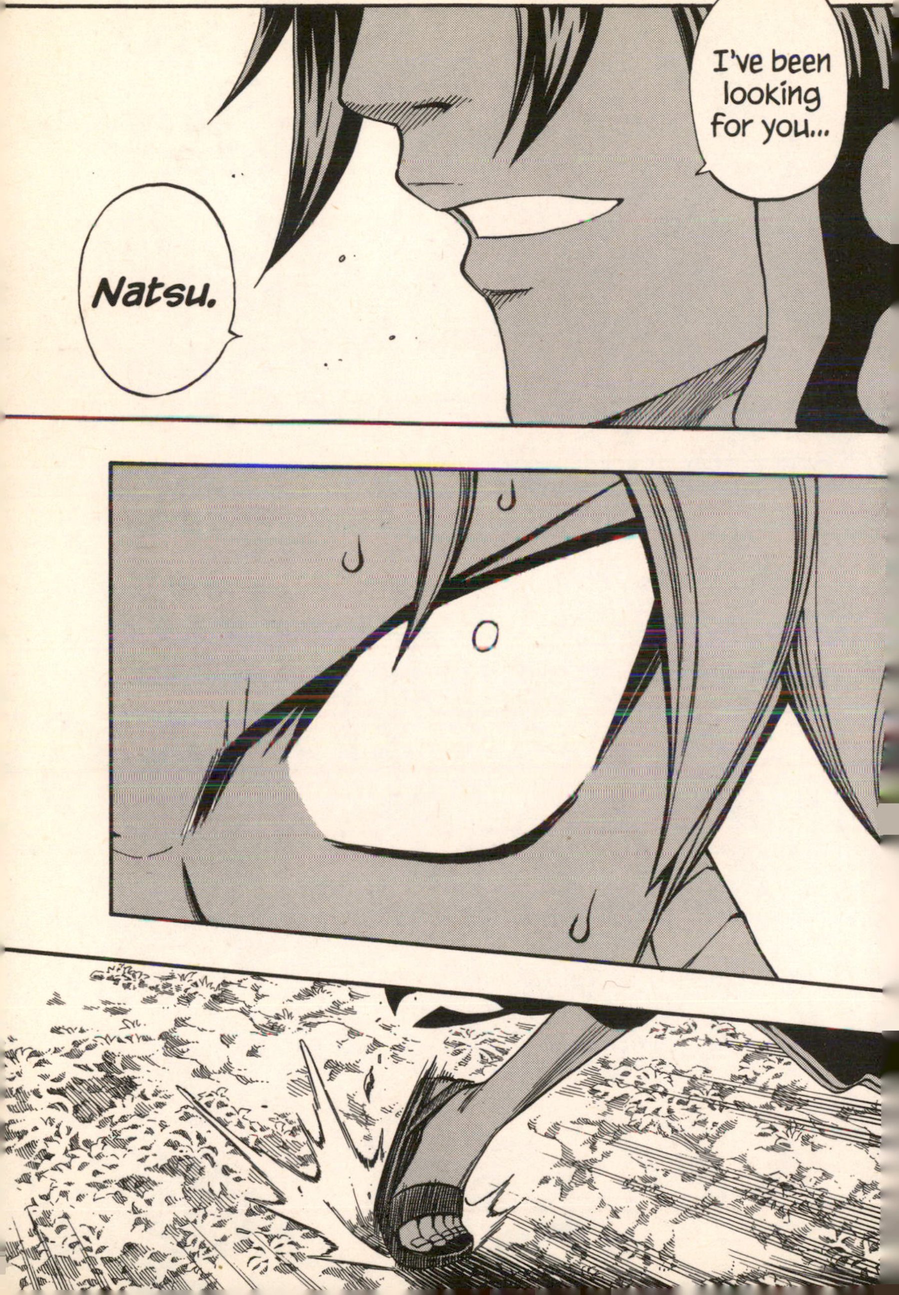
I've been looking for you...
Natsu.

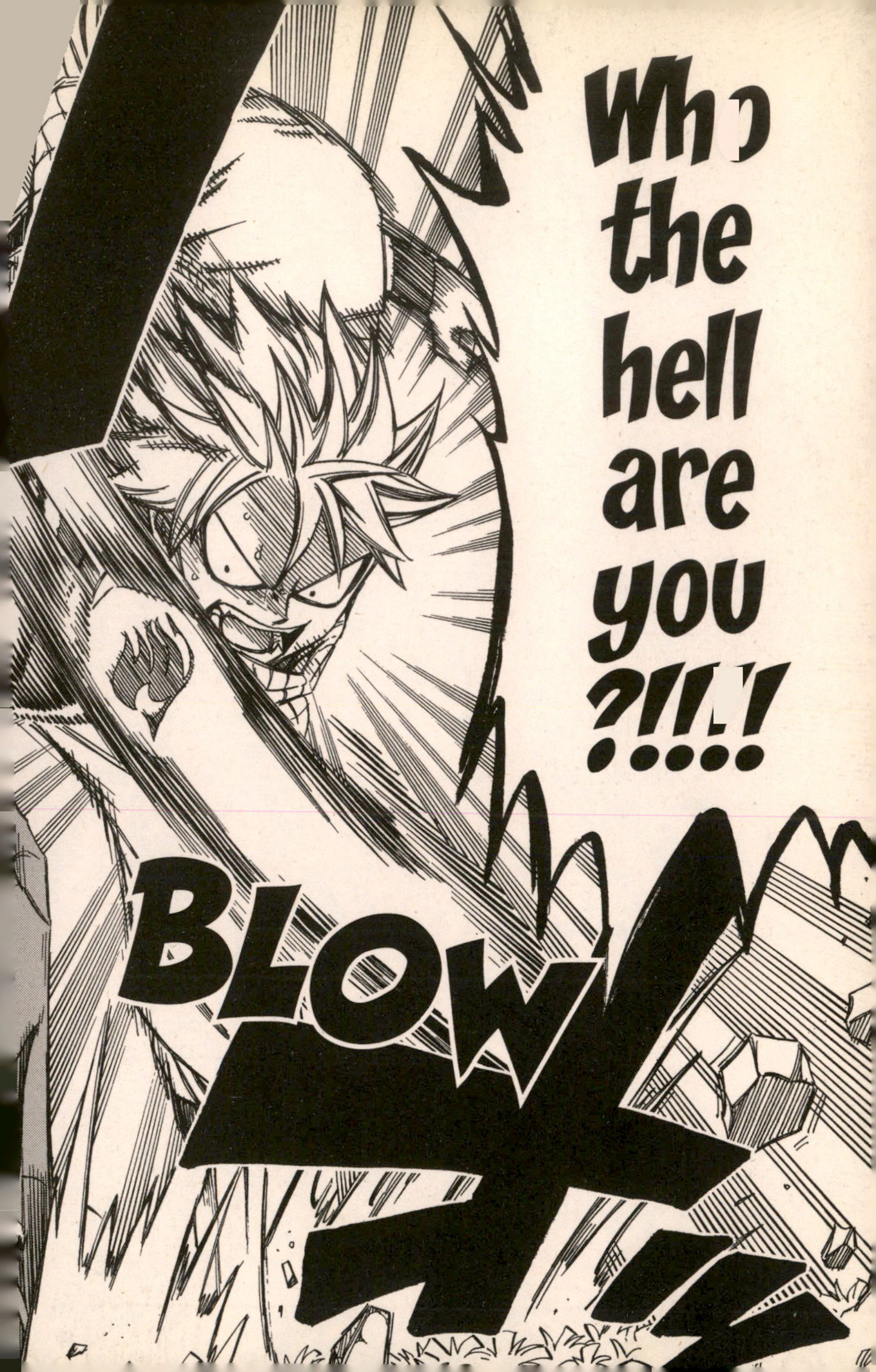
Who the hell are you?!!!!
BLOW

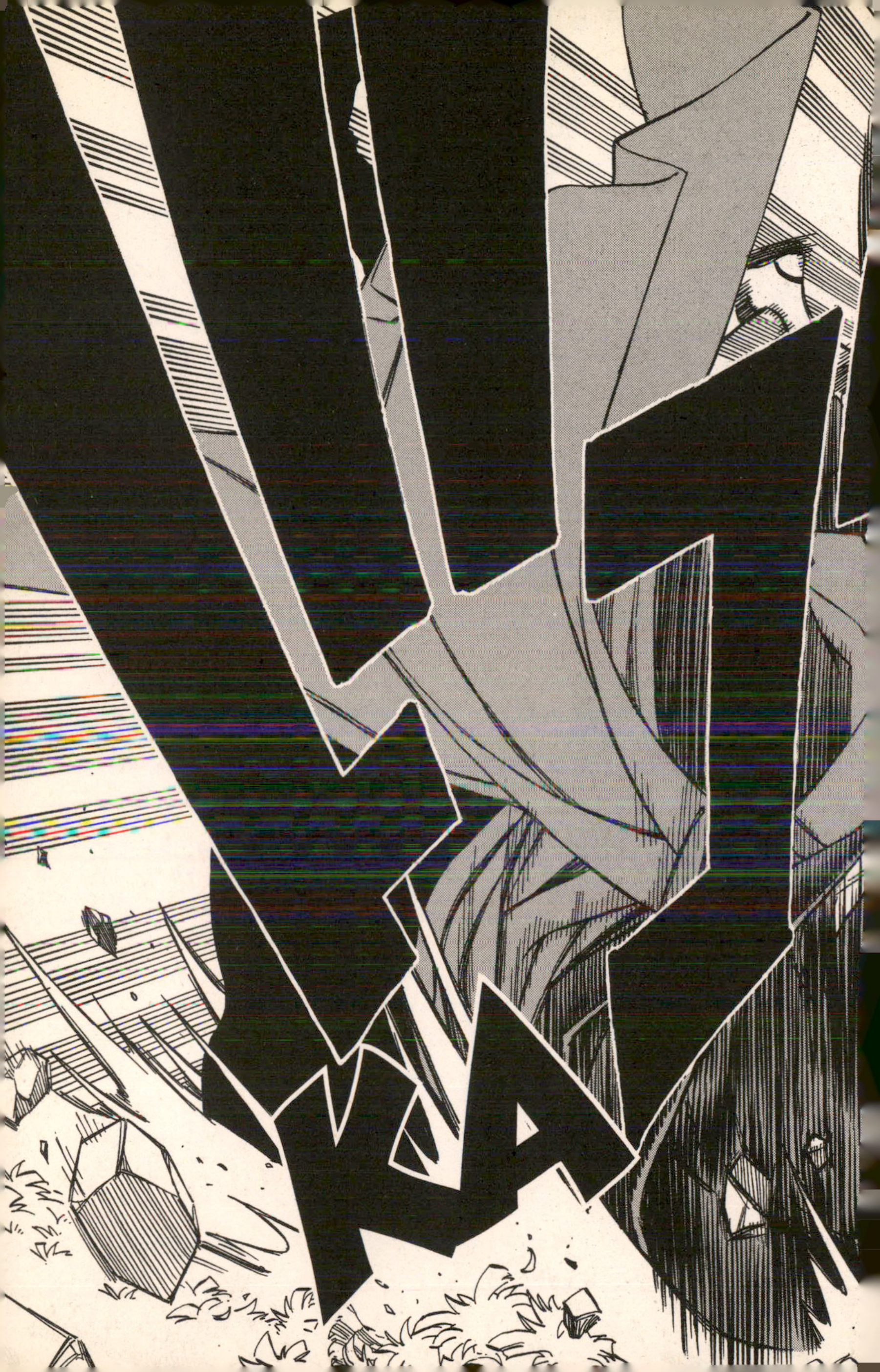

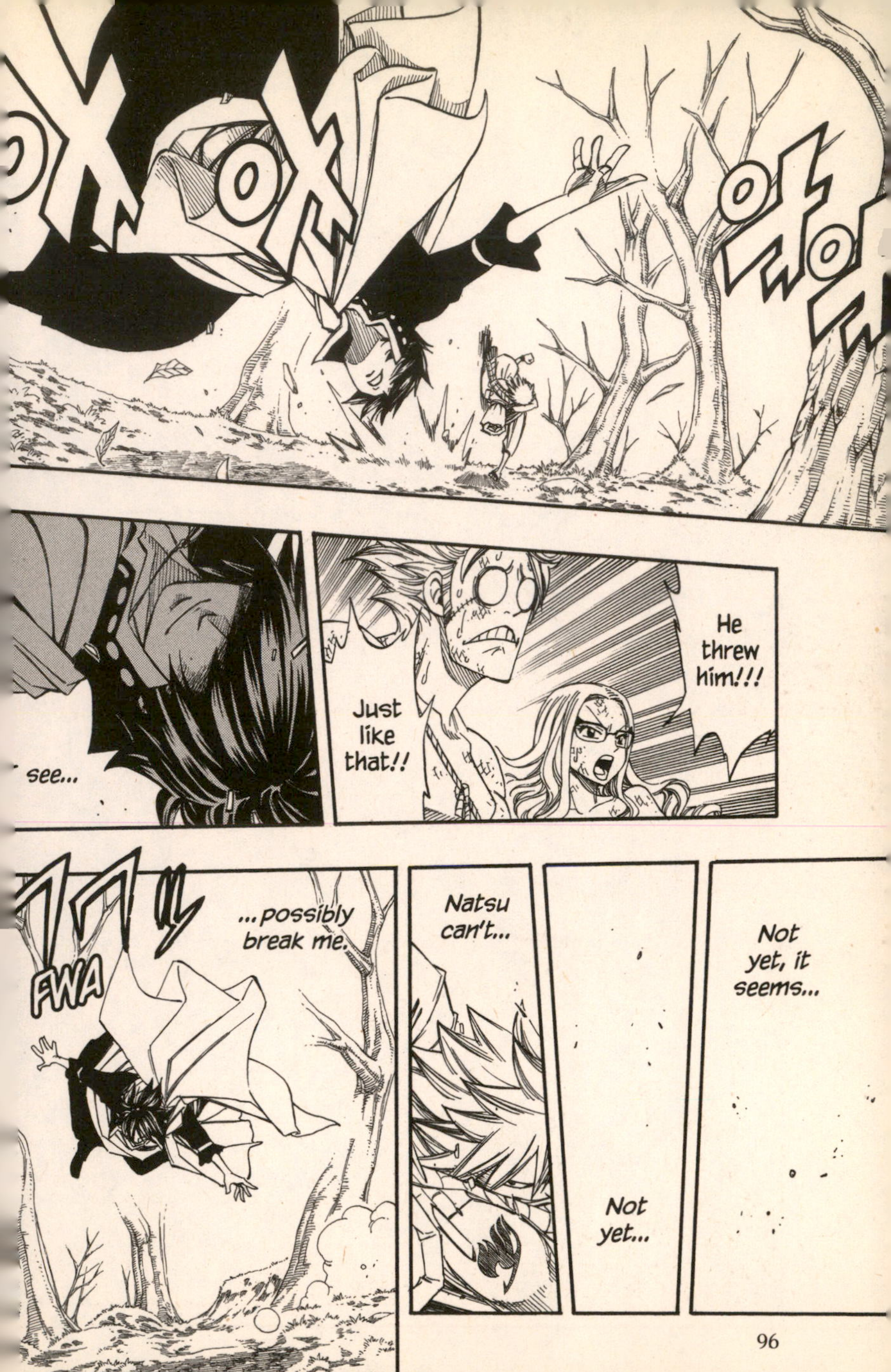
He threw him!!!
Just like that!!
see...
Not yet, it seems...
Not yet...
Natsu can't...
...possibly break me.
FWA

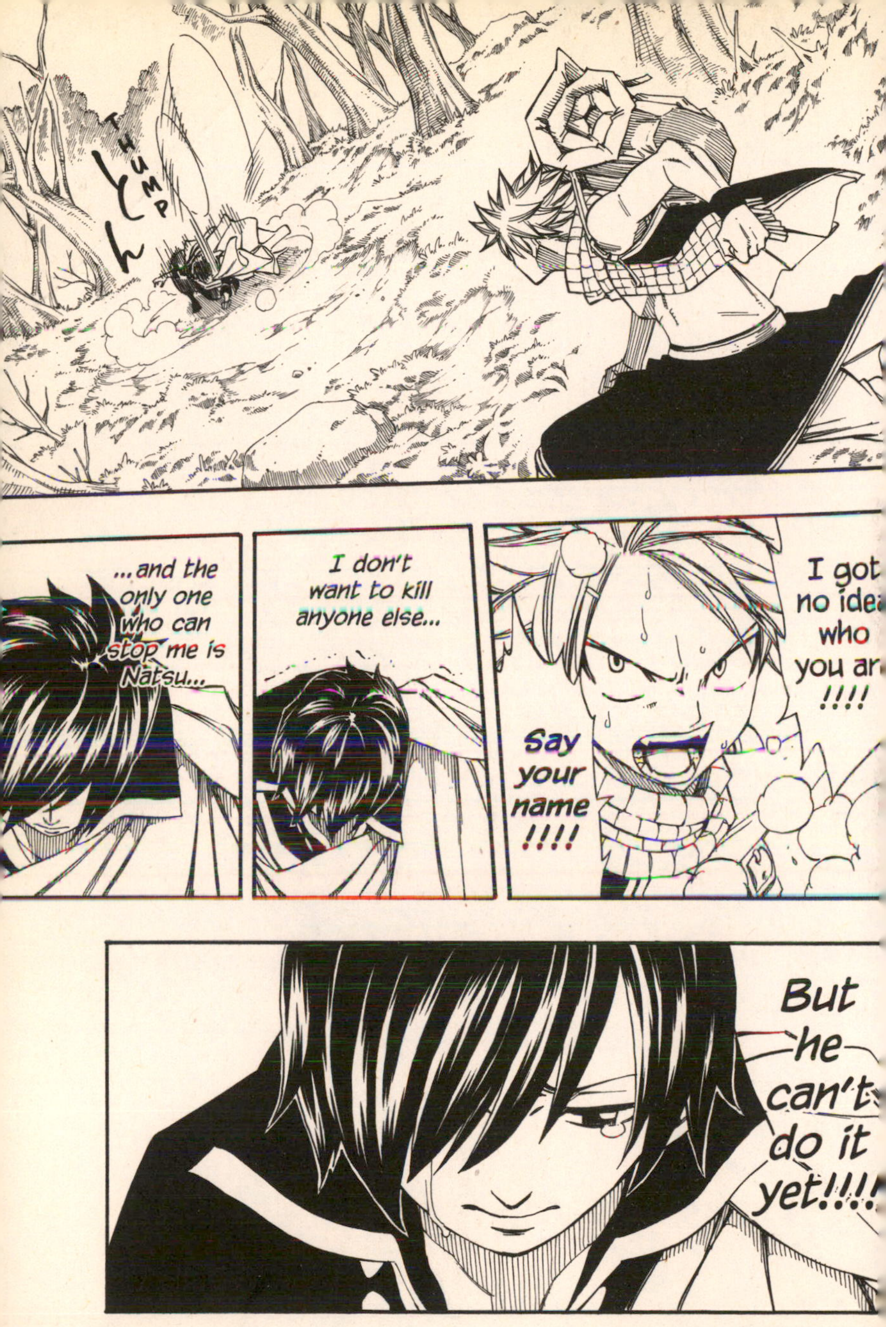
THUMP
I got no idea who you ar!!!!
Say your name!!!!
I don't want to kill anyone else...
...and the only one who can stop me is Natsu...
But he can't do it yet!!!!

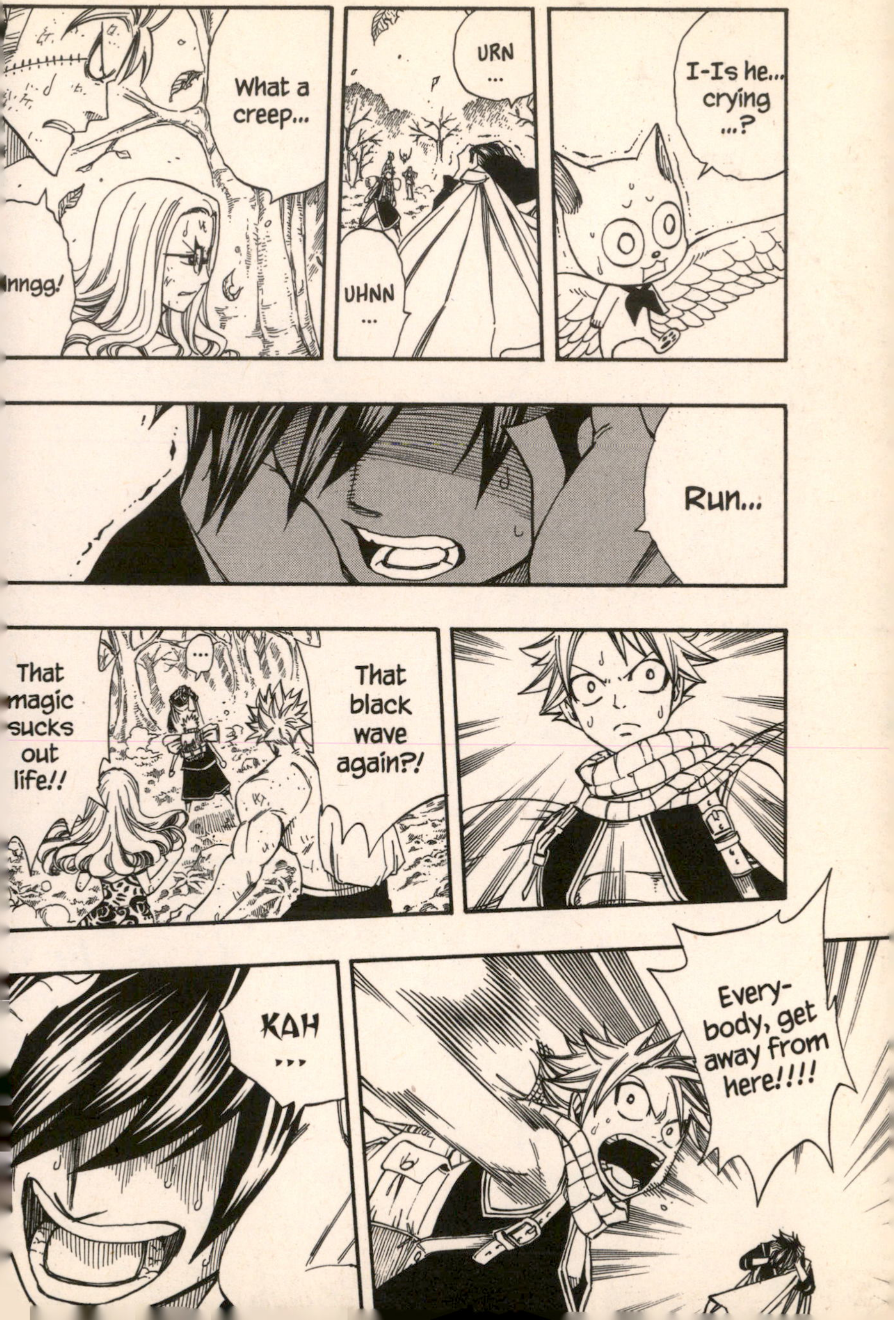
I-Is he... crying ...?
URN ...
UHNN ...
What a creep...
nnngg!
Run...
That black wave again?!
...
That magic sucks out life!!
Every-body, get away from here!!!!
KAH ...

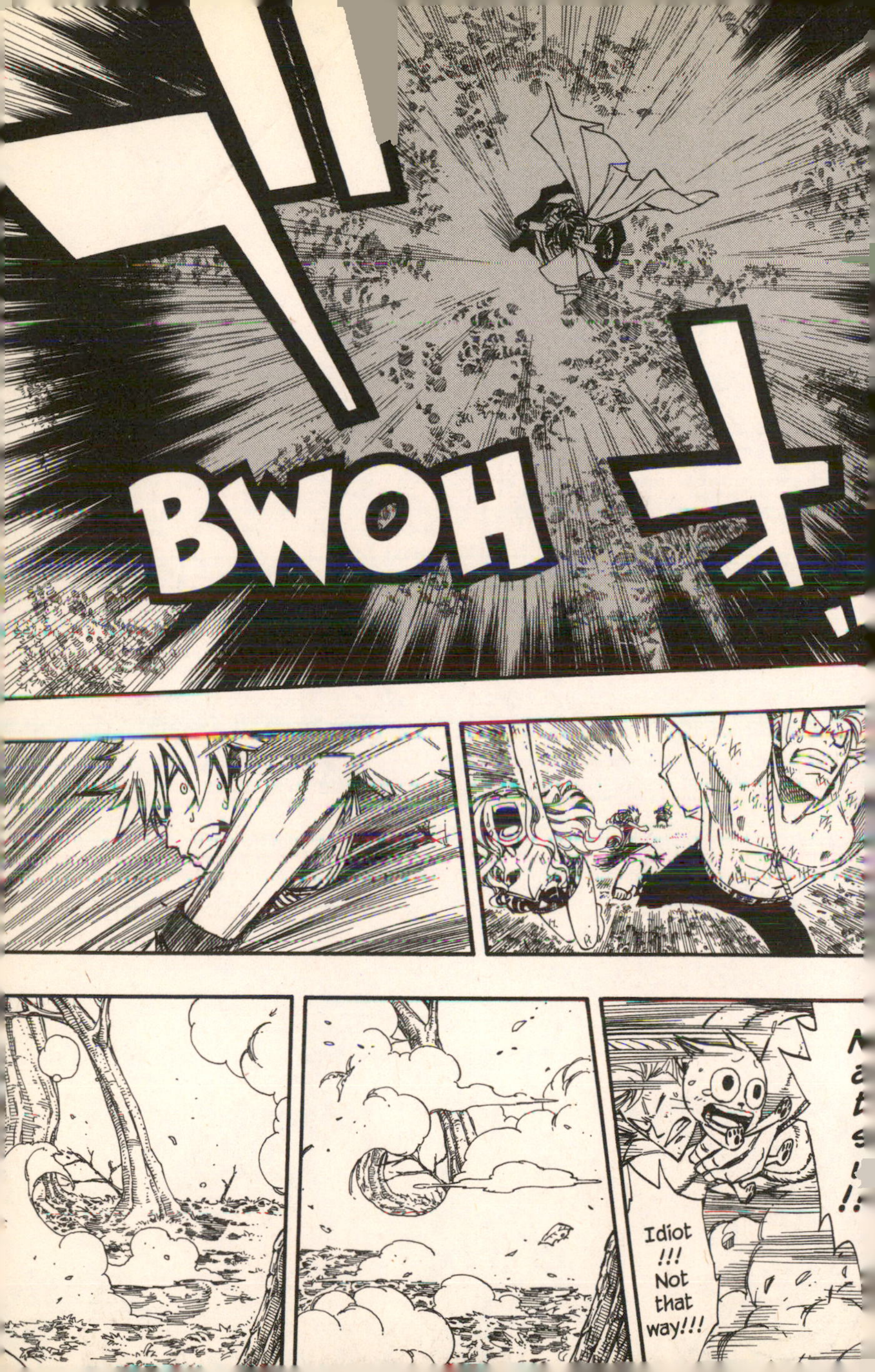
BWOH
Natsu!!
Idiot!!! Not that way!!!

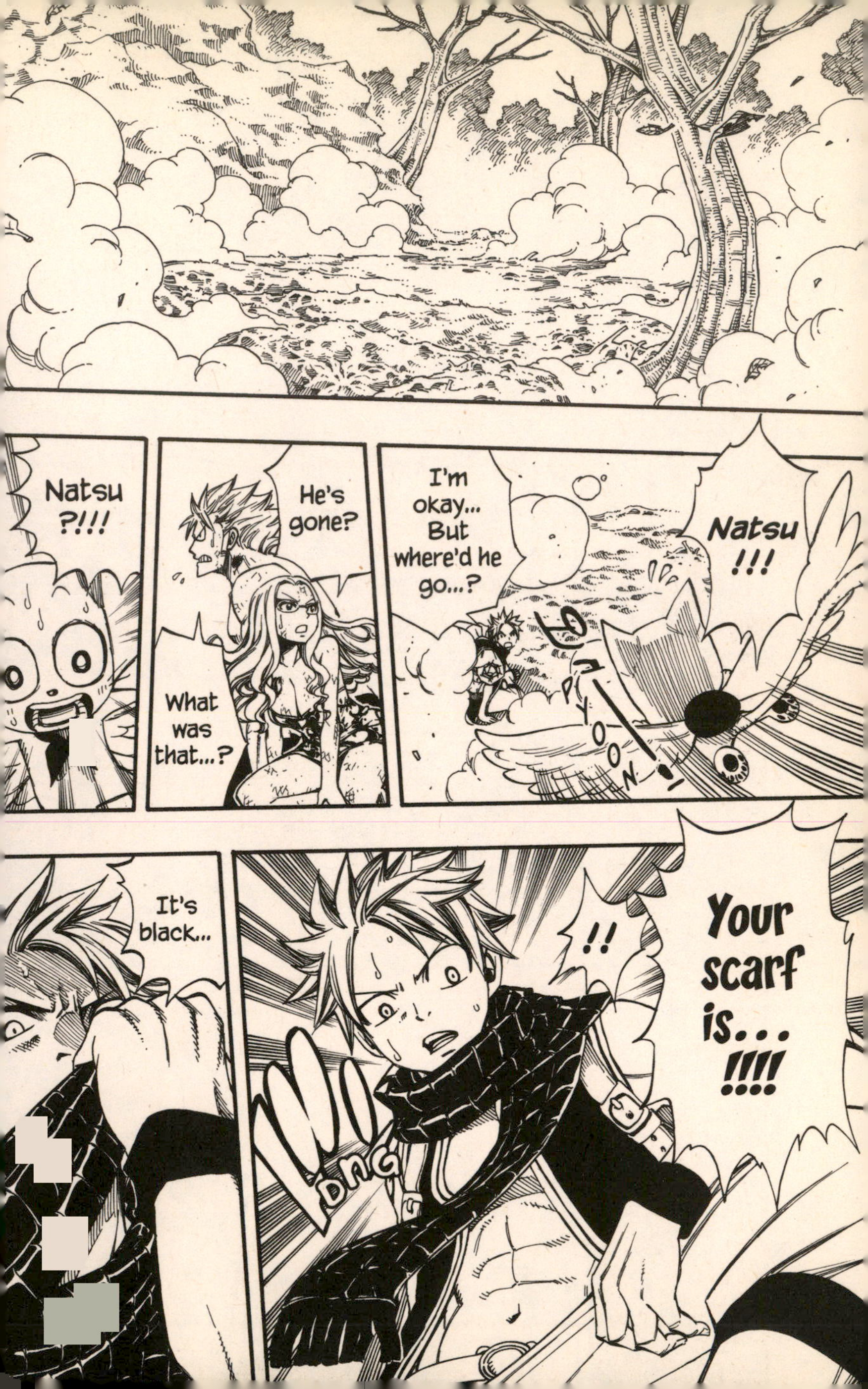
Natsu !!!
I'm okay... But where'd he go...?
DOPYOON!
He's gone?
What was that...?
Natsu ?!!!
Your scarf is.... !!!!
!!
DNG
It's black...

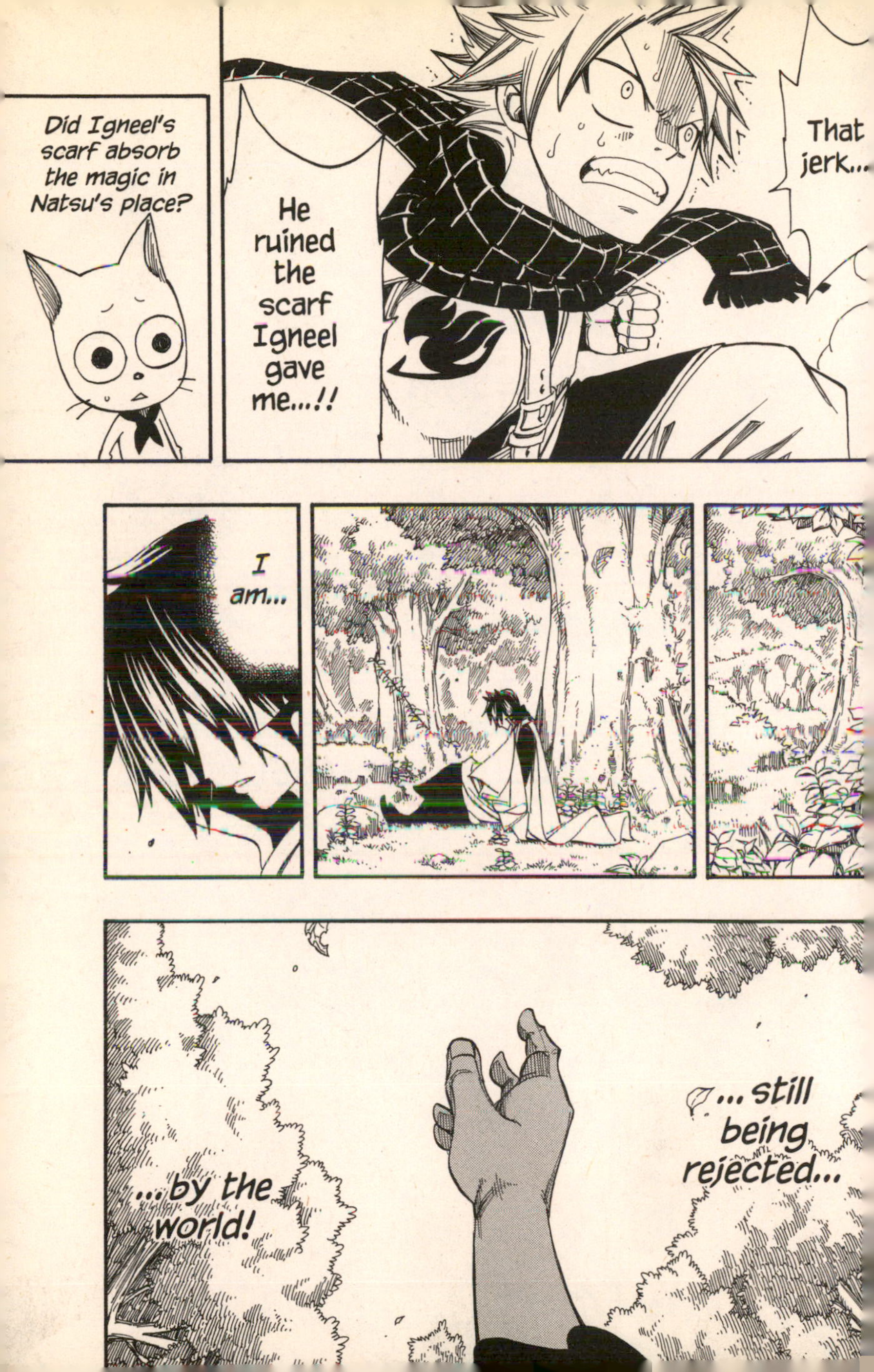
That jerk...
He ruined the scarf Igneel gave me...!!
Did Igneel's scarf absorb the magic in Natsu's place?
I am...
...still being rejected...
...by the world!

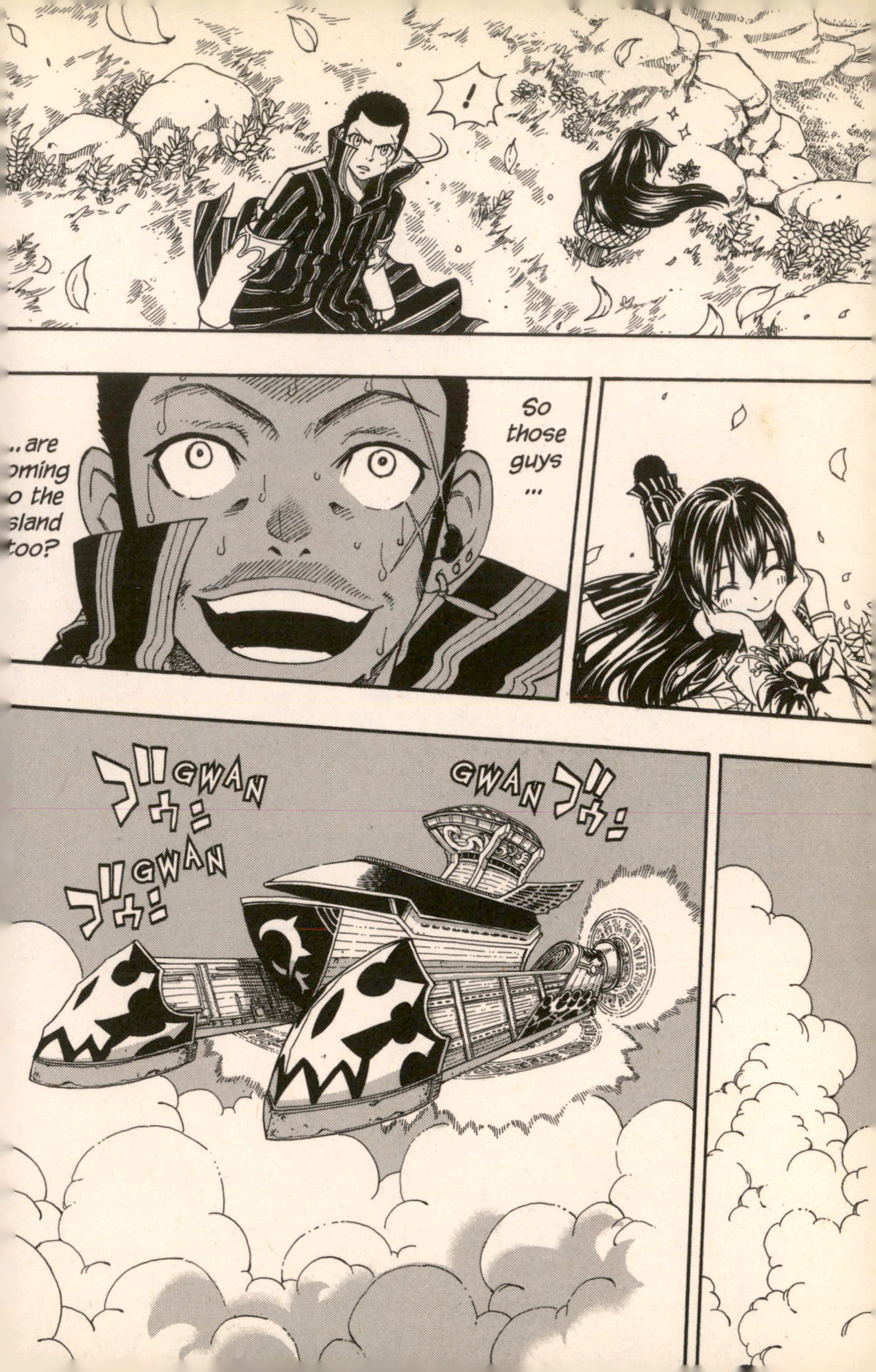
!
So those guys ...
..are
oming
o the
sland
too?
GWAN
GWAN
GWAN

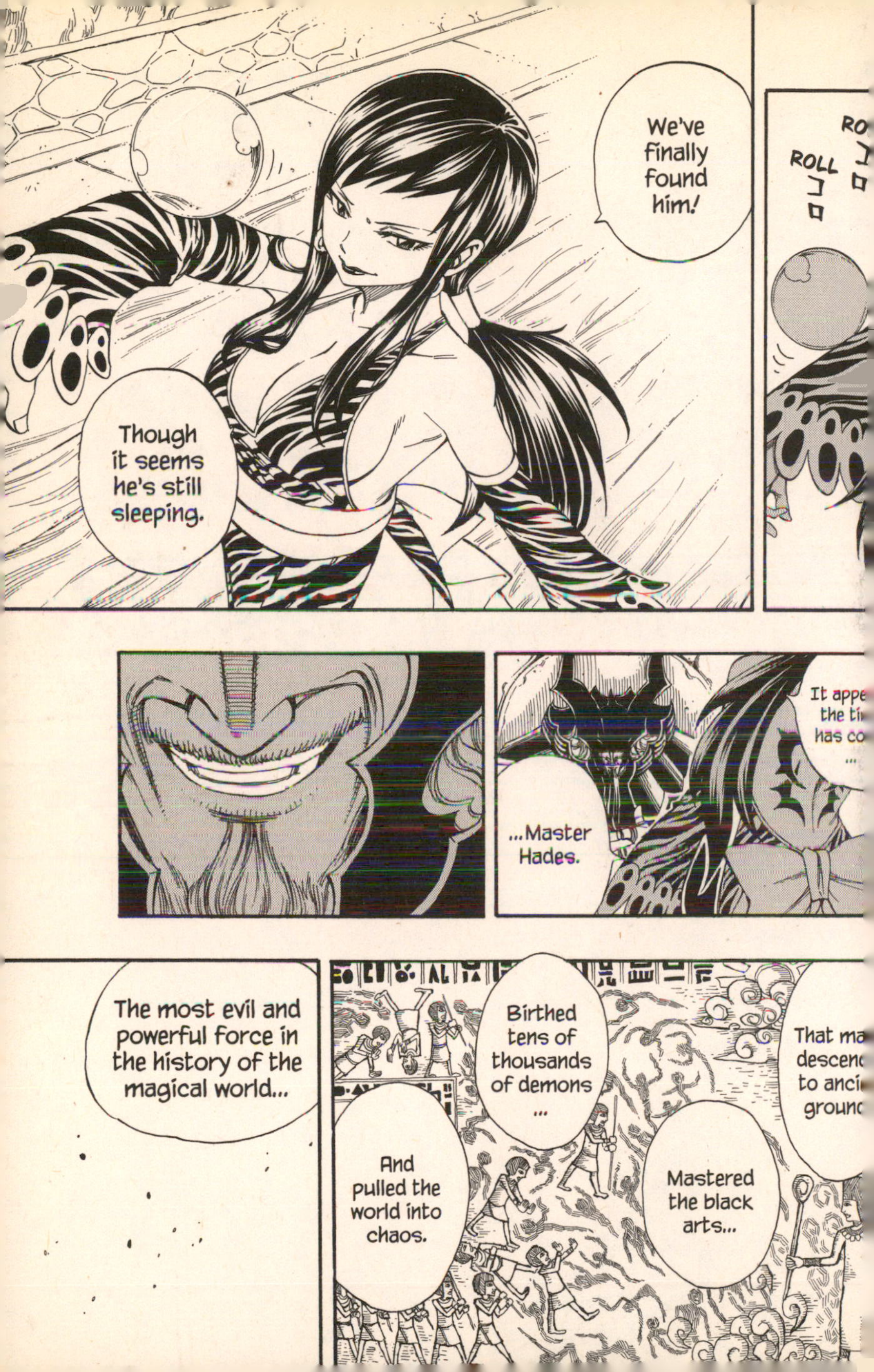
RO
ROLL
We've finally found him!
Though it seems he's still sleeping.
It appe the ti has co ...
...Master Hades.
That ma descenc to anci grounc
Mastered the black arts...
Birthed tens of thousands of demons ...
And pulled the world into chaos.
The most evil and powerful force in the history of the magical world...

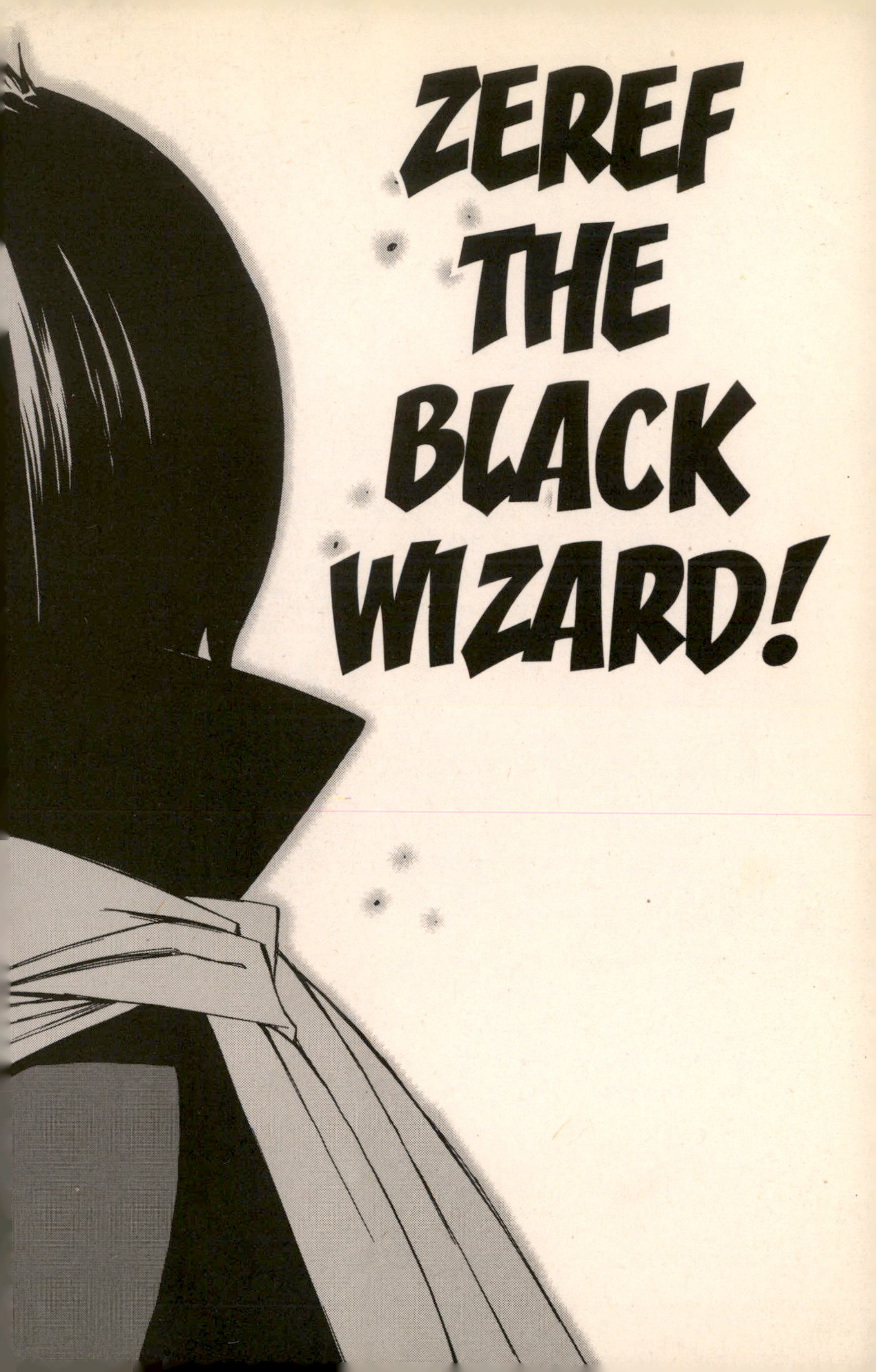
ZEREF THE BLACK WIZARD!

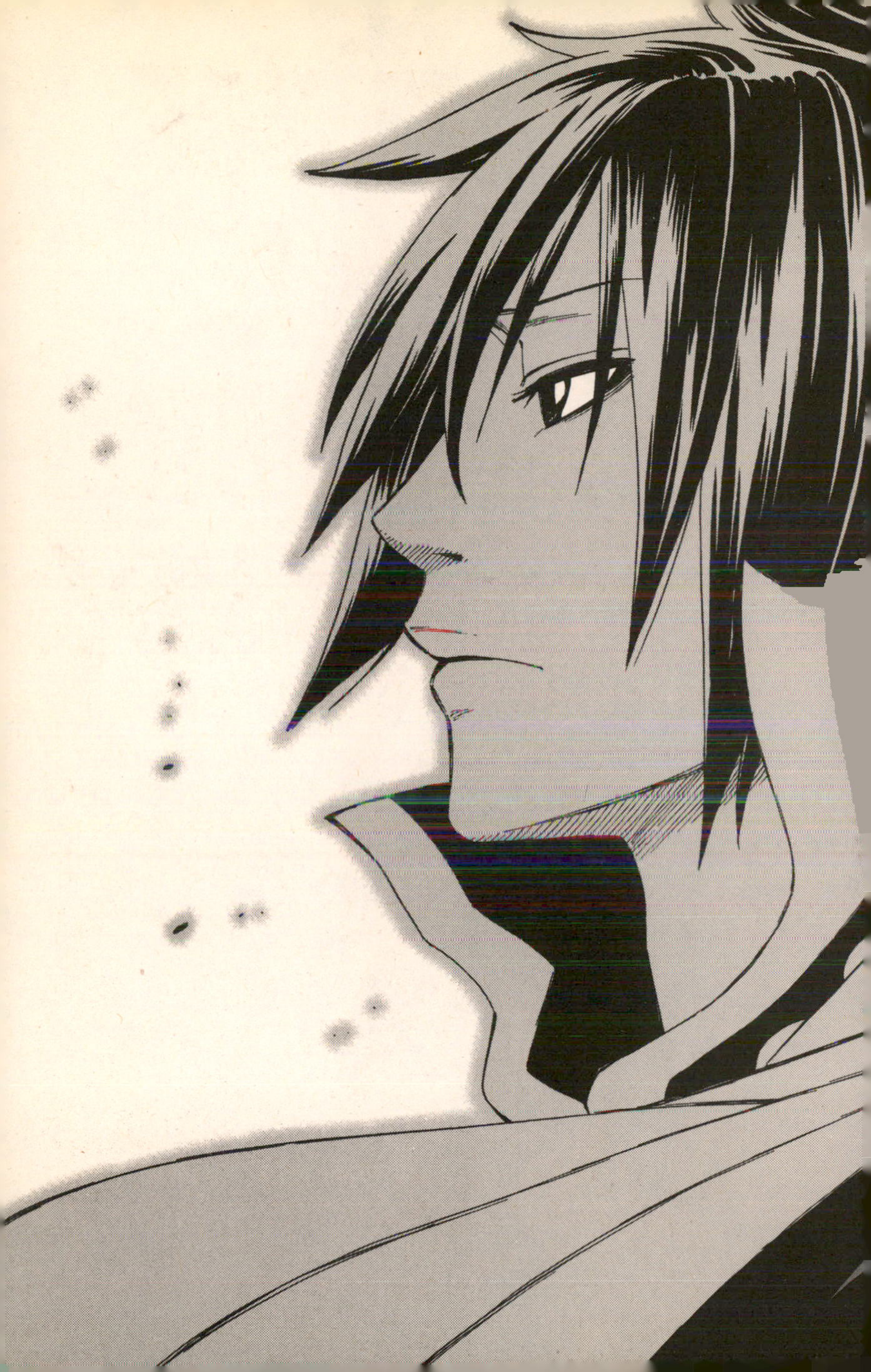

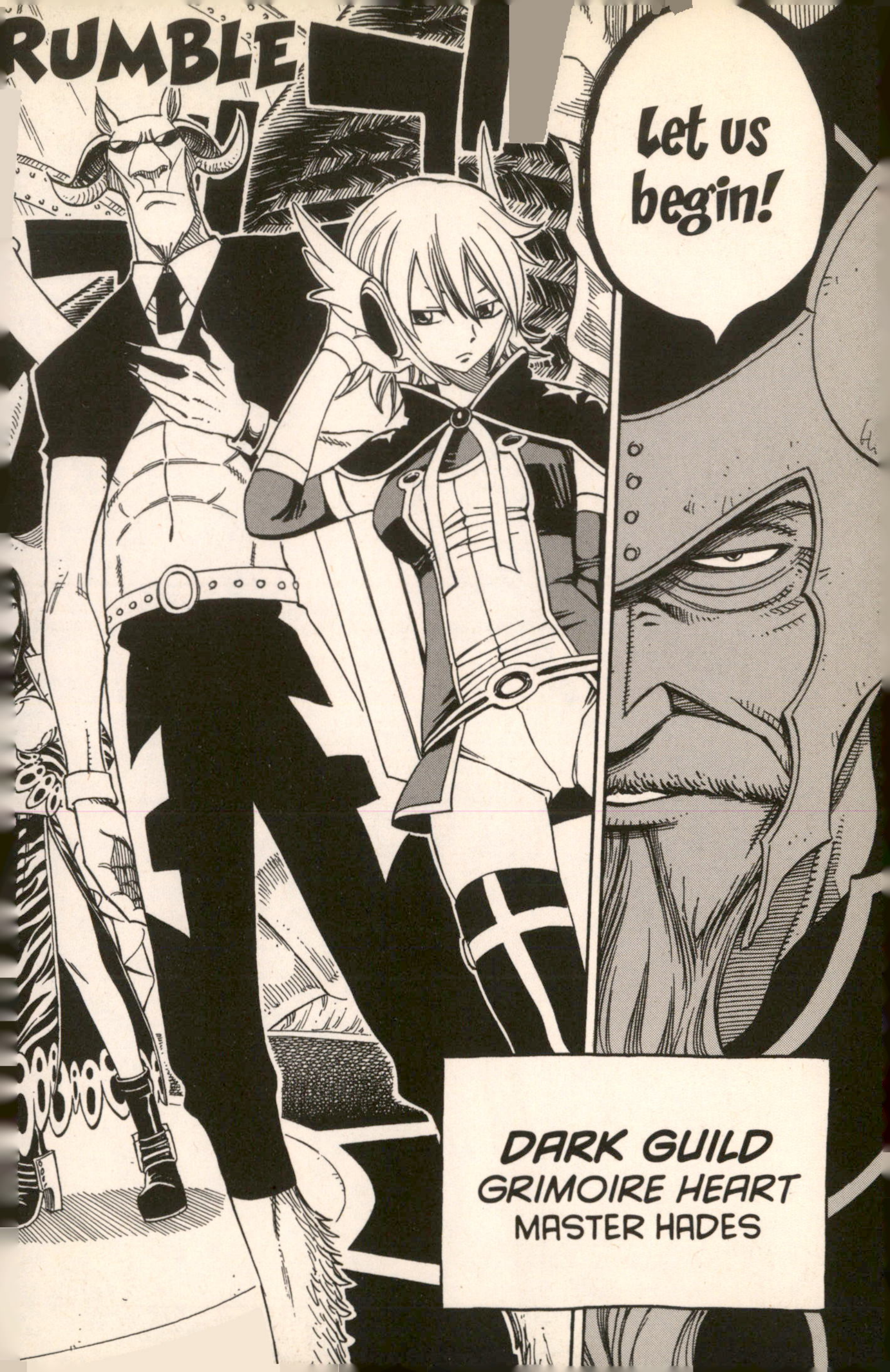
Let us begin!
DARK GUILD GRIMOIRE HEART MASTER HADES
RUMBLE

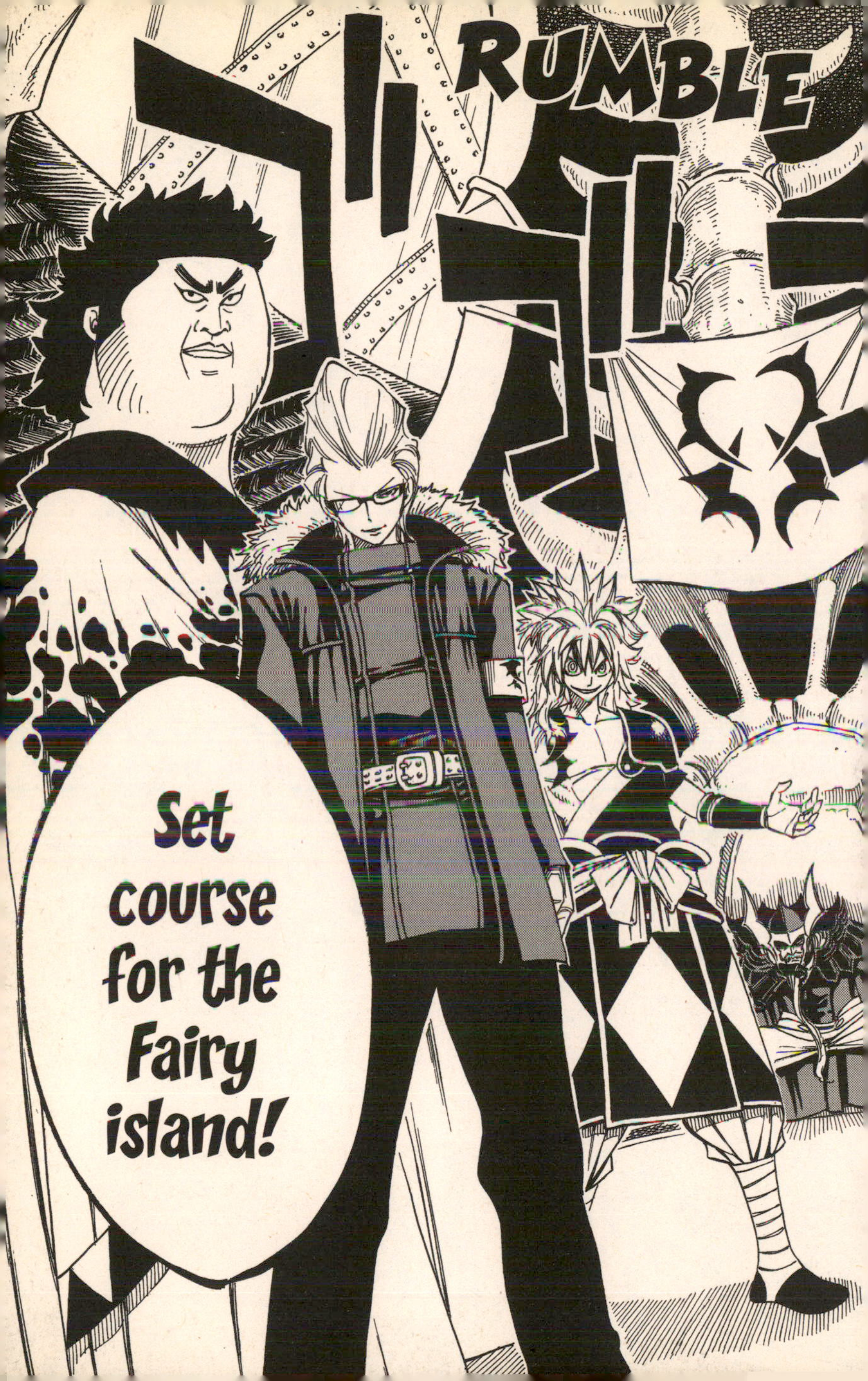
RUMBLE
Set course for the Fairy island!

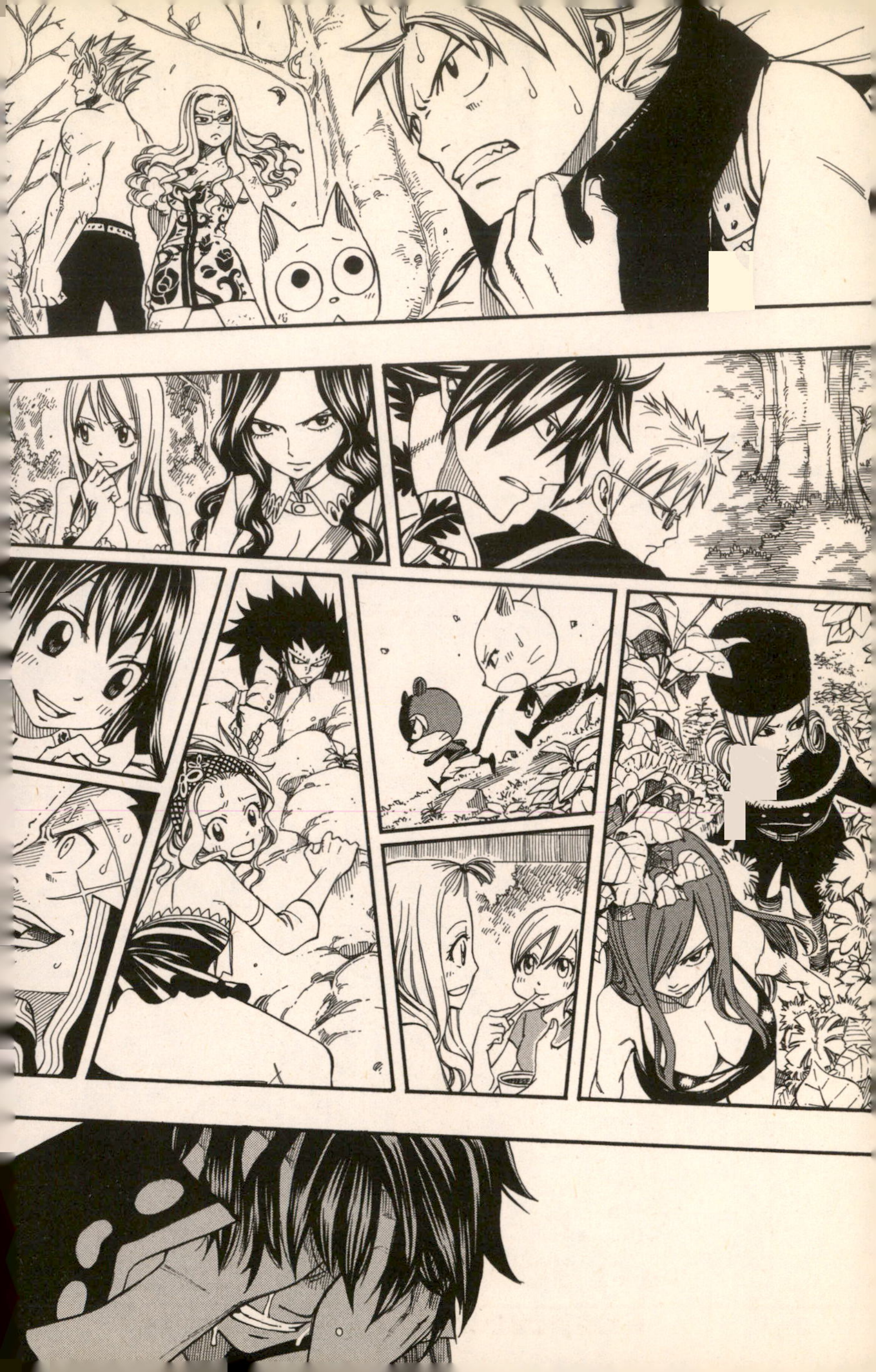

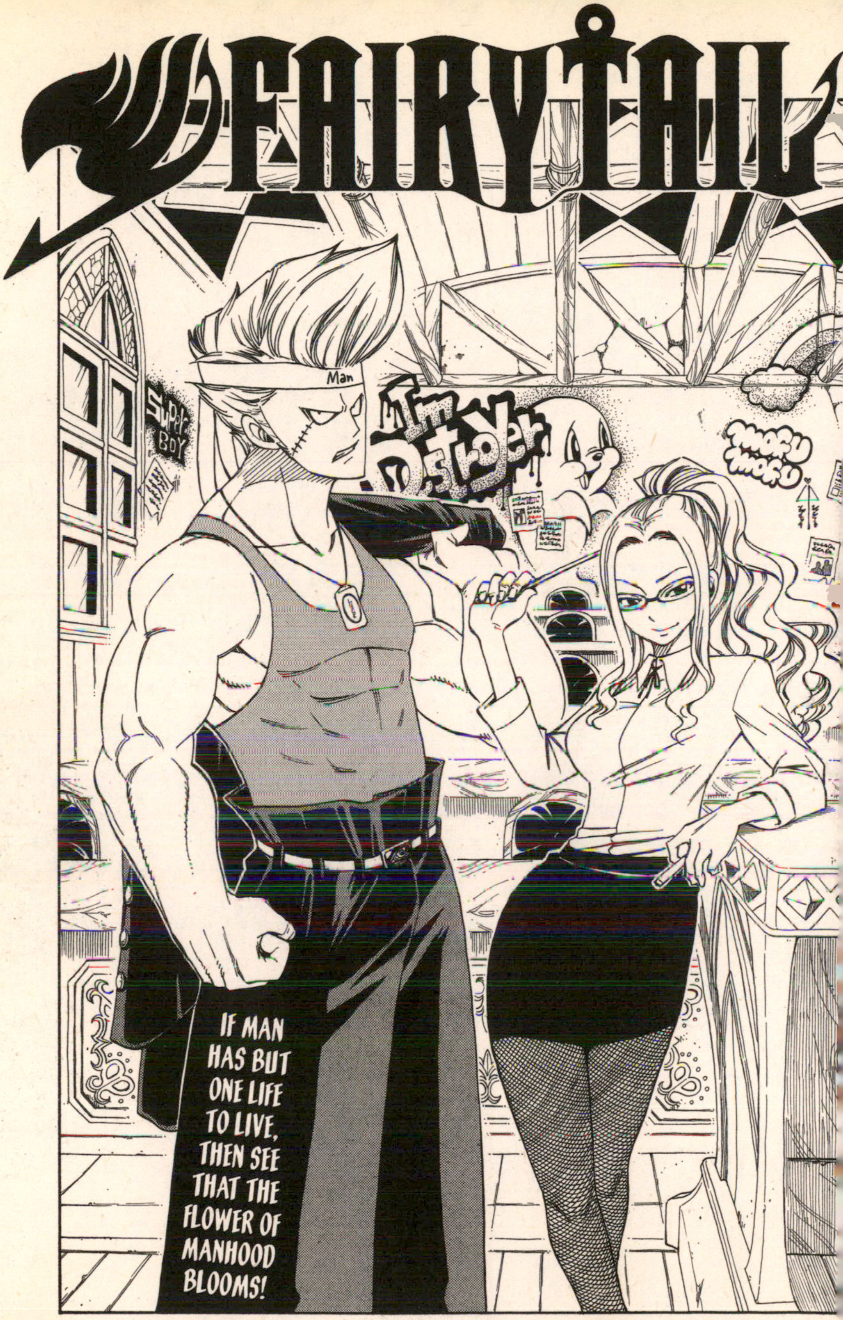
FAIRY TAIL
Man
I'm Destroyer
MOFU MOFU
IF MAN HAS BUT ONE LIFE TO LIVE, THEN SEE THAT THE FLOWER OF MANHOOD BLOOMS!

Chapter 210, Stupid Gajeel

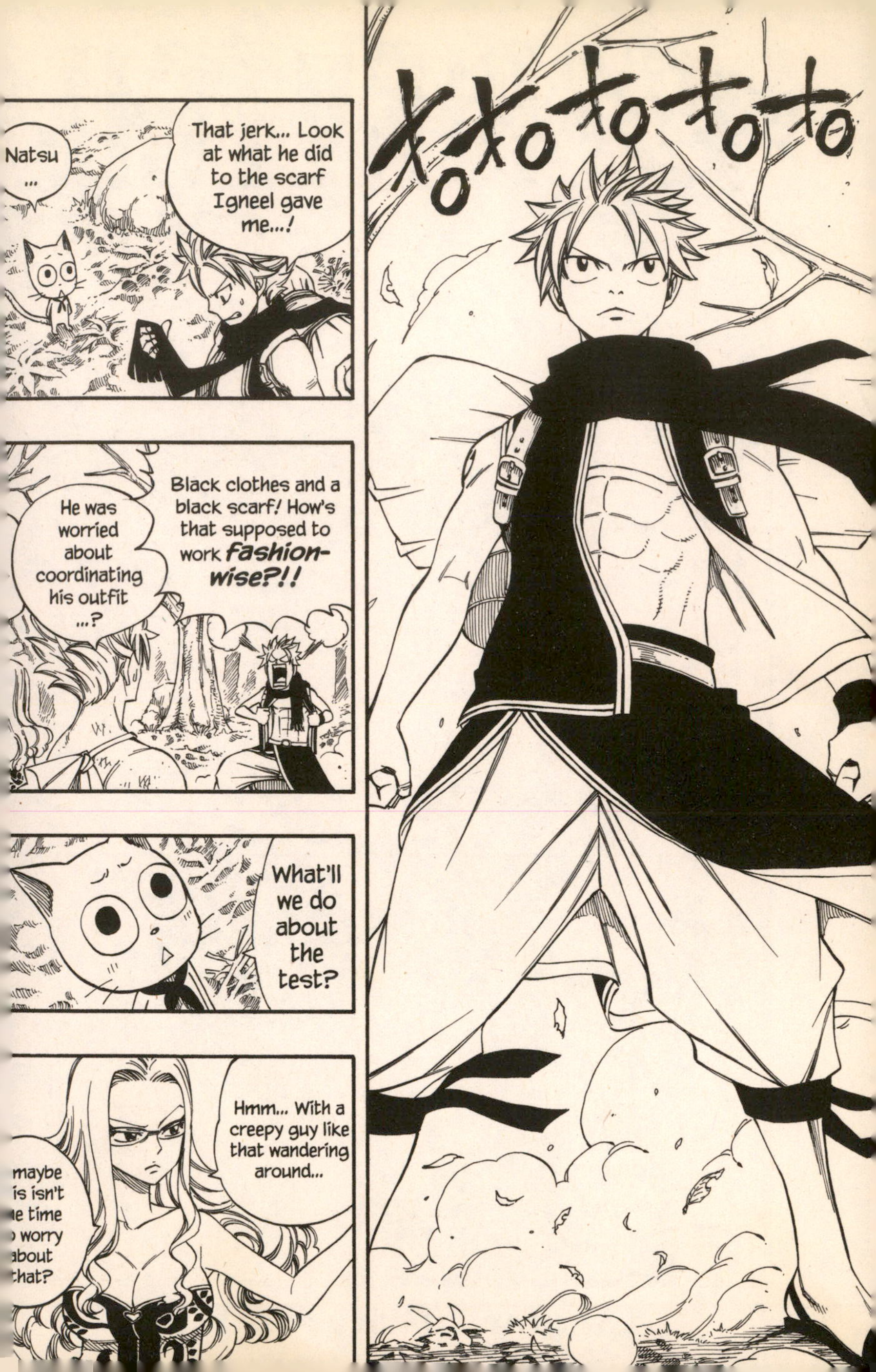
That jerk... Look at what he did to the scarf Igneel gave me...!
Natsu ...
Black clothes and a black scarf! How's that supposed to work ***fashion-wise?!!***
He was worried about coordinating his outfit ...?
What'll we do about the test?
Hmm... With a creepy guy like that wandering around...
maybe is isn't e time worry about that?

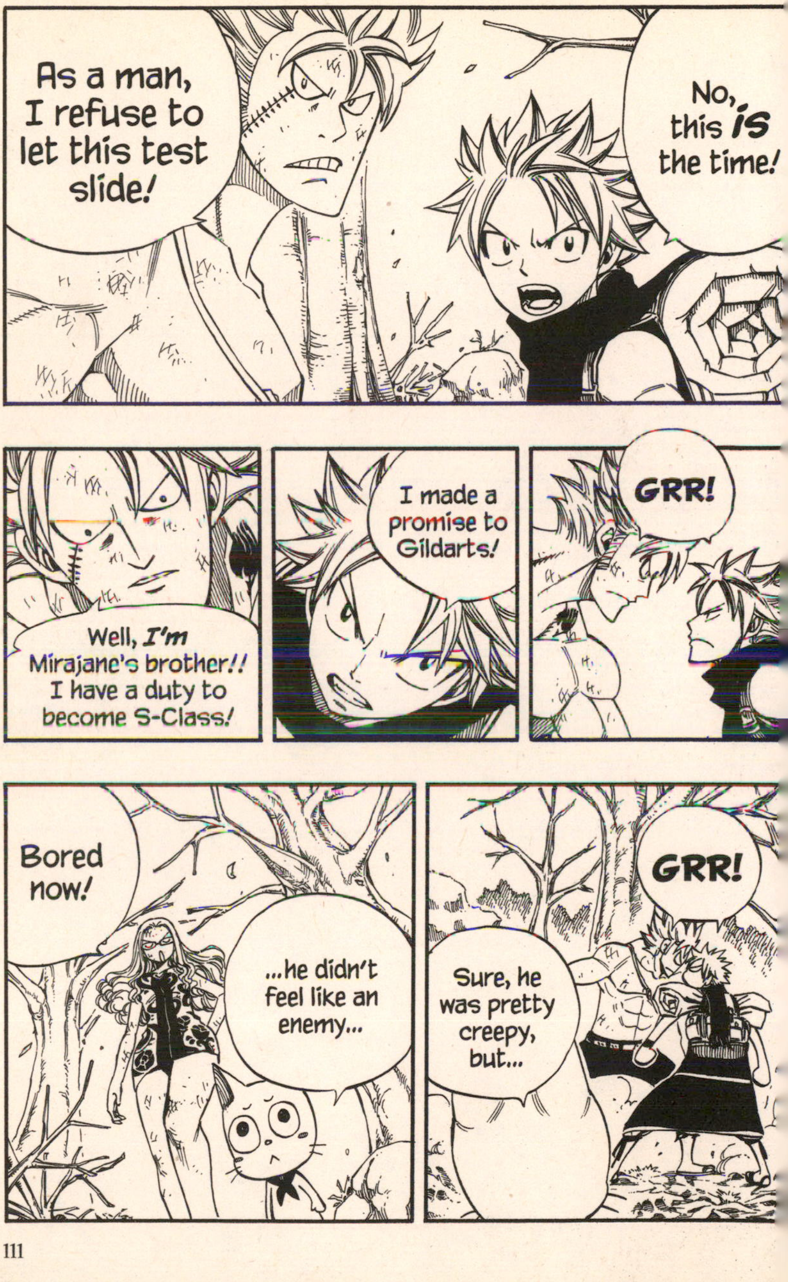
No, this *IS* the time!
As a man, I refuse to let this test slide!
GRR!
I made a promise to Gildarts!
Well, *I'm* Mirajane's brother!! I have a duty to become S-Class!
GRR!
Sure, he was pretty creepy, but...
...he didn't feel like an enemy...
Bored now!

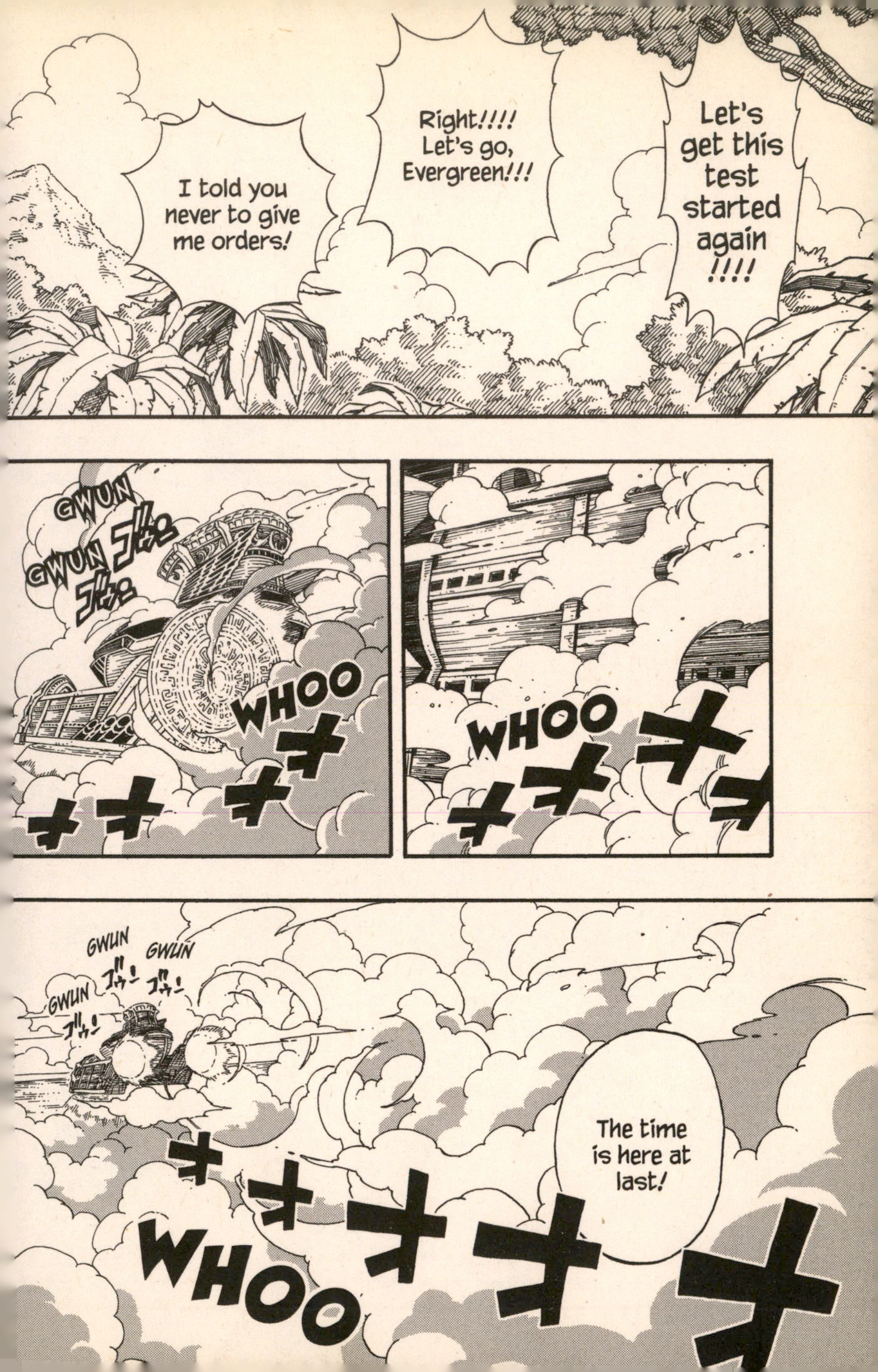
Let's get this test started again!!!!
Right!!!! Let's go, Evergreen!!!
I told you never to give me orders!
WHOO
GWUN
GWUN
WHOO
GWUN
GWUN
GWUN
The time is here at last!
WHOO

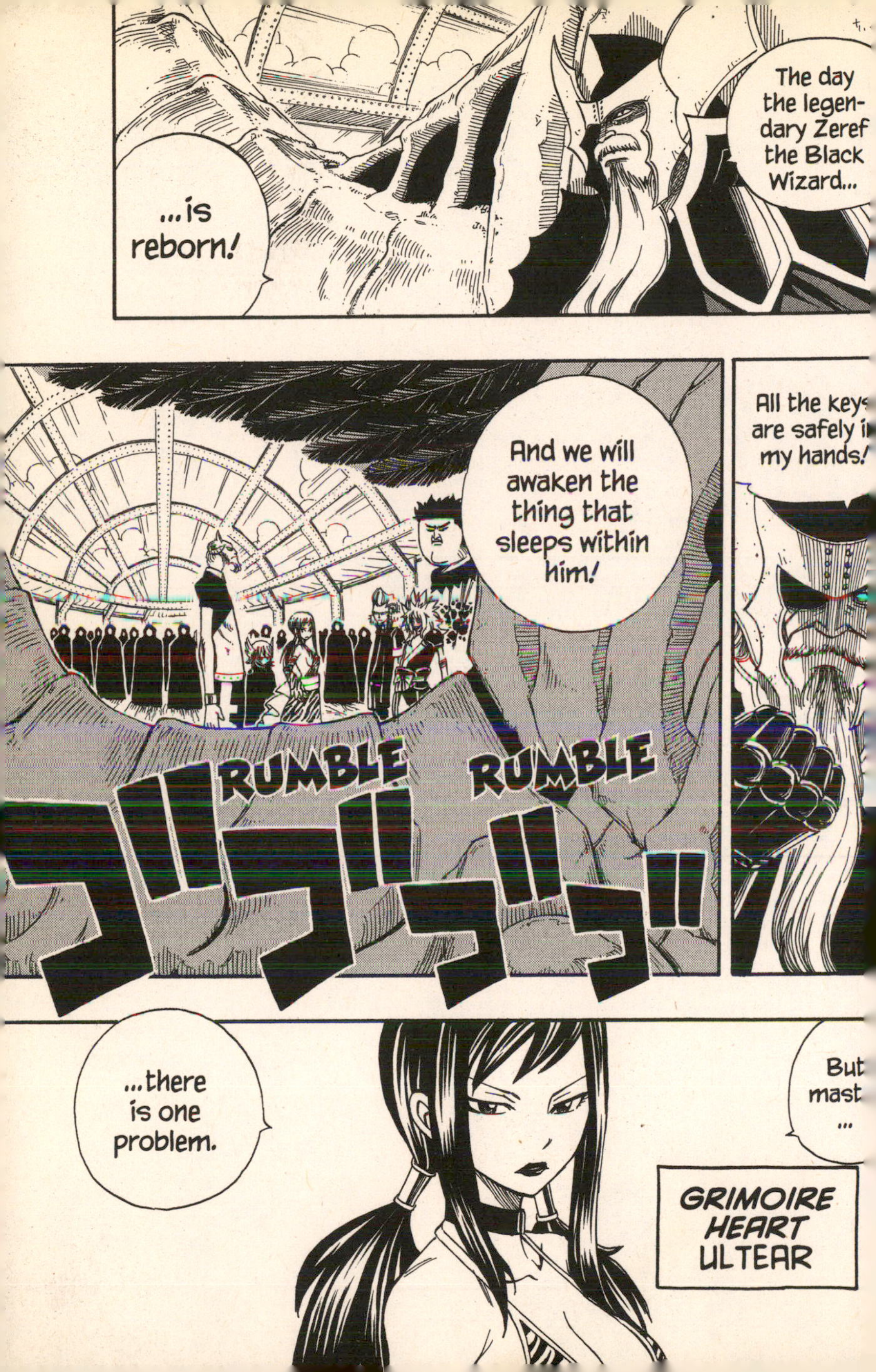

The day the legendary Zeref the Black Wizard...
...is reborn!
All the keys are safely i my hands!
And we will awaken the thing that sleeps within him!
RUMBLE
RUMBLE
But mast ...
...there is one problem.
GRIMOIRE HEART ULTEAR

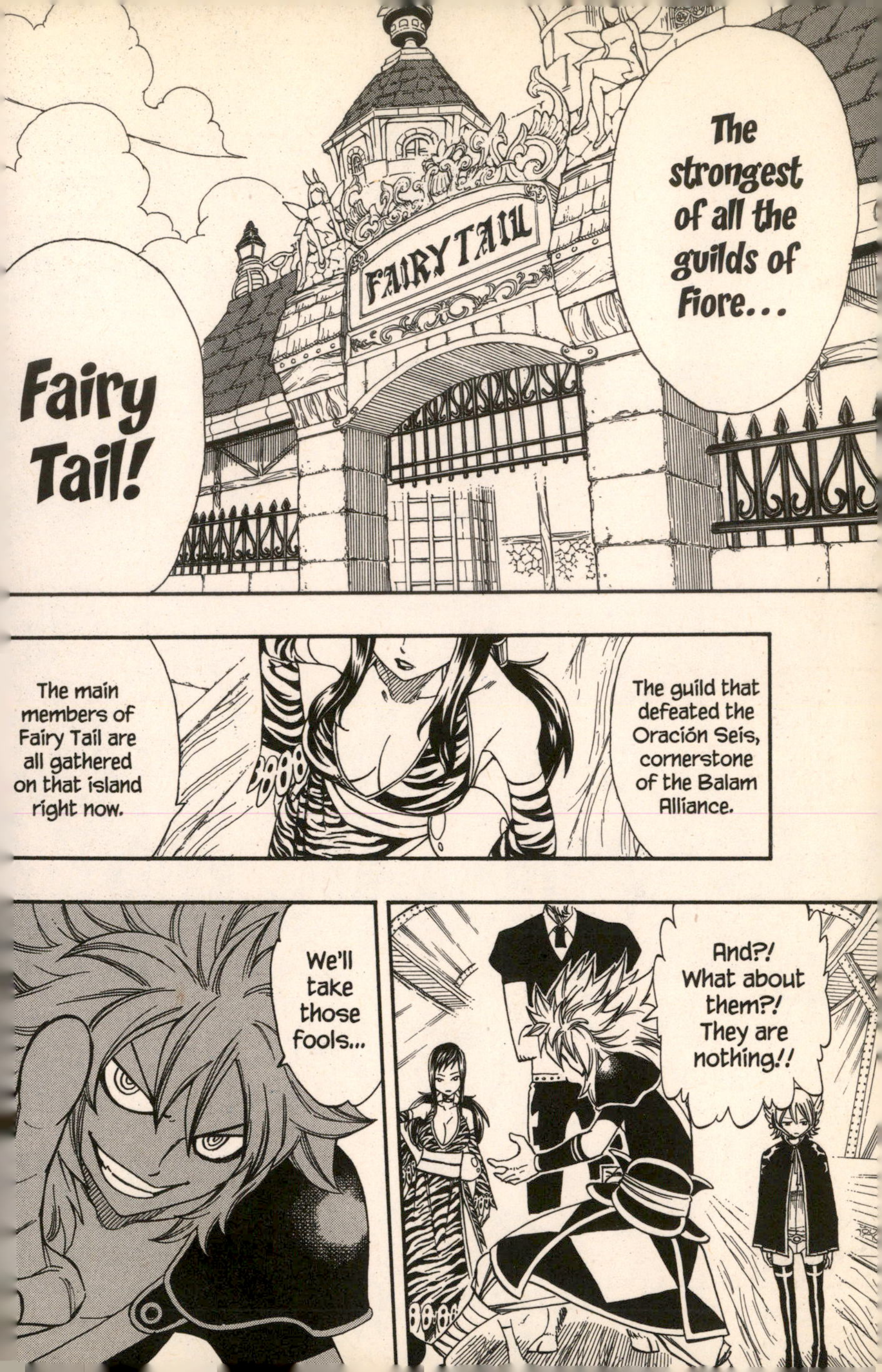
The strongest of all the guilds of Fiore...
FAIRY TAIL
Fairy Tail!
The guild that defeated the Oración Seis, cornerstone of the Balam Alliance.
The main members of Fairy Tail are all gathered on that island right now.
And?! What about them?! They are nothing!!
We'll take those fools...

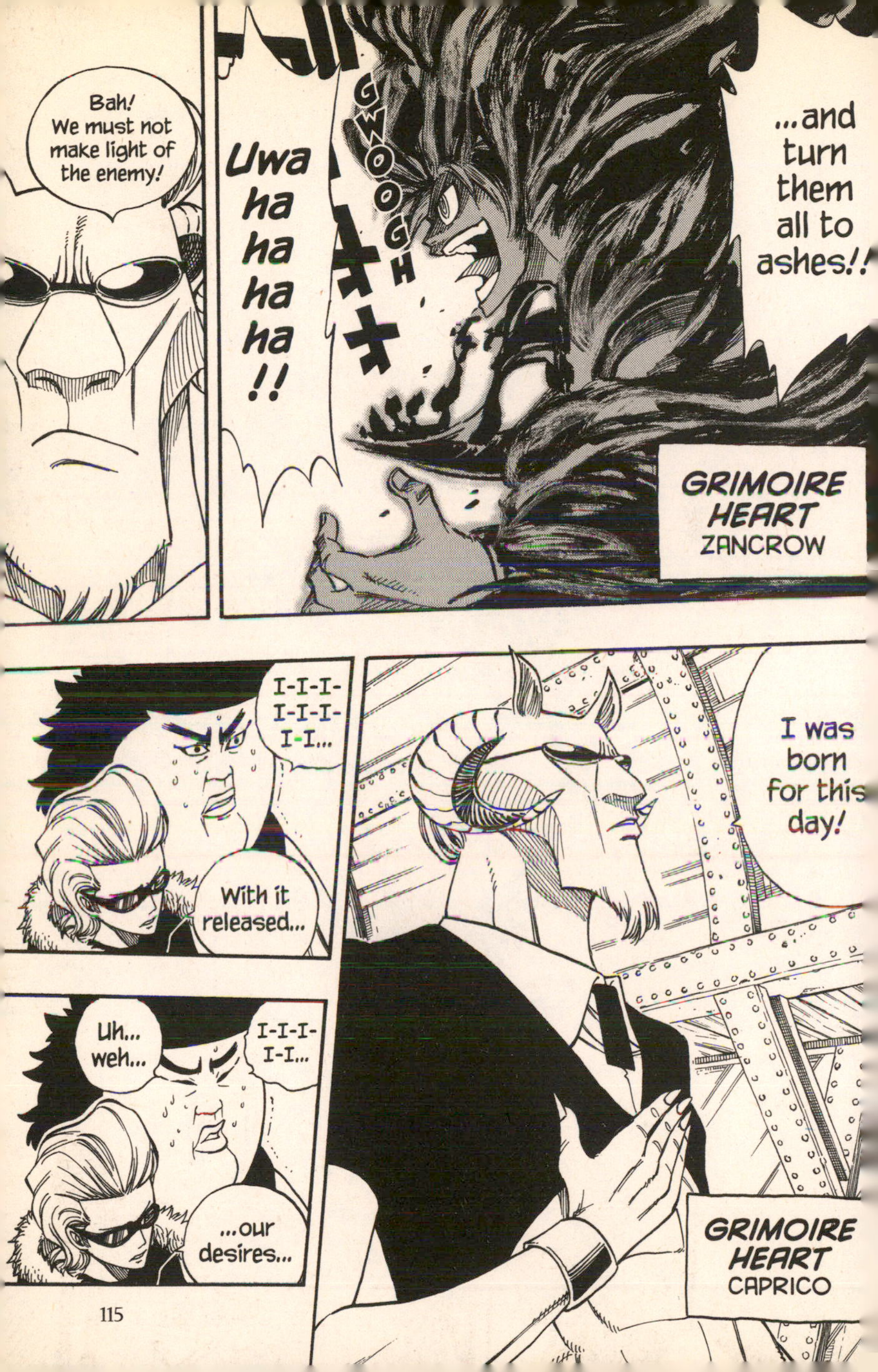
...and turn them all to ashes!!
GWOOOGH
Uwa ha ha ha ha!!
GRIMOIRE HEART ZANCROW
Bah! We must not make light of the enemy!
I was born for this day!
GRIMOIRE HEART CAPRICO
I-I-I- I-I-I- I-I...
With it released...
I-I-I- I-I...
Uh... weh...
...our desires...

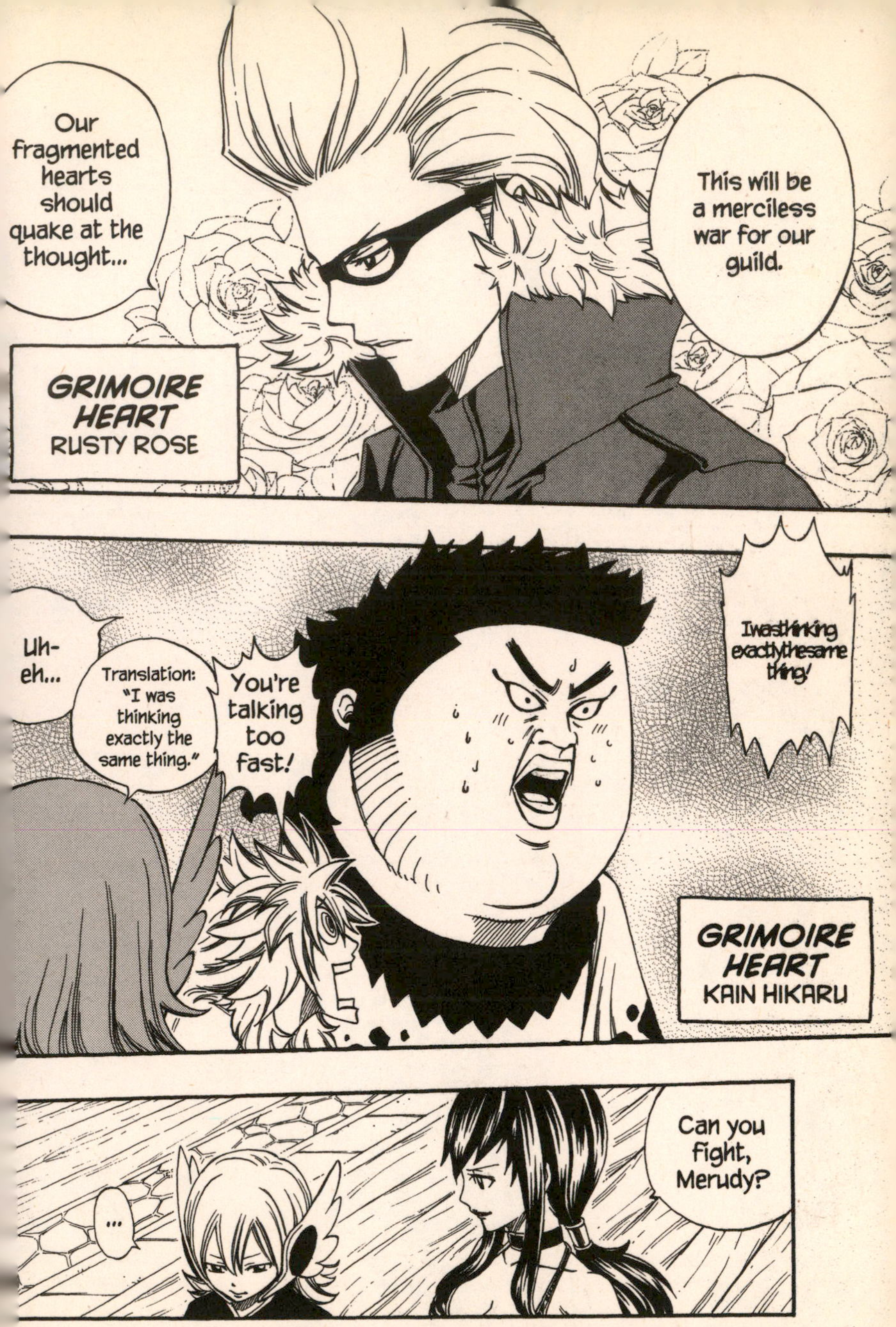
This will be a merciless war for our guild.
Our fragmented hearts should quake at the thought...
GRIMOIRE HEART RUSTY ROSE
Iwasthinking exactlythesame thing!
GRIMOIRE HEART KAIN HIKARU
You're talking too fast!
Translation: "I was thinking exactly the same thing."
Uh-eh...
Can you fight, Merudy?
...

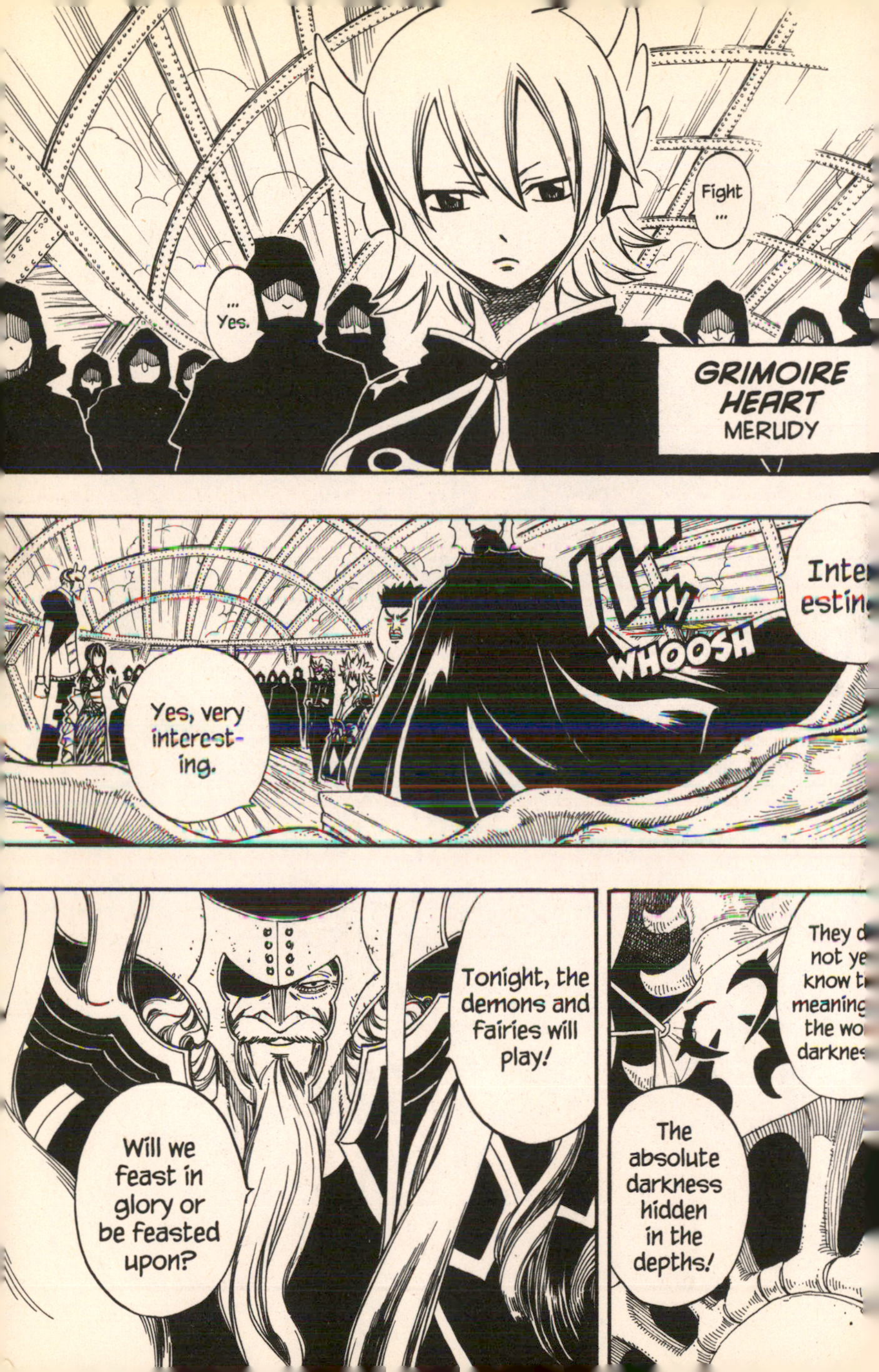
Fight ...
... Yes.
GRIMOIRE HEART MERUDY
Inter estin
WHOOSH
Yes, very interesting.
They d not ye know t meaning the wo darkne
The absolute darkness hidden in the depths!
Tonight, the demons and fairies will play!
Will we feast in glory or be feasted upon?

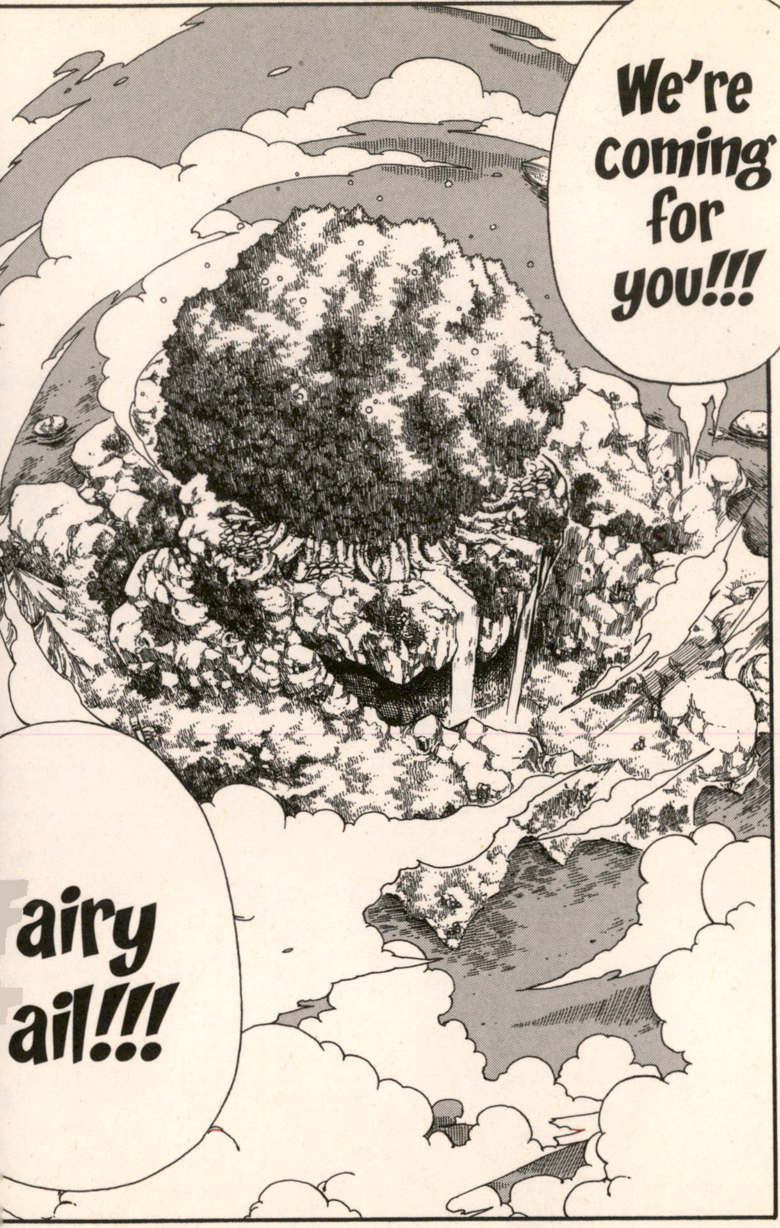
We're coming for you!!!
airy ail!!!

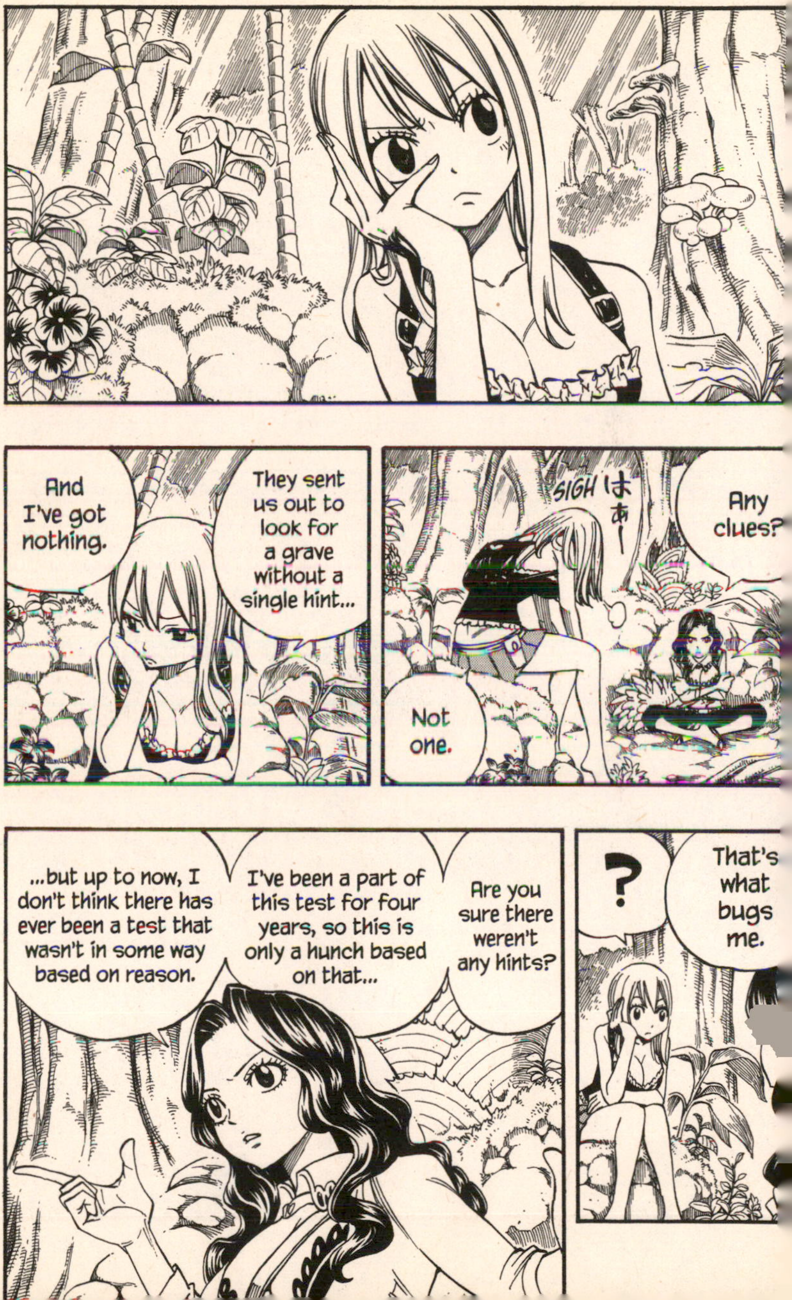

Any clues?
SIGH
はあー
Not one.
They sent us out to look for a grave without a single hint...
And I've got nothing.
That's what bugs me.
?
Are you sure there weren't any hints?
I've been a part of this test for four years, so this is only a hunch based on that...
...but up to now, I don't think there has ever been a test that wasn't in some way based on reason.

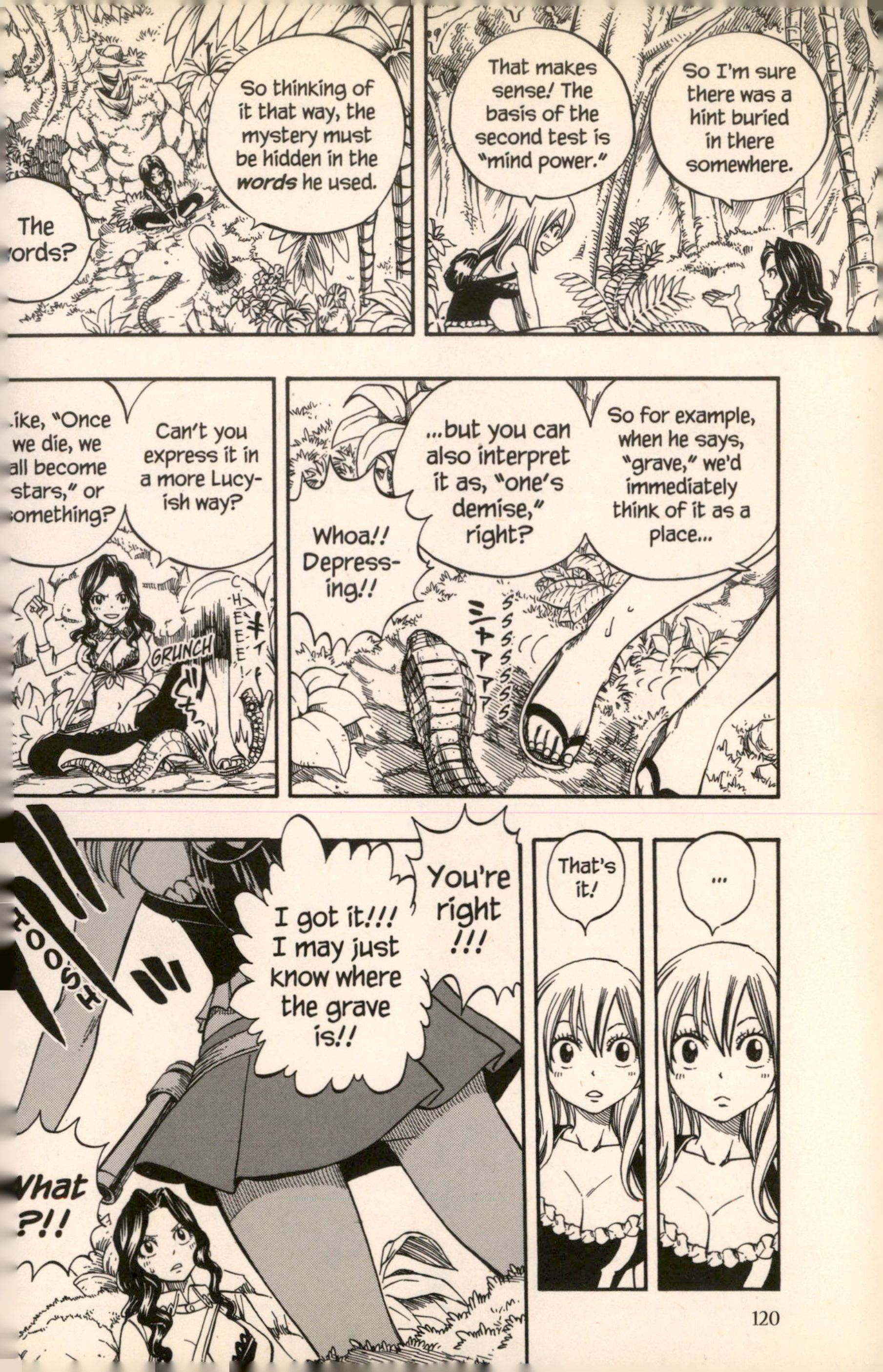
So I'm sure there was a hint buried in there somewhere.
That makes sense! The basis of the second test is "mind power."
So thinking of it that way, the mystery must be hidden in the words he used.
The words?
So for example, when he says, "grave," we'd immediately think of it as a place...
...but you can also interpret it as, "one's demise," right?
Whoa!! Depress-ing!!
SSSSSSSS
シャアア
Can't you express it in a more Lucy-ish way?
Like, "Once we die, we all become stars," or something?
CHEEEE!
キイ
GRUNCH
...
That's it!
You're right!!!
I got it!!! I may just know where the grave is!!
TOOSH
What?!!

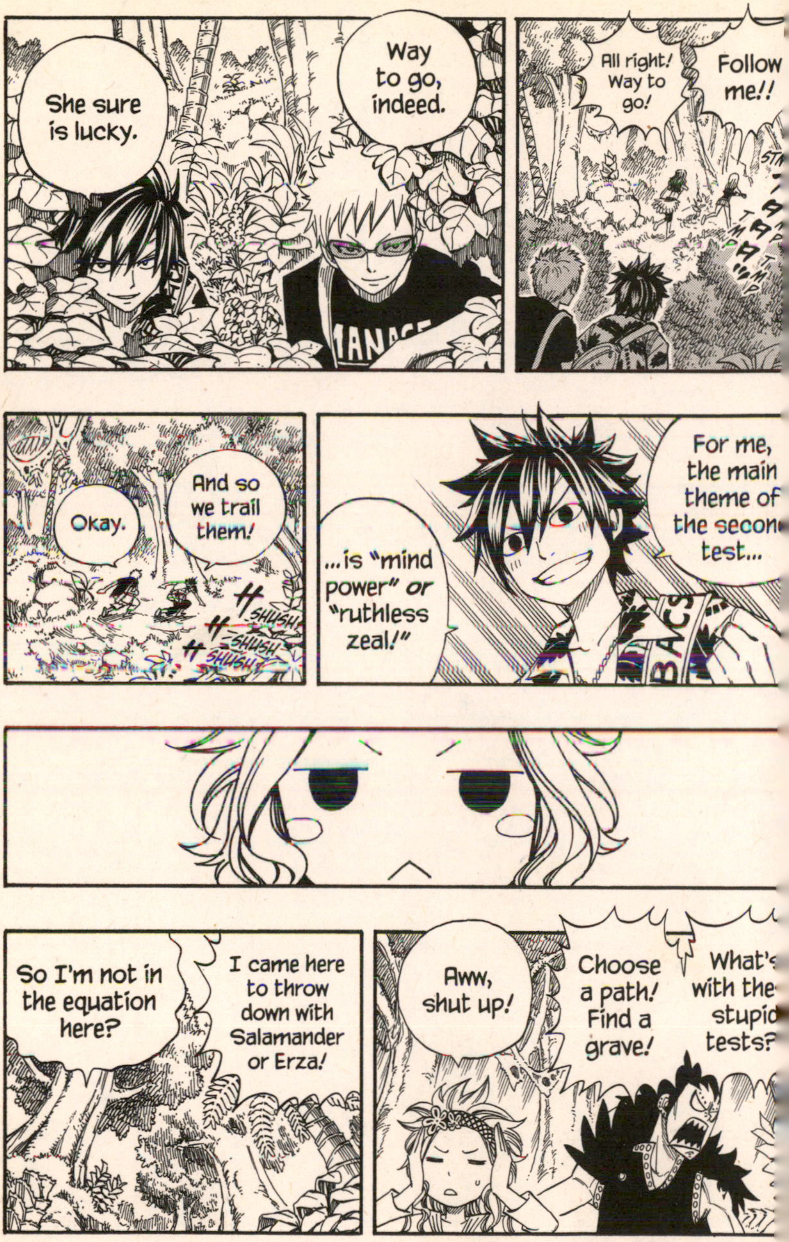
All right! Way to go!
Follow me!!
STMP
TMP
TMP
Way to go, indeed.
She sure is lucky.
For me, the main theme of the secon test...
...is "mind power" or "ruthless zeal!"
And so we trail them!
Okay.
SHUSH
SHUSH
SHUSH
What's with the stupid tests?
Choose a path! Find a grave!
Aww, shut up!
I came here to throw down with Salamander or Erza!
So I'm not in the equation here?

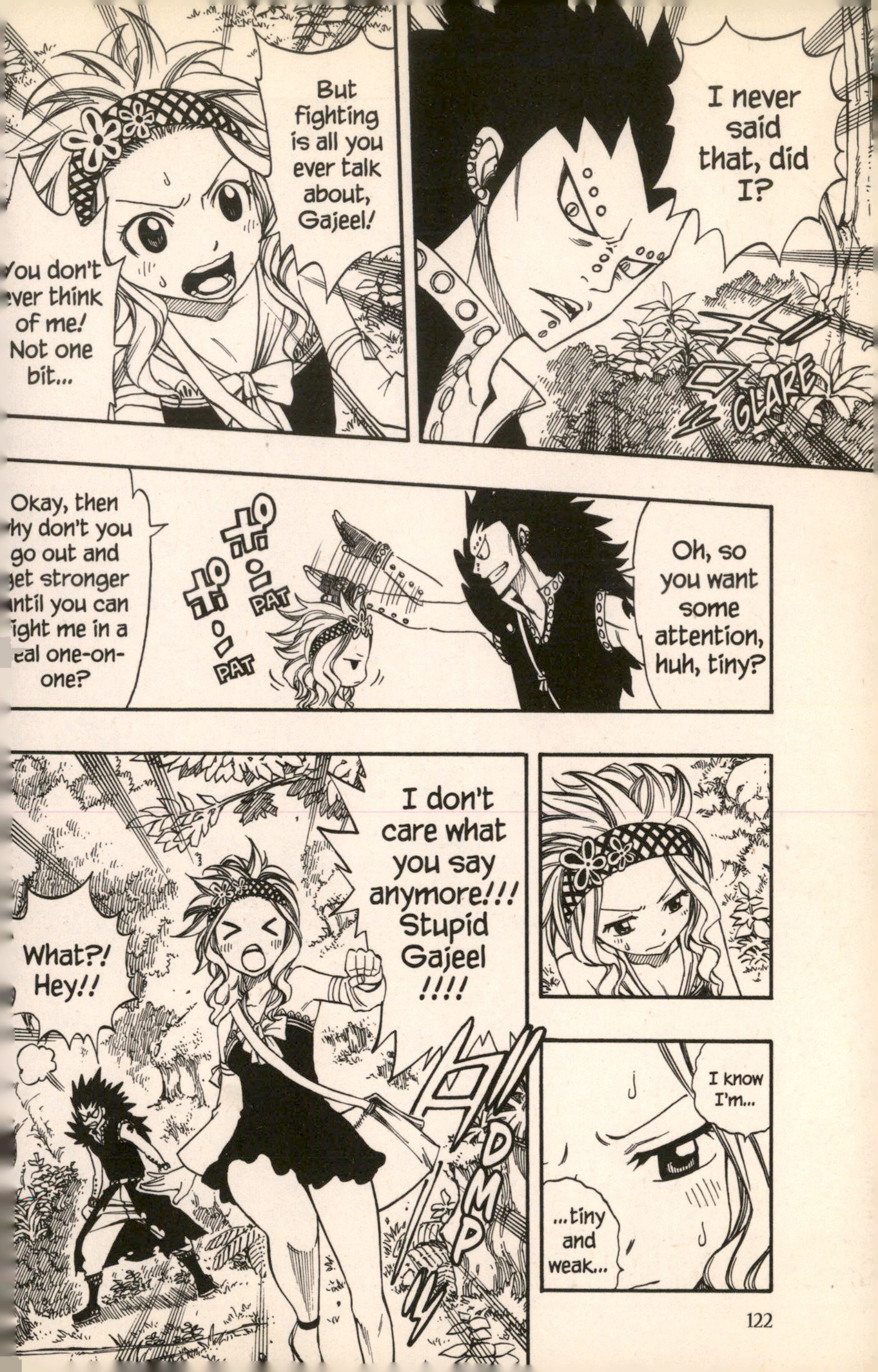
I never said that, did I?
GLARE
But fighting is all you ever talk about, Gajeel!
You don't ever think of me! Not one bit...
Oh, so you want some attention, huh, tiny?
PAT
PAT
Okay, then hy don't you go out and jet stronger ıntil you can ight me in a eal one-on-one?
I know I'm...
...tiny and weak...
I don't care what you say anymore!!! Stupid Gajeel !!!!
DMMP
What?! Hey!!

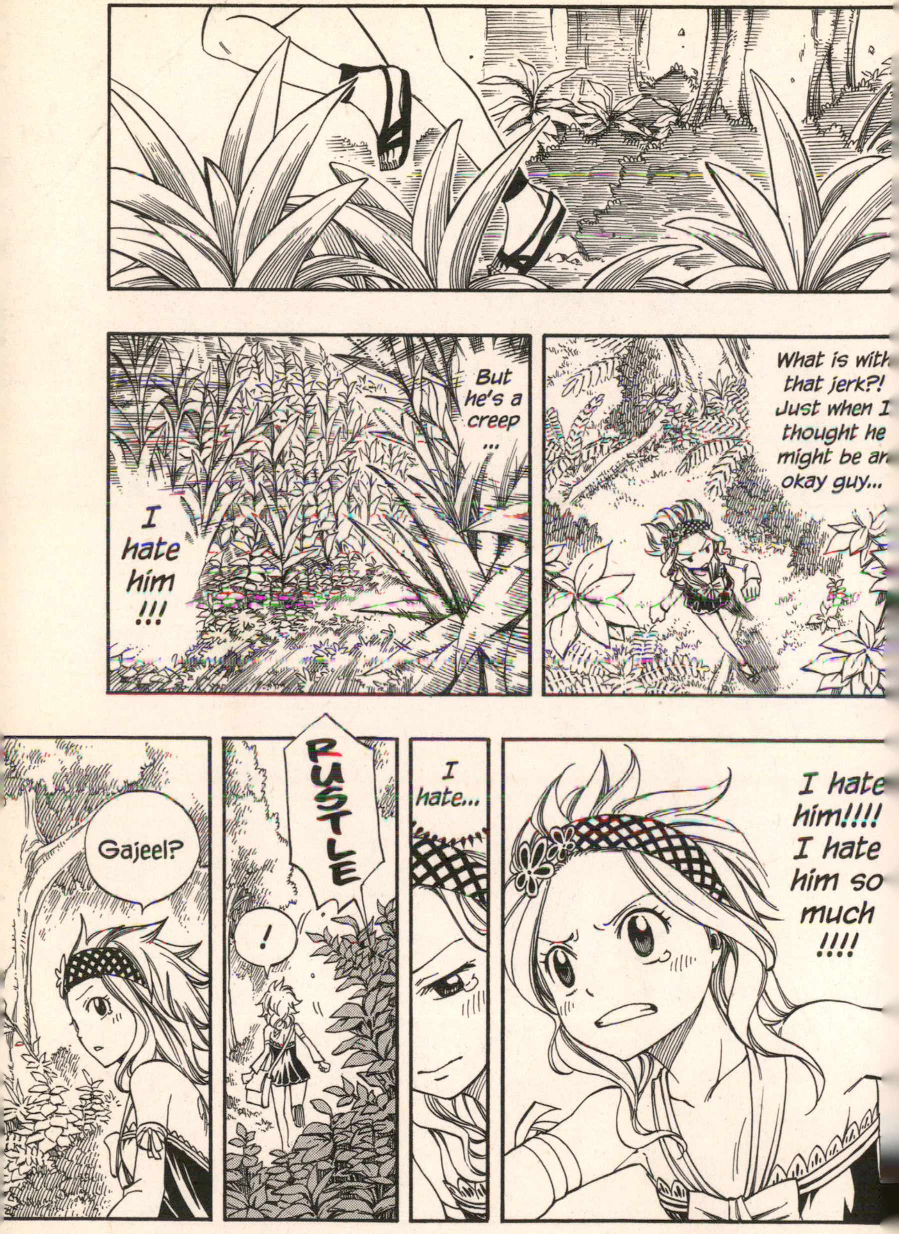
What is with that jerk?! Just when I thought he might be an okay guy...
But he's a creep ...
I hate him !!!
I hate him!!!! I hate him so much !!!!
I hate...
RUSTLE
!
Gajeel?

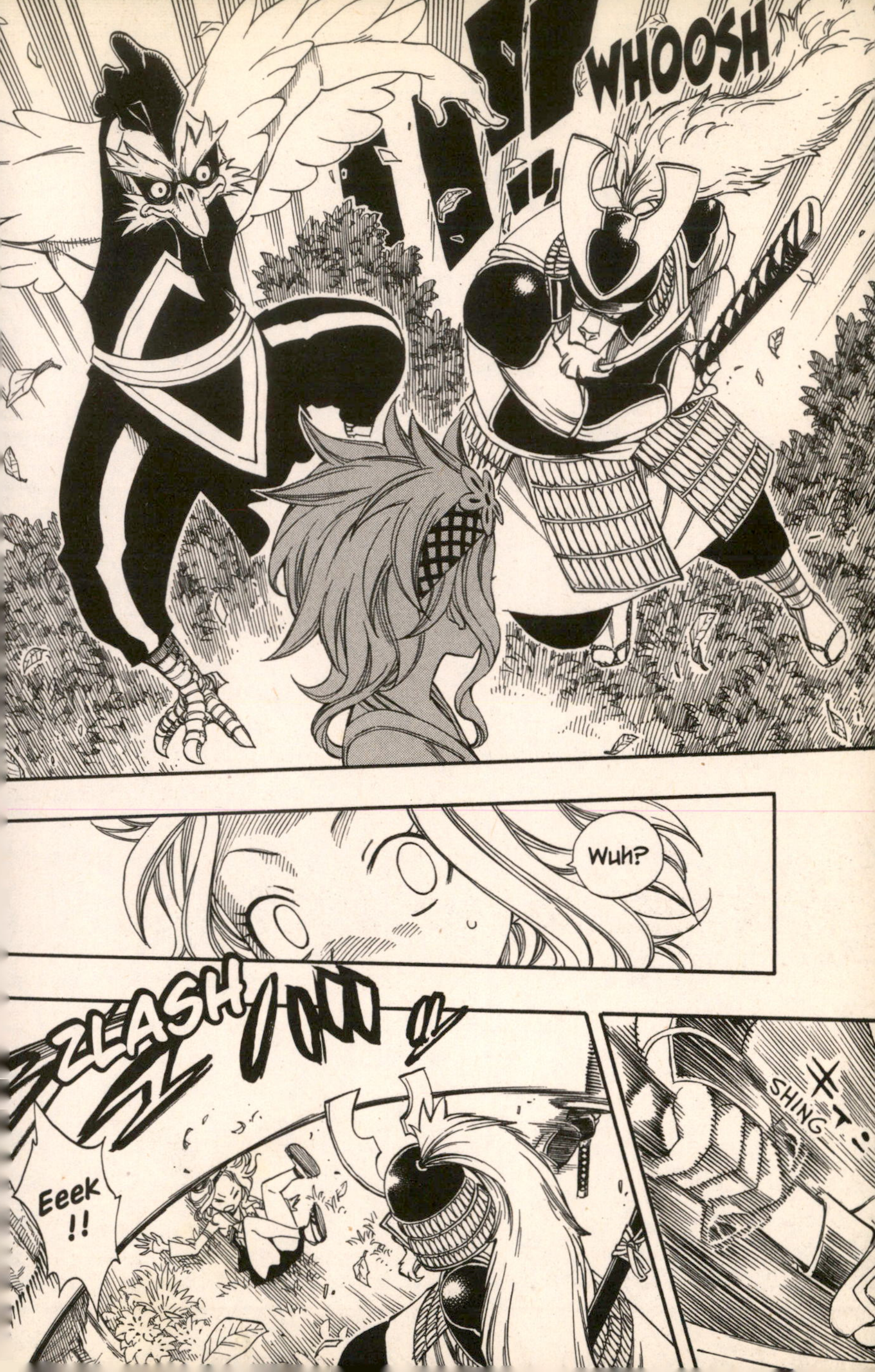
WHOOSH
Wuh?
SHING
ZZLASH
Eeek !!

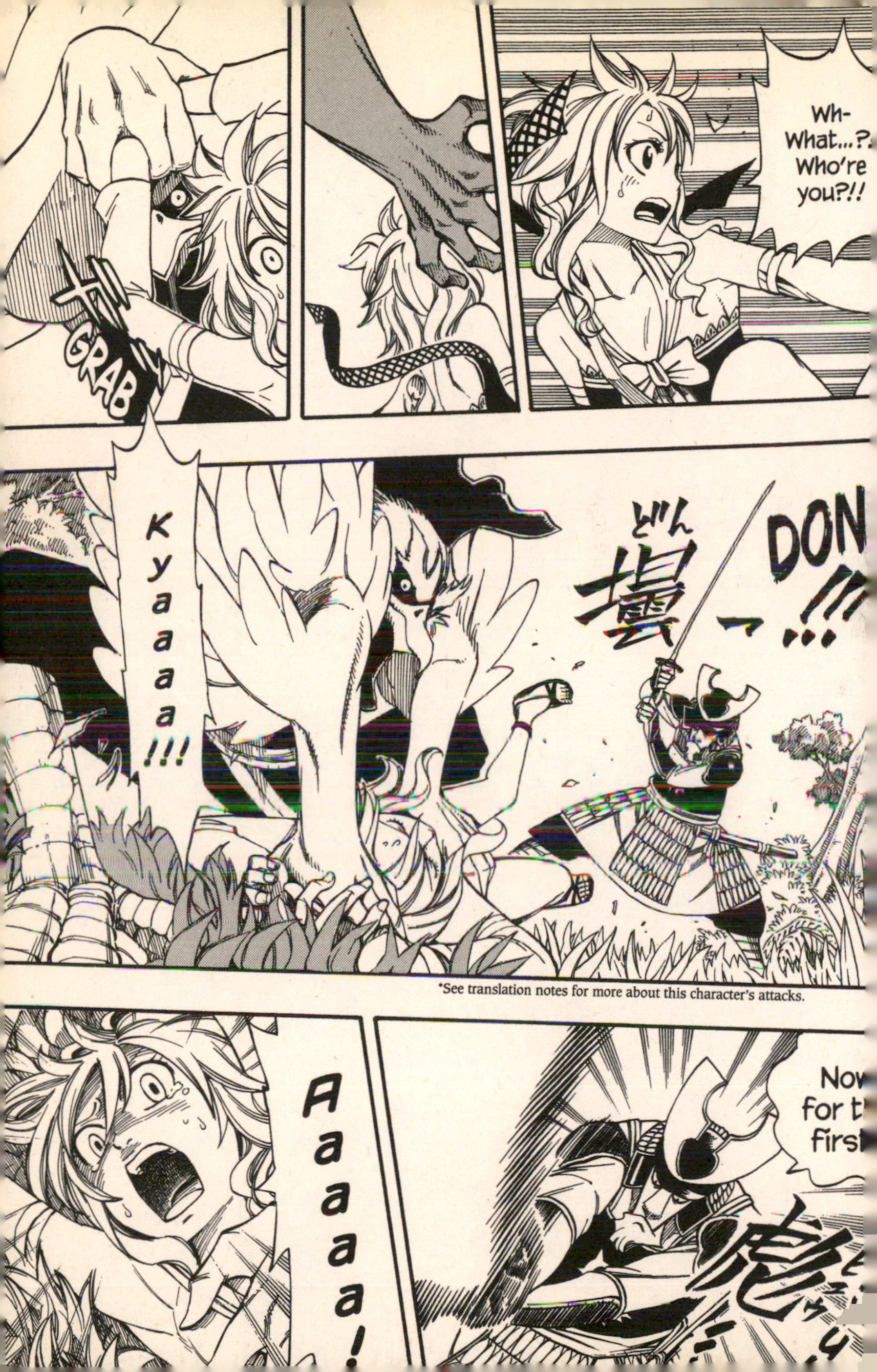
Wh- What...?! Who're you?!!
GRAB
DON!!!
Kyaaaaa!!!
Now for t first
Aaaaaa!

*See translation notes for more about this character's attacks.

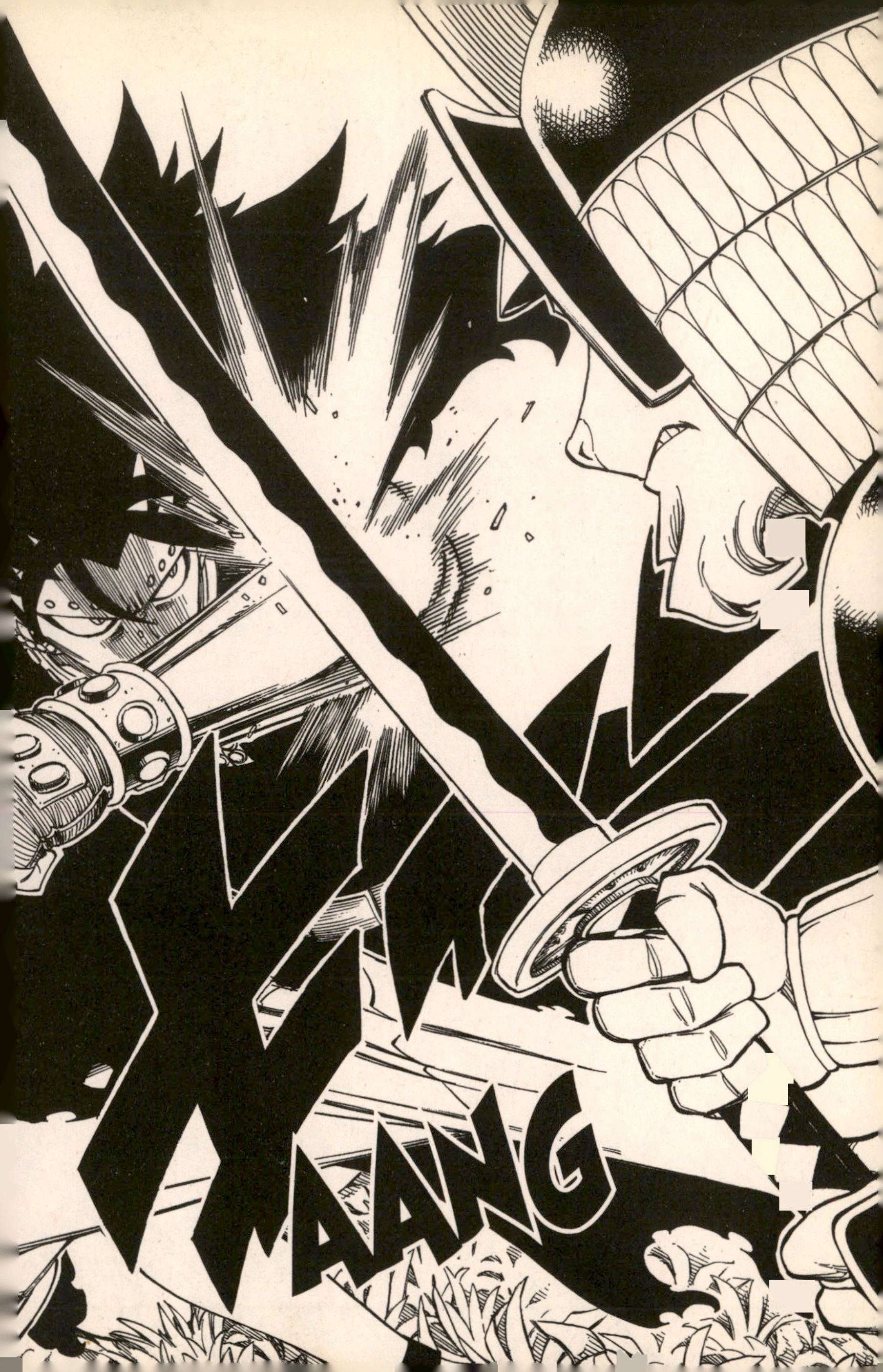
KWAANG

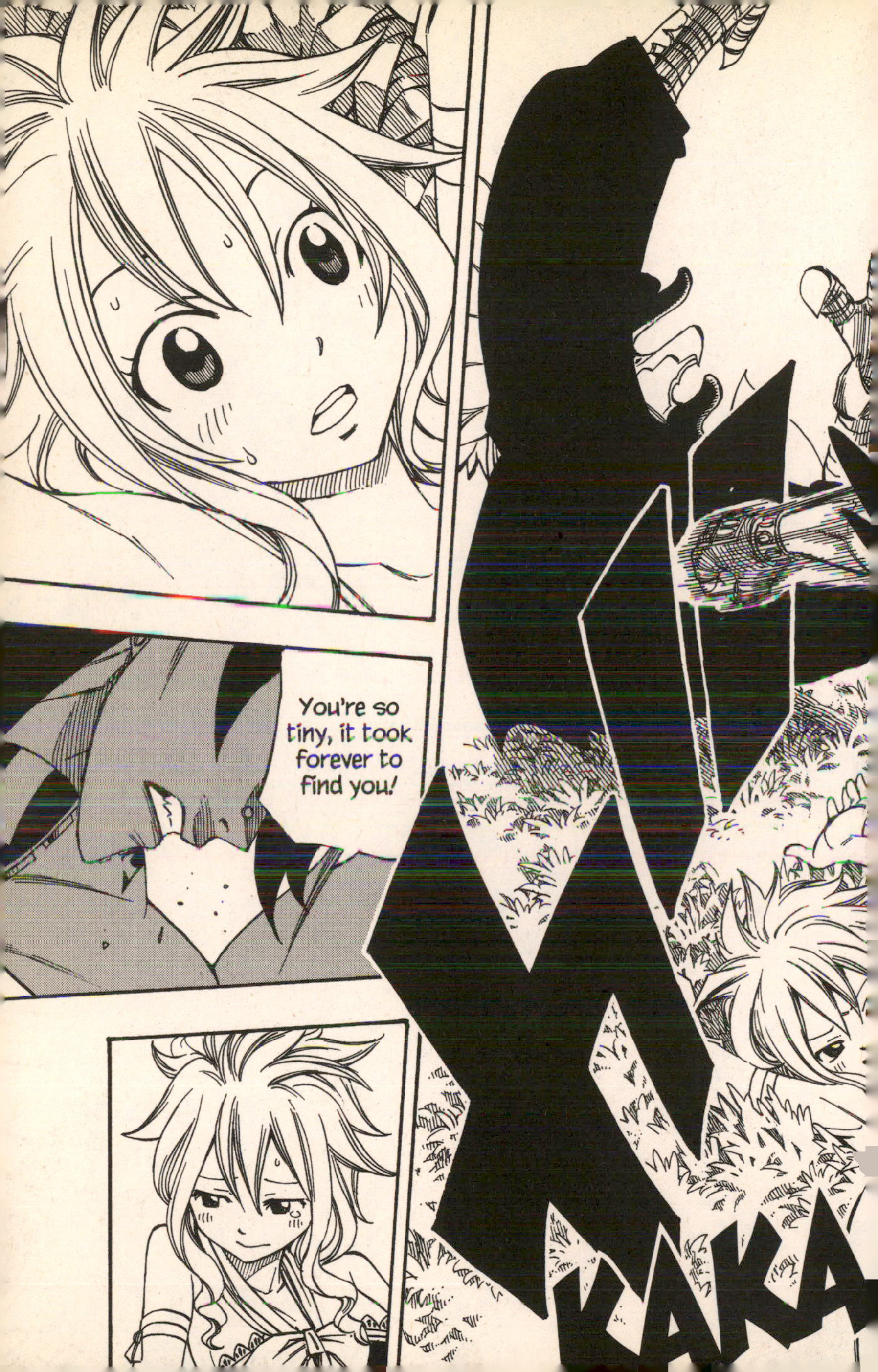
You're so tiny, it took forever to find you!
KAKA

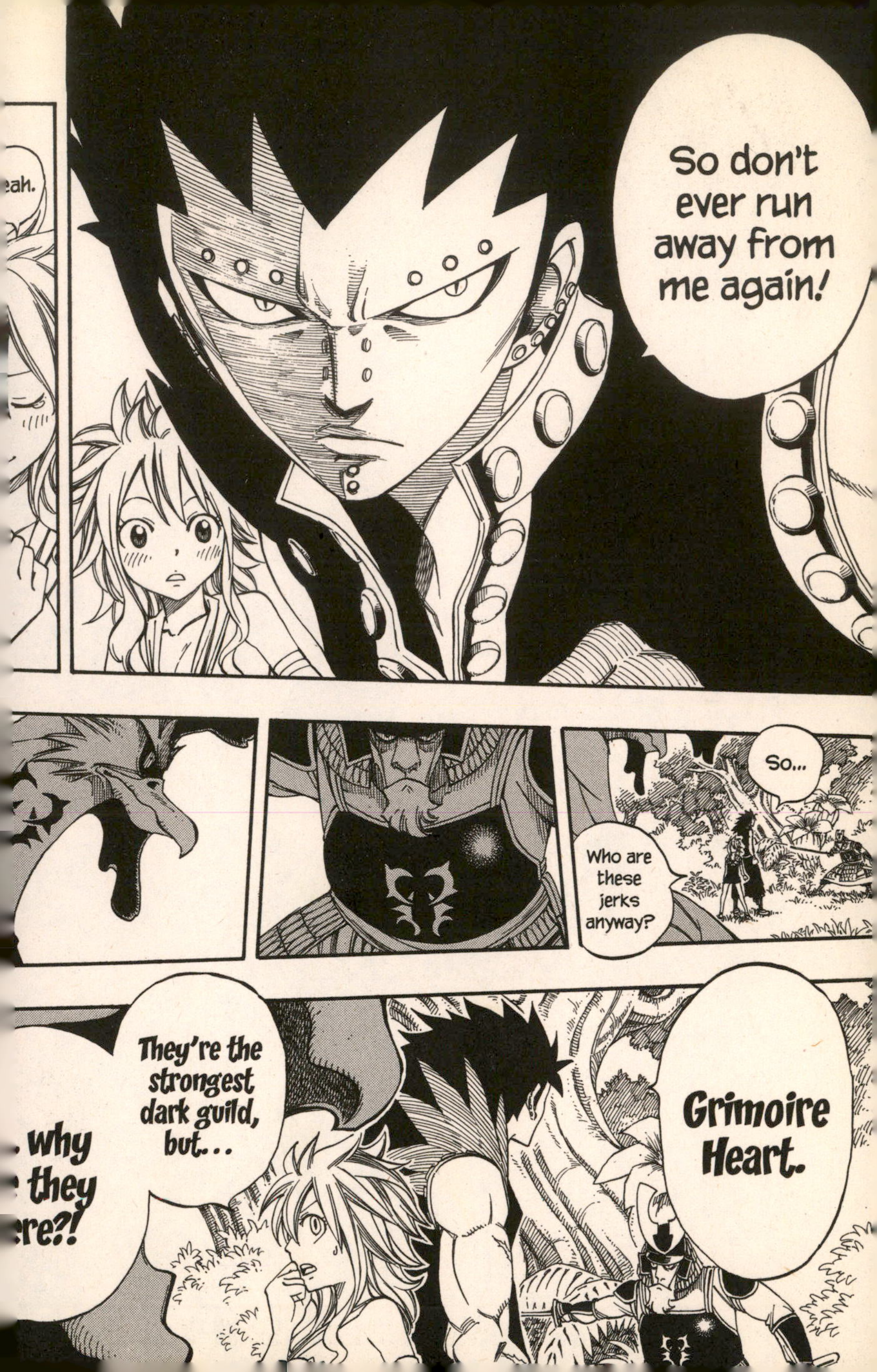
So don't ever run away from me again!
eah.
So...
Who are these jerks anyway?
Grimoire Heart.
They're the strongest dark guild, but...
why
they
re?!

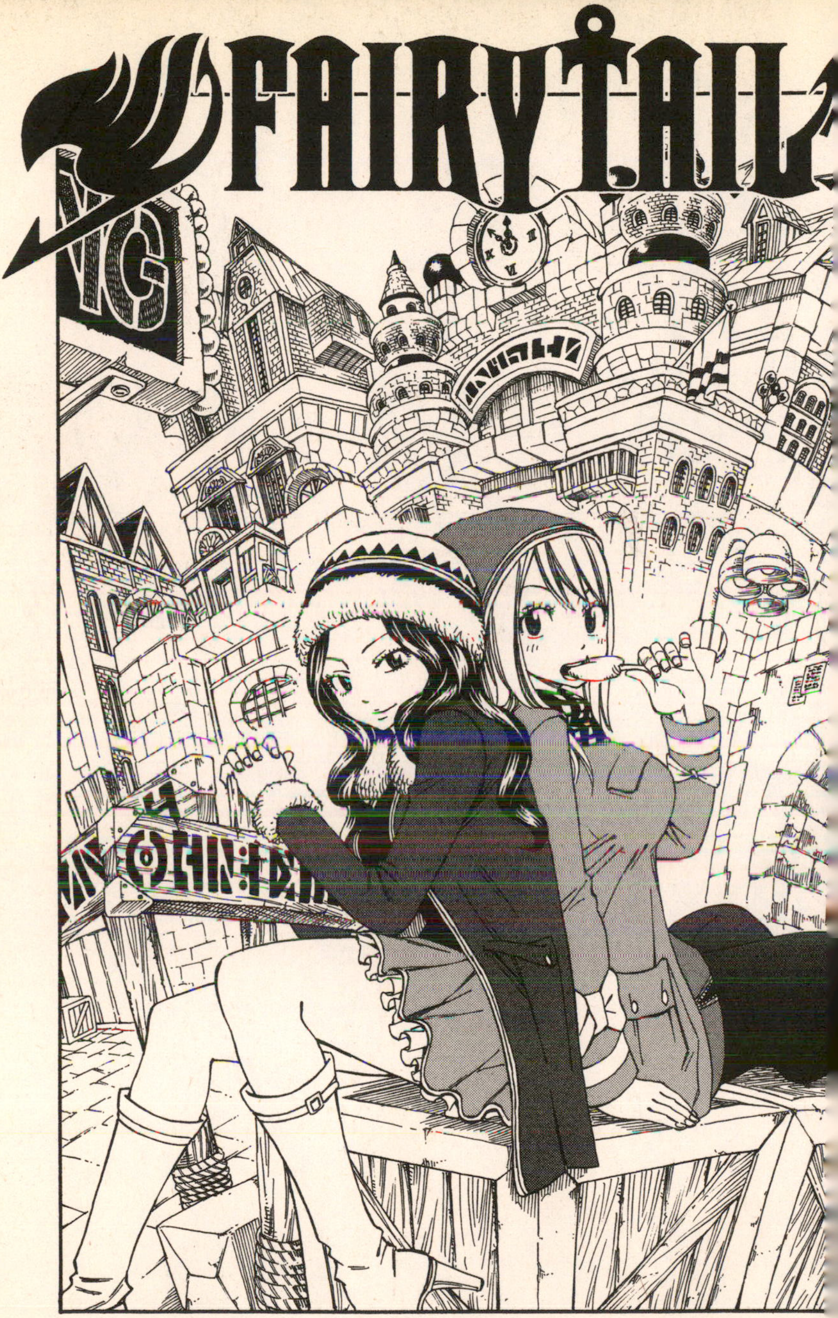
FAIRY TAIL

Chapter 211: Kawazu and Yomazu

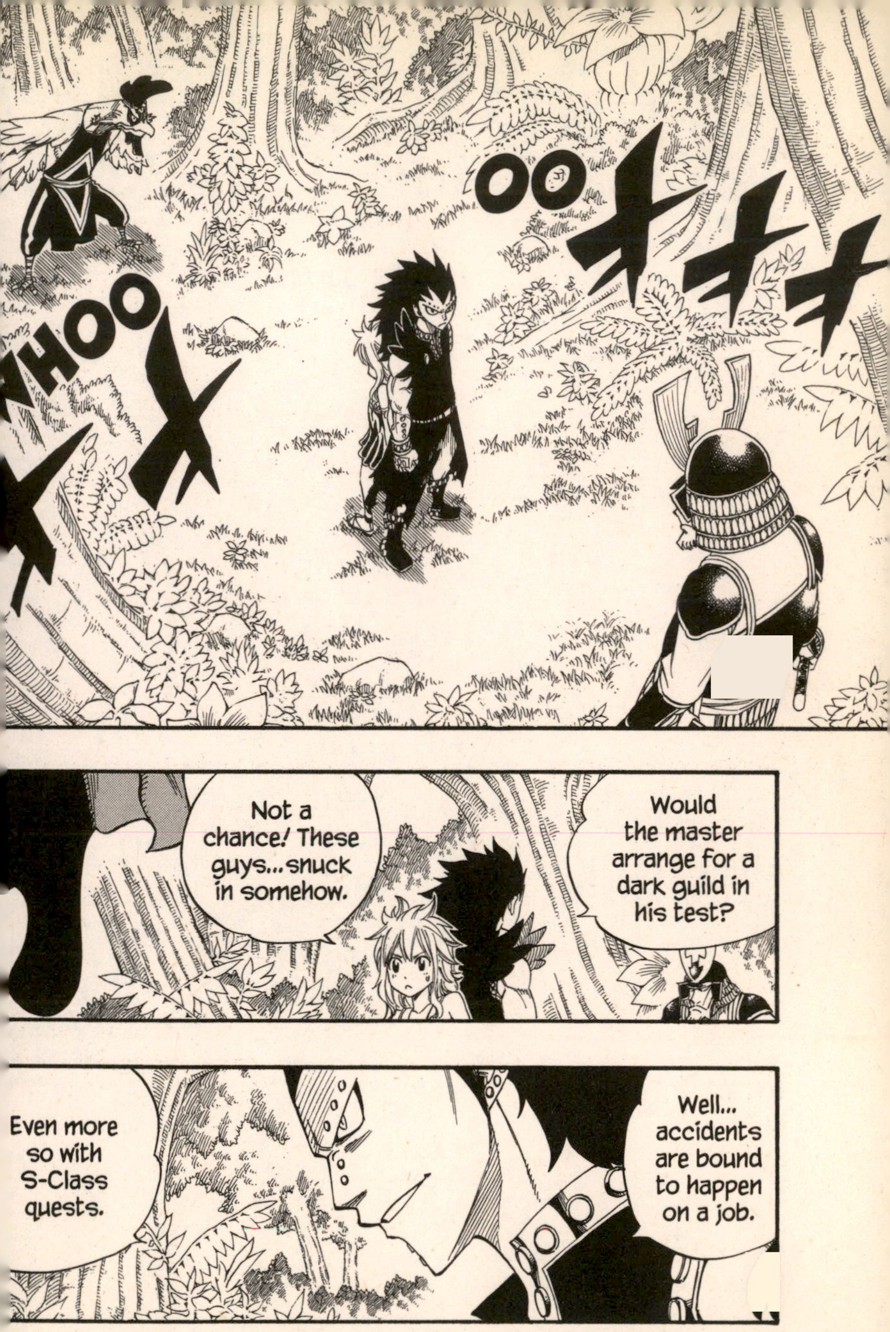
OO
WHOO
Would the master arrange for a dark guild in his test?
Not a chance! These guys...snuck in somehow.
Well... accidents are bound to happen on a job.
Even more so with S-Class quests.

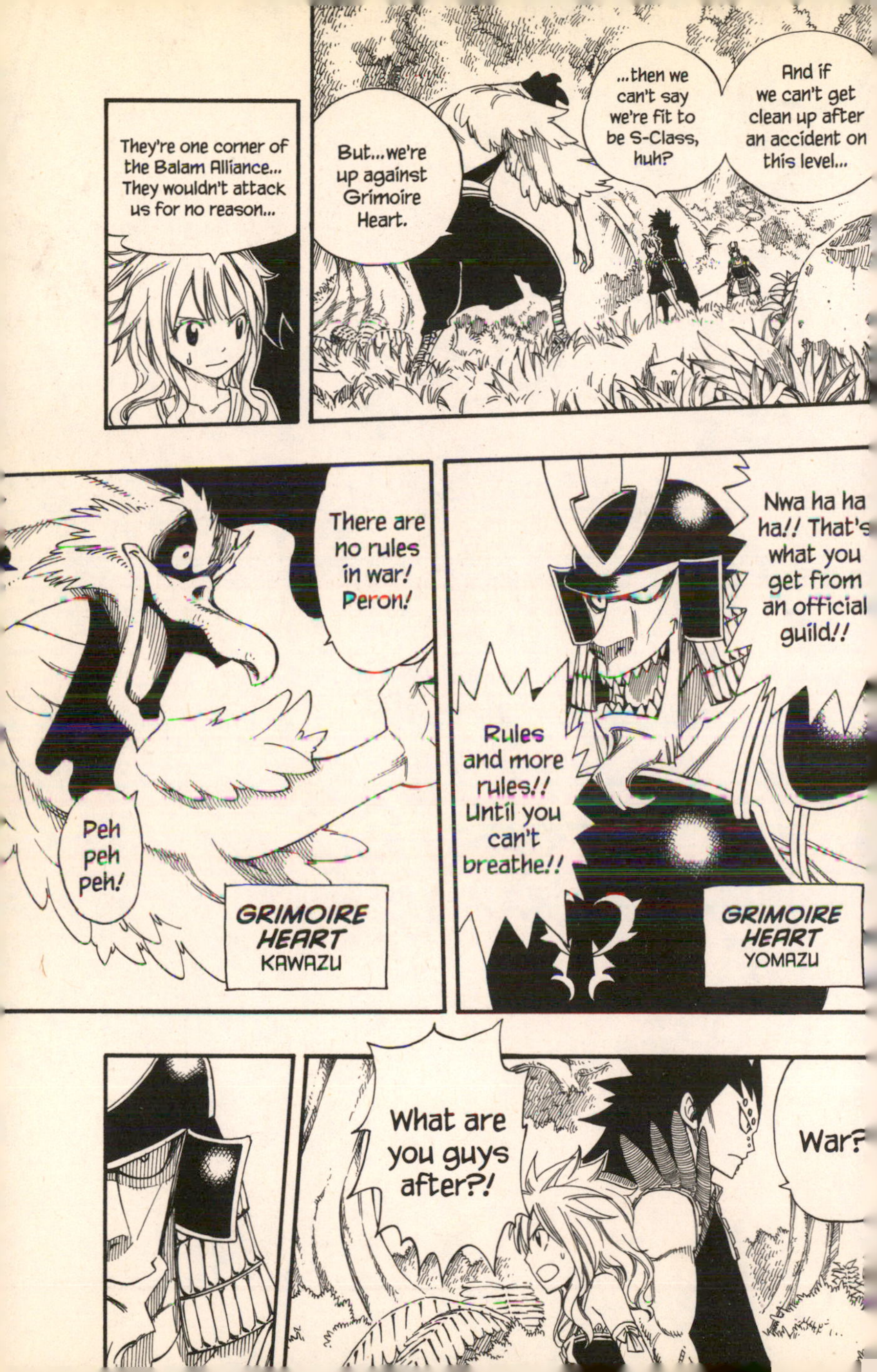
And if we can't get clean up after an accident on this level...
...then we can't say we're fit to be S-Class, huh?
But...we're up against Grimoire Heart.
They're one corner of the Balam Alliance... They wouldn't attack us for no reason...
Nwa ha ha!! That's what you get from an official guild!!
Rules and more rules!! Until you can't breathe!!
GRIMOIRE HEART YOMAZU
There are no rules in war! Peron!
Peh peh peh!
GRIMOIRE HEART KAWAZU
War?
What are you guys after?!

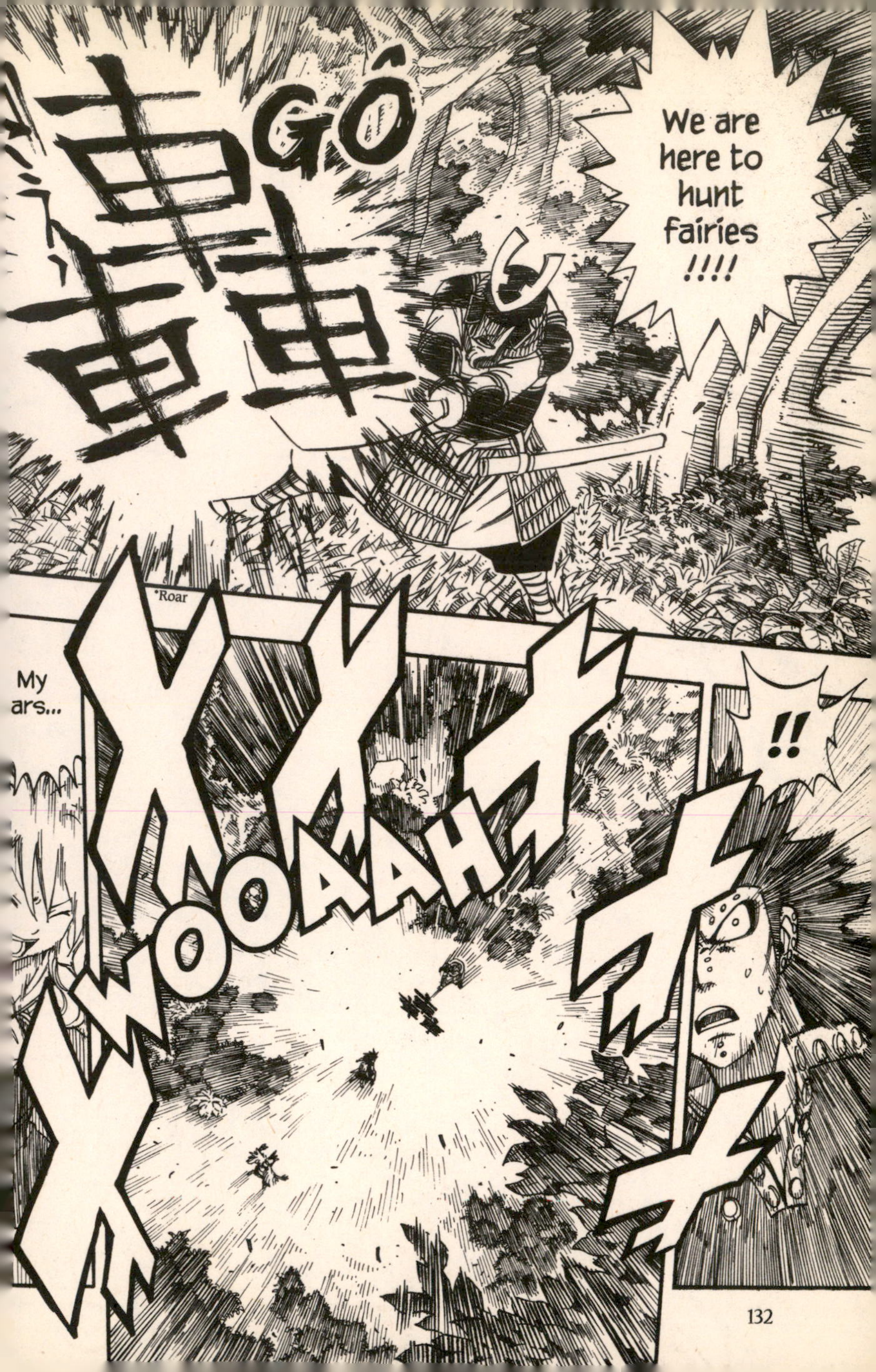
We are here to hunt fairies !!!!
GŌ
!!
WOOAAH
*Roar
My ars...

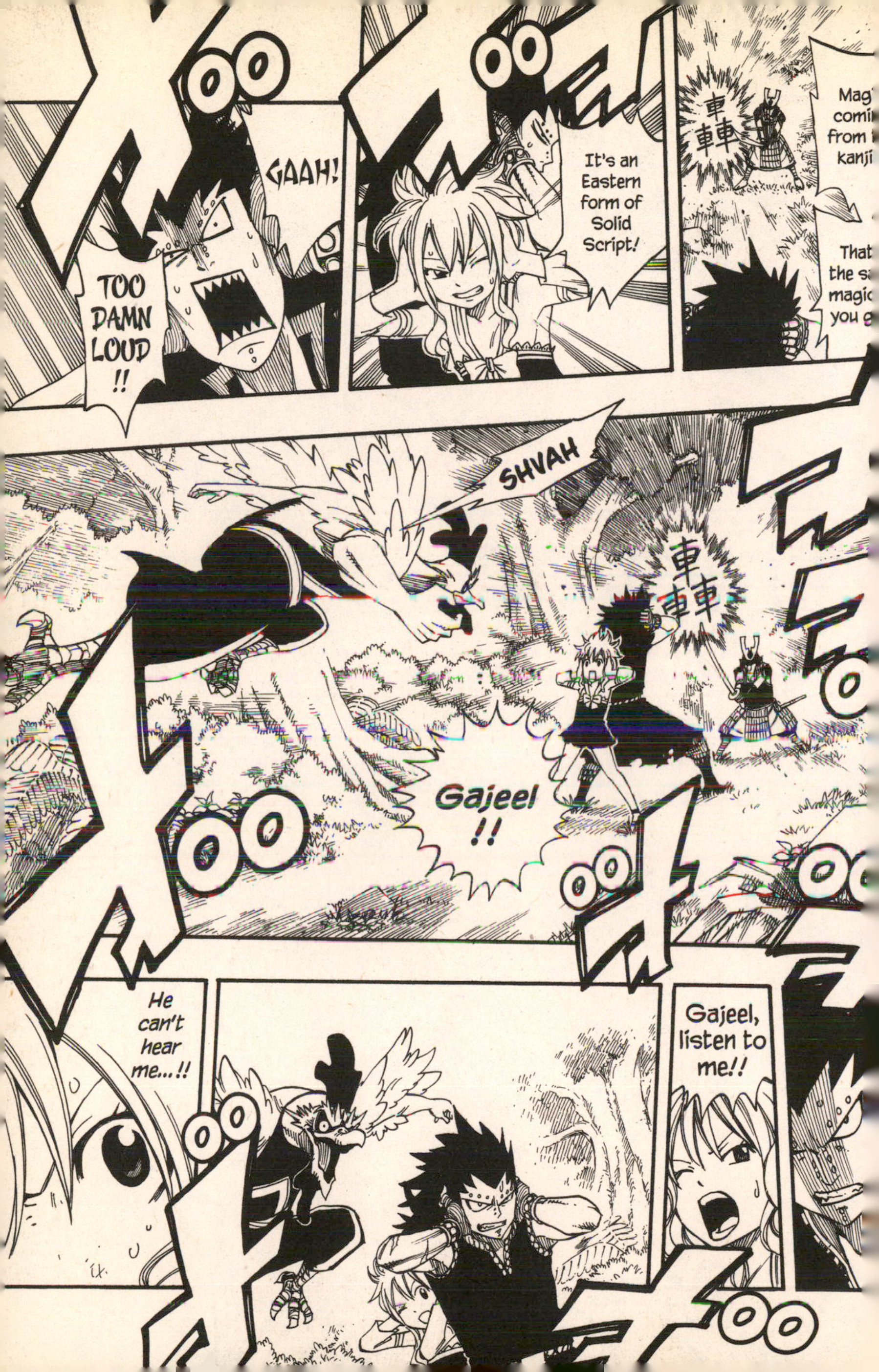

車車
It's an Eastern form of Solid Script!
GAAH!
TOO DAMN LOUD !!
車車
SHVAH
Gajeel !!
Gajeel, listen to me!!
He can't hear me...!!

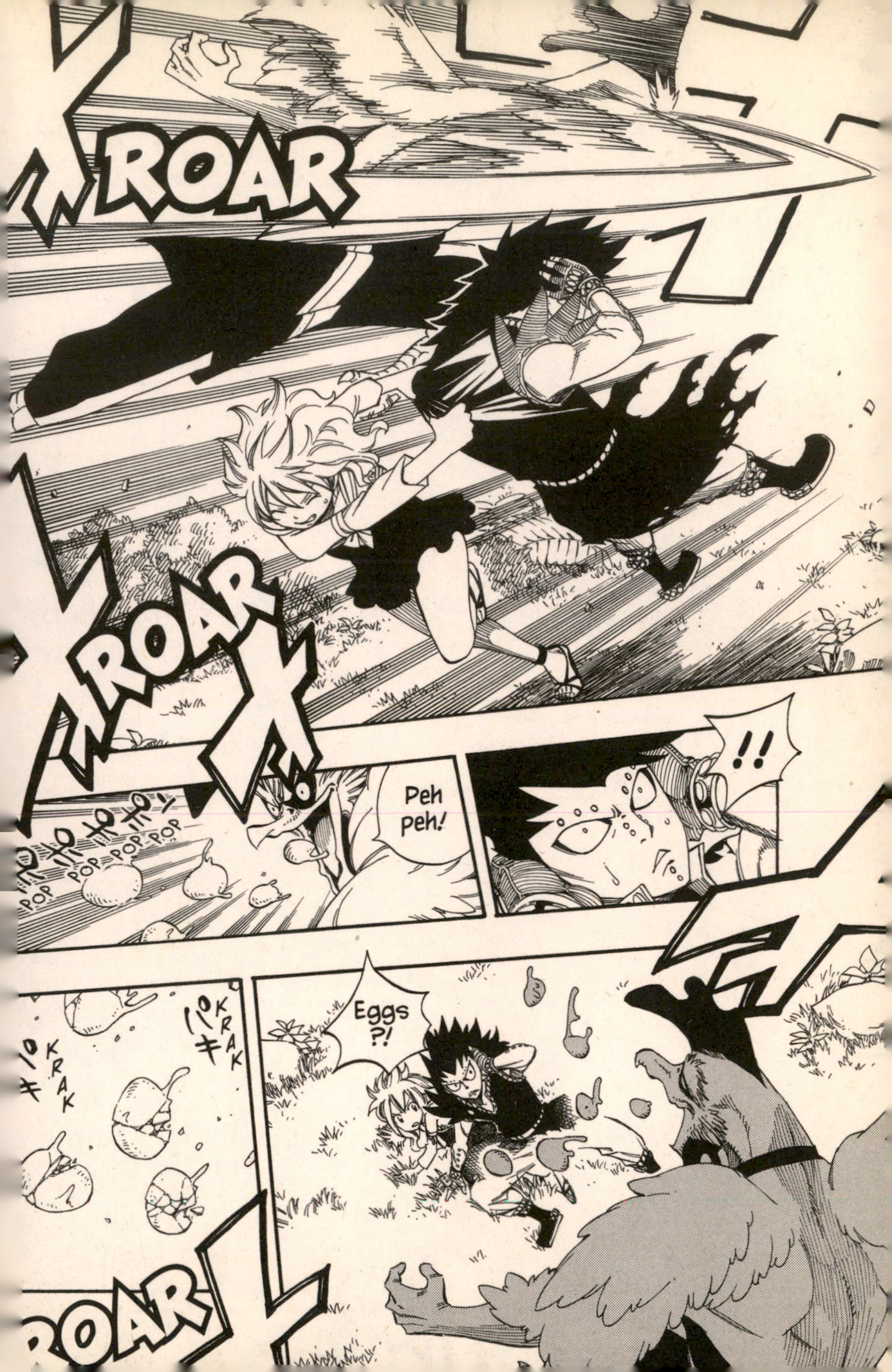
ROAR
ROAR
!!
Peh peh!
POP POP POP POP
Eggs?!
ROAR
KRAK
KRAK

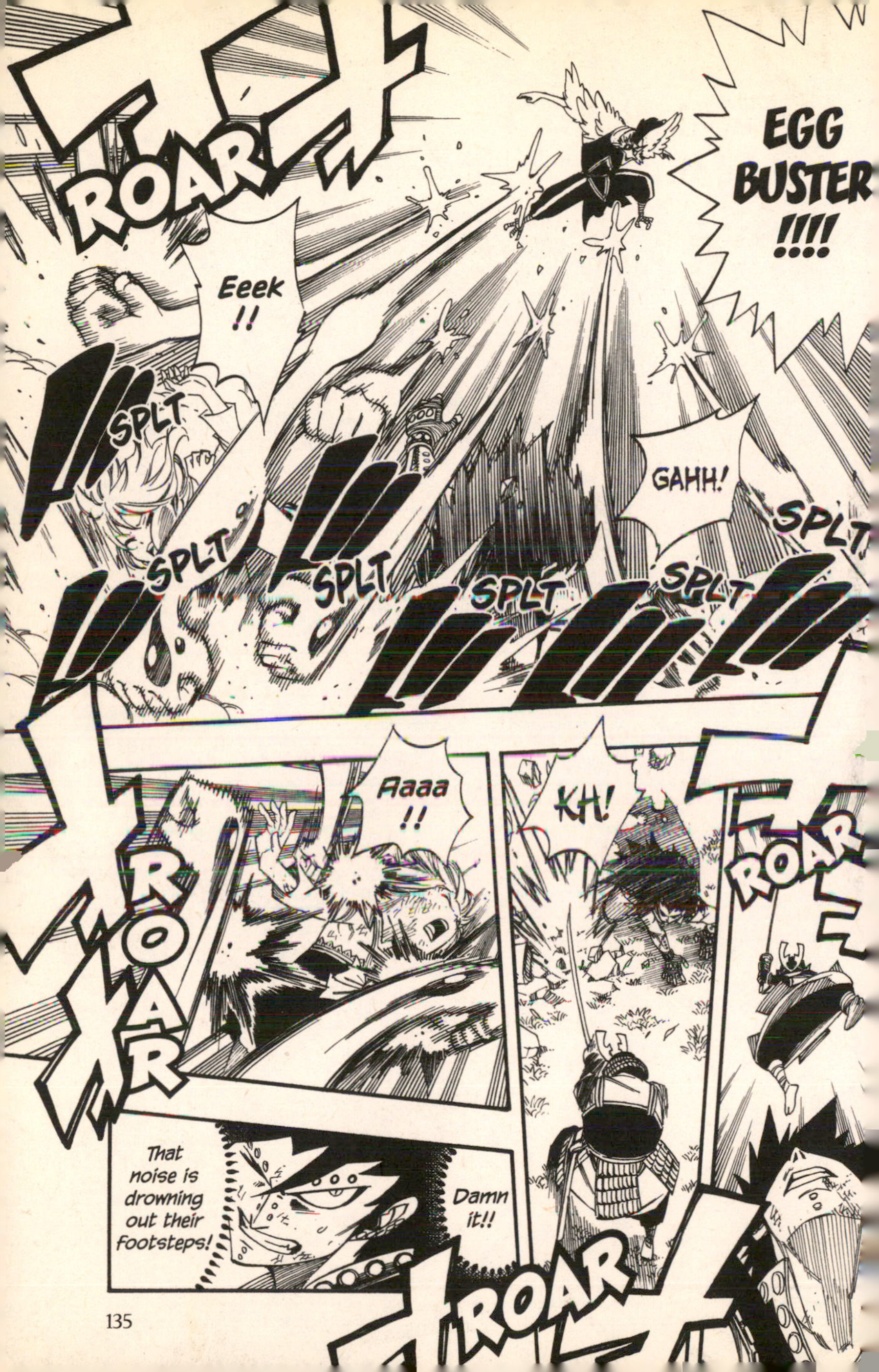
EGG BUSTER !!!!
ROAR
Eeek !!
SPLT
GAHH!
SPLT
SPLT
SPLT
SPLT
SPLT
SPLT
ROAR
KH!
Aaaa !!
ROAR
Damn it!!
That noise is drowning out their footsteps!
ROAR

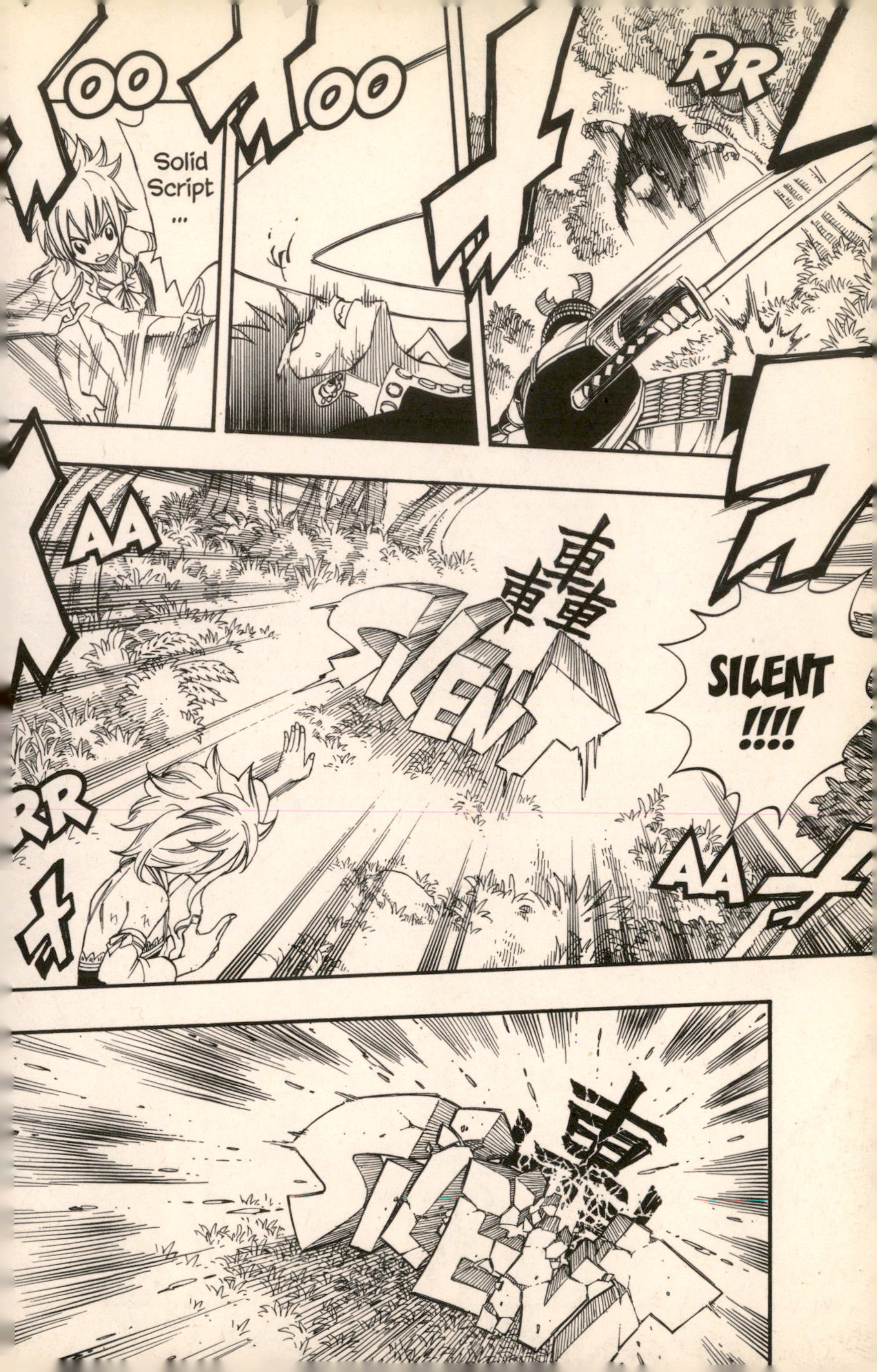
RR
OO
OO
Solid Script ...
SILENT !!!!
AA
AA
RR

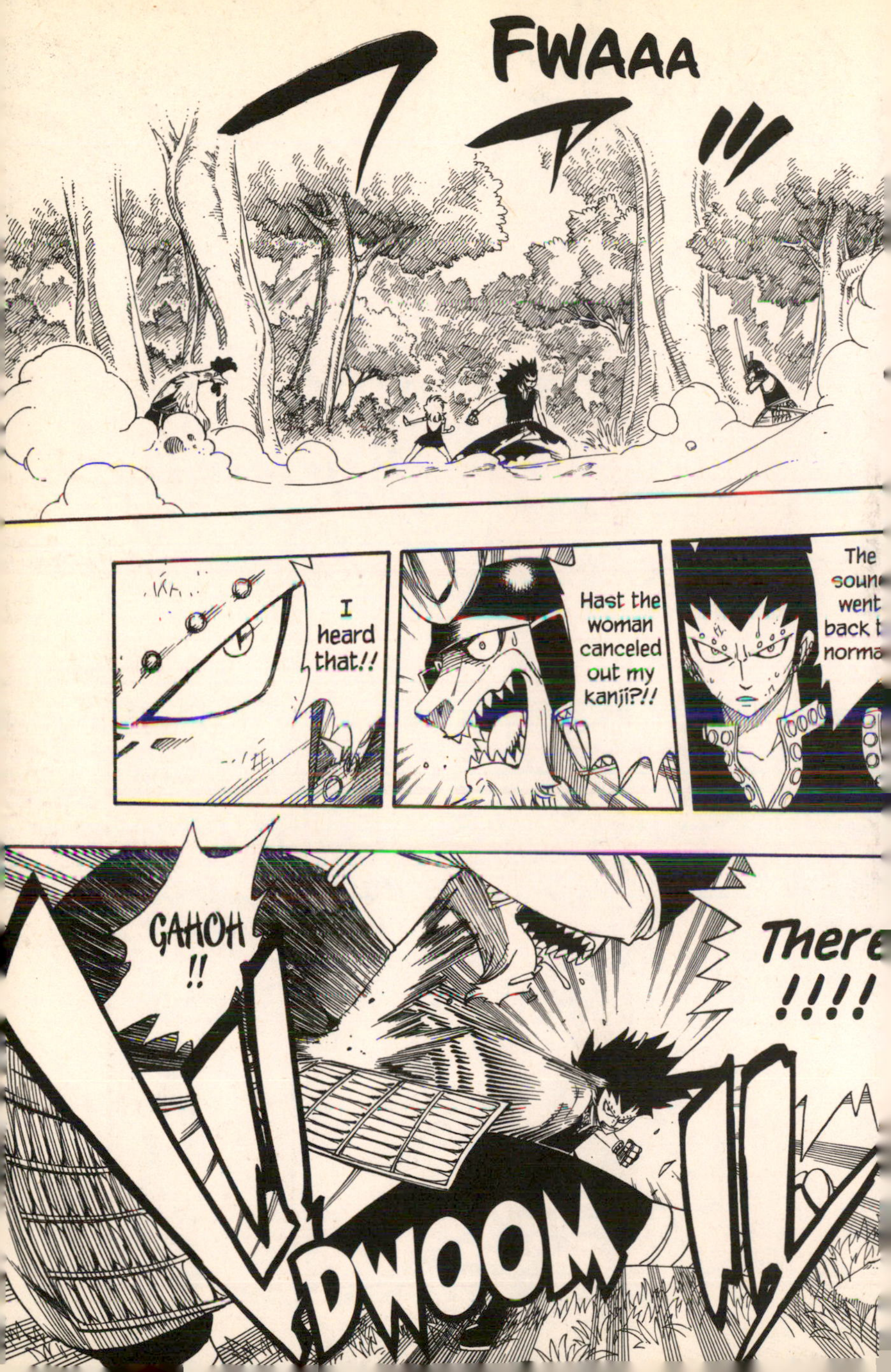
FWAAAAP!!!
The soun went back t norma
Hast the woman canceled out my kanji?!!
I heard that!!
There !!!!
GAHOH !!
DWOOM

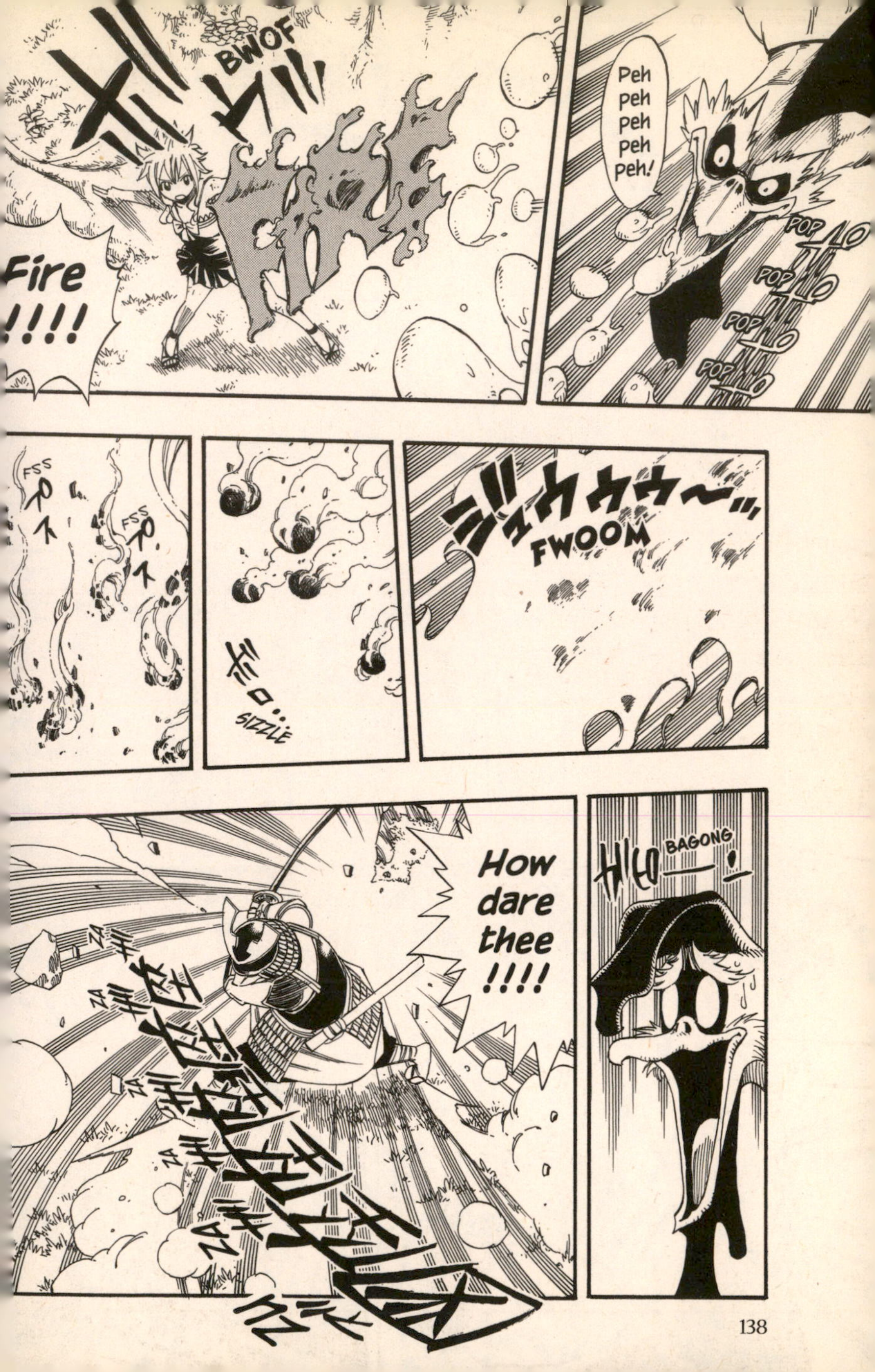

Peh peh peh peh peh!
POP
POP
POP
POP
BWOF
Fire !!!!
FWOOM
SIZZLE
FSS
FSS
BAGONG
How dare thee !!!!
ZA
ZA
ZA
ZA
ZA

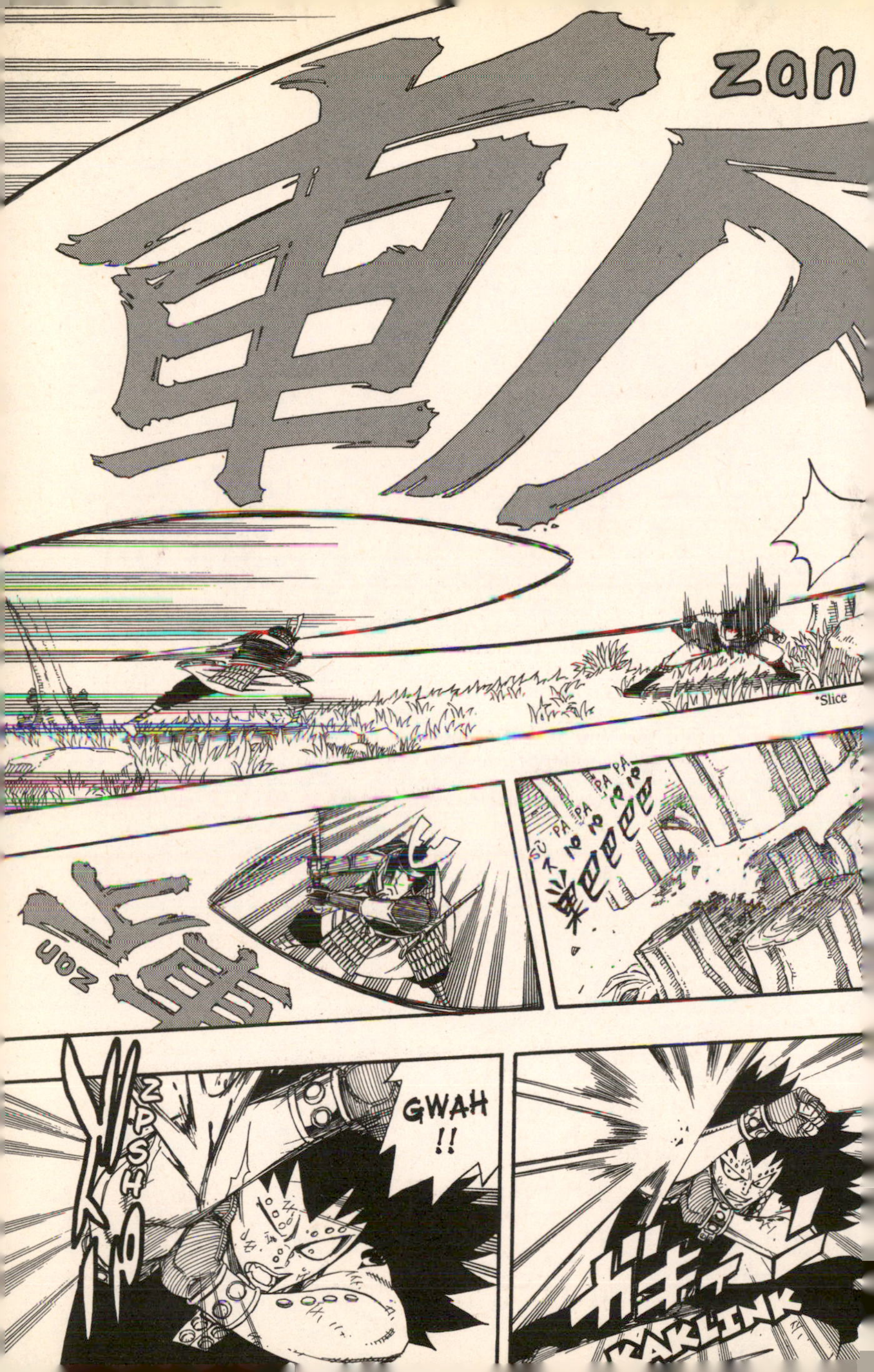

斬
zan
*Slice
SU PA PA PA PA
zon
KAKLINK
GWAH !!
ZPSH

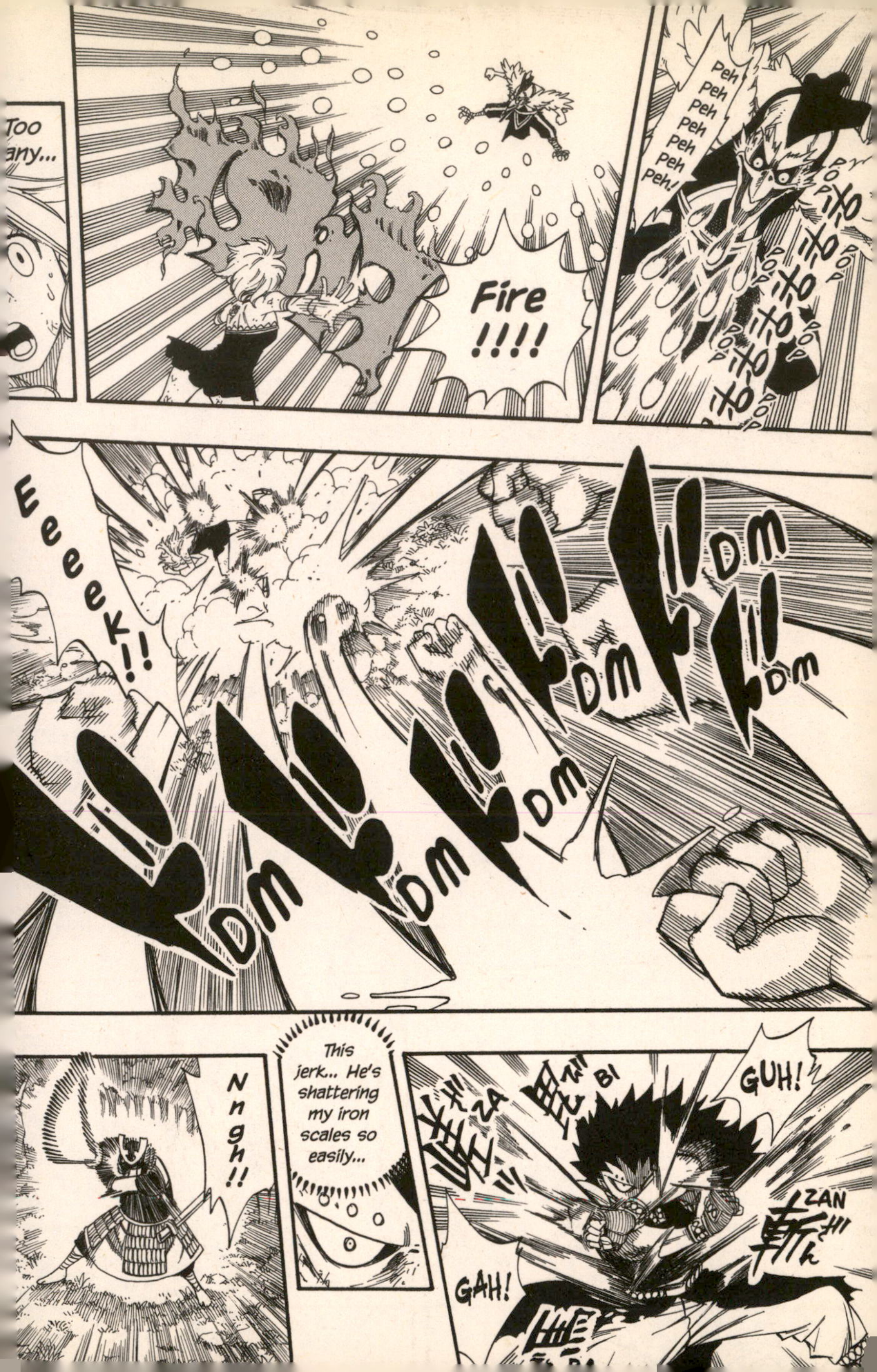

Peh peh peh peh peh peh peh!
Fire !!!!
Too many...
Eeeeek!!
DM DM DM DM DM DM DM
GUH!
BI
ZAN
GAH!
This jerk... He's shattering my iron scales so easily...
Nngh!!

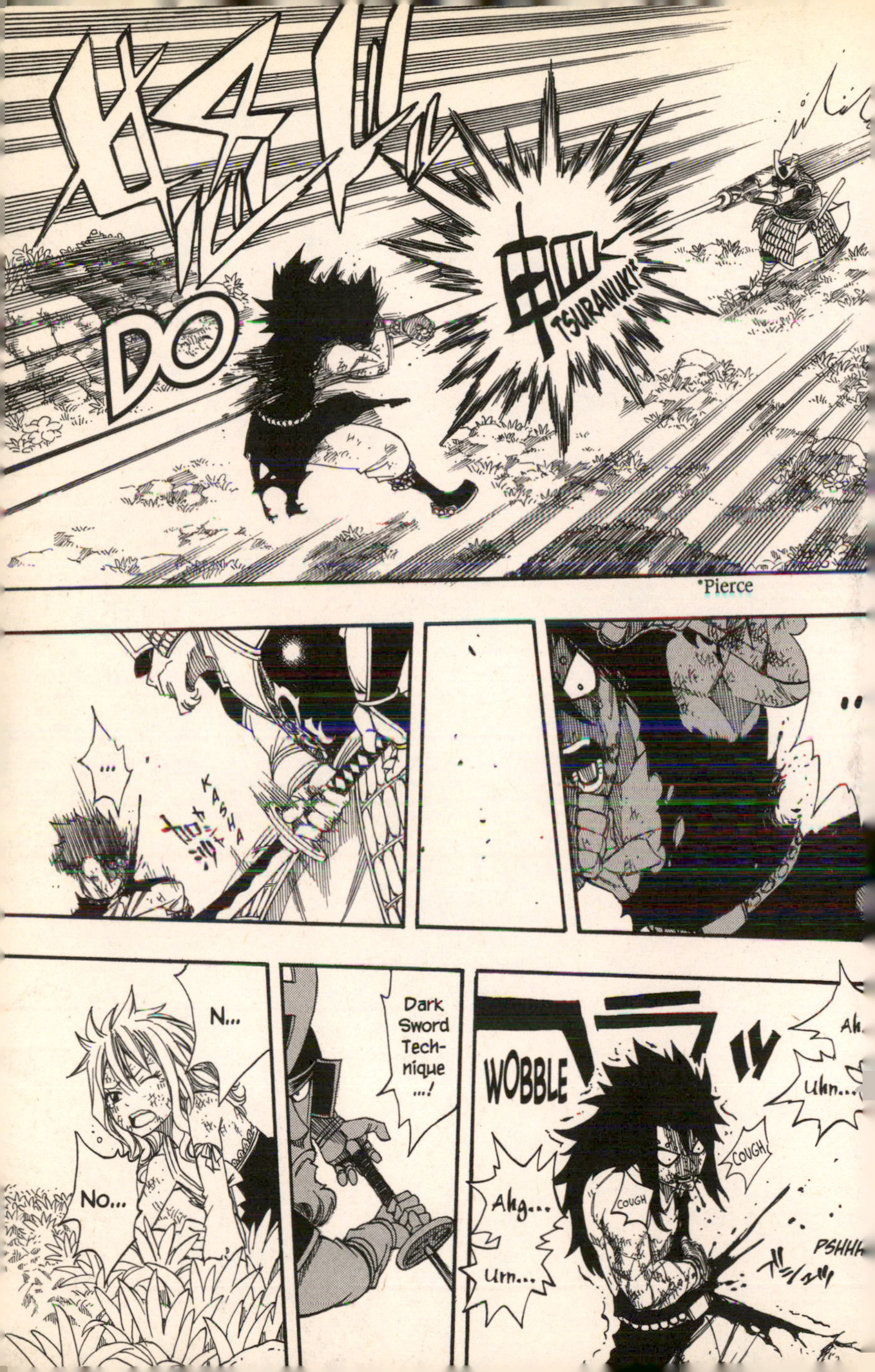
TSURANUKI*
DO
*Pierce
..
...
KASHA
Ah...
Uhn...
COUGH
COUGH
WOBBLE
Ahg...
Urn...
PSHHH
Dark Sword Technique...!
N...
No...

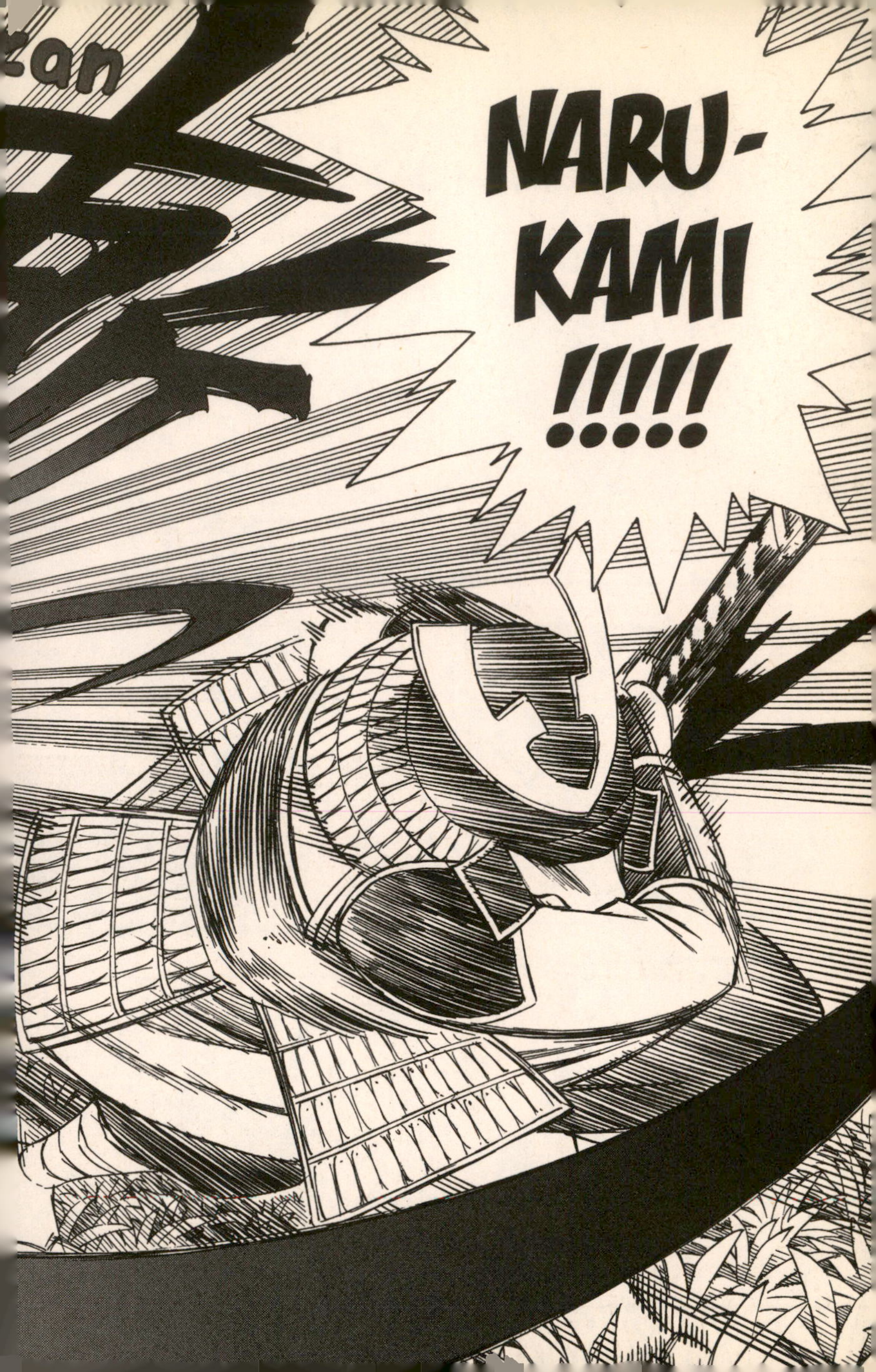
NARU-KAMI!!!!!
zan

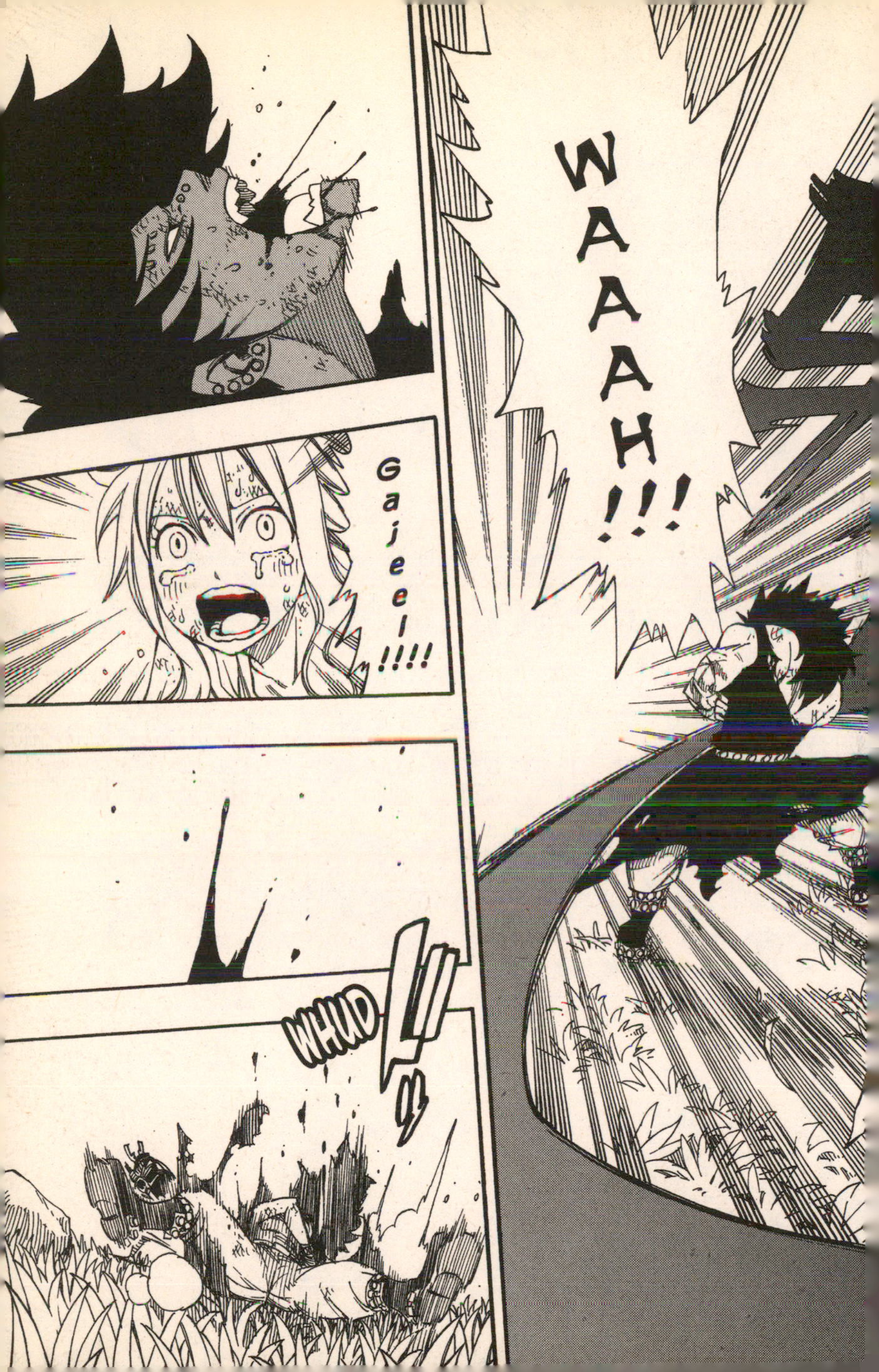
WAAAH!!!
Gajeeel!!!!
WHUD

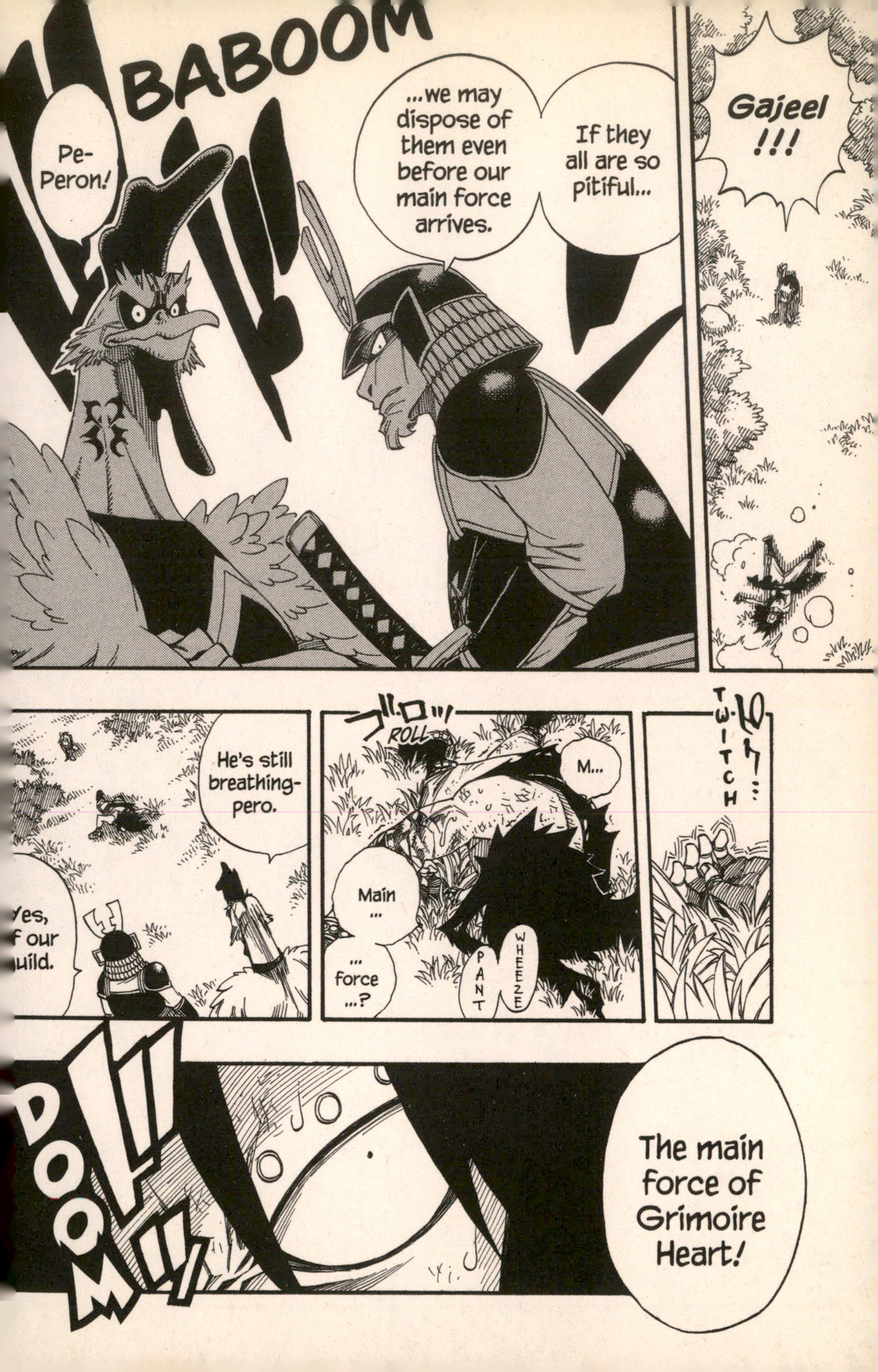
Gajeel !!!
If they all are so pitiful...
...we may dispose of them even before our main force arrives.
BABOOM
Pe-Peron!
TWITCH
ROLL
M...
Main ...
... force ...?
WHEEZE
PANT
He's still breathing-pero.
yes, f our uild.
The main force of Grimoire Heart!
DOOM!!!

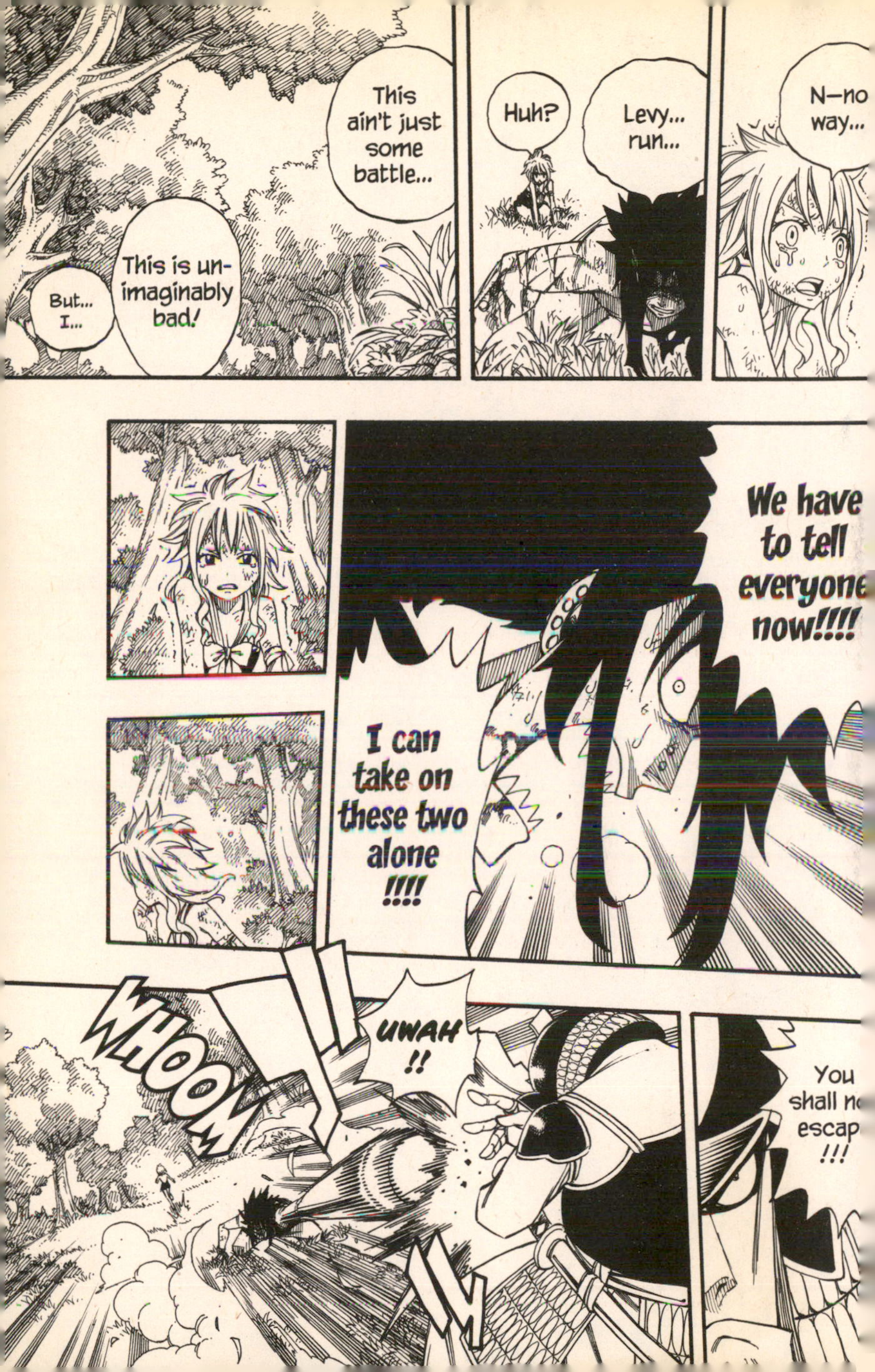
N—no way...
Levy... run...
Huh?
This ain't just some battle...
This is un-imaginably bad!
But... I...
We have to tell everyone now!!!!
I can take on these two alone !!!!
You shall n escap !!!
UWAH !!
WHOOM

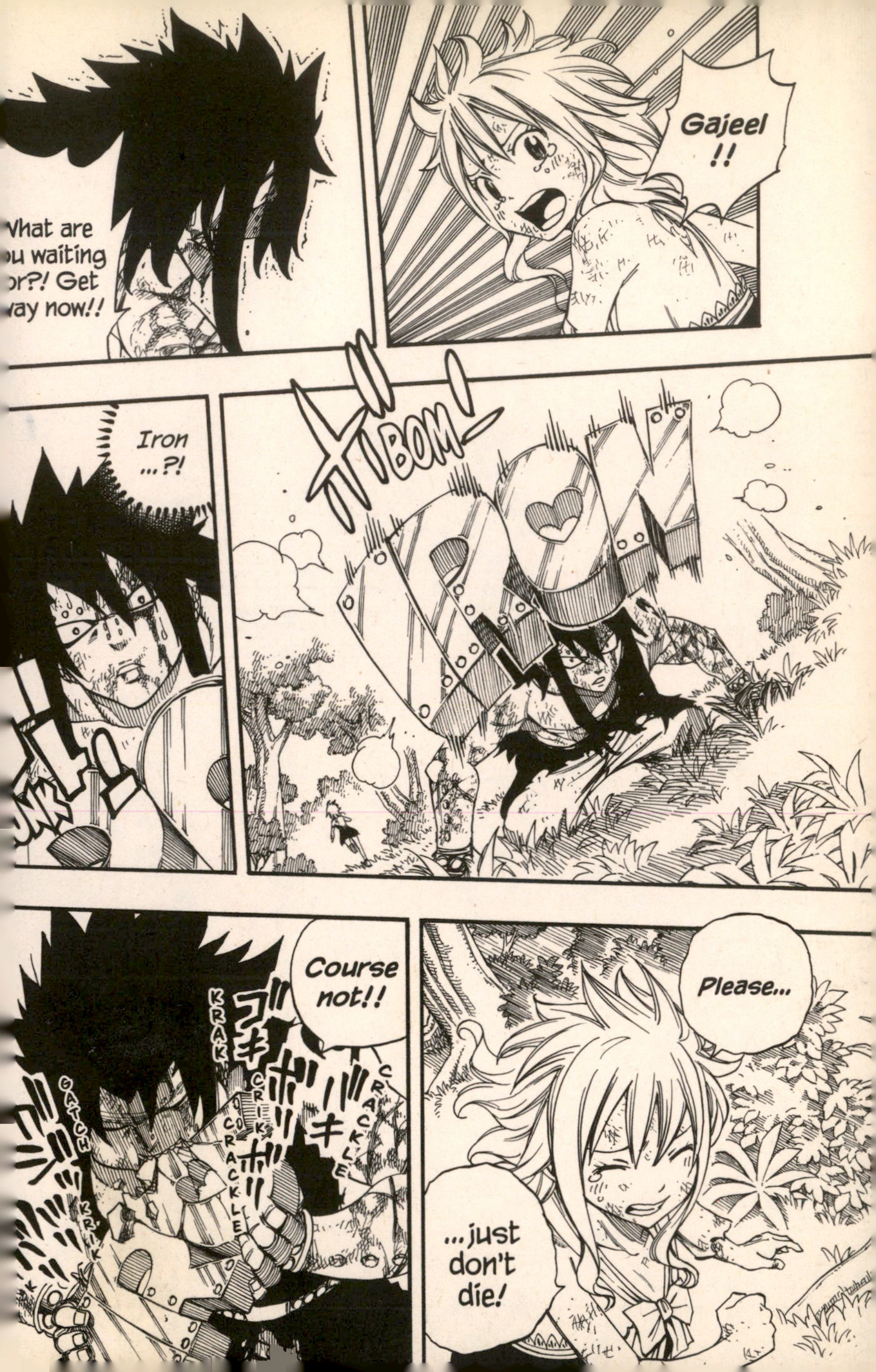
Gajeel !!
What are ou waiting or?! Get way now!!
BOM
Iron ...?!
Please...
...just don't die!
Course not!!
KRAK
CRIK
CRACKLE
CRACKLE
GATCH
KRIK

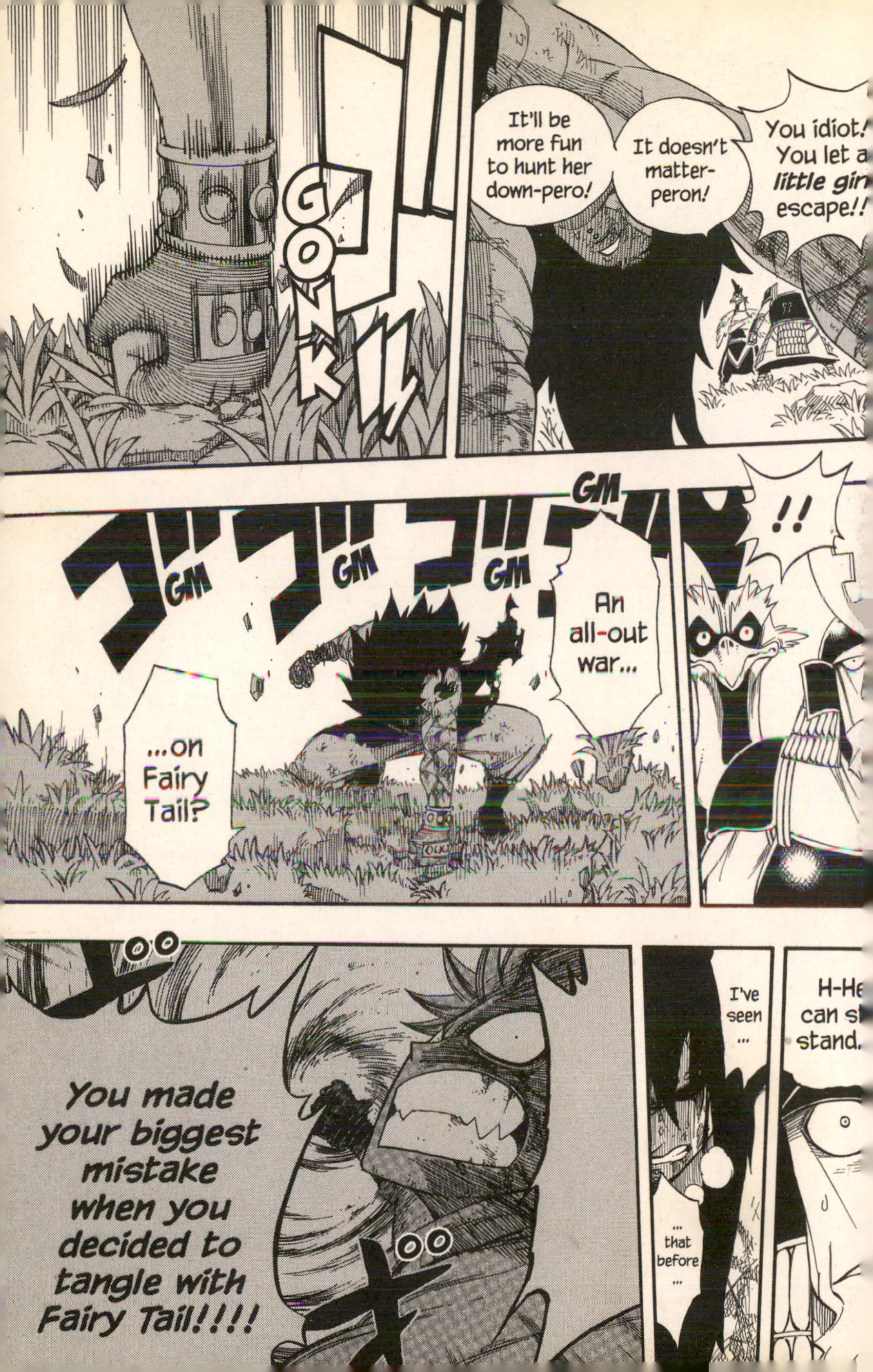
You idiot! You let a little gir escape!!
It doesn't matter-peron!
It'll be more fun to hunt her down-pero!
GONK!!
!!
GM GM GM GM
An all-out war...
...on Fairy Tail?
H-He can s stand.
I've seen ...
... that before ...
You made your biggest mistake when you decided to tangle with Fairy Tail!!!!

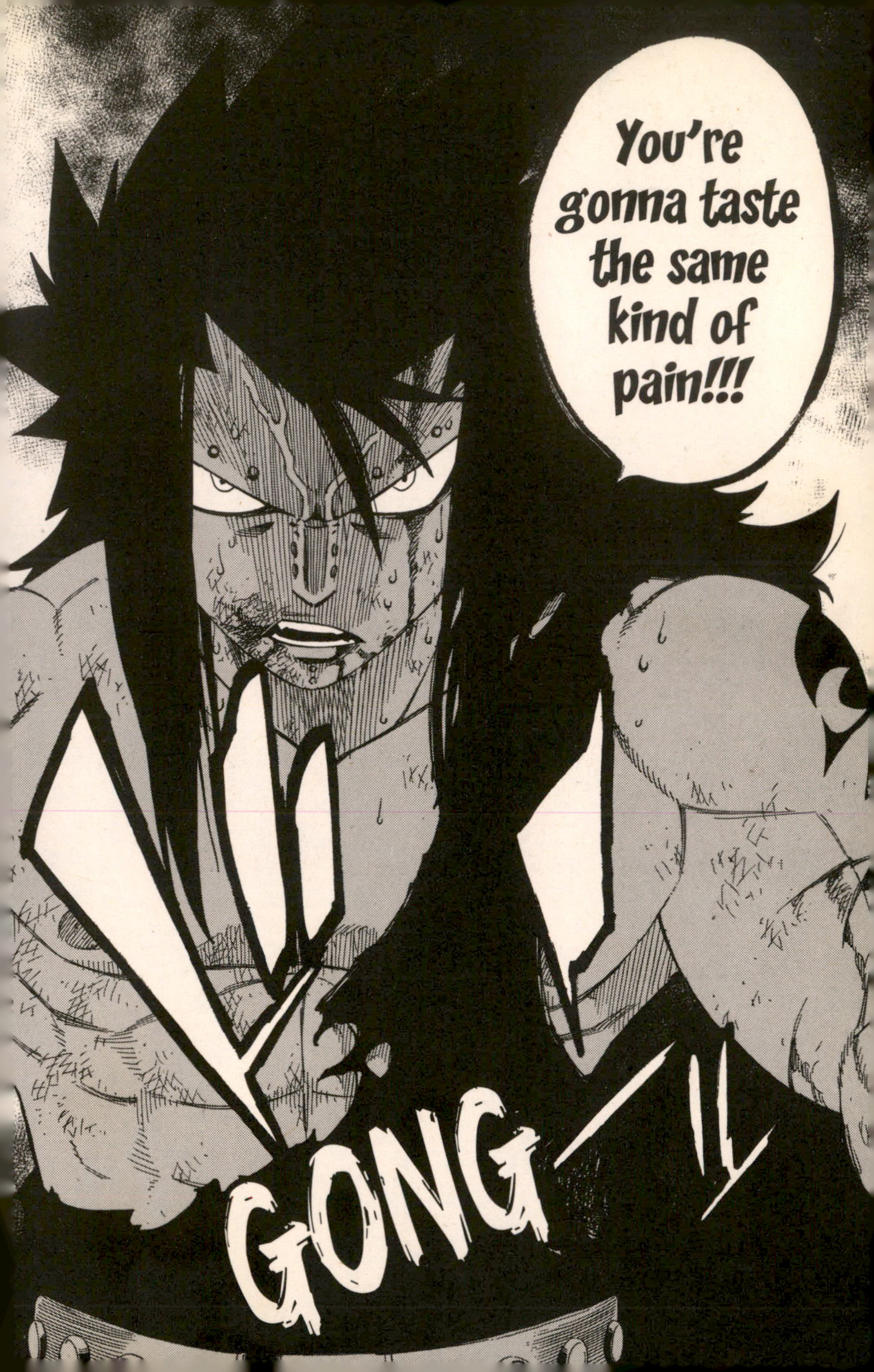
You're gonna taste the same kind of pain!!!
GONG

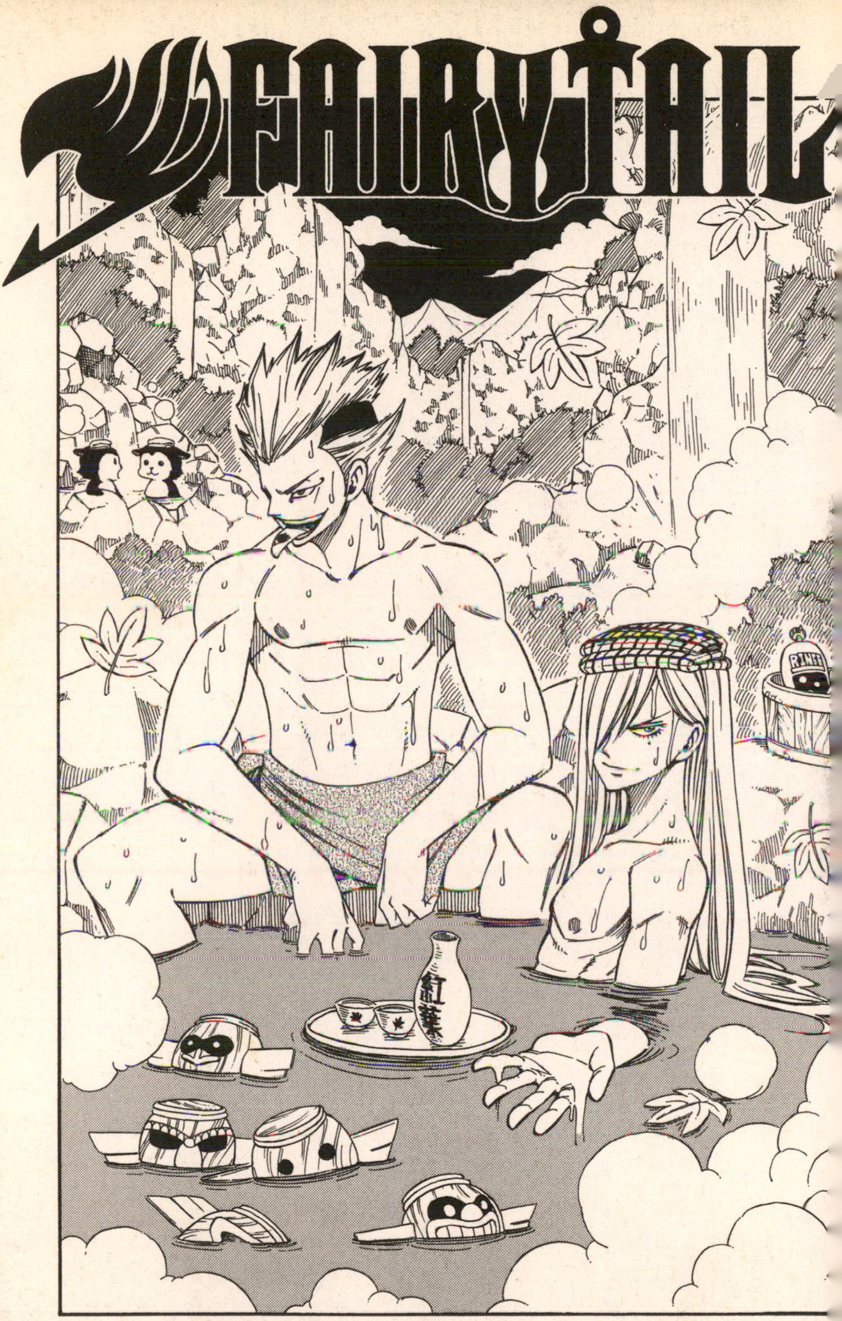
FAIRY TAIL
紅葉

Chapter 212: Soul of Iron

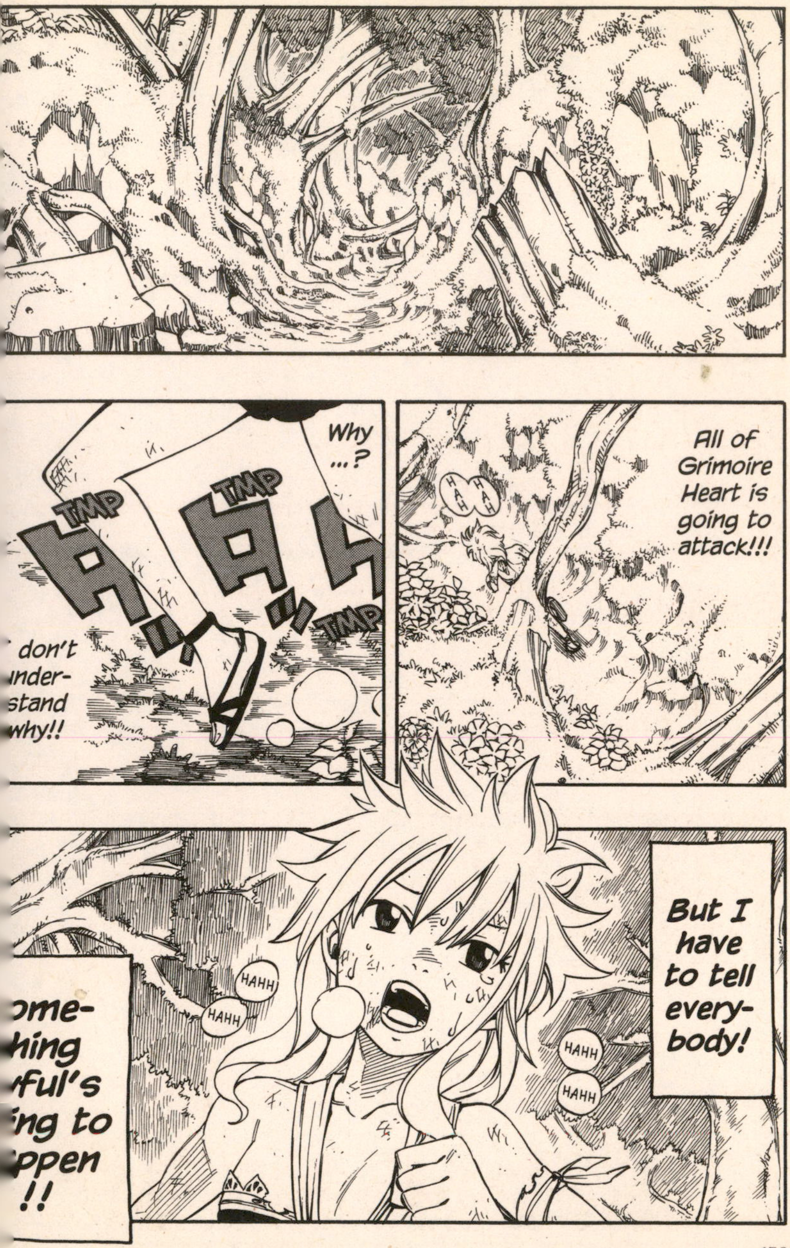

All of Grimoire Heart is going to attack!!!
HAH
HAH
Why ...?
TMP
TMP
TMP
don't nder-stand why!!
But I have to tell every-body!
HAHH
HAHH
HAHH
HAHH
ome-hing ful's ing to ppen !!

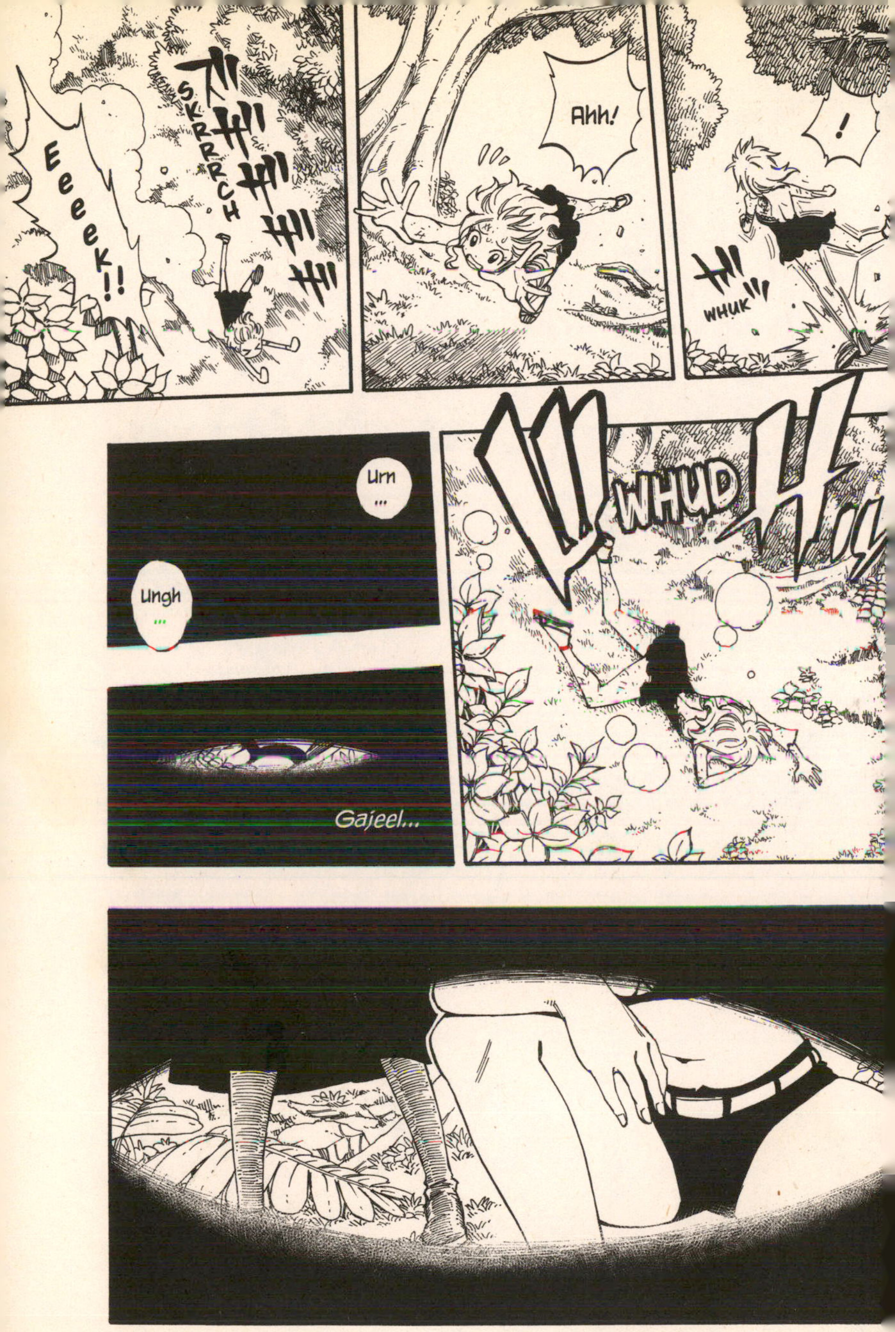

!
WHUK
Ahh!
Eeeek!!
SKRRRCH
WHUD
Urn...
Ungh...
Gajeel...

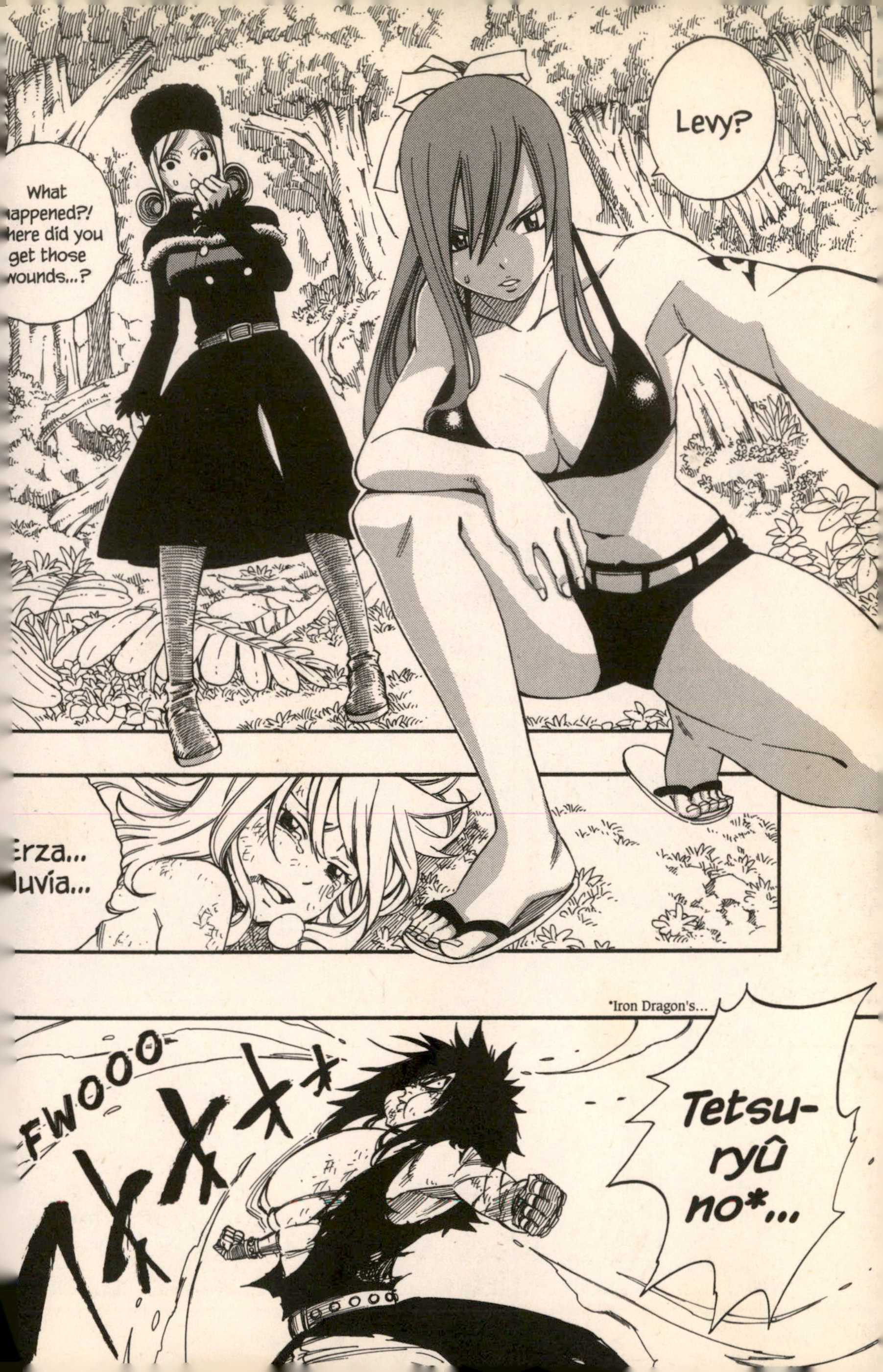
Levy?
What appened?! here did you get those wounds...?
Erza... uvia...
Tetsu-ryû no*...
FWOOO
*Iron Dragon's...

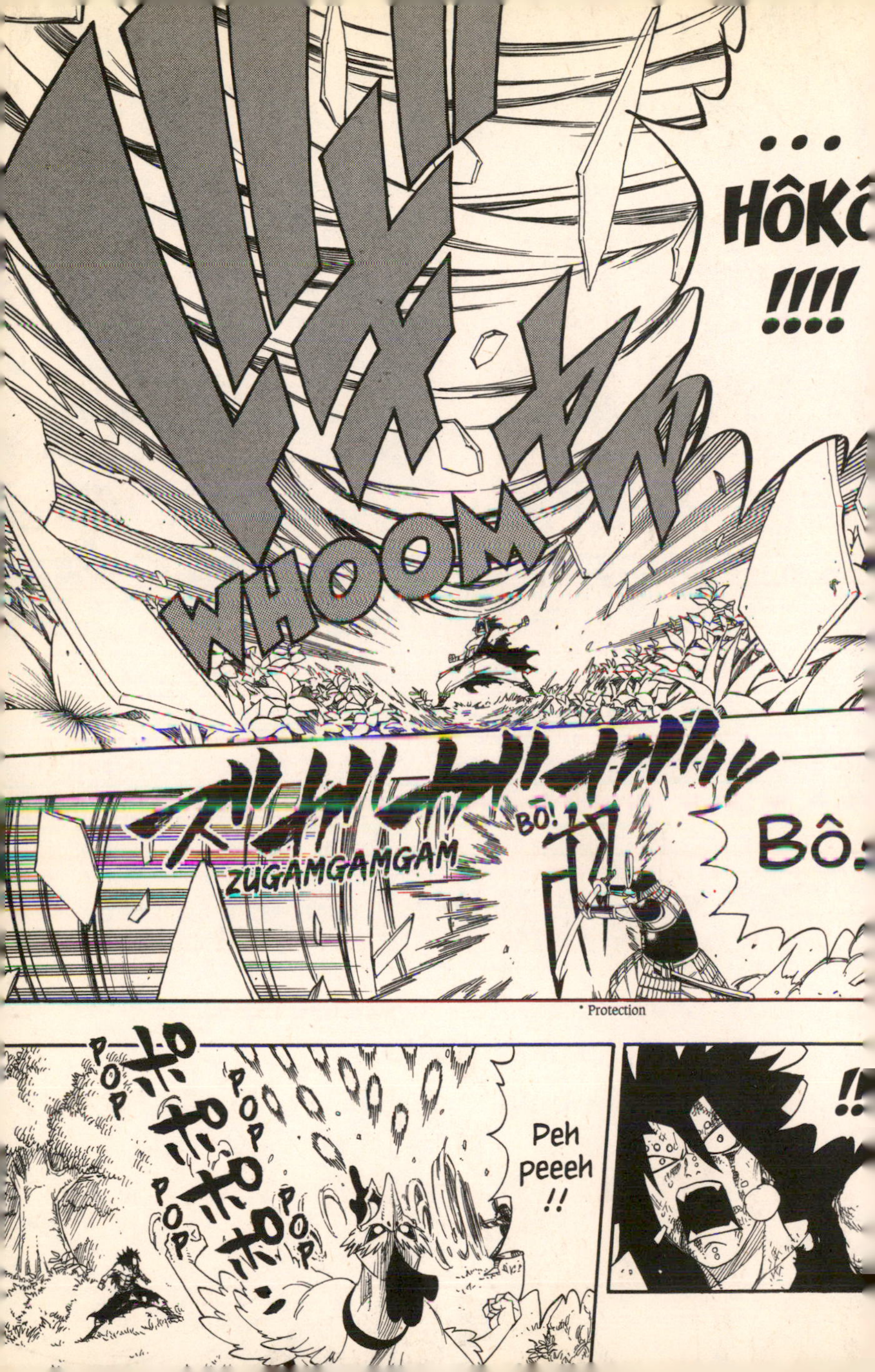
... HÔKÔ !!!!
WHOOM
Bô.
BÔ!
ZUGAMGAMGAM
!!
Peh peeeh !!
POP
POP
POP
POP
POP
POP
* Protection

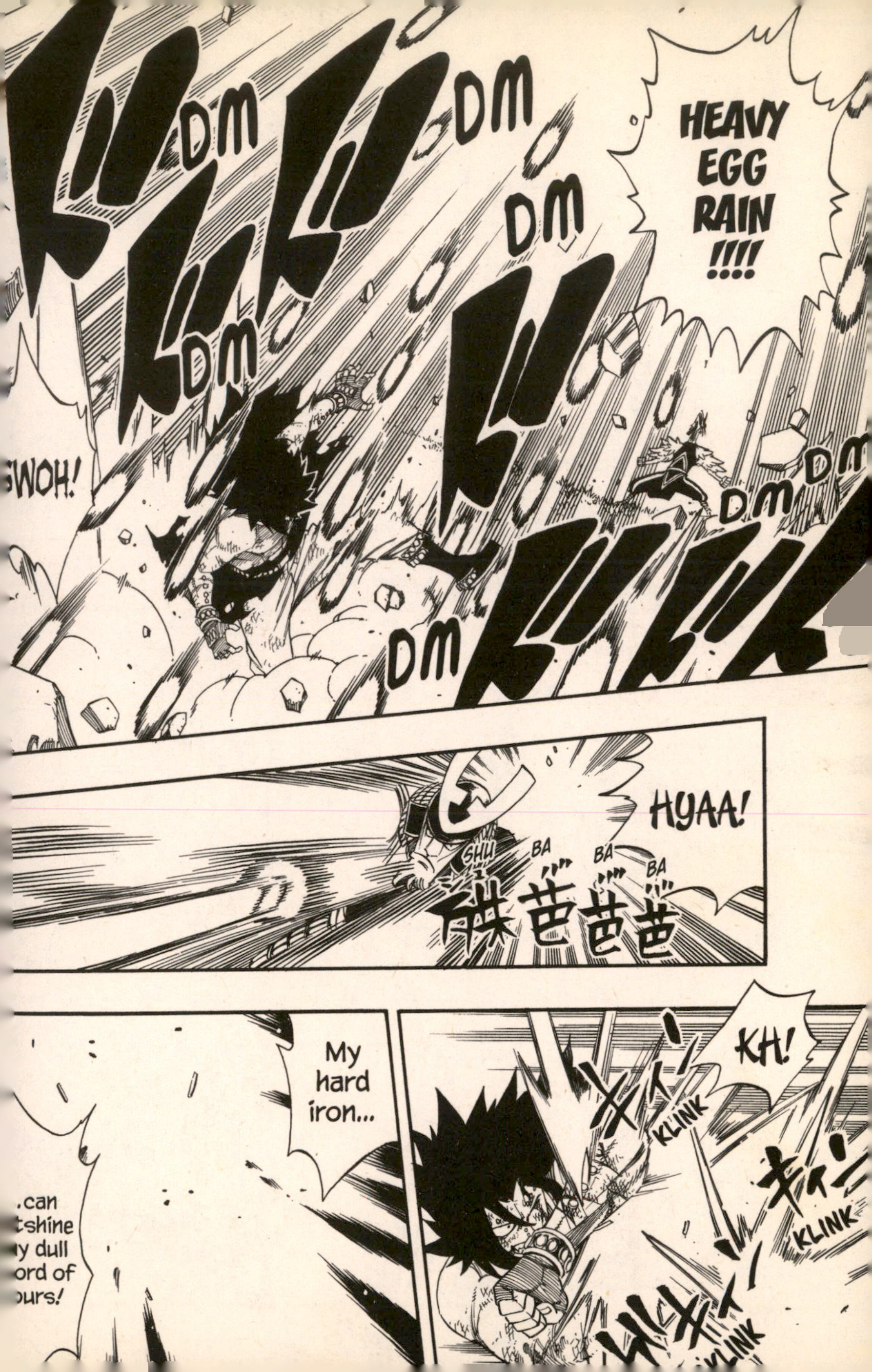

HEAVY EGG RAIN!!!!
DM DM DM DM DM DM DM DM DM
SWOH!
HYAA!
SHU BA BA BA
KH!
KLINK
KLINK
KLINK
My hard iron...
.can tshine y dull ord of ours!

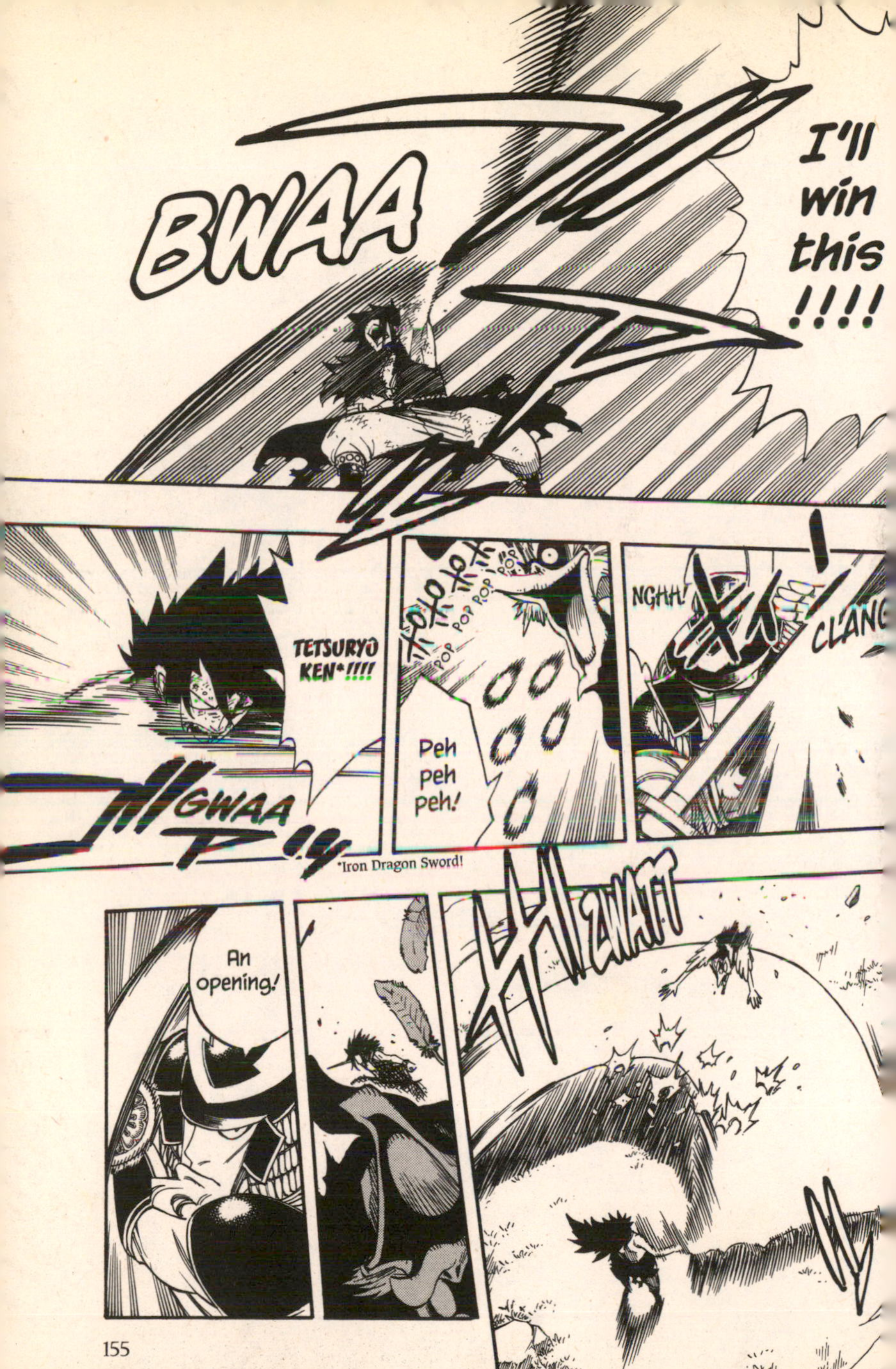
I'll win this!!!!
BWAA
NGHH!
CLANG
POP POP POP POP
Peh peh peh!
TETSURYO KEN*!!!!
MGWAAP
An opening!

*Iron Dragon Sword!

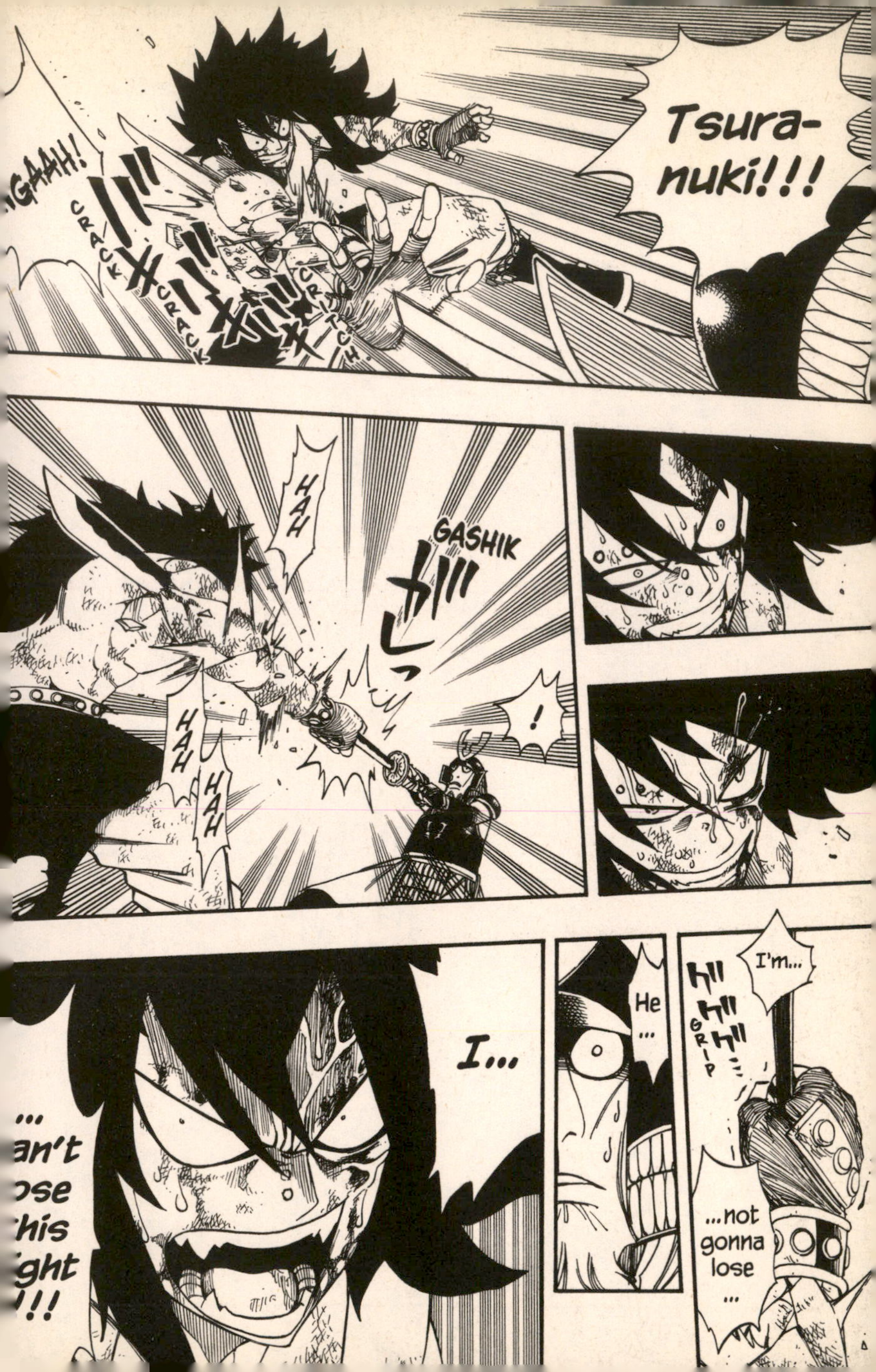
Tsura-
nuki!!!
CRUTCH
CRACK
CRACK
GAAH!
!
HAH
GASHIK
HAH
HAH
I'm...
GRIP
...not
gonna
lose
...
He
...
I...
...
an't
ose
this
ight
!!

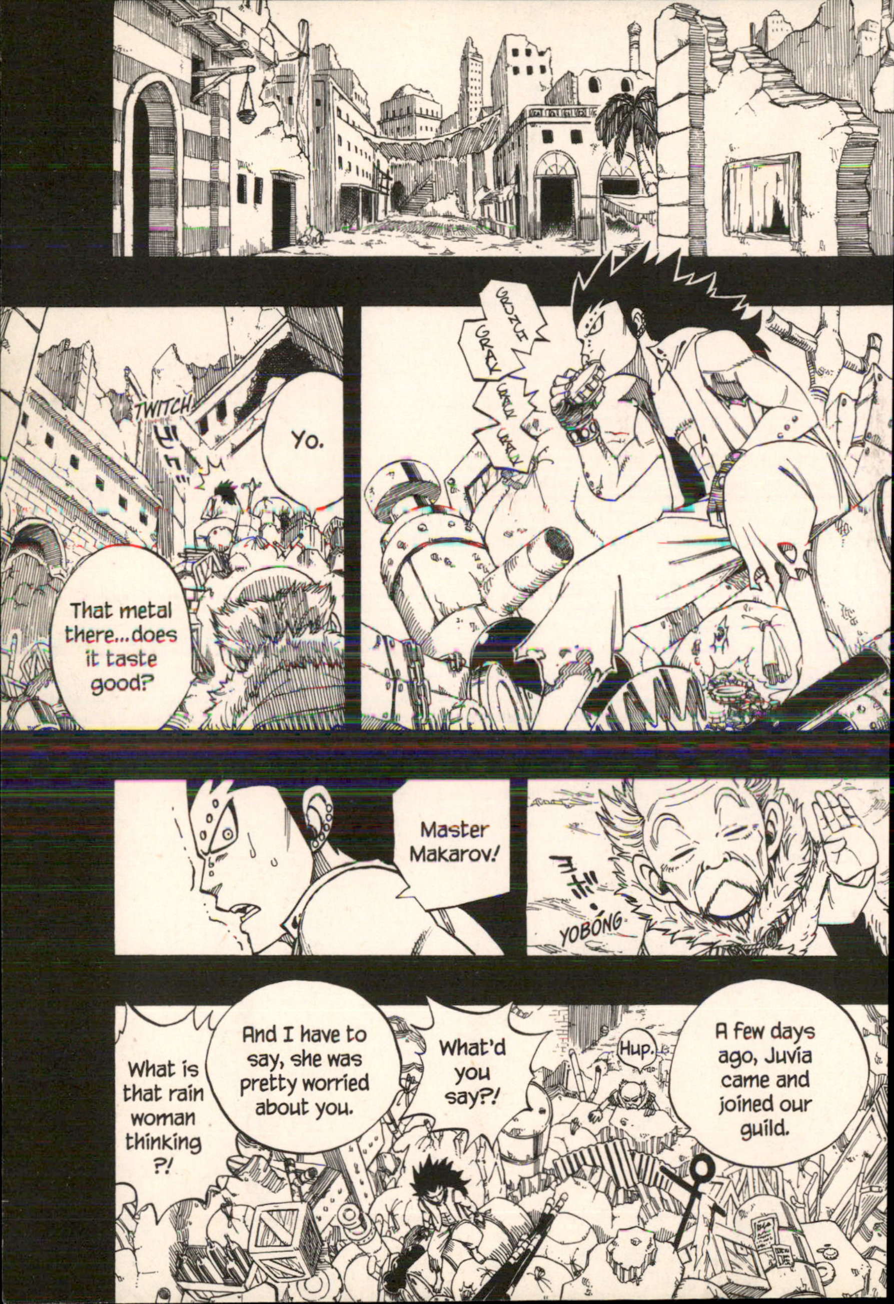
CRUNCH
CRACK
TWITCH
Yo.
That metal there...does it taste good?
YOBONG
Master Makarov!
A few days ago, Juvia came and joined our guild.
Hup.
What'd you say?!
And I have to say, she was pretty worried about you.
What is that rain woman thinking?!

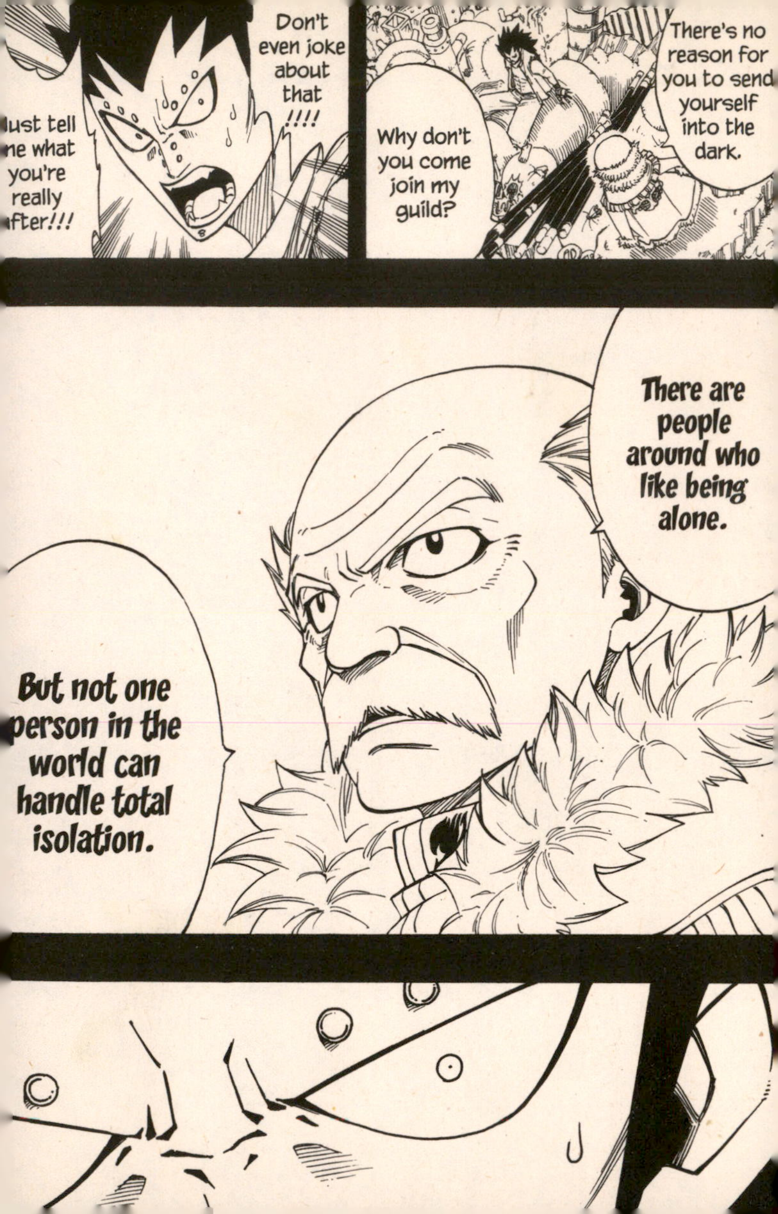
There's no reason for you to send yourself into the dark.
Why don't you come join my guild?
Don't even joke about that!!!!
Just tell me what you're really after!!!
There are people around who like being alone.
But not one person in the world can handle total isolation.

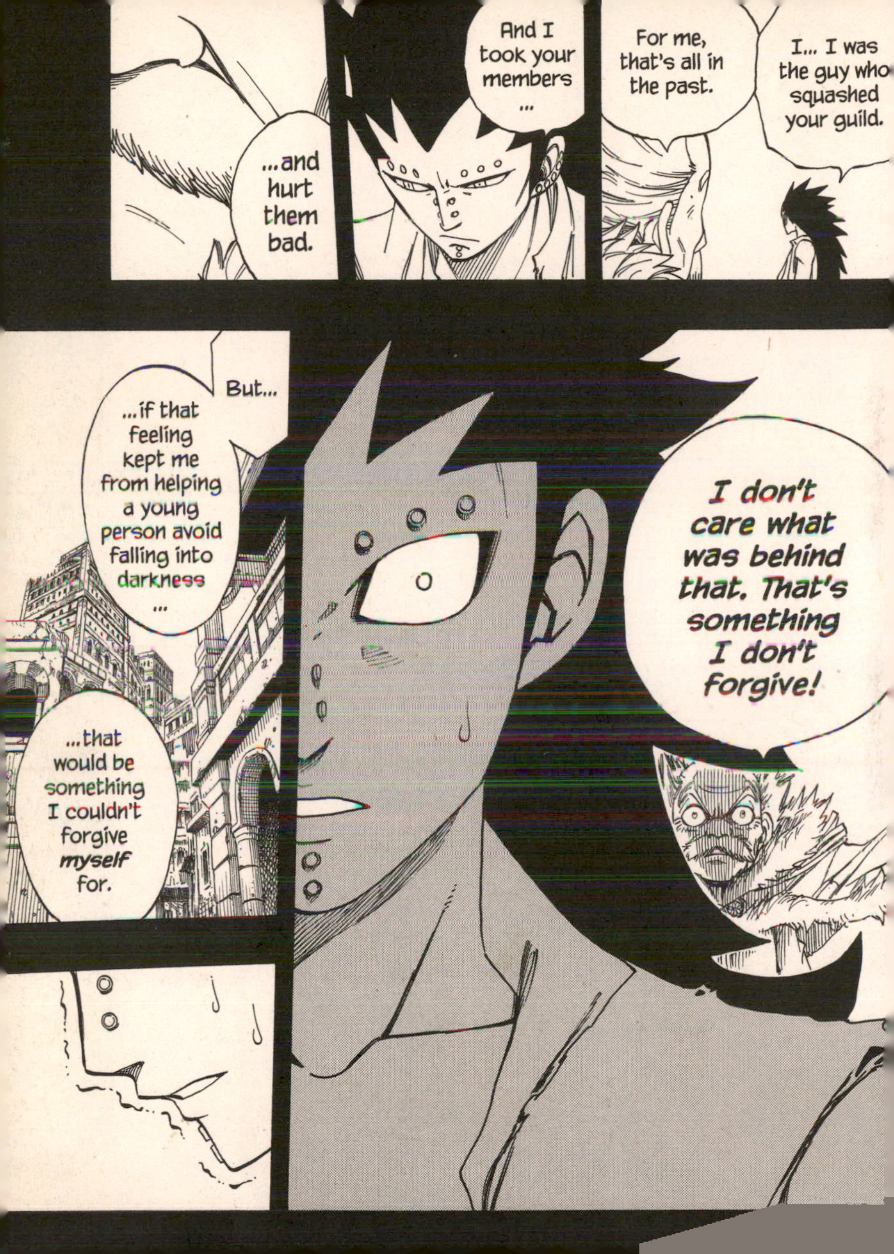
I... I was the guy who squashed your guild.
For me, that's all in the past.
And I took your members ...
...and hurt them bad.
I don't care what was behind that. That's something I don't forgive!
But...
...if that feeling kept me from helping a young person avoid falling into darkness ...
...that would be something I couldn't forgive *myself* for.

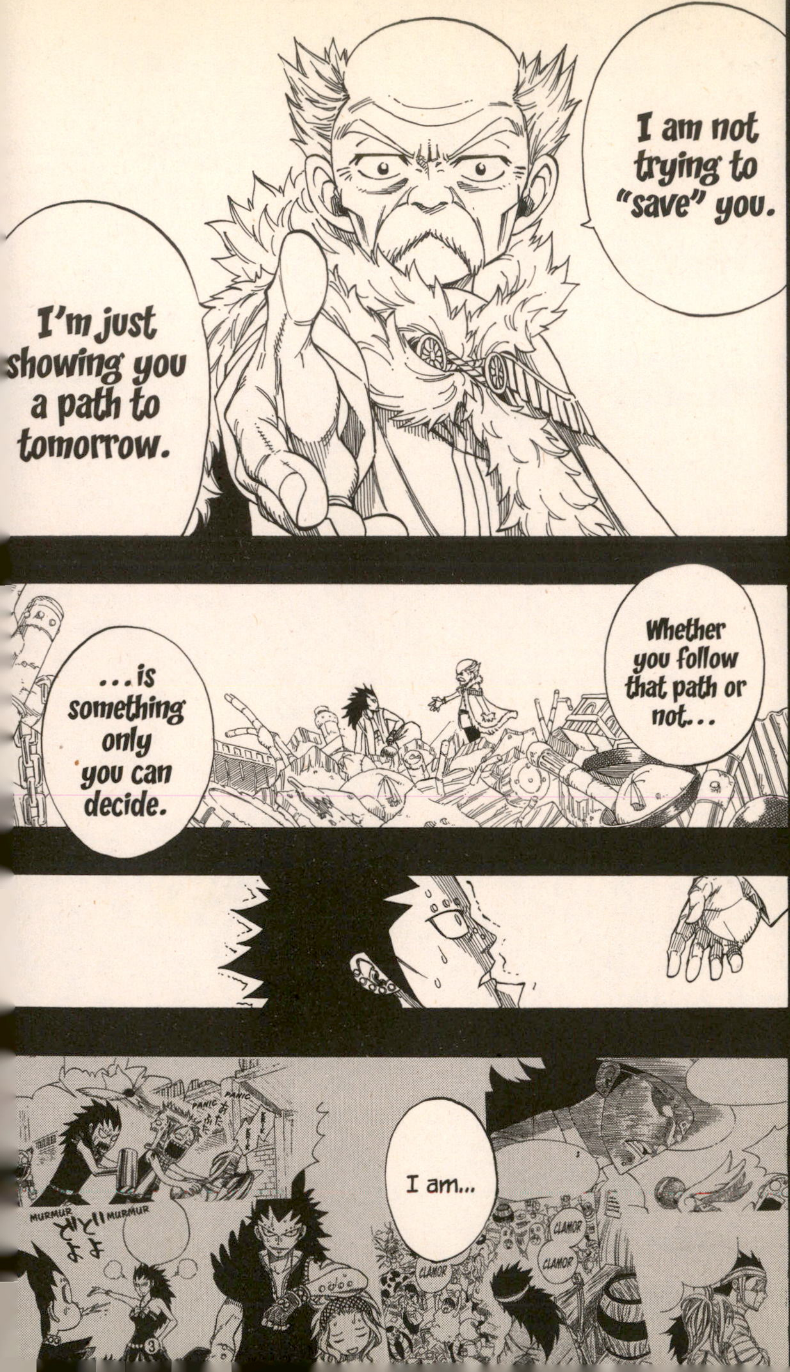
I am not trying to "save" you.
I'm just showing you a path to tomorrow.
Whether you follow that path or not...
...is something only you can decide.
PANIC
PANIC
I am...
CLAMOR
CLAMOR
CLAMOR
MURMUR
MURMUR

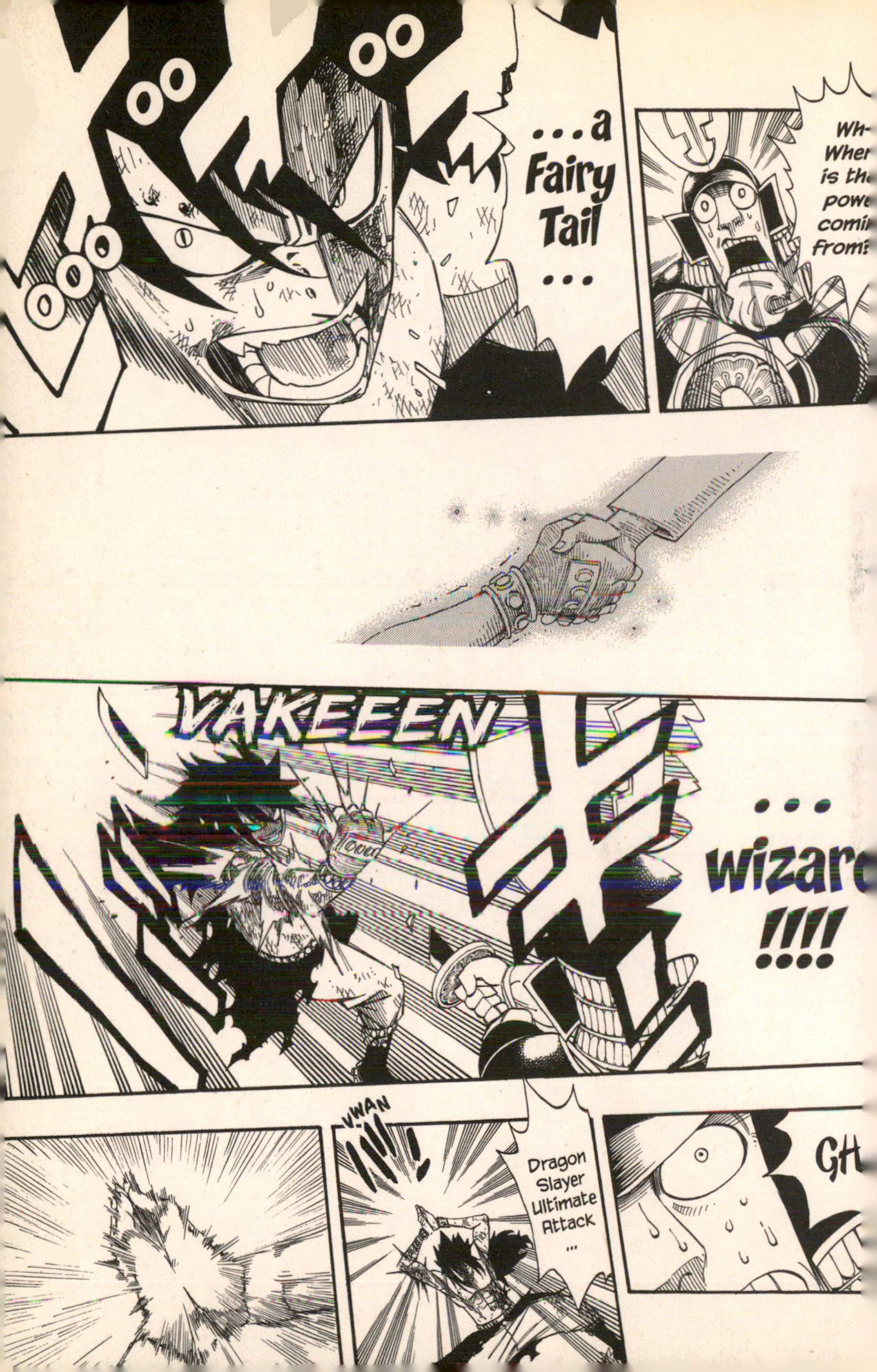
Wh- Wher is th powe comi from!?
...a Fairy Tail ...
VAKEEEN
... wizar !!!!
GH
Dragon Slayer Ultimate Attack ...
V-WAN

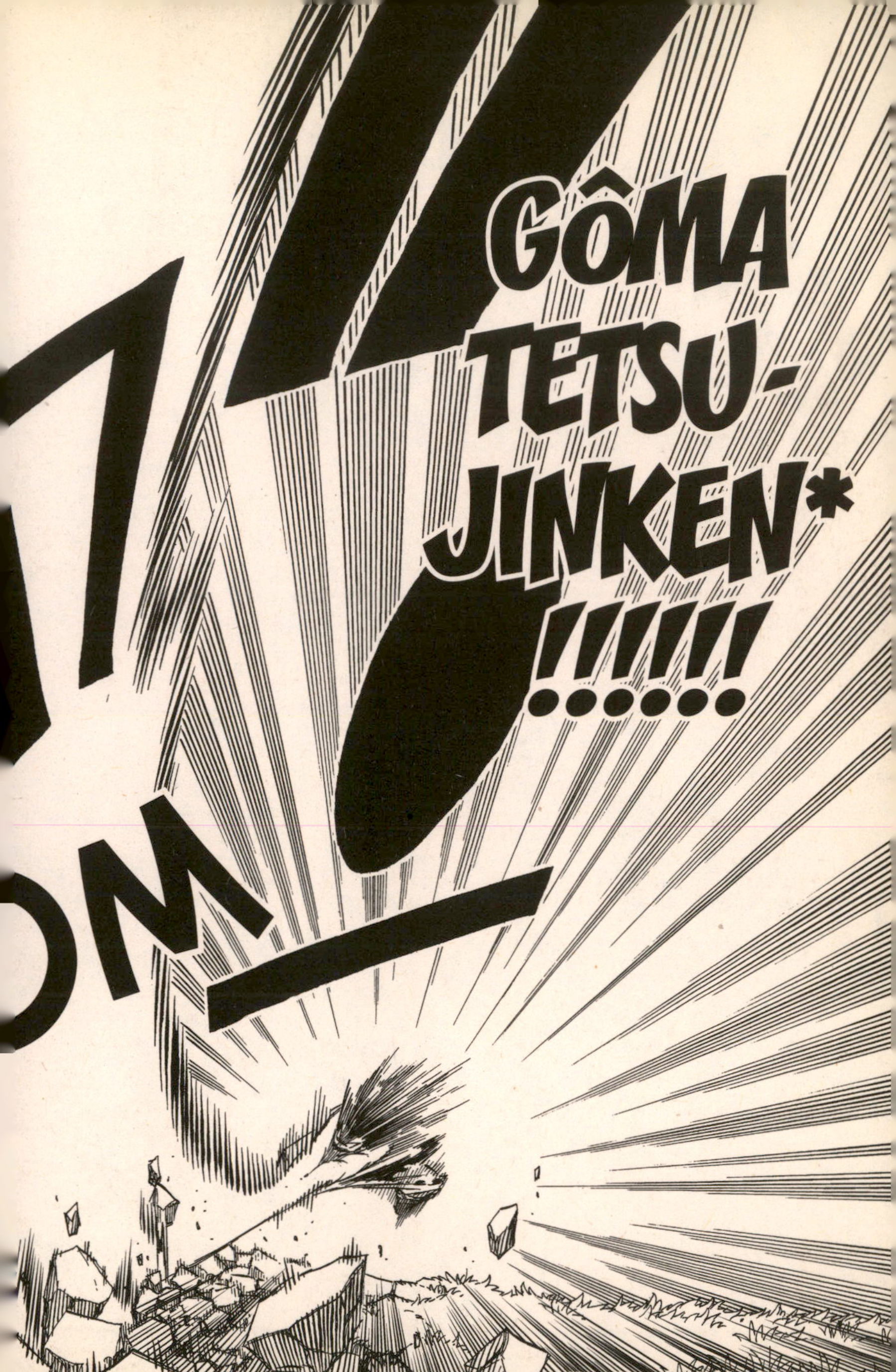
GÔMA TETSU-JINKEN* !!!!!!
*Karma Demon: Iron God Sword!

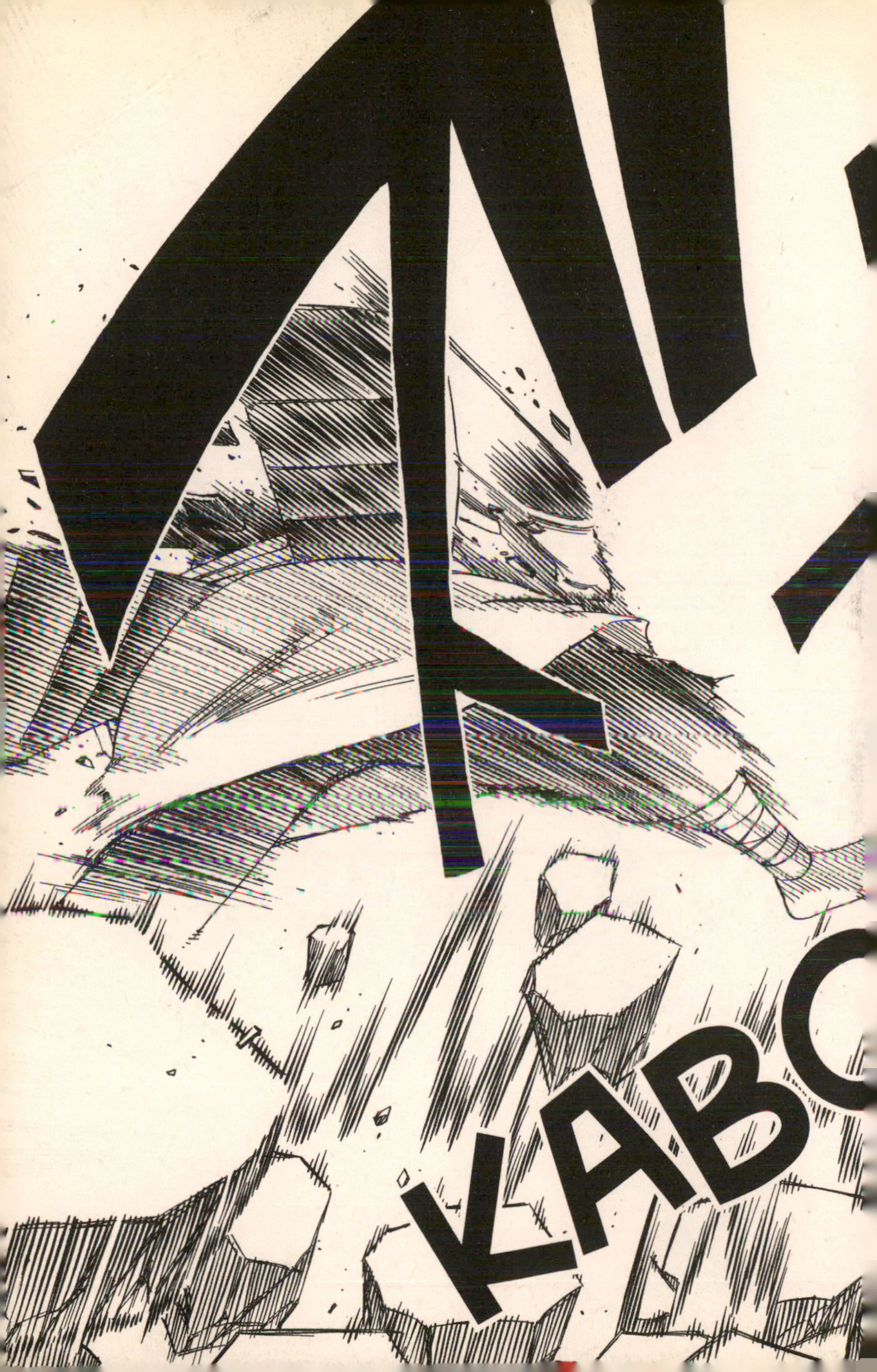
KAB

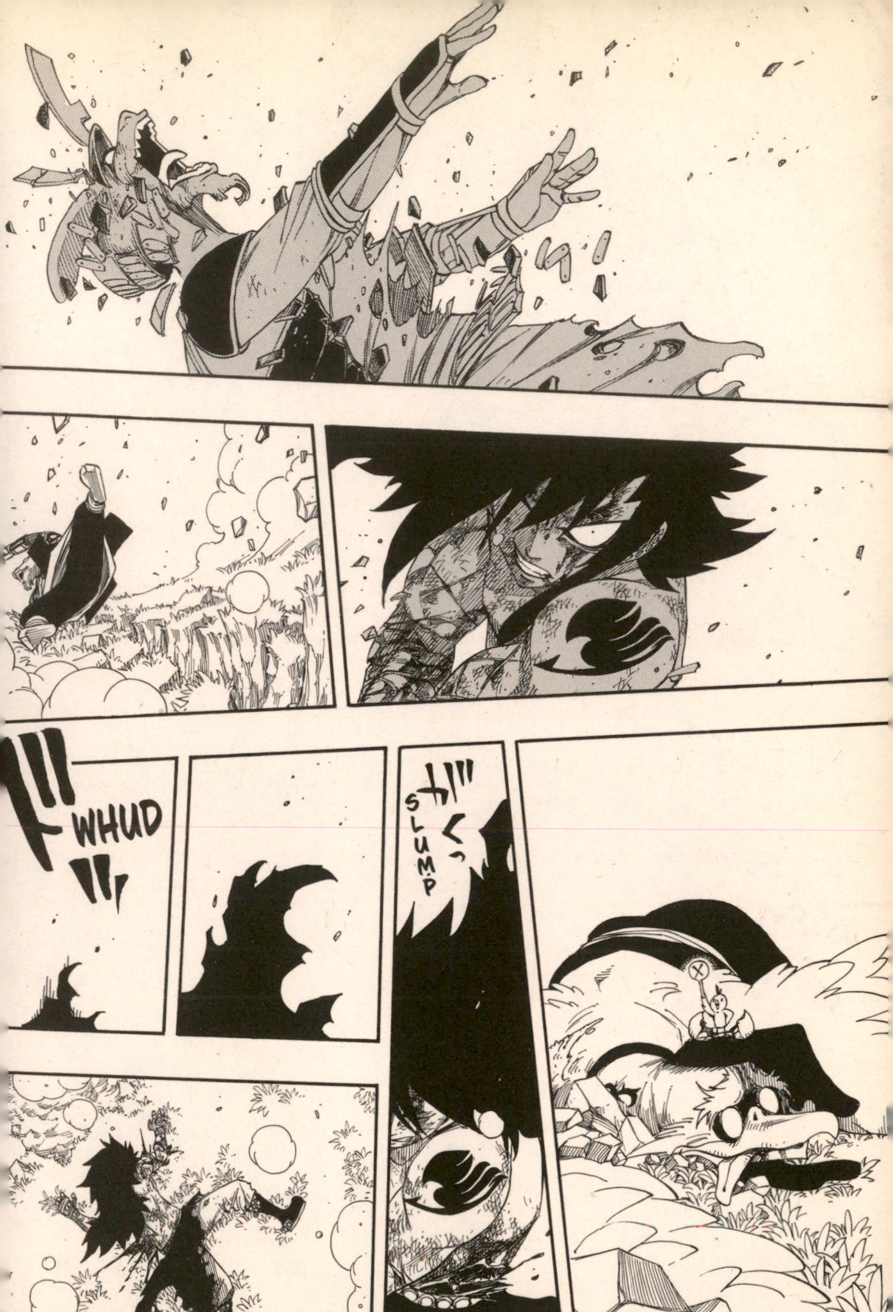
SLUMP
WHUD

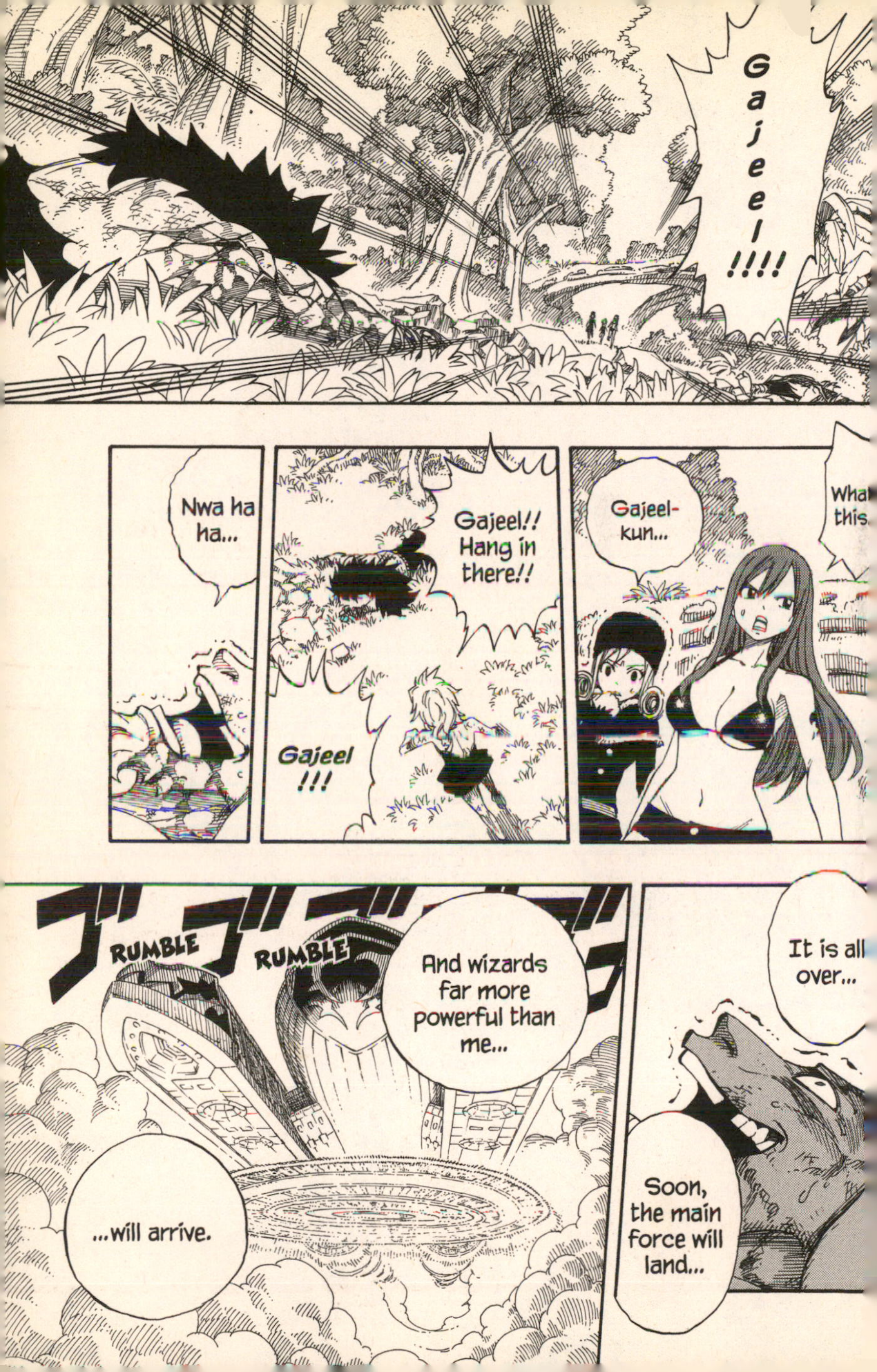
Gajeel!!!!
Wha this.
Gajeel-kun...
Gajeel!! Hang in there!!
Gajeel!!!
Nwa ha ha...
It is all over...
Soon, the main force will land...
RUMBLE
RUMBLE
And wizards far more powerful than me...
...will arrive.

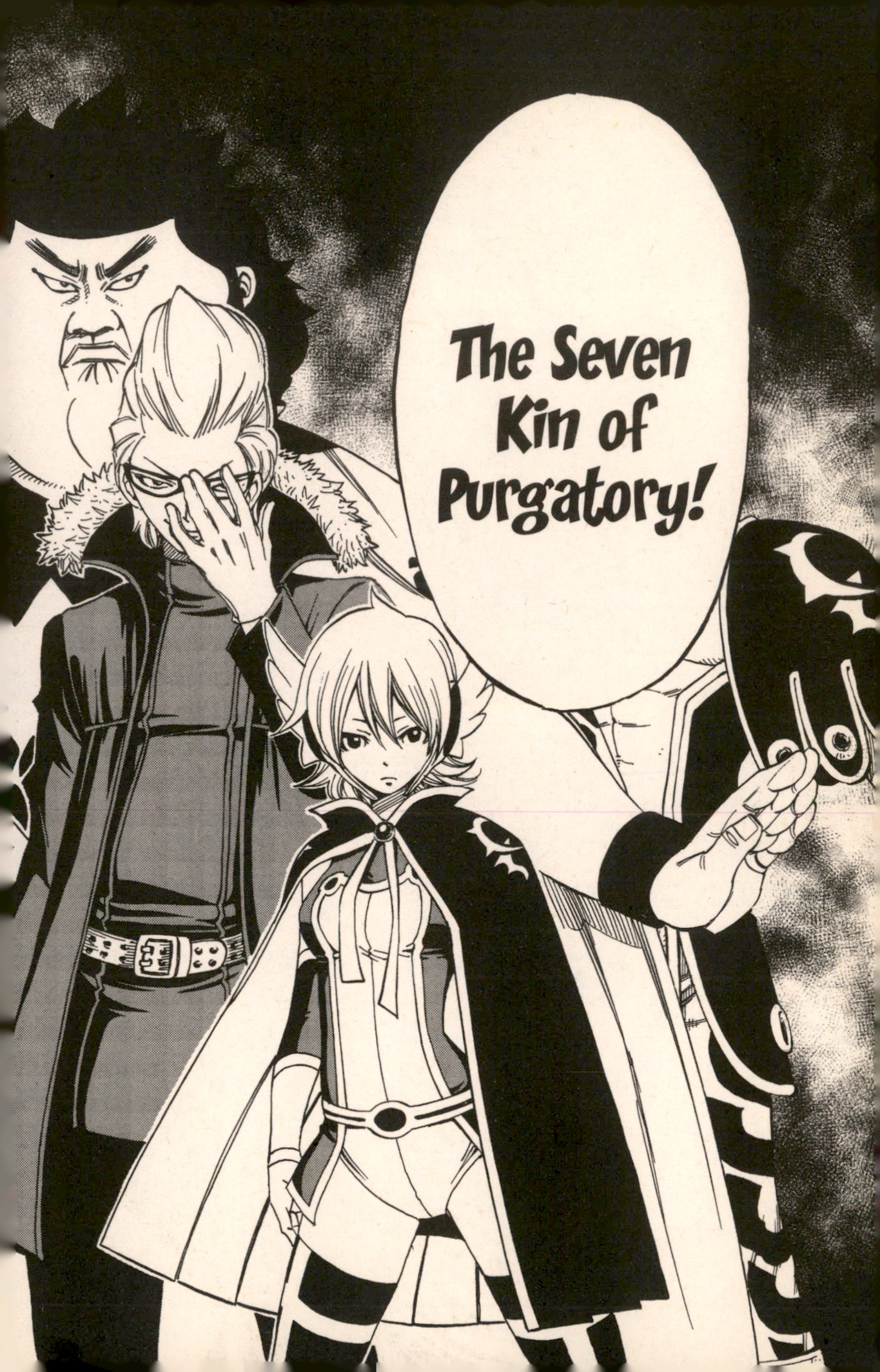
The Seven Kin of Purgatory!

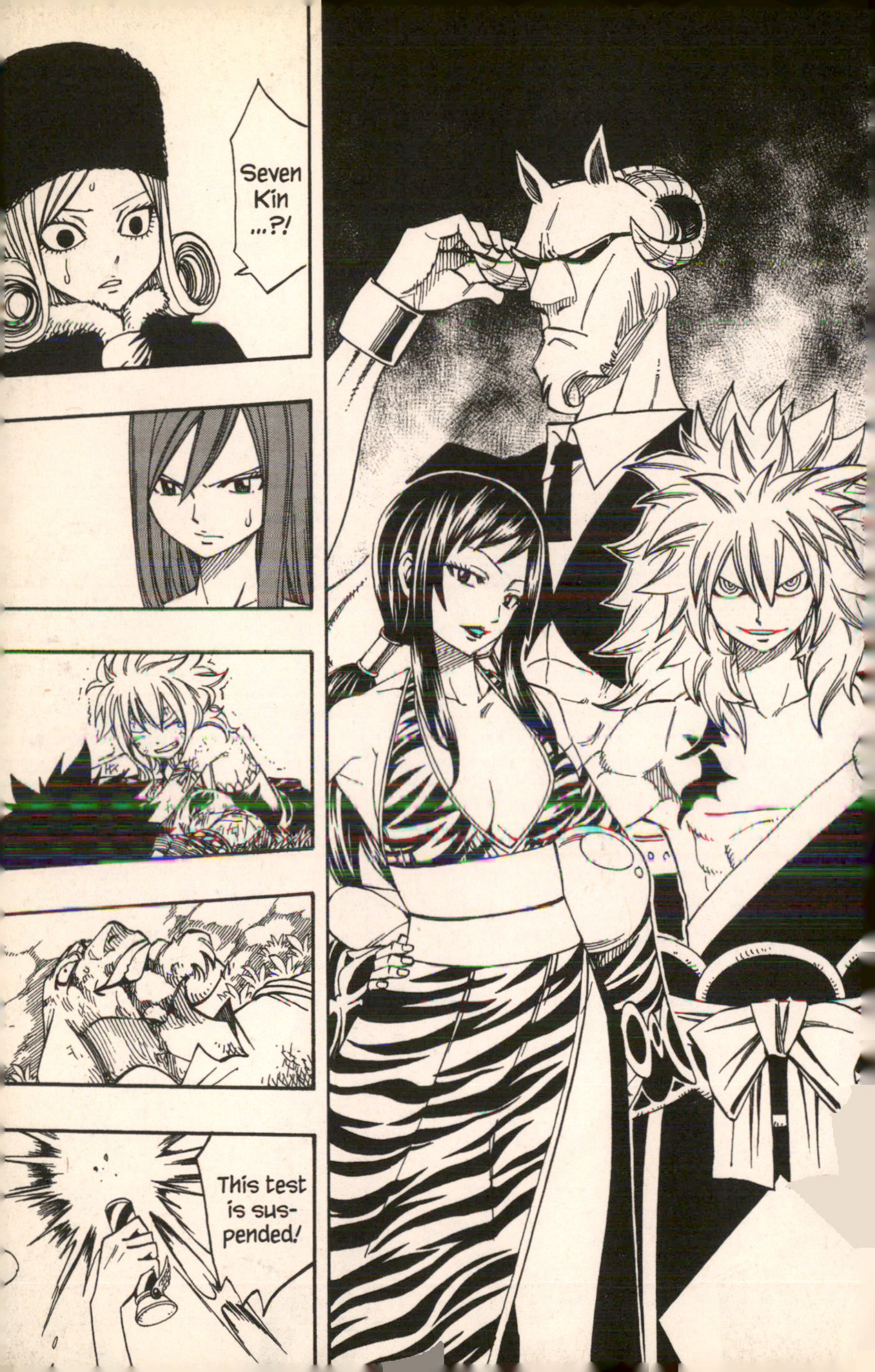
Seven Kin ...?!
This test is suspended!

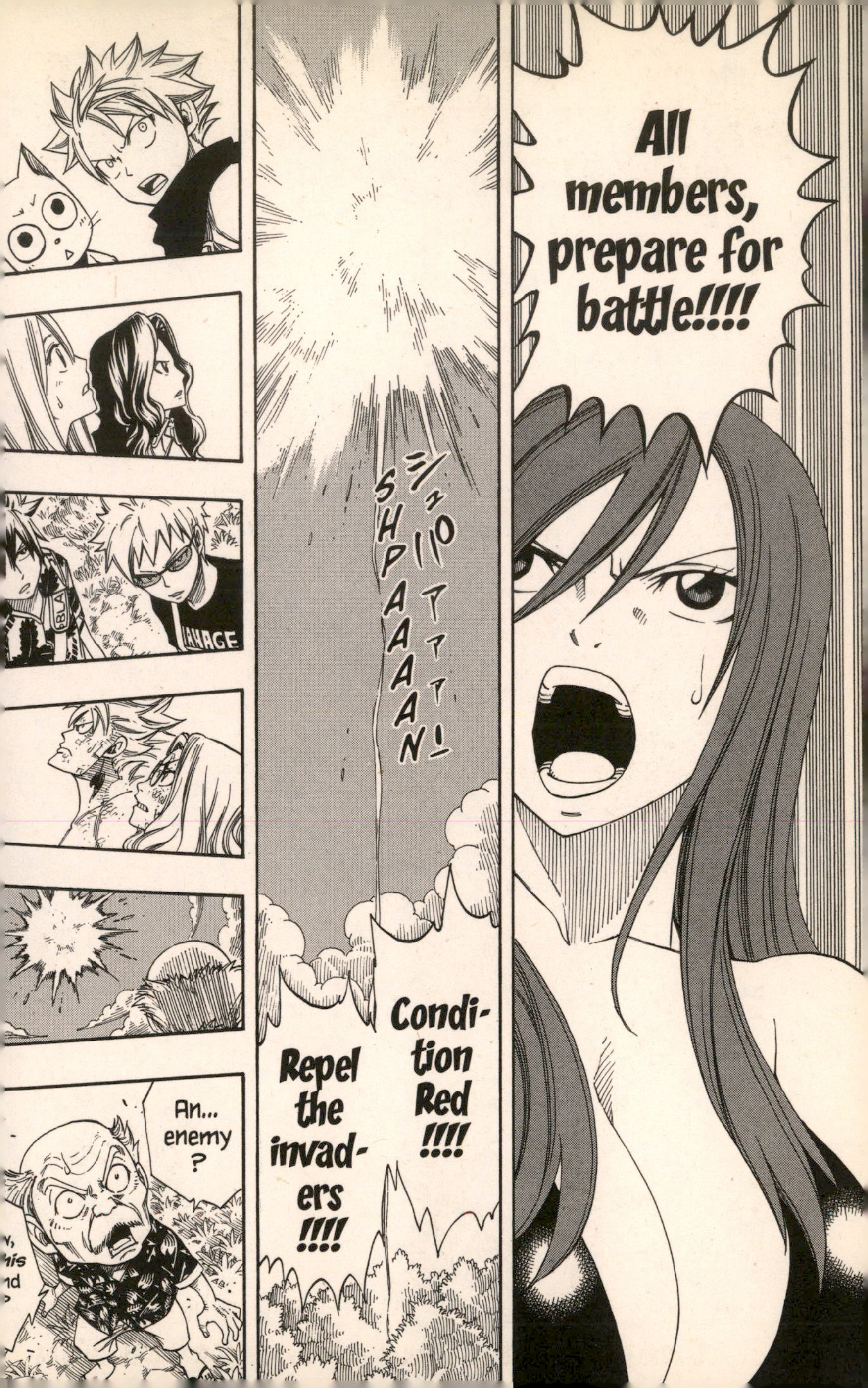
All members, prepare for battle!!!!
SHPAAAAAN
Condition Red!!!!
Repel the invaders!!!!
An... enemy?

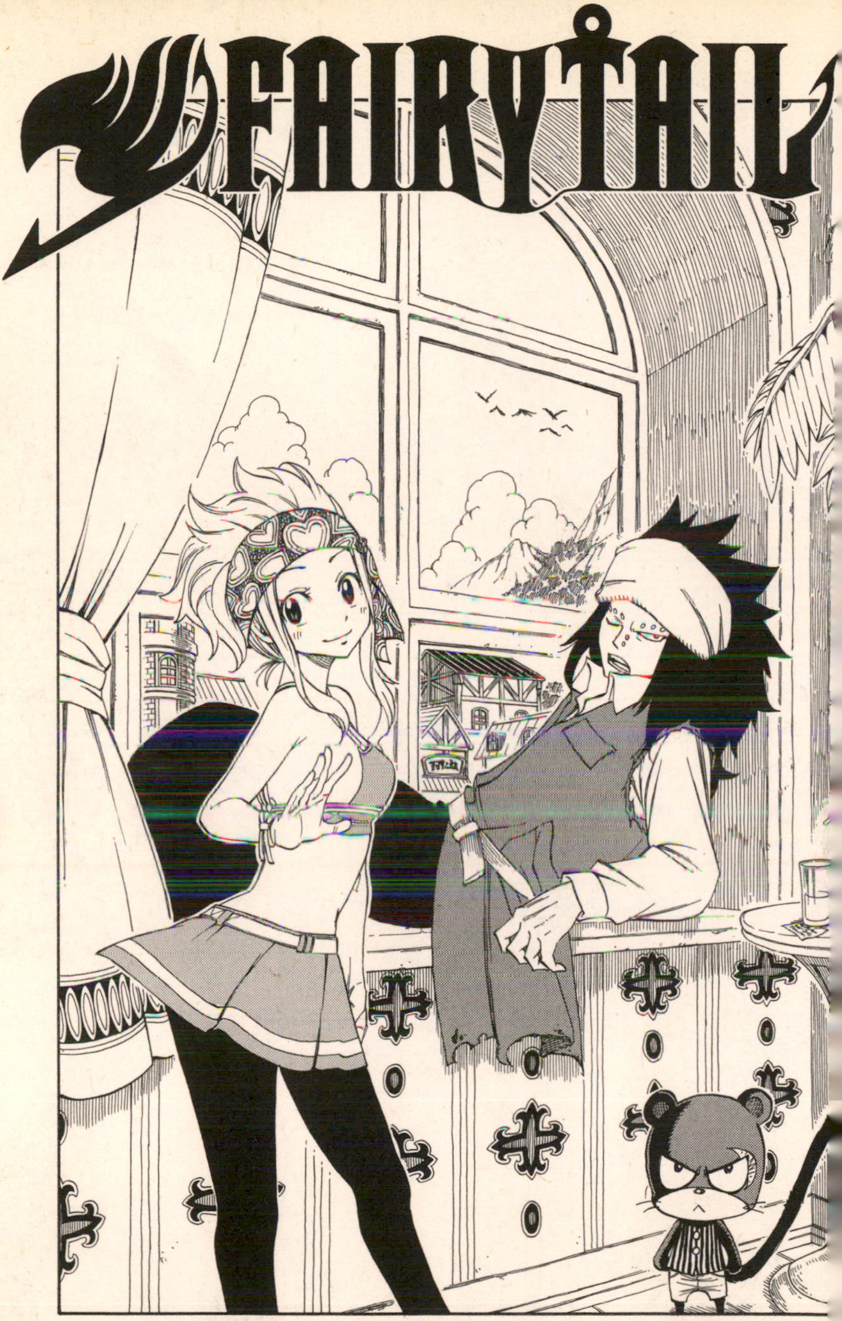
FAIRY TAIL

Chapter 213: One of the Seven Kin

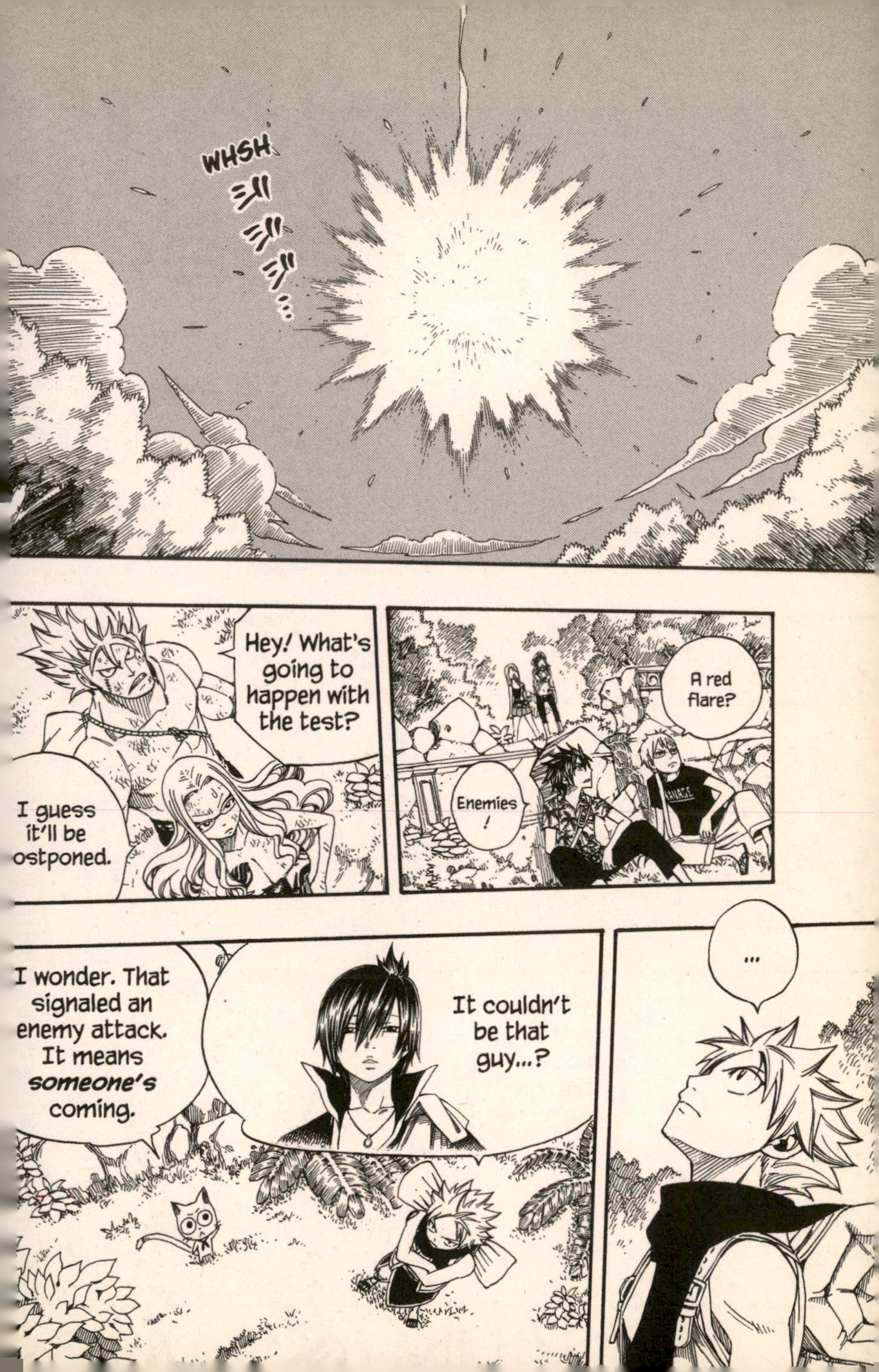
WHSH
A red flare?
Enemies!
Hey! What's going to happen with the test?
I guess it'll be ostponed.
...
It couldn't be that guy...?
I wonder. That signaled an enemy attack. It means *someone's* coming.

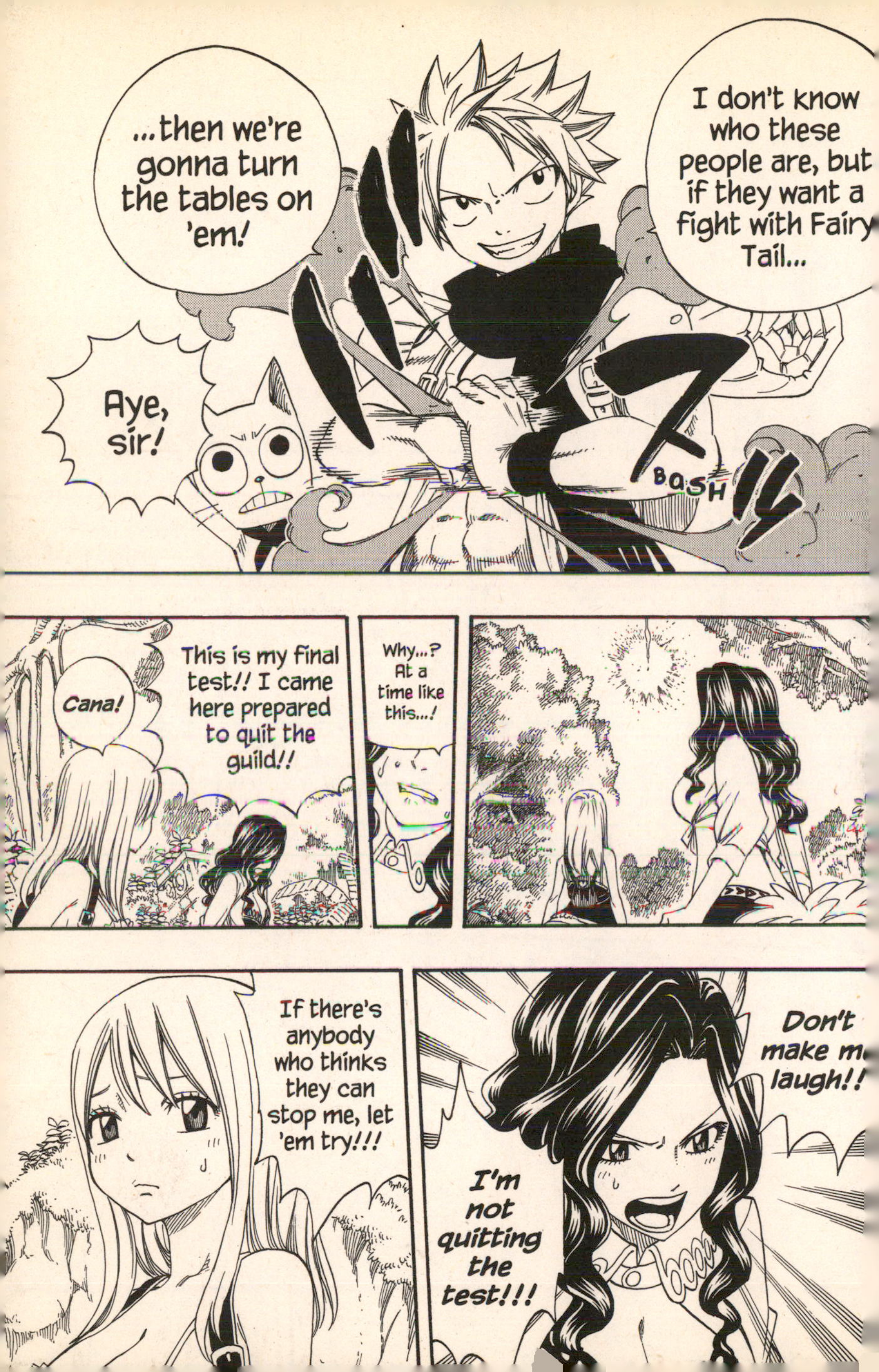
I don't know who these people are, but if they want a fight with Fairy Tail...
...then we're gonna turn the tables on 'em!
Aye, sir!
BASH
Why...? At a time like this...!
This is my final test!! I came here prepared to quit the guild!!
Cana!
Don't make m laugh!!
I'm not quitting the test!!!
If there's anybody who thinks they can stop me, let 'em try!!!

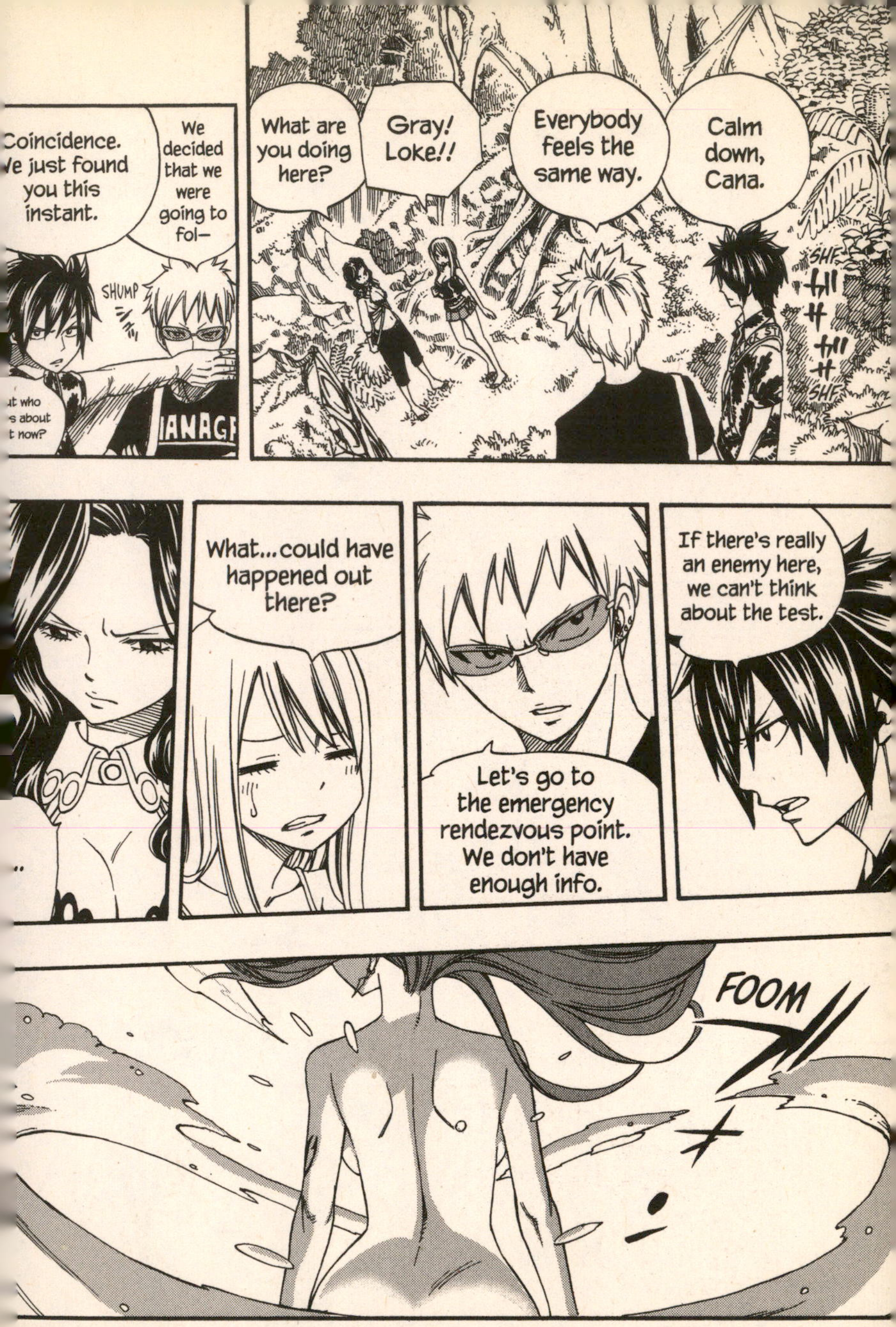
Calm down, Cana.
Everybody feels the same way.
Gray! Loke!!
What are you doing here?
SHF
SHF
We decided that we were going to fol—
Coincidence. e just found you this instant.
SHUMP
IANAGE
If there's really an enemy here, we can't think about the test.
Let's go to the emergency rendezvous point. We don't have enough info.
What...could have happened out there?
FOOM

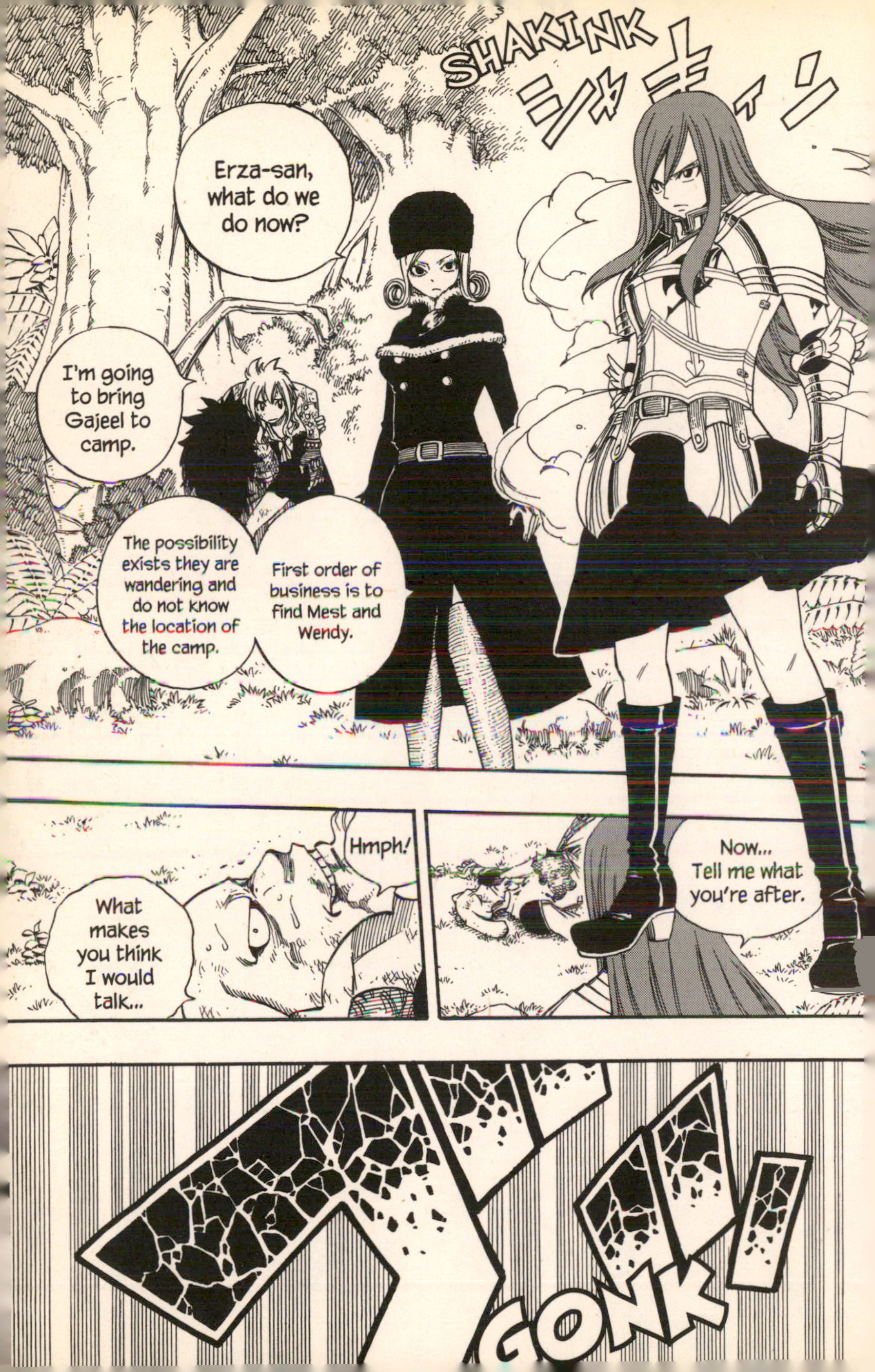
SHAKINK
シャキィン
Erza-san, what do we do now?
First order of business is to find Mest and Wendy.
The possibility exists they are wandering and do not know the location of the camp.
I'm going to bring Gajeel to camp.
Now... Tell me what you're after.
Hmph!
What makes you think I would talk...
GONK!

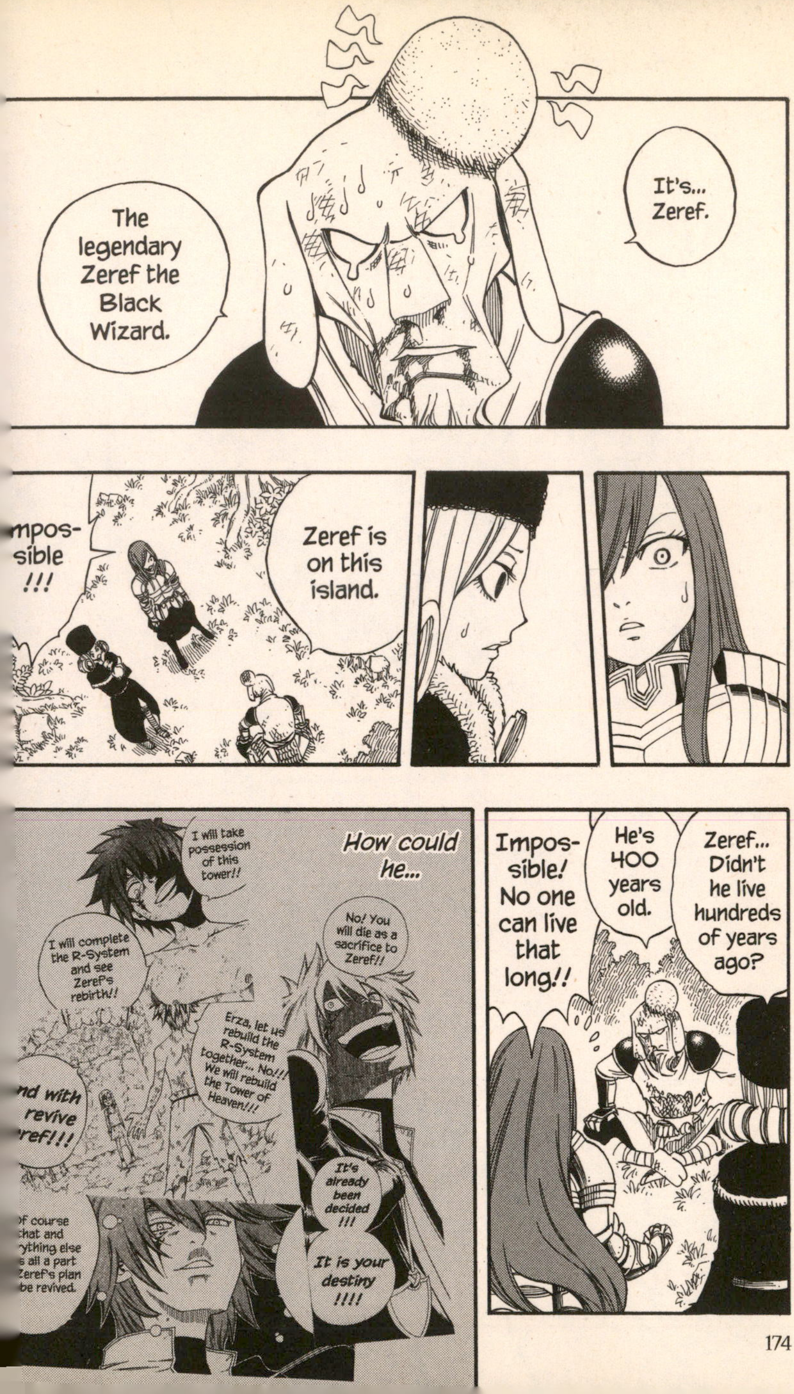
It's... Zeref.
The legendary Zeref the Black Wizard.
Zeref is on this island.
mpos-sible !!!
Zeref... Didn't he live hundreds of years ago?
He's 400 years old.
Impos-sible! No one can live that long!!
How could he...
I will take possession of this tower!!
No! You will die as a sacrifice to Zeref!!
I will complete the R-System and see Zeref's rebirth!!
Erza, let us rebuild the R-System together... No!!! We will rebuild the Tower of Heaven!!!
It's already been decided!!!
It is your destiny!!!!

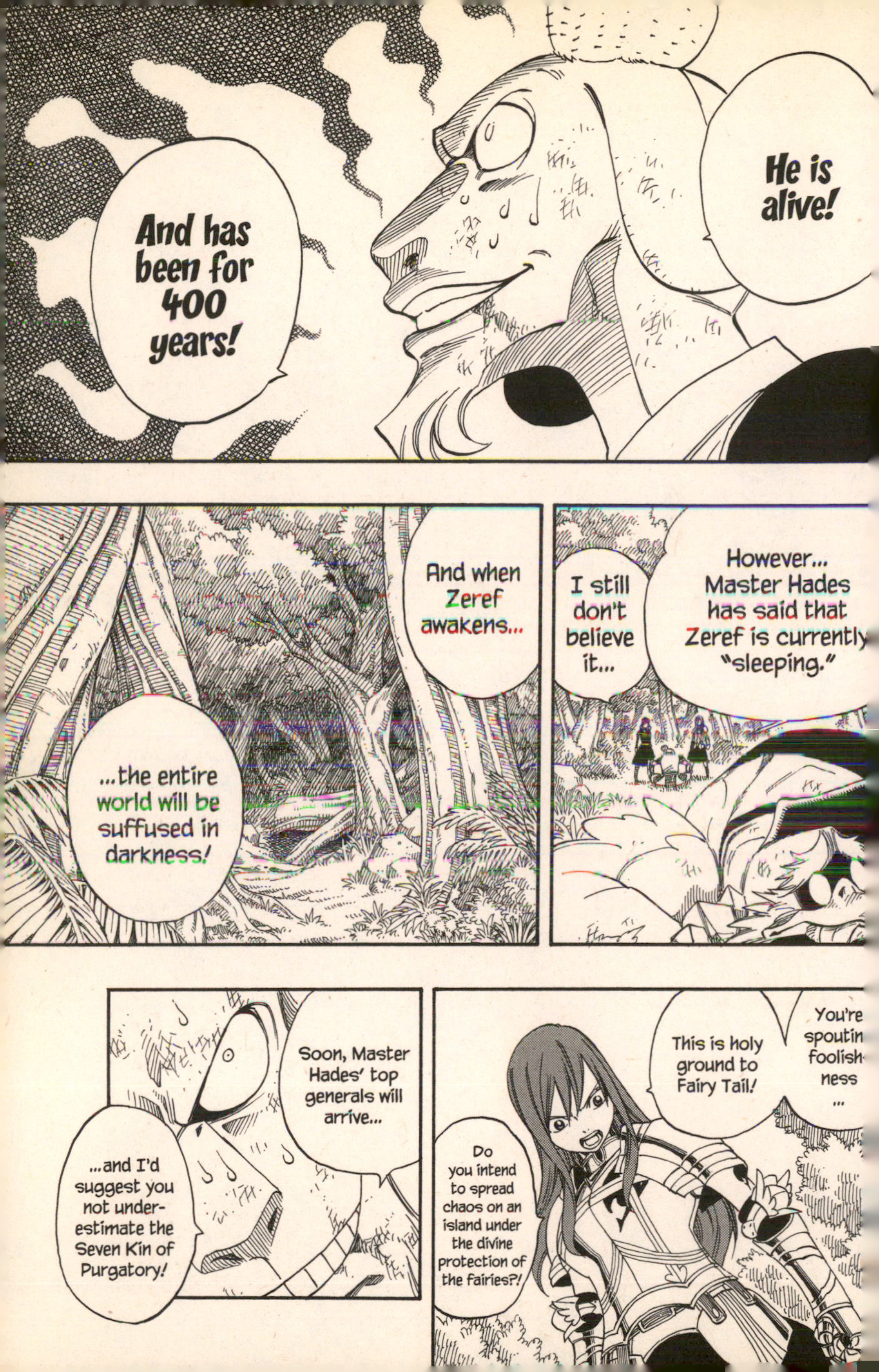
He is alive!
And has been for 400 years!
However... Master Hades has said that Zeref is currently "sleeping."
I still don't believe it...
And when Zeref awakens...
...the entire world will be suffused in darkness!
You're spoutin foolish-ness ...
This is holy ground to Fairy Tail!
Do you intend to spread chaos on an island under the divine protection of the fairies?!
Soon, Master Hades' top generals will arrive...
...and I'd suggest you not under-estimate the Seven Kin of Purgatory!

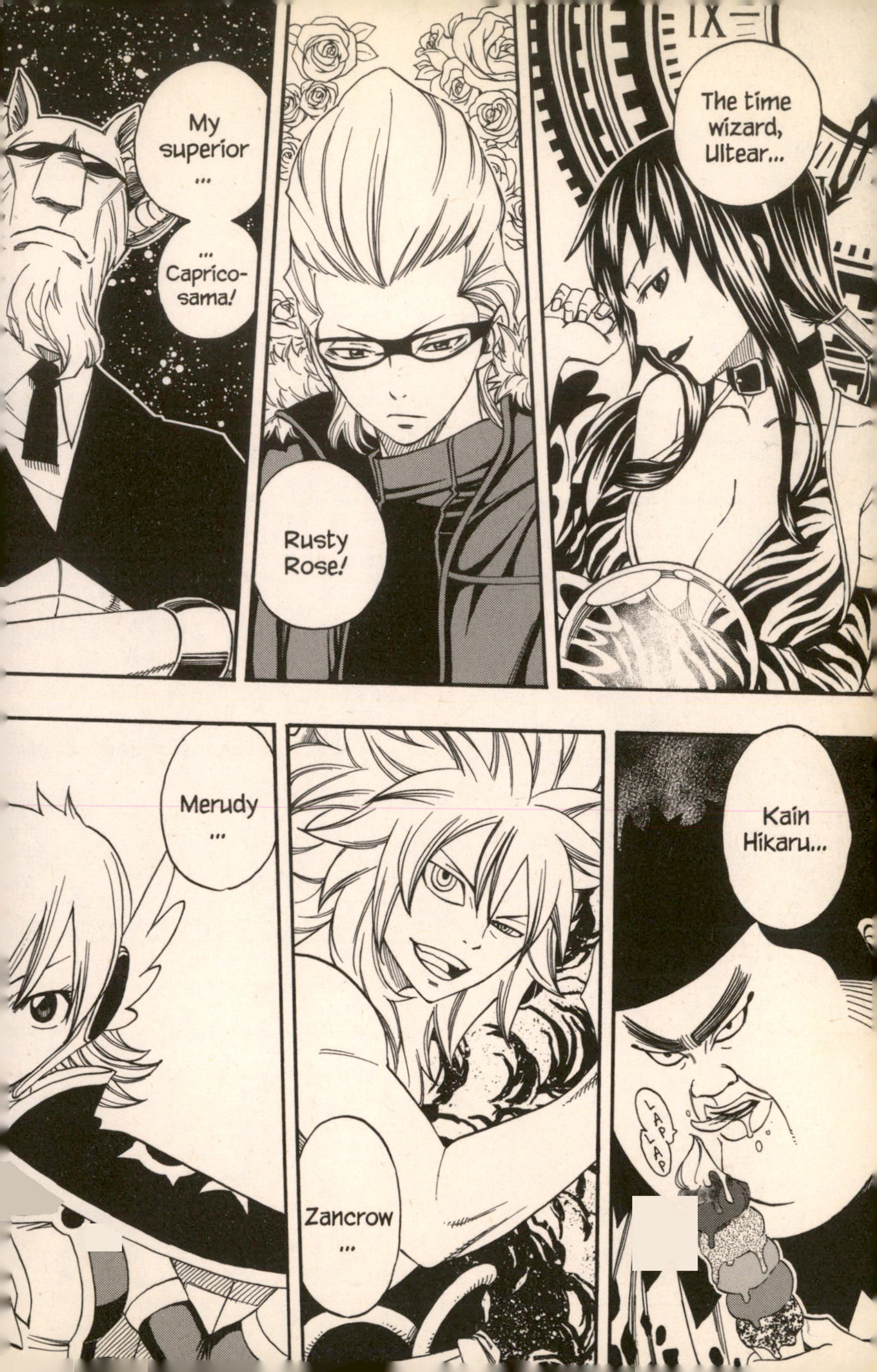
The time wizard, Ultear...
Rusty Rose!
My superior ...
... Caprico-sama!
Kain Hikaru...
LAP LAP
Zancrow ...
Merudy ...

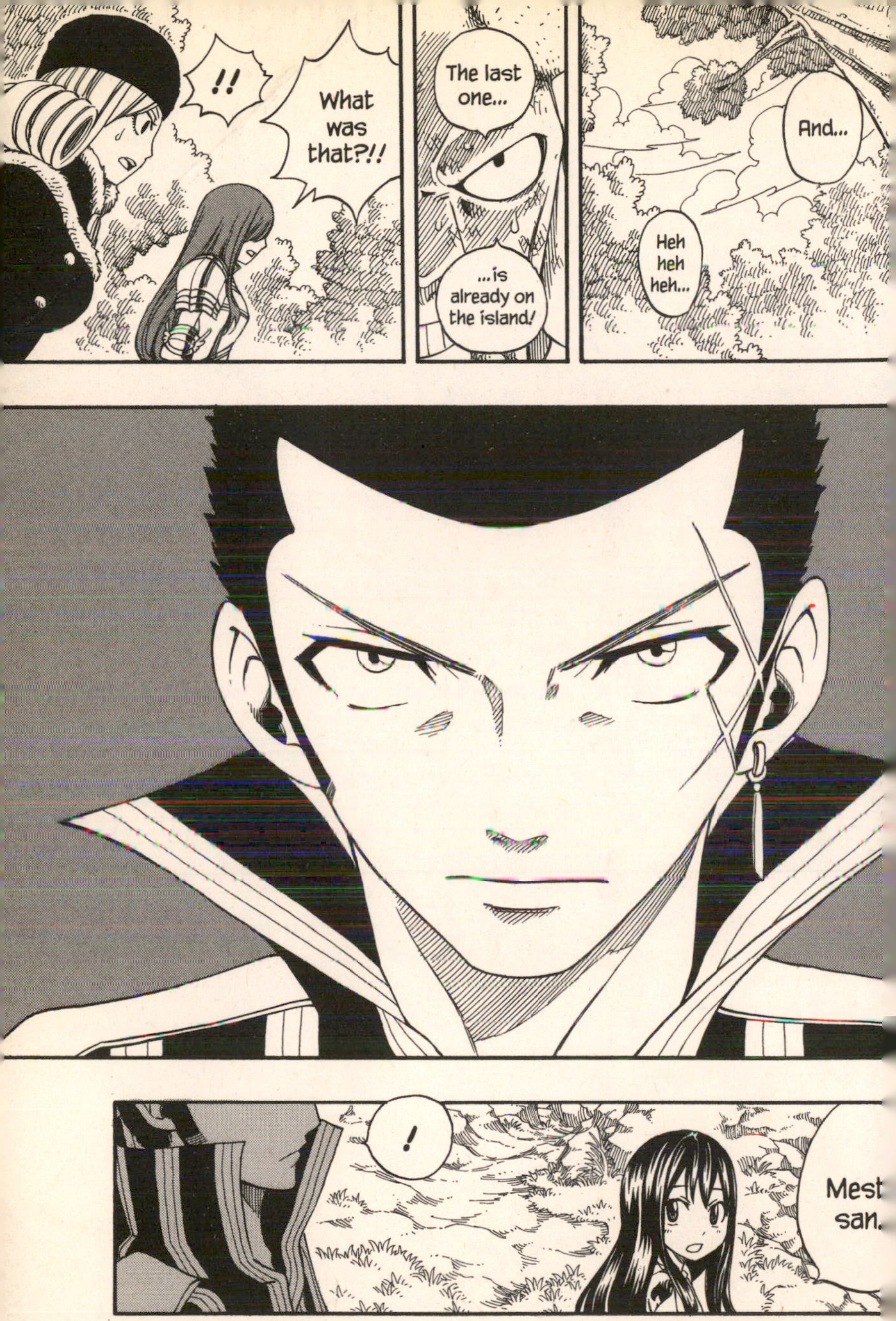
And...
Heh heh heh...
The last one...
...is already on the island!
!!
What was that?!!
Mest san.
!

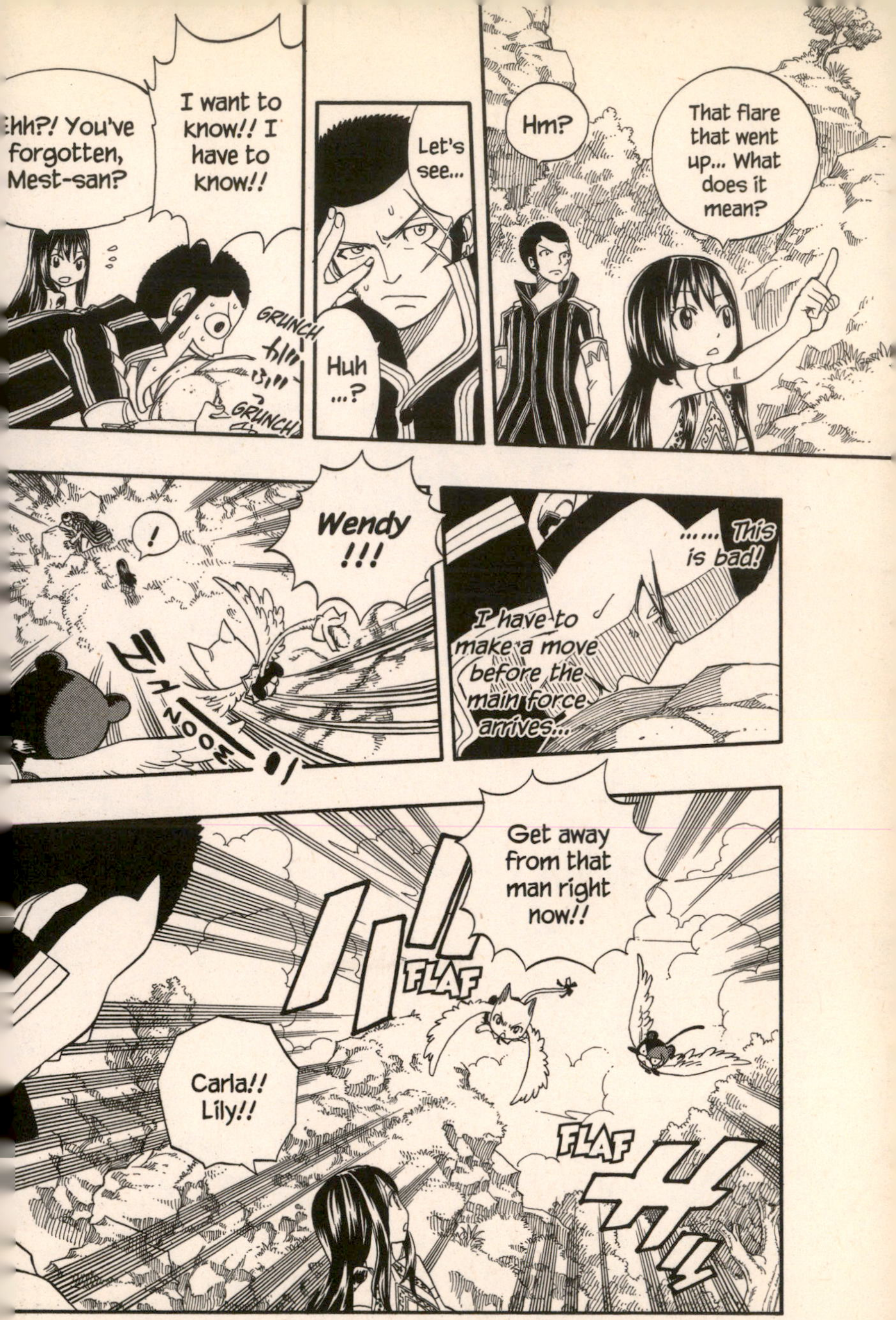
That flare that went up... What does it mean?
Hm?
Let's see...
Huh ...?
I want to know!! I have to know!!
GRUNCH
GRUNCH
hh?! You've forgotten, Mest-san?
...... This is bad!
I have to make a move before the main force arrives...
Wendy !!!
!
Get away from that man right now!!
FLAF
FLAF
Carla!! Lily!!

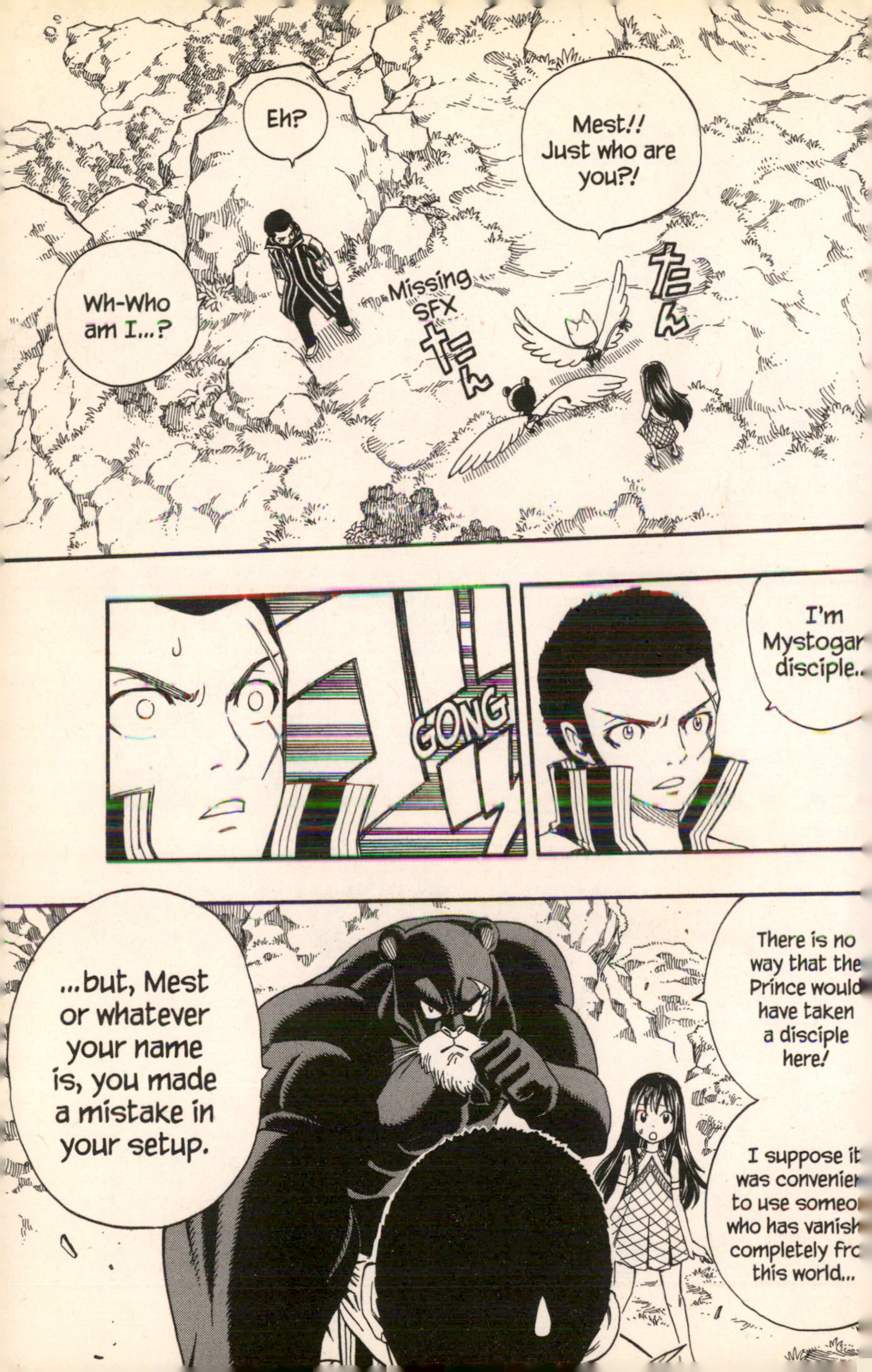
Mest!! Just who are you?!
Eh?
たん
Missing SFX
たん
Wh-Who am I...?
I'm Mystogar disciple..
GONG
There is no way that the Prince would have taken a disciple here!
I suppose it was convenien to use someo who has vanish completely fro this world...
...but, Mest or whatever your name is, you made a mistake in your setup.

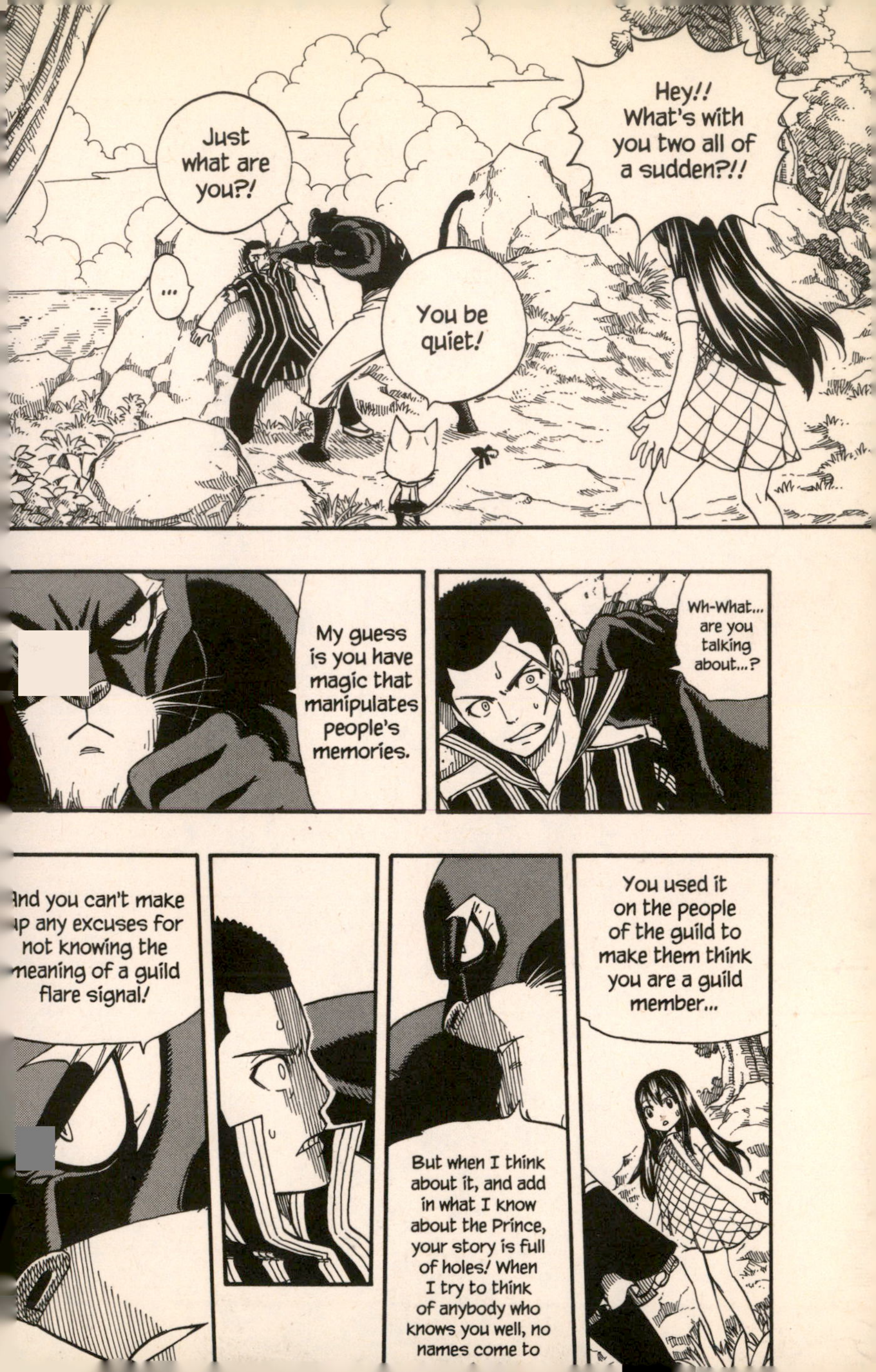

Hey!! What's with you two all of a sudden?!!
Just what are you?!
...
You be quiet!
Wh-What... are you talking about...?
My guess is you have magic that manipulates people's memories.
You used it on the people of the guild to make them think you are a guild member...
But when I think about it, and add in what I know about the Prince, your story is full of holes! When I try to think of anybody who knows you well, no names come to
And you can't make up any excuses for not knowing the meaning of a guild flare signal!

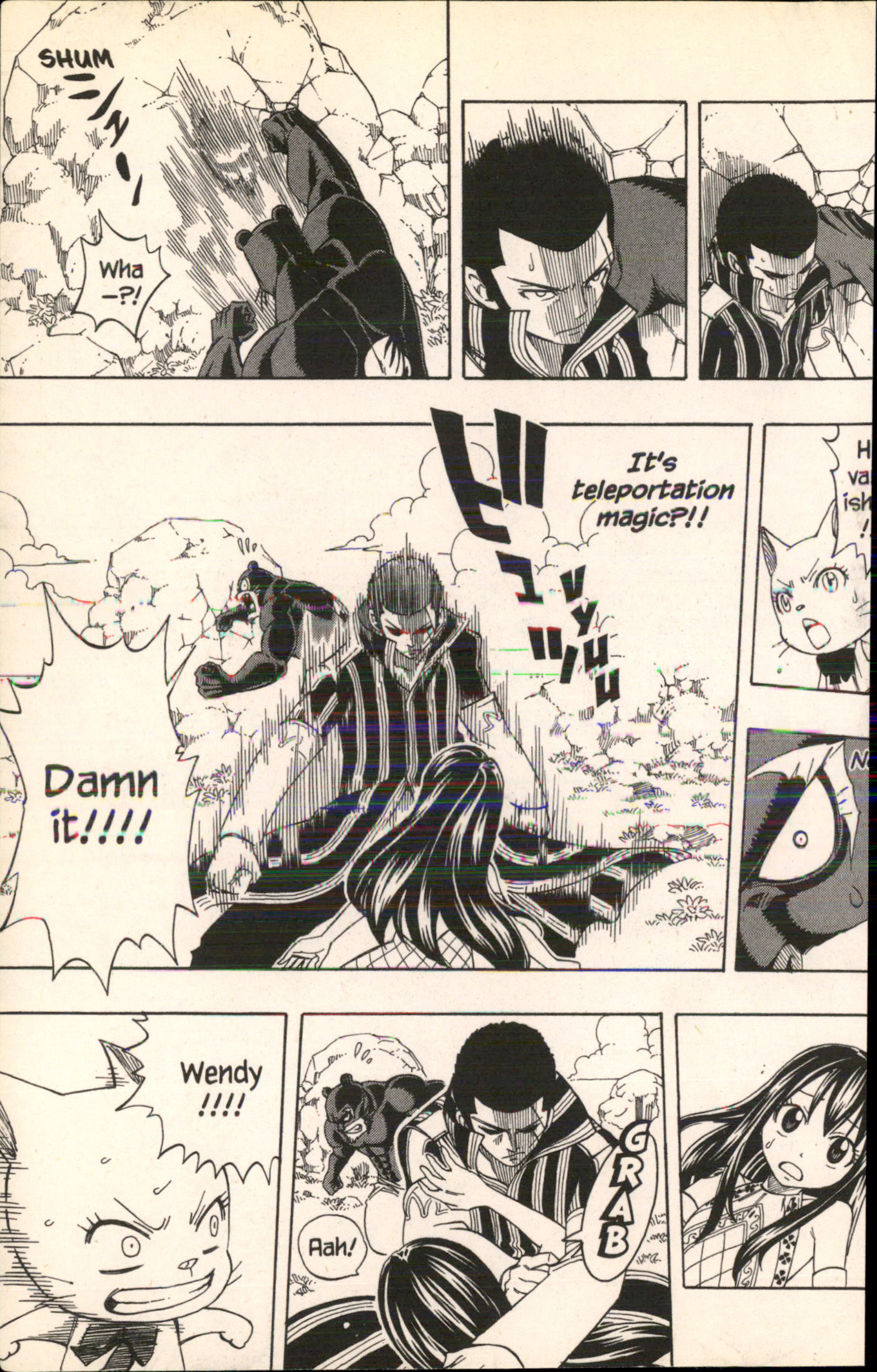
SHUM
Wha—?!
It's teleportation magic?!!
VYUU
Damn it!!!!!
GRAB
Aah!
Wendy!!!!

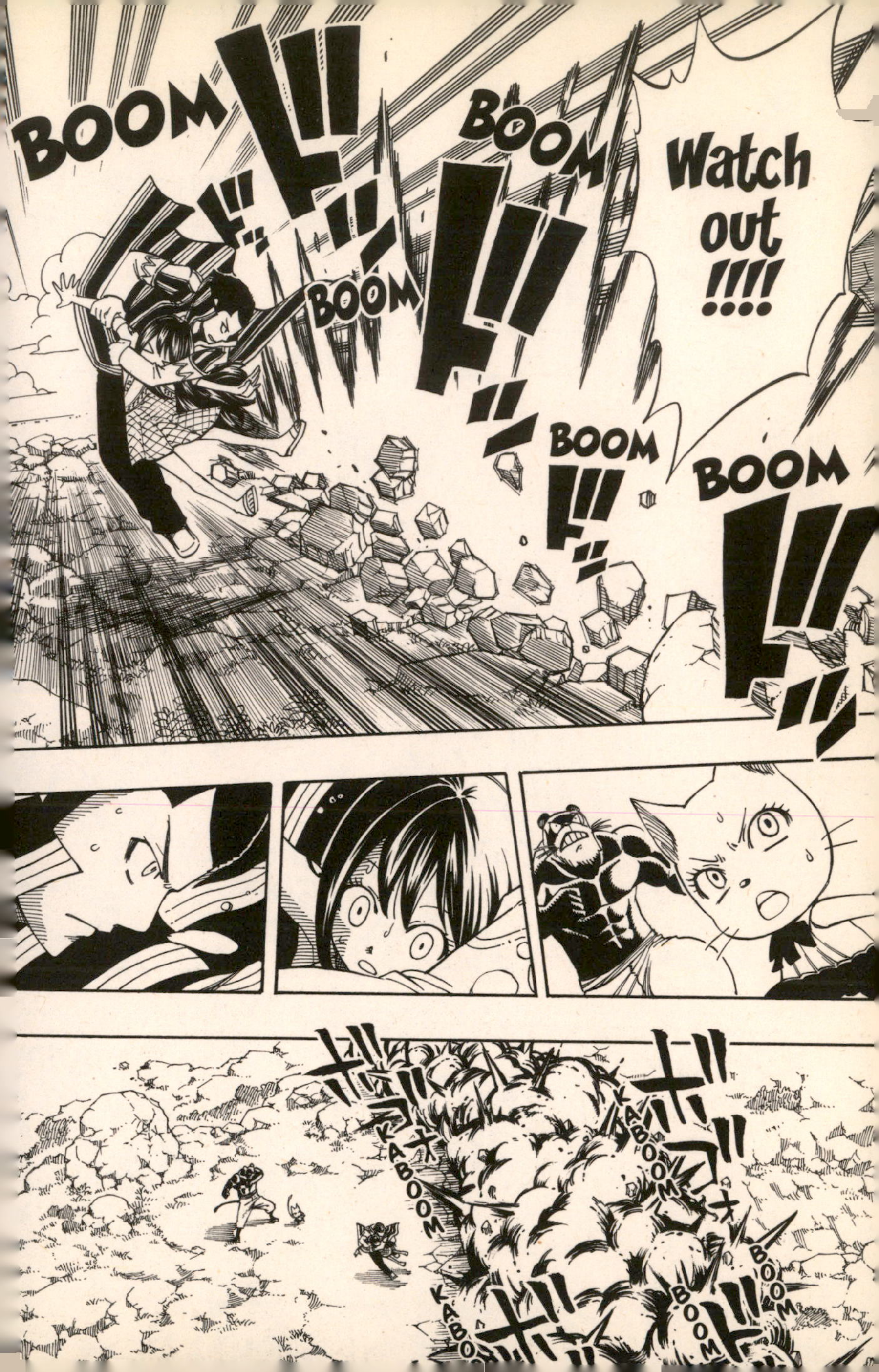

Watch out!!!!
BOOM!!
BOOM!!
BOOM!!
BOOM!!
BOOM!!
BOOM!!
KABOOM
BOOM
BOOM
KABOOM
KABOOM

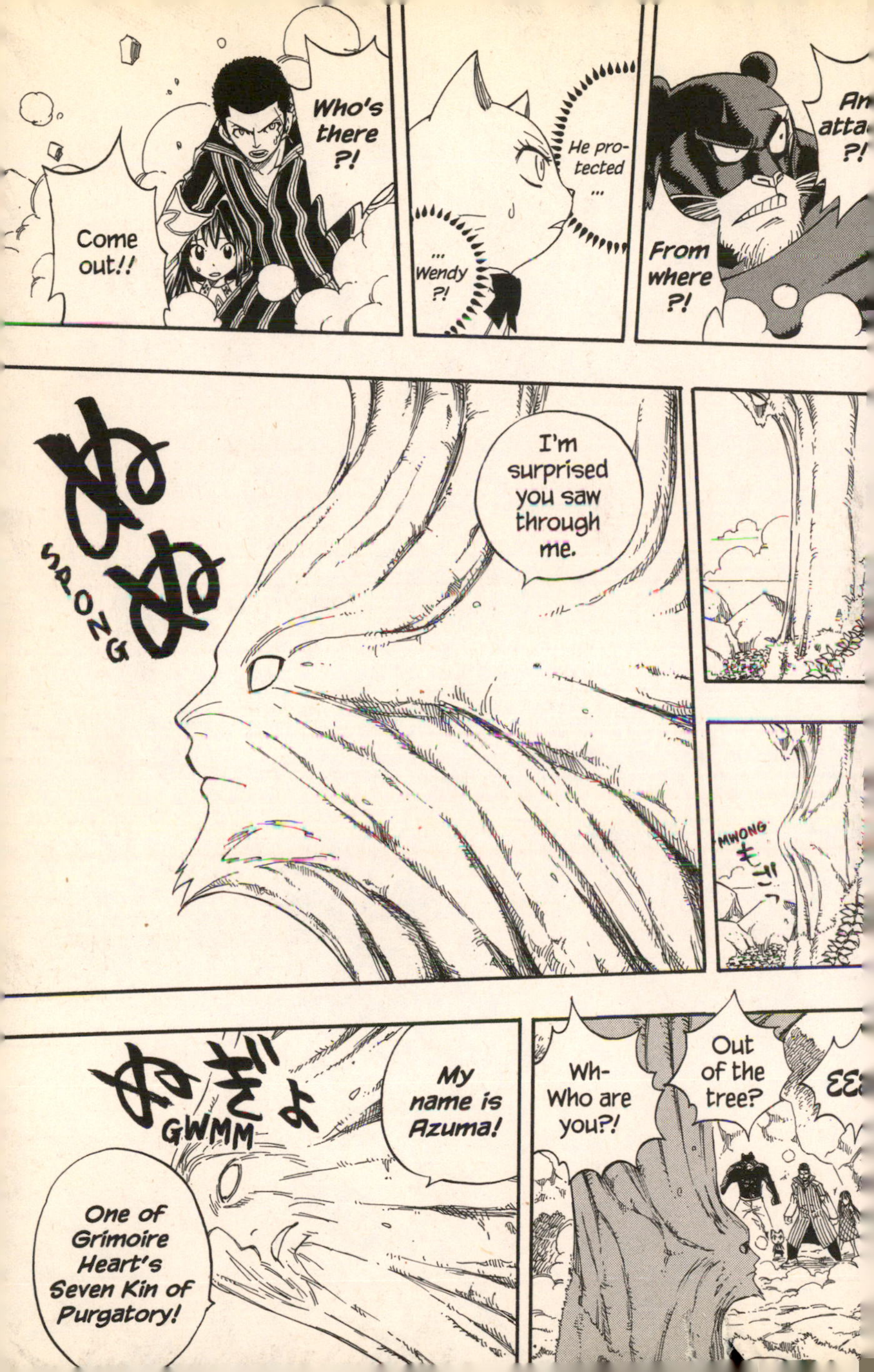
An attac
?!
From where ?!
He protected ...
... Wendy ?!
Who's there ?!
Come out!!
MWONG
SPONG
I'm surprised you saw through me.
Out of the tree?
Wh- Who are you?!
My name is Azuma!
GWMM
One of Grimoire Heart's Seven Kin of Purgatory!

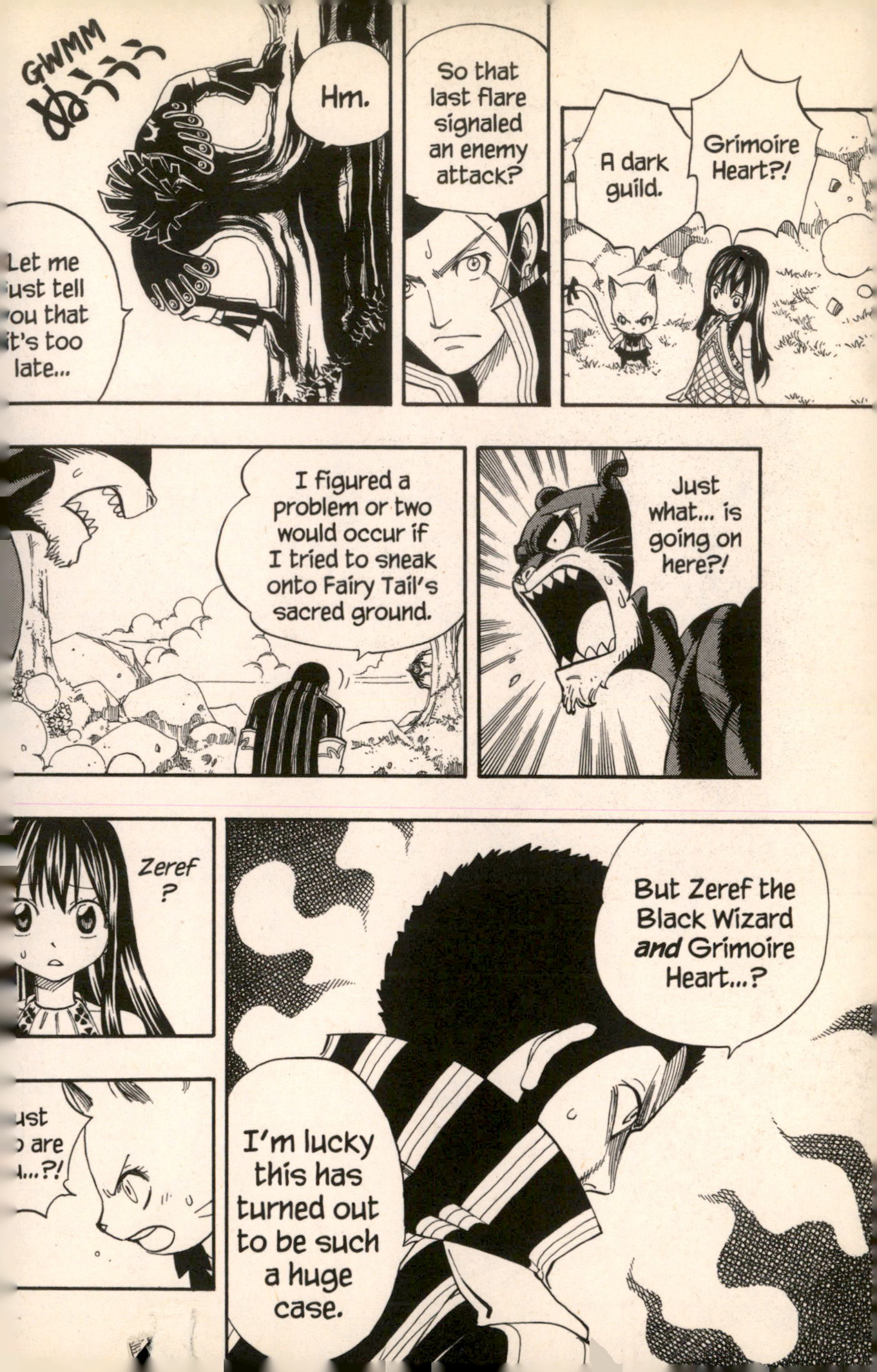
Grimoire Heart?!
A dark guild.
So that last flare signaled an enemy attack?
Hm.
GWMM
ぬううう
Let me ust tell ou that t's too late...
Just what... is going on here?!
I figured a problem or two would occur if I tried to sneak onto Fairy Tail's sacred ground.
But Zeref the Black Wizard *and* Grimoire Heart...?
I'm lucky this has turned out to be such a huge case.
Zeref ?
ust are ...?!

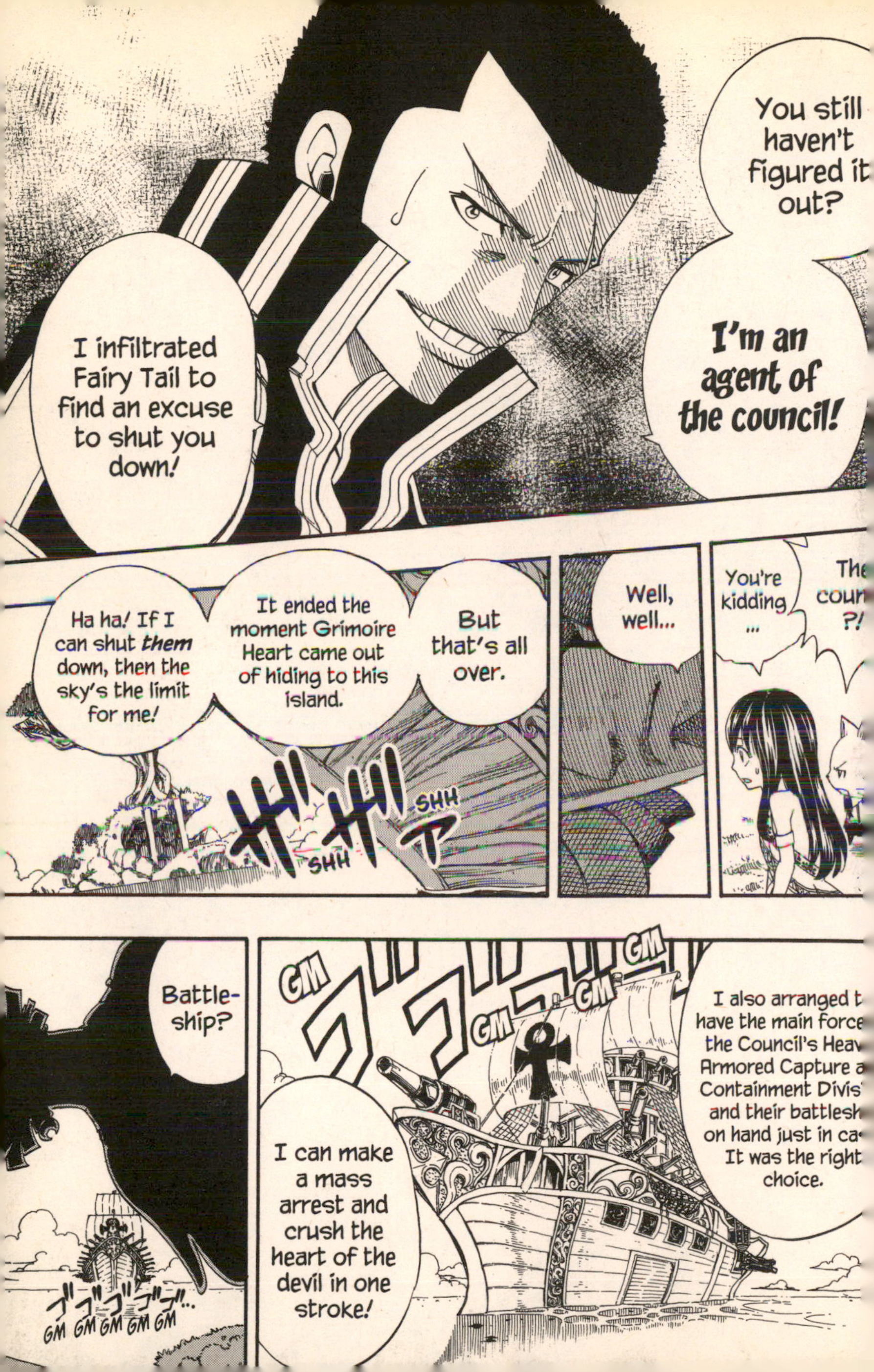
You still haven't figured it out?
I'm an agent of the council!
I infiltrated Fairy Tail to find an excuse to shut you down!
The coun ?!
You're kidding ...
Well, well...
But that's all over.
It ended the moment Grimoire Heart came out of hiding to this island.
Ha ha! If I can shut *them* down, then the sky's the limit for me!
SHH SHH
GM GM GM GM
I also arranged t have the main force the Council's Heav Armored Capture a Containment Divis and their battlesh on hand just in ca It was the right choice.
I can make a mass arrest and crush the heart of the devil in one stroke!
Battle-ship?
GM GM GM GM GM

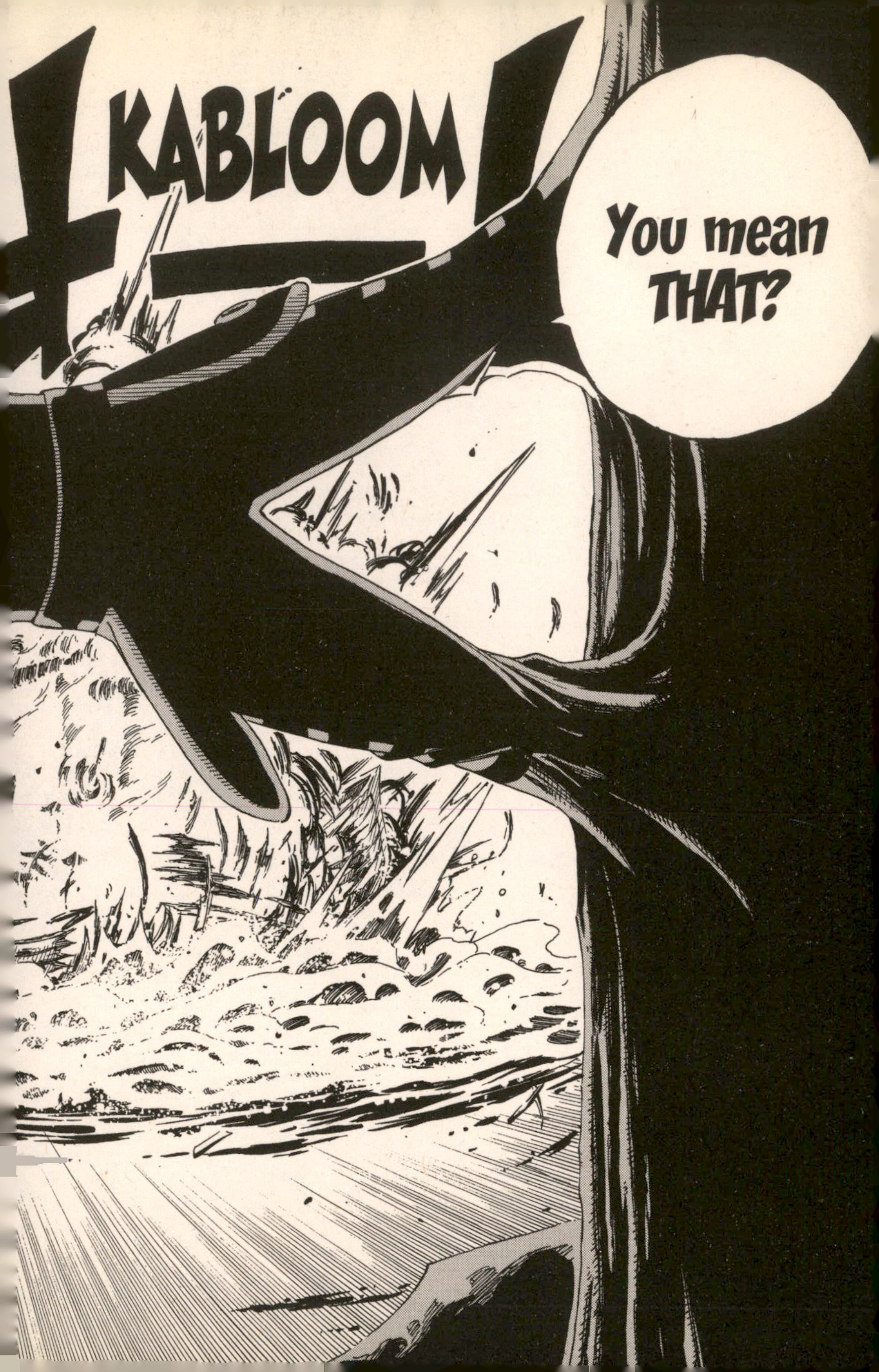
KABLOOM
You mean THAT?

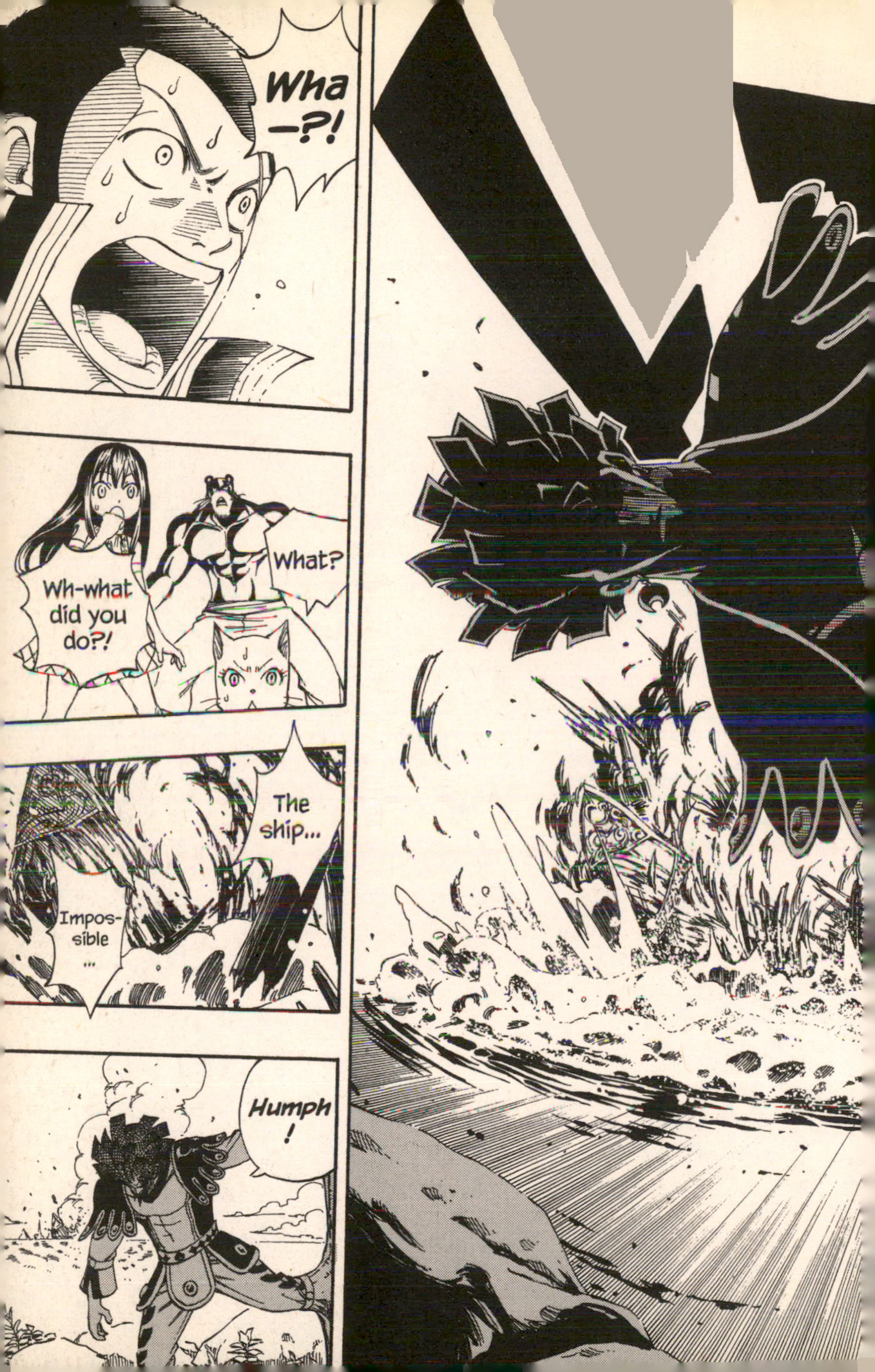
Wha—?!
What?
Wh-what did you do?!
The ship...
Impos-sible...
Humph!

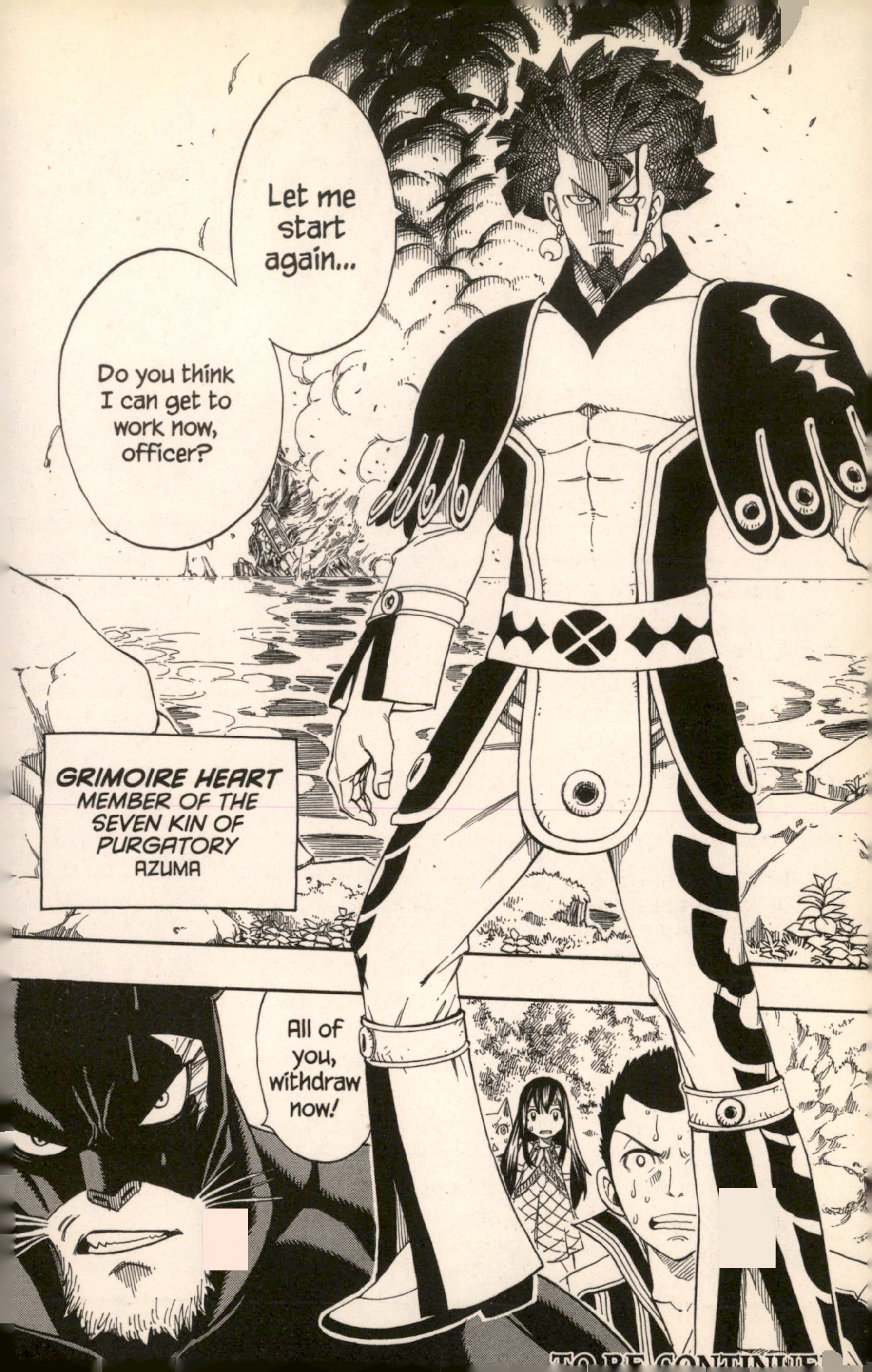
Let me start again...
Do you think I can get to work now, officer?
GRIMOIRE HEART MEMBER OF THE SEVEN KIN OF PURGATORY AZUMA
All of you, withdraw now!

あとがき

Afterword

Ahhhhhh!! The famous hidden one-shot short story "Welcome to Fairy Hills!!" will be included in the **Special Japanese Edition of Volu** **26,** and you will soon be able to read it in a small booklet edition!! On to that, there will be a "Welcome to Fairy Hills!!" **anime DVD** also includ Not only that, but a **Happy Cell Phone Strap** will also come in the package for only **1980 yen!!*** Yahoo!! What a feast! Come to think of i I'm putting on a few pounds myself. (cries) Anyway, I'm sorry for the suc advertisement, but Volume 26 is becoming an irresistible volume! It's got much going for it!! There are a lot of scenes you could consider a bit sexy some I think may seem a bit too much for the anime…! Or so I thought u saw what they did with the anime…! The story of "Welcome to Fairy Hill is about the Fairy Tail women's dorm, and how Lucy gets into a treasure inside the dorm. When it was printed in the magazine, it had a huge imp on the readership, and I must say, it's a story I'm very fond of myself. So you all to please check it out!

Ah! Also there will be two different editions for Volume 26, the **Norma Edition** and the **Special Edition**, each with their own packaging. M sure you don't get confused thinking they're two different books! The ma story running in the books will be exactly the same. The Normal Edition be a *tankobon* exactly like they always are. But with the Special Edition all its added extras, it'd be really easy to mistakenly buy both editions! If do, please don't inundate the editorial office with complaints, okay? Because there aren't many extra pages in this volume, this bonus section didn't turn out to be much more than an advertisement!
Sorry!!

*A little over $20.

TAIL d'ART

The Fairy Tail Guild d'Art is looking for illustrations! Please send in your art on a postcard or at postcard size, and do it in black pen, okay? Those chosen to be published will get a signed mini poster! ♪ Make sure you write your real name and address on the back of your illustration!

wa Prefecture, Akira Hasegawa

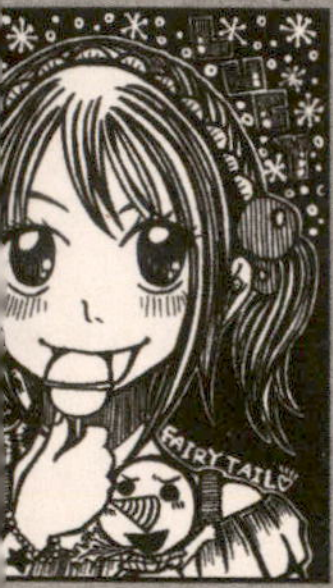
FAIRY TAIL

ou know, I really seeing girls eating ething. Is it just me?

Saitama Prefecture, Mafuyu Nakayama

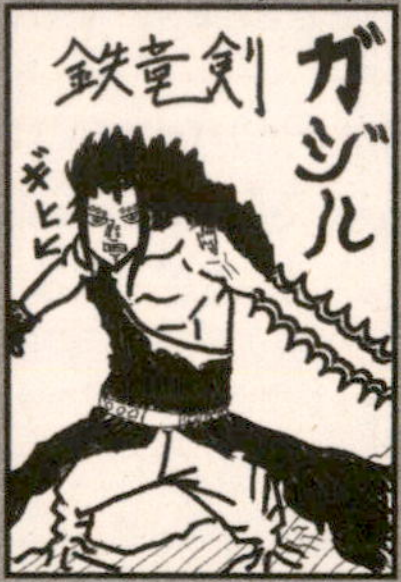
鉄竜剣
ガジル

▲You saw Gajeel-kun do a lot this time! What do you think?

Chiba Prefecture, Tori

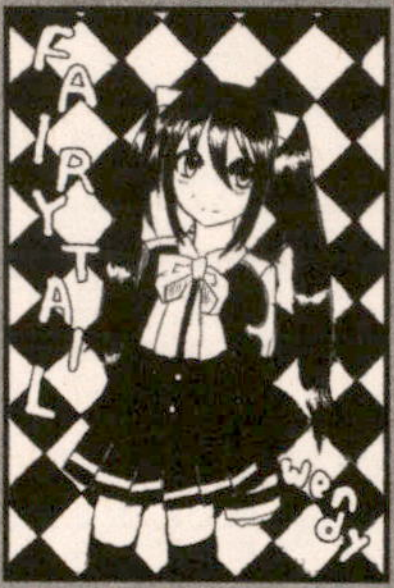
FAIRY TAIL

▲Ohh! Cute! Do you think those clothes could be popular?

Hokkaido, Eri

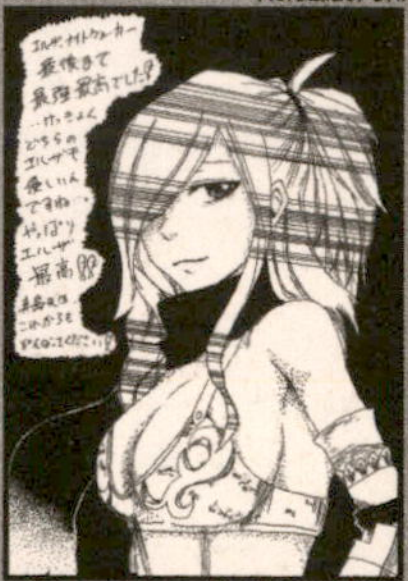

▲I guess it's true that there are Erza Nightwalker fans out there!

wa Prefecture, Runa Shinohara

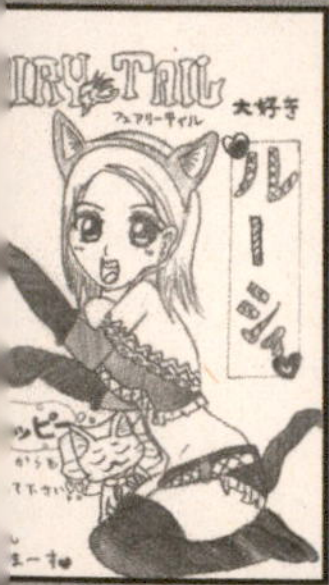
FAIRY TAIL
大好き
フェアリーテイル

atch for the manga on of this costume e special edition of ne 26!

Okayama Prefecture, Misaki Ishii

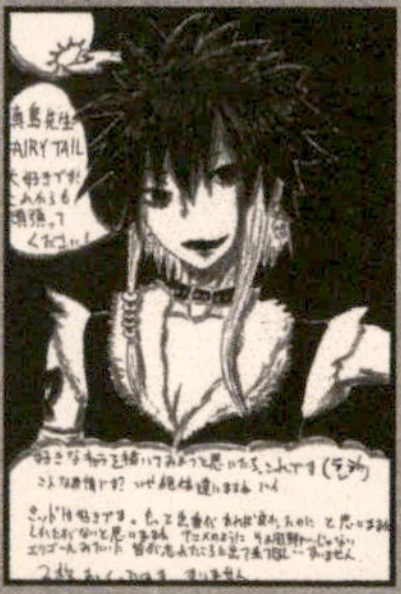
FAIRY TAIL

▲Ohh!! That's well drawn! And that guy makes me kind of nostalgic.

Aichi Prefecture, Ikumi Takashima

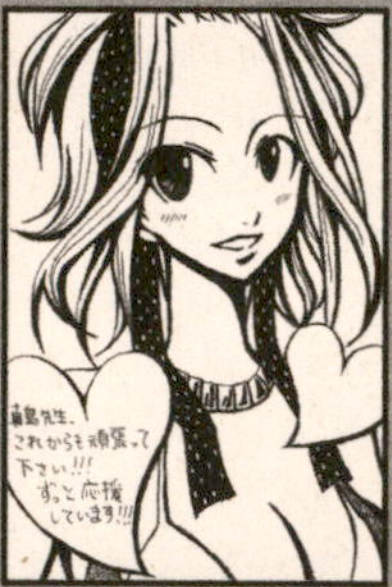
真島先生、
これからも頑張って
下さい!!!
ずっと応援
しています!!!

▲And here's Levy-san, who worked pretty hard this time, huh?

Tochigi Prefecture, Henzel

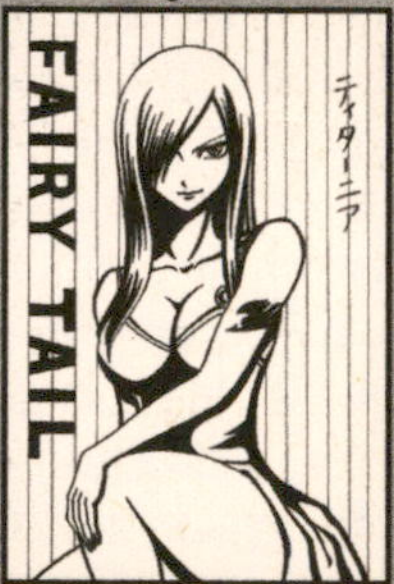
FAIRY TAIL
ティターニア

▲Wow!! That's good!! And the balance between black and white is excellent!

Send to Hiro Mashima, Kodansha Comics
451 Park Ave. South, 7th Floor New York, NY 10016

FAIRY GUILD

Miyagi Prefecture, Takuya Wagatsuma

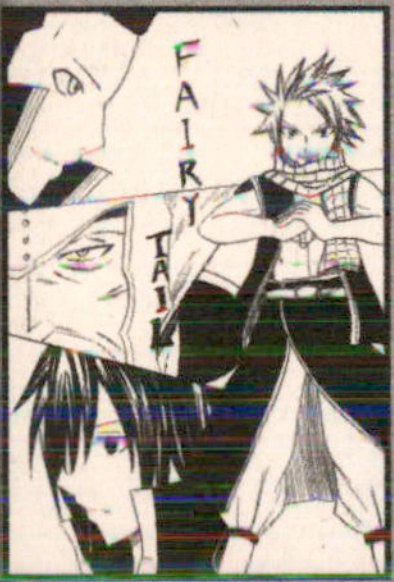
FAIRY TAIL

▲It's a really recent illustration, huh? From now on, things get interesting!

Nagasaki Prefecture, Den-chan

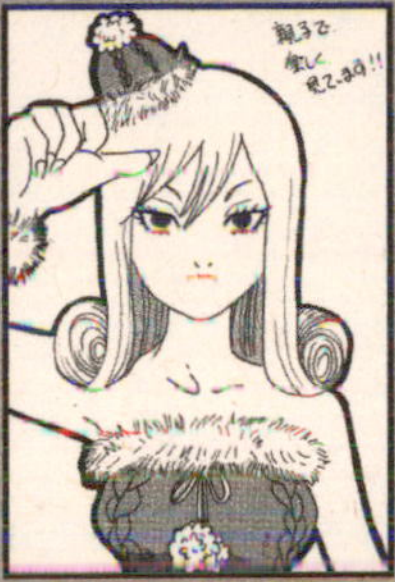

▲I wonder what she'll do for Fairy Tail during this series?

Kagawa Prefecture, Shin Miyamoto

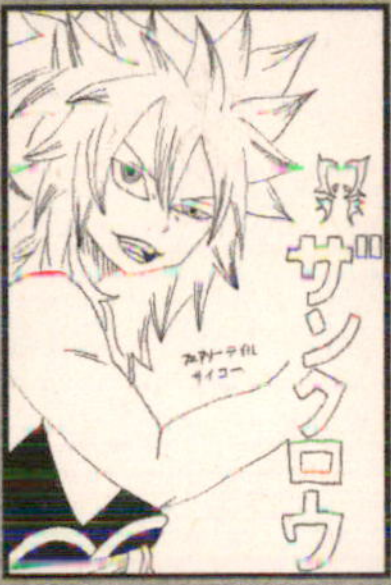
ザンクロウ

▲That was quick! Zancrow!!

Aichi Prefecture, Yuki Kos

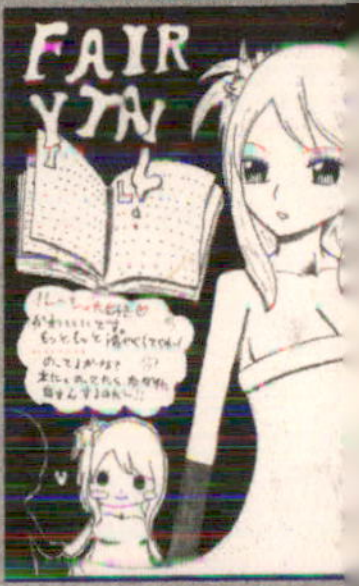
FAIRY TAIL

▲This is so nice! It's so simple and refreshing!

Saitama Prefecture, Pudding

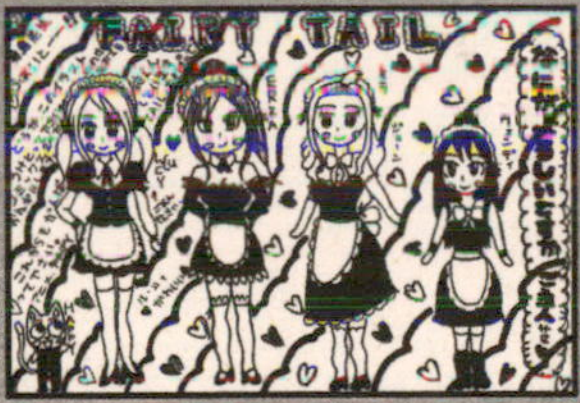
FAIRY TAIL

▲Everybody's maids!! They're all like Virgo!!

REJECTION CORNER

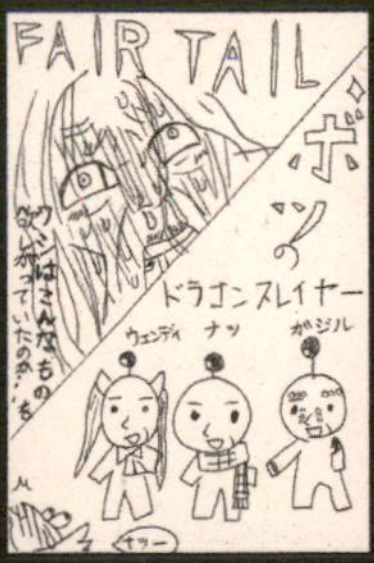
FAIR TAIL
ドラゴンスレイヤー
ウェンディ ナツ ガジル

Saitama Prefecture, Satan Soul

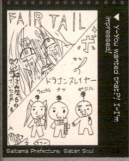

▲Y-You wanted that?! I-I'm impressed!

Niigata Prefecture, Baba-

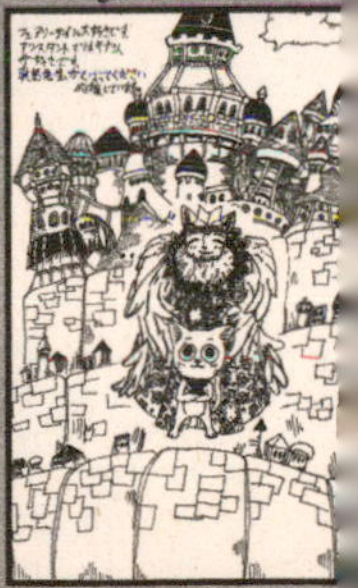

▲That castle must have been a pain to draw, huh A great effort!!

By sending in letters or postcards you give us permission to give your name, address, postal code and any other information you include to the author as is. Please keep that in mind.

Pretty Ominous, Huh...?

With the amount of work greater than twice normal, everyone, of course, enters Exhaustion Mode.
Exhaustion Level 8
Like in this area.
Ue-chan is so exhausted his arm muscles start to twitch. It's obvious how much those muscles need protein.
Kina-san's overall straps fall to different lengths.
Exhaustion Level 5
But someone in the maximum defensive posture won't notice the state of one's overalls.
The cold compresses on the back of Bobby's neck get all scrunched up.
BOB
Exhaustion Level 10
This is extreme exhaustion. The scrunchyness of the compresses is his archenemy.
And obsessed with that, sleep does not come all night.
イラ… GRR
GRR イラ…
It's just distracting! The way he puts on those compresses! Just distracting...

Shô Nakamura

Amazing Power of Good-Looking Men

With three installments at once, the workplace is busier than normal.
Hat: Mashima
But even that fails to alleviate my self-loathing.
I can't draw! I just want to disappear and never come back!
Vanish if you like, just do it after all the work is finished this time.
It's hard both physically and emotionally...
...
But...
The new character is so good-looking, it saved me! Let's all be simple-minded!
That expression just tickles a young girl's fancy!
WHO CARES?!! JUST DO YOUR WORK!!!

Kina Kobayashi

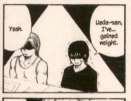

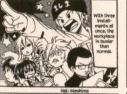

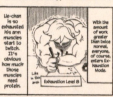

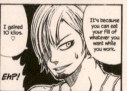

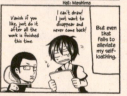

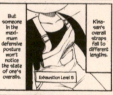

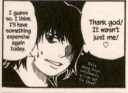

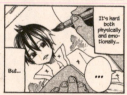

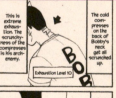

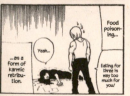

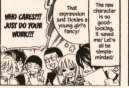

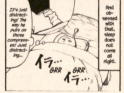

Three Meals at Once Letting his instincts lead his life.

Ueda-san, I've... gained weight.
Yeah.
It's because you can eat your fill of whatever you want while you work.
I gained 10 kilos. ♡
Eh?!
Thank god! It wasn't just me! ♡
I guess so. I think I'll have something expensive again today.
We're doing three installments so I can eat for three!
Food poisoning...
Eating for three is way too much for you!
Yeah...
...as a form of karmic retribution.

Kain

FAIRY TAIL 25

This is a record of a hero (Hiro Mashima) and his brave warriors (assistants) that appeared in Weekly Shonen Magazine, Issue 2010, Number 42 when three installments were all drawn at once!

25-Year-Old Dreamer

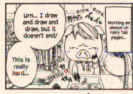

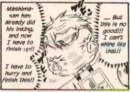

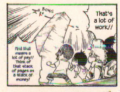

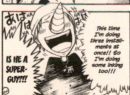

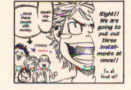

Right!! We are going to put out three install-ments at once!!
I'm all fired up!!
Mashi-ma-san...
...hired these people with money.
OHHHH!
That's a lot of work!!
BONG
And that means a lot of pay!! Think of that stack of pages as a stack of money!
SKRITCH
Mo-ney!
Mo-ney!
Mo-neeey!
Bobby Ōsawa (25). His dream is...
PHEEEEW
...to become a manga artist who can bring dreams and hope to his readers!

Bobby Ōsawa

SuperGuy

Working as always on Fairy Tail pages...
OINK OINK
Um... I draw and draw and draw, but it doesn't end!
This is really hard...
SKRITCH
..... But this is no good!!! I can't whine like that!!
Mashima-san has already did his inking, and now I have to finish up!!
I have to hurry and finish this!!
Besides... I'm sure that Mashi-ma-san is much more tired than I am...
SKRITCH
H-Huh? Didn't Mashima-san already finish inking his part of the pages...?
Hm?
HA HA
This time I'm doing three install-ments at once!! So I'm doing some inking too!!!
AH HA
IS HE A SUPER-GUY?!!

Yui Ueda

HIRO MASHIMA

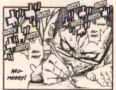

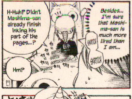

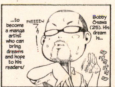

FROM HIRO MASHIMA

The above drawing is from when I was looking at a bookend at home and suddenly wanted to draw it. I don't remember when I bought it, but it's a bookend with a kind of orange-colored dog, or maybe bear.

Come to think of it, I really don't remember when I bought it. How long has this thing been in my house? This weird-colored animal!

Original Jacket Design: Hisao Ogawa

Translation Notes:

Japanese is a tricky language for most Westerners, and translation is often more art than science. For your edification and reading pleasure, here are notes on some of the places where we could have gone in a different direction with our translation of the work, or where a Japanese cultural reference is used.

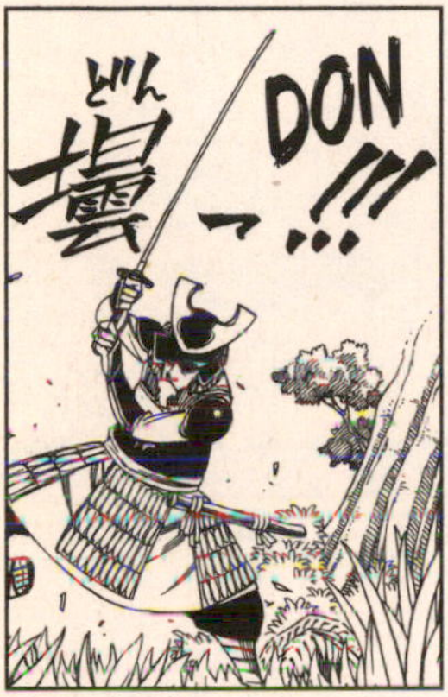
どん
DON
!!!

Page 125, Don

Yomazu's attack is like Levy's Solid Script, except it use the Chinese characters called *kanji* that make up part of the Japanese writing system. Mashima-sensei uses some of the characters strictly because they're pronounced like sound effects. (Some have real meanings and these are translated in the book.) This *kanji* mean "turtle," and the sound effect, don, sounds like striking dramatic pose.

Page 125, Hyuu

This *kanji* means "little tiger," and sounds like somethi whizzing through the air.

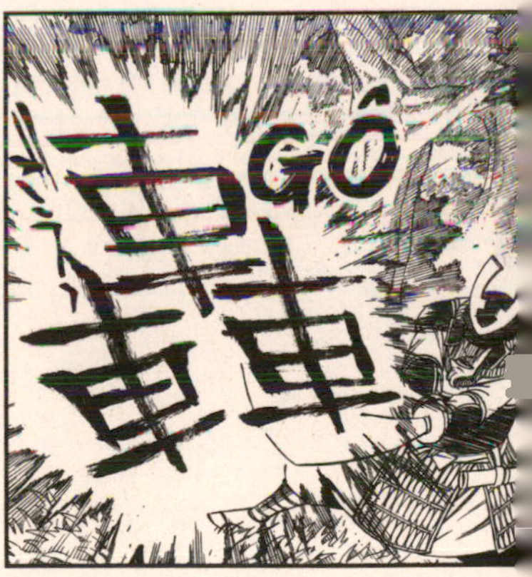
GÔ

Page 132, Gô

This *kanji* means "thunder" and is pronounced *gô*, the Japanese sound for thunder. In fact, it probably came to mean thunder because of its pronunciation, not the other way around.

Page 138, Zu-Za Za Za Za Za

Here we have a series of *kanji* that sound like the Japanese sound effect for a swinging sword. The *kanji* mean "design" followed by a bunch of *kanji* meaning "seat" – so, as you can see, the meaning doesn't matter. Only the pronunciation is important.

Page 139, Zan

This *kanji* means "cut" or "behead," and it really is pronounced "zan."

Page 139, Su-Pa Pa Pa Pa

Like *Zu-Za Za Za Za* above, these *kanji* were chosen for their sounds rather than their meanings. The first, *su*, means "nest," and the *pa* sounds mean "twirl."

Page 140, Bi, Za, Ba

Here the *bi kanji* means "assist." The *kanji* for *za* means "steep." The *kanji* for *ba* means "horse," and is the first character in the common Japanese insult *baka* (the *ka* in *baka* means "deer").

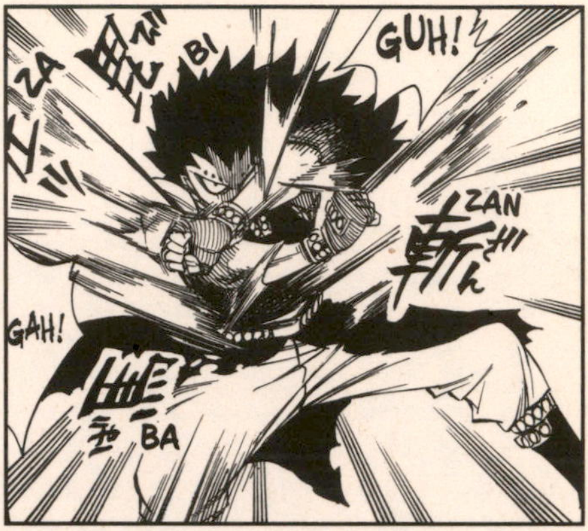
GUH!
BI
ZA
ZAN
GAH!
BA

Page 141, Tsuranuki

The *kanji* for *tsuranuki* means "pierce."

Page 141, Do

Do is a *kanji* that means "anger" or "rage."

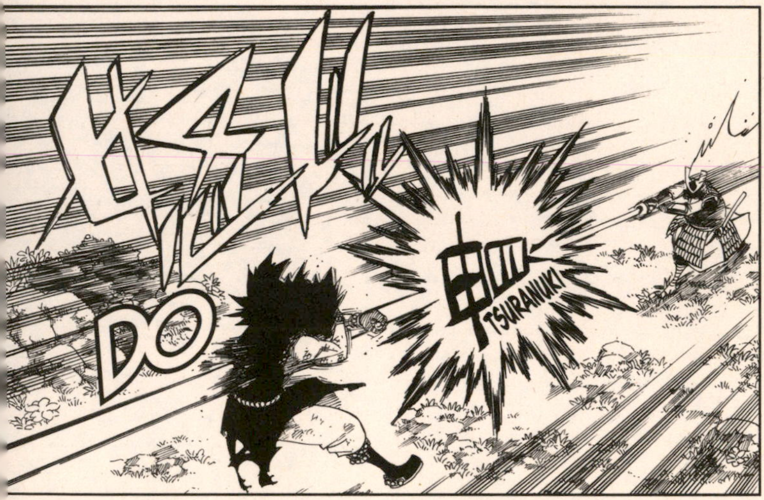
TSURANUKI
DO

Page 141, Kasha

The first *kanji*, ka, means "to add," and the second *kanji*, *sha*, means "pebbles."

Page 153, Bô

This *kanji* seems to have been chosen both for its sound and meaning. The *kanji bô* means "protection."

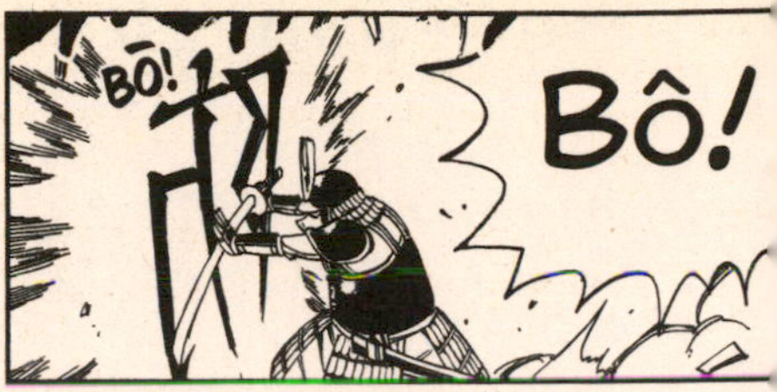
BŌ!
Bô!

Page 154, Shu-Ba Ba Ba

The phrase *shu-ba -ba ba* was probably chosen for its sound. The *kanji* for *shu* means "exceptional," and the *ba kanji* refers to certain kinds of banana and is the first character in the name of the famous haiku poet, Basho.

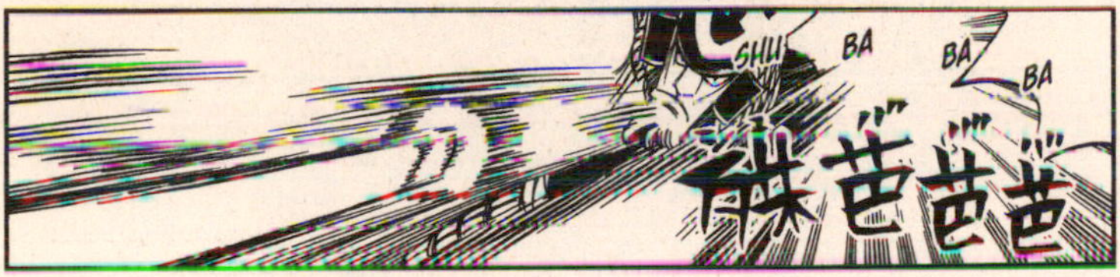
SHU
BA
BA
BA

Preview of *Fairy Tail*, volume 26

We're pleased to present you with a preview from Fairy Tail, volume 26, now available digitally from Kodansha Comics. Check our Web site (www.kodanshacomics.com) for details!

FAIRY TAIL
26
Hiro Mashima
Creator of Rave Master

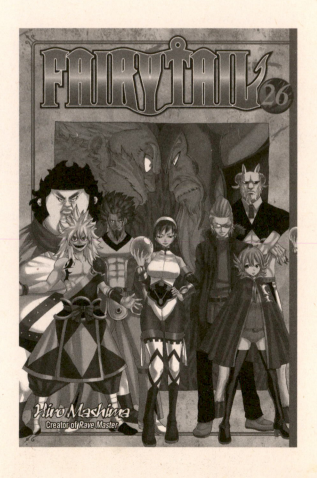

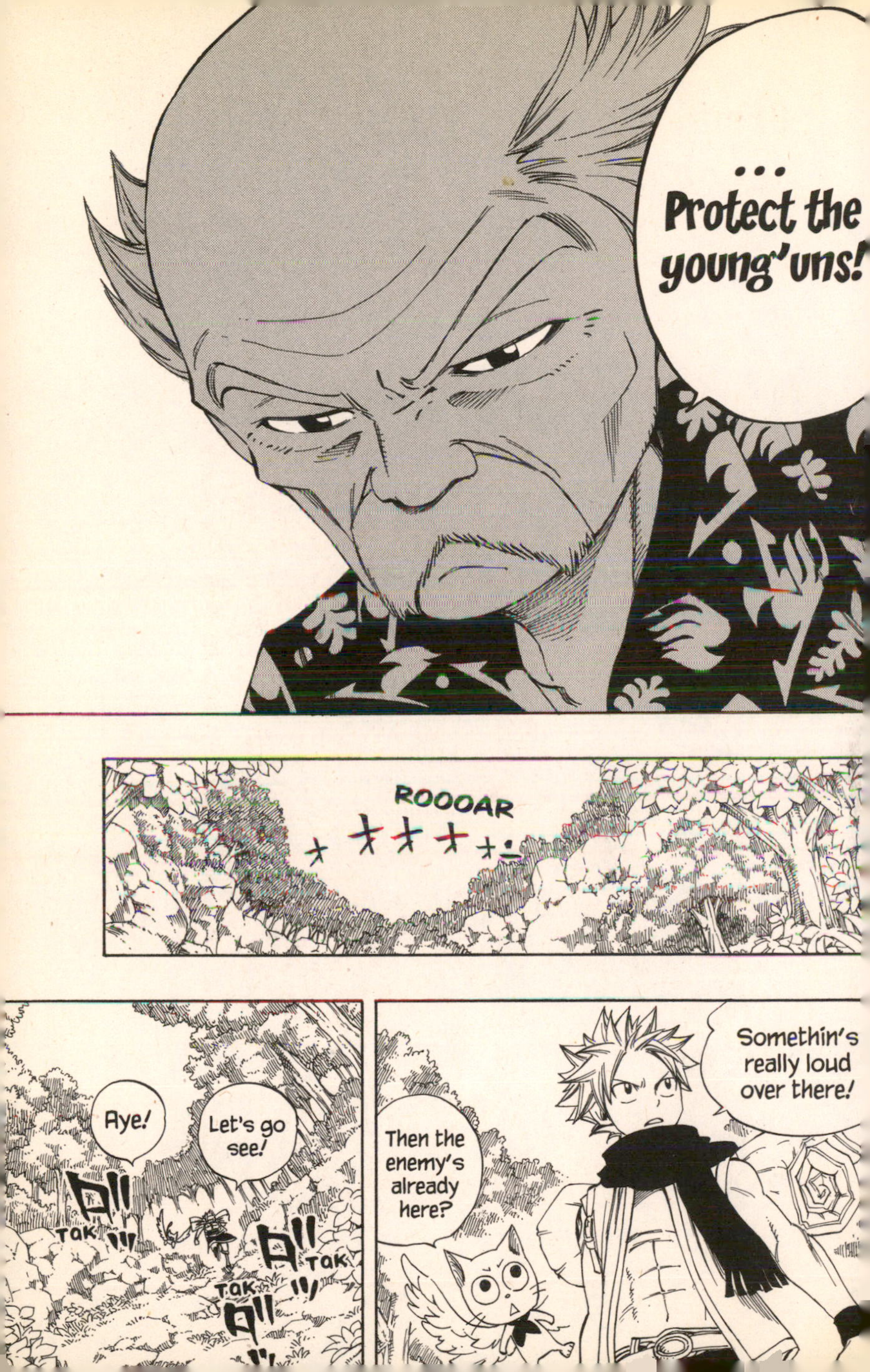
...
Protect the young'uns!
ROOOAR
Somethin's really loud over there!
Then the enemy's already here?
Let's go see!
Aye!
TAK
TAK
TAK

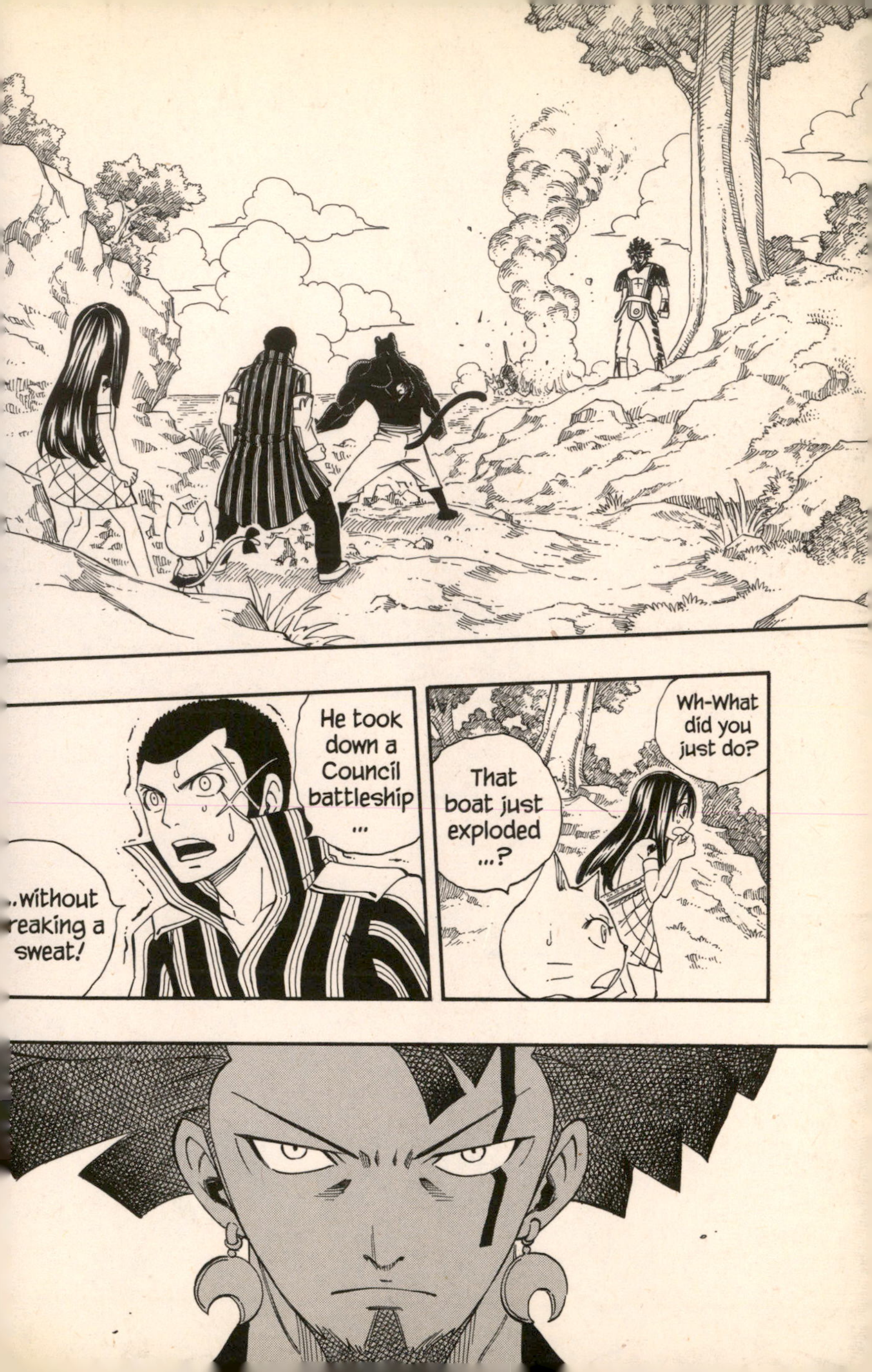
Wh-What did you just do?
That boat just exploded ...?
He took down a Council battleship ...
..without reaking a sweat!

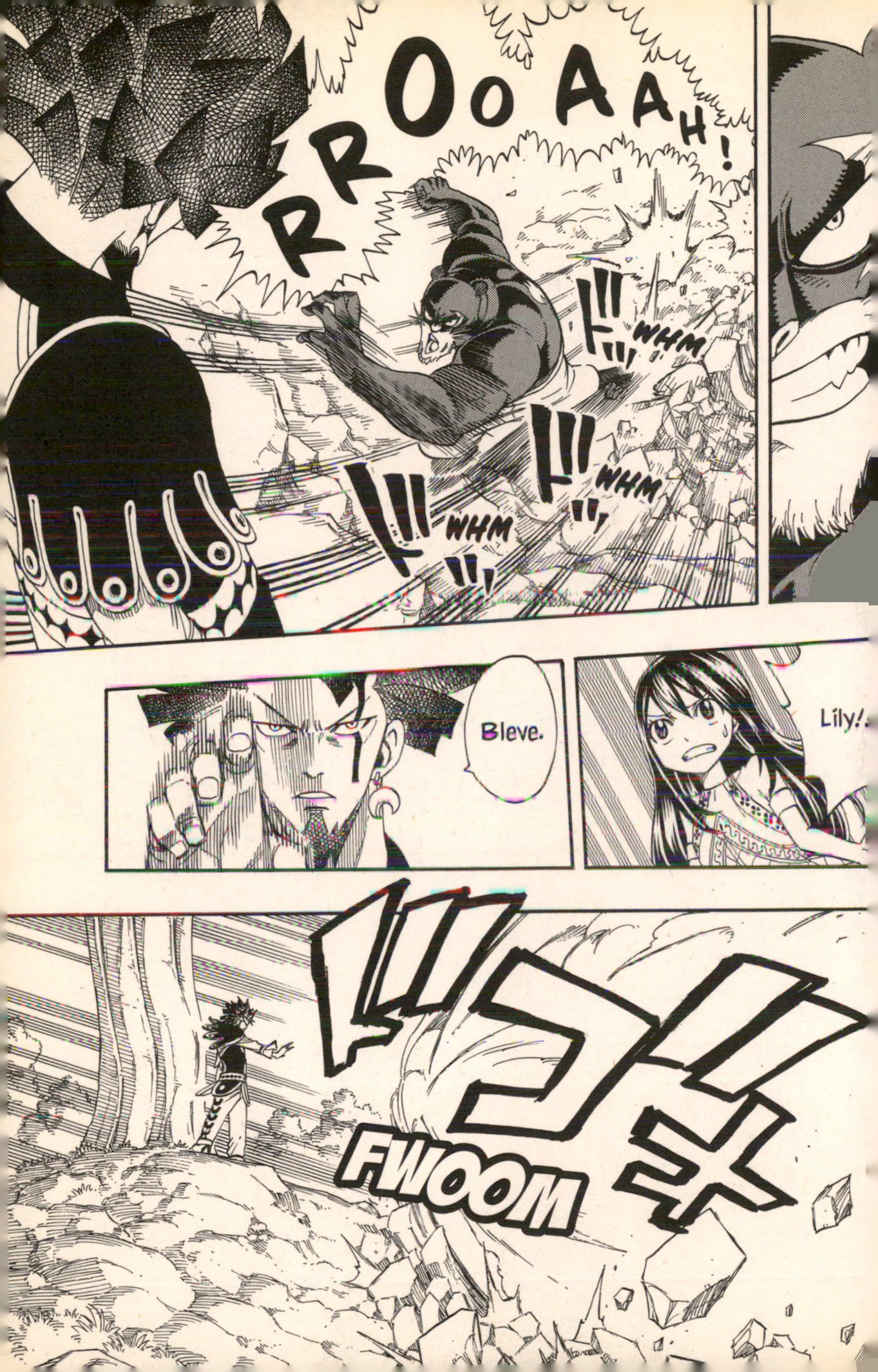
RROOAAH!
WHM
WHM
WHM
Lily!
Bleve.
FWOOM

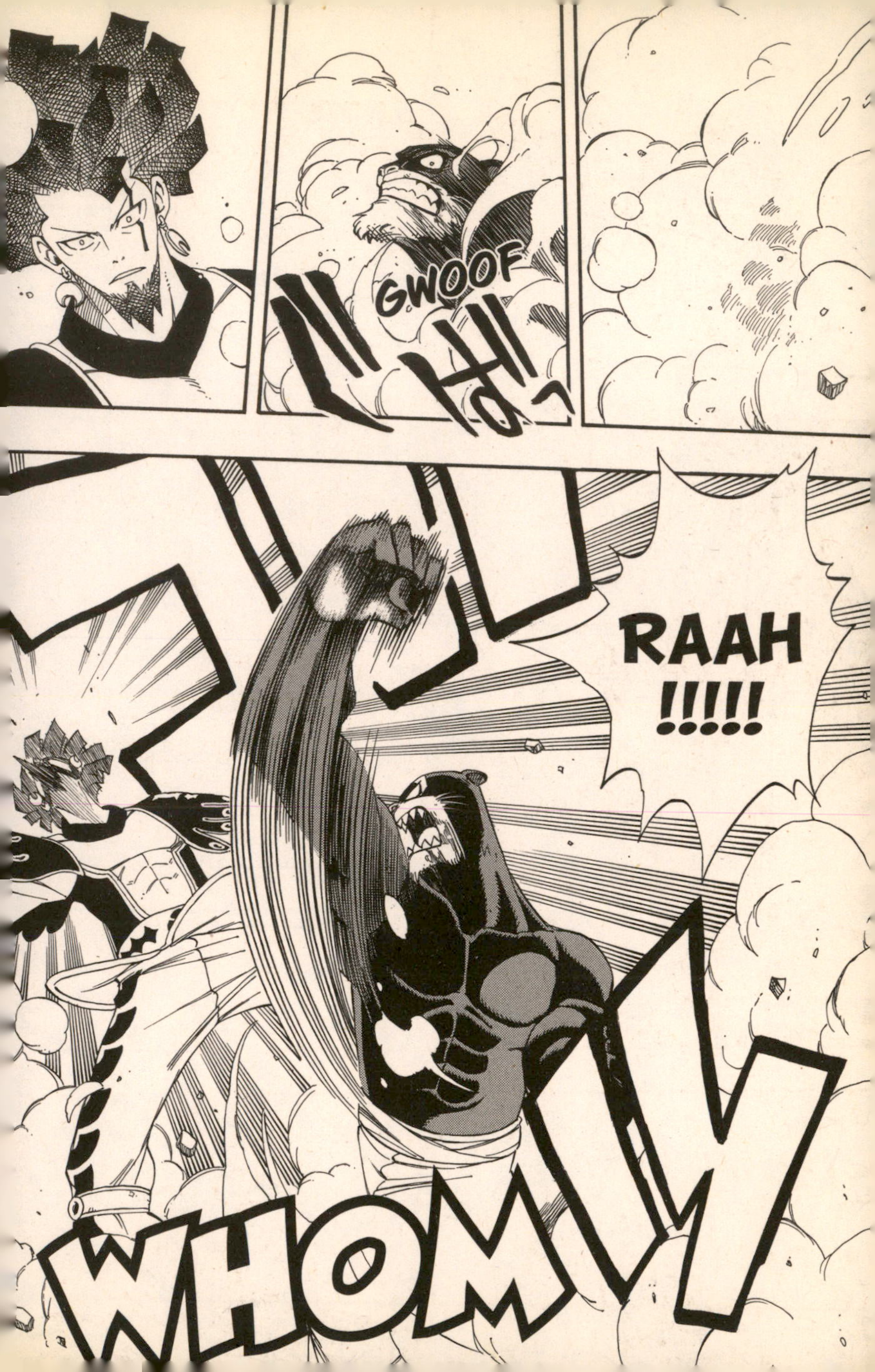
GWOOF
RAAH !!!!!
WHOMP

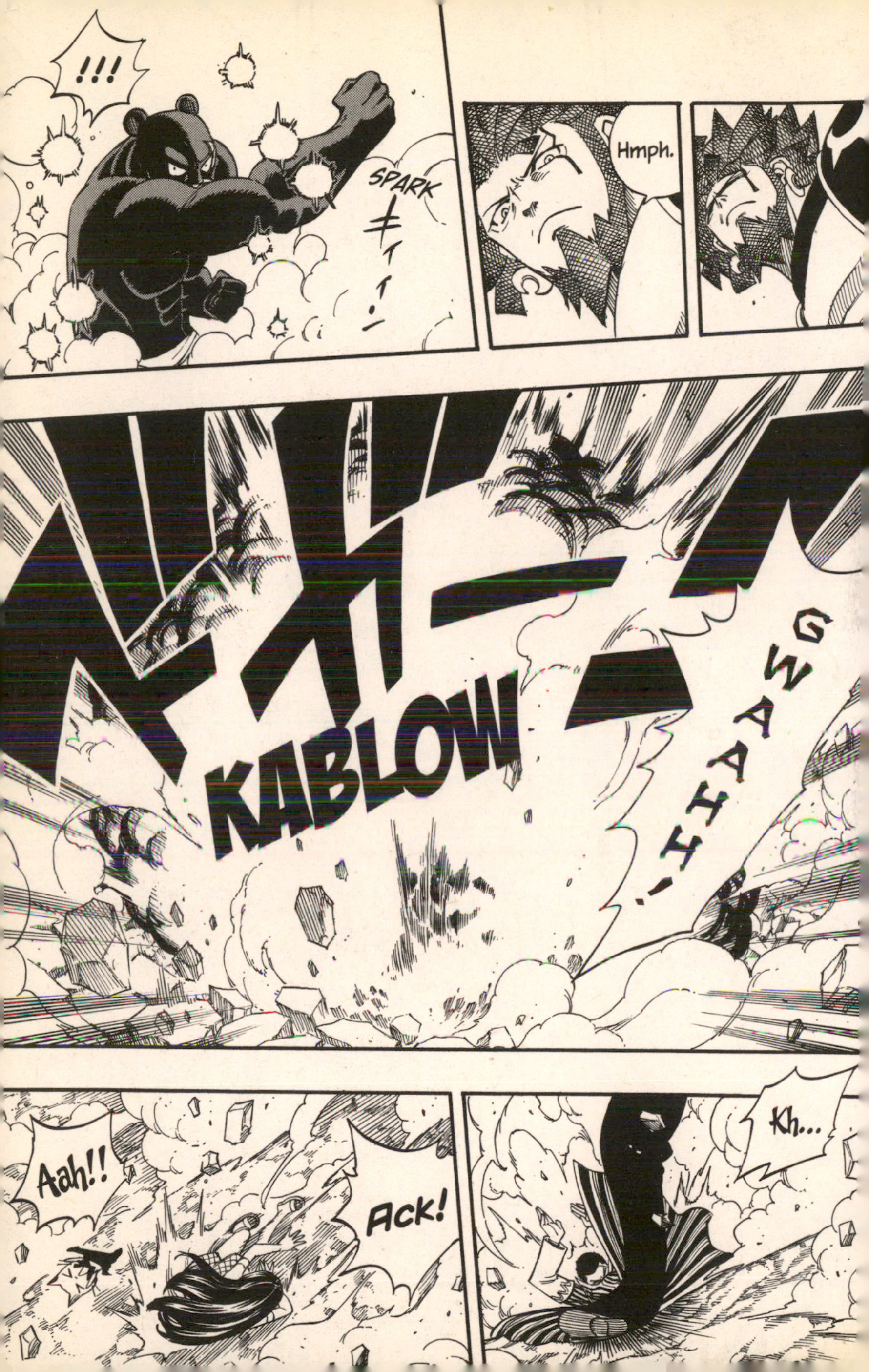
Hmph.
!!!
SPARK
KABLOW
GWAAHH!
Kh...
Aah!!
Ack!

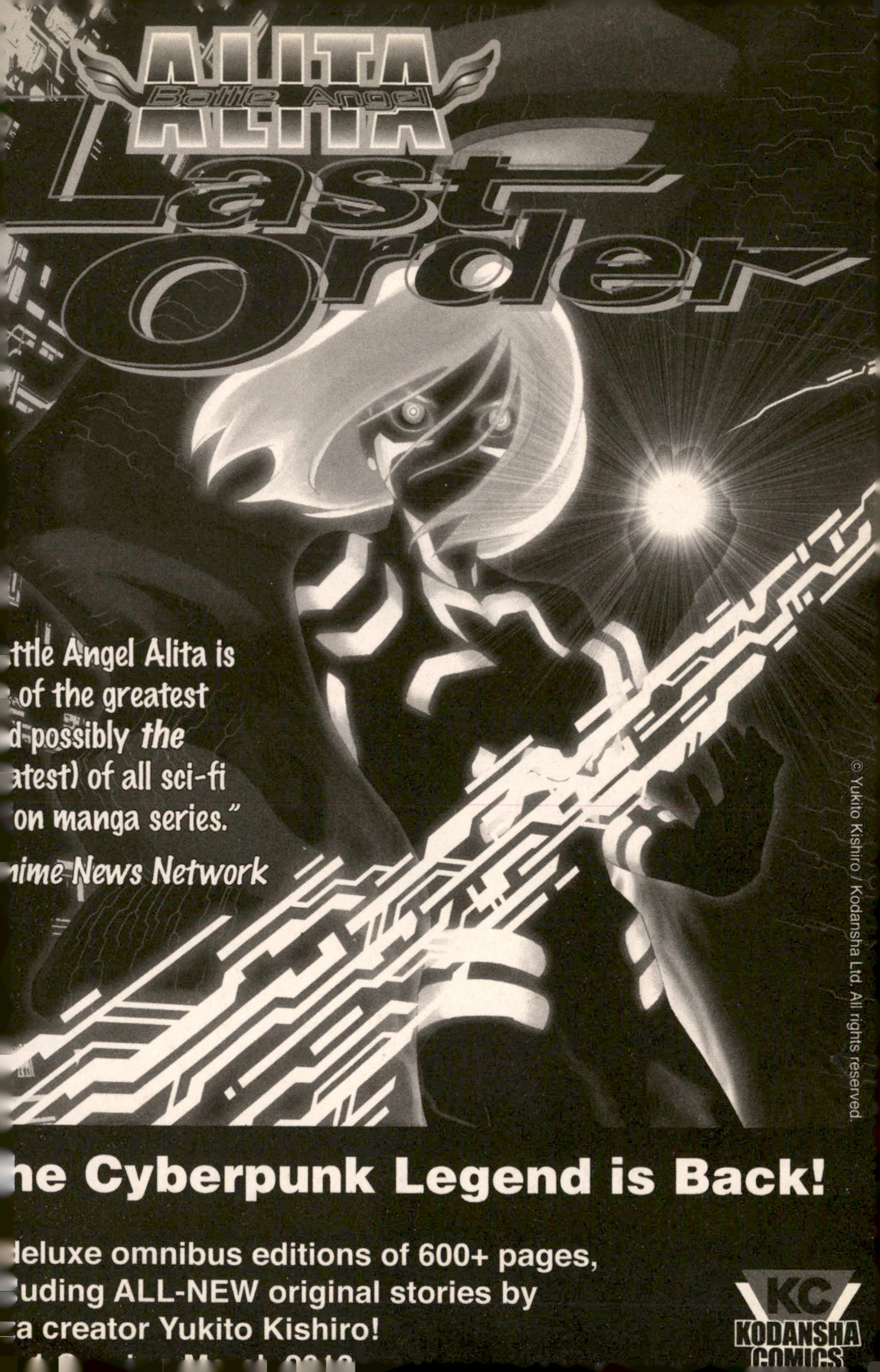
ALITA
Battle Angel
ALITA
Last Order
ttle Angel Alita is
of the greatest
d possibly *the*
atest) of all sci-fi
on manga series."
nime News Network
© Yukito Kishiro / Kodansha Ltd. All rights reserved.
he Cyberpunk Legend is Back!
deluxe omnibus editions of 600+ pages,
uding ALL-NEW original stories by
a creator Yukito Kishiro!
KC
KODANSHA COMICS

ATTACK ON TITAN

Winner of a 2011 Kodansha Manga Award

Humanity has been decimated!

A century ago, the bizarre creatures known as Titans devoured most of the world's population, driving the remainder into a walled stronghold. Now, the appearance of an immense new Titan threatens the few humans left, and one restless boy decides to seize the chance to fight for his freedom, and the survival of his species!

KODAN COMI

ANIMAL LAND

MAKOTO RAIKU

WELCOME TO THE JUNGLE

In a world of animals where the strong eat the weak, Monoko the tanuki stumbles across a strange creature the like of which has never been seen before - **a human baby!**

While the newborn has no claws or teeth to protect itself, it does have the rare ability to speak to and understand all the different animal.

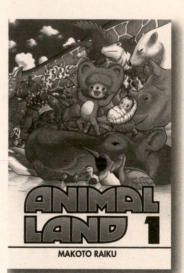

Special extras in each volume! Read them all!

VISIT WWW.KODANSHACOMICS.COM TO:
- View release date calendars for upcoming volumes
- Find out the latest about new Kodansha Comics series

KODANSHA COMICS

Fairy Tail volume 25 is a work of fiction. Names, characters, places, and inciden are the products of the author's imagination or are used fictitiously. Any resemblance to actual events, locales, or persons, living or dead, is entirely coincidental.

A Kodansha Comics Trade Paperback Original.

Published in the United States by Kodansha Comics, an imprint of Kodansha USA Publishing, LLC, New York.

Publication rights for this English edition arranged through Kodansha Ltd., Tokyo.

First published in Japan in 2011 by Kodansha Ltd., Tokyo
ISBN 978-1-61262-267-5

Printed in the United States of America.

www.kodanshacomics.com

9 8 7 6 5 4 3 2

Translator: William Flanagan
Lettering: AndWorld Design

TOMARE!

止まれ

[STOP!]

You're going the wrong way!

Manga is a completely different
type of reading experience.

To start at the *beginning,*
go to the *end!*

It's right! Authentic manga is read the traditional Japanese way—
m right to left, exactly the *opposite* of how American books are
d. It's easy to follow: Just go to the other end of the book and read
h page—and each panel—from right side to left side, starting at
top right. Now you're experiencing manga as it was meant to be!